Blackstone's

Police Station Handbook

Blackstone's

Police Station Handbook

Anthony Edwards
Matthew Hardcastle

OXFORD
UNIVERSITY PRESS

OXFORD
UNIVERSITY PRESS

Great Clarendon Street, Oxford, OX2 6DP,
United Kingdom

Oxford University Press is a department of the University of Oxford. It furthers the University's objective of excellence in research, scholarship, and education by publishing worldwide. Oxford is a registered trade mark of Oxford University Press in the UK and in certain other countries

First Edition published in 2015

Published in the United States of America by Oxford University Press
198 Madison Avenue, New York, NY 10016, United States of America

British Library Cataloguing in Publication Data
Data available

Library of Congress Control Number: 2015934061

ISBN 978–0–19–872266–3

Foreword

This is the third invaluable handbook published in the invaluable Blackstone series, beginning with the Magistrates' Court Handbook and continued with the Youth Court Handbook and now culminating in this Police Station Handbook.

The current complexity of the criminal justice system has made increasing demands on practitioners, and certainly not least on those who attend police stations, often at the earliest stages of the process. At the police station the practitioner has to deal first with a client, whose reactions are usually unpredictable and frequently variable, ranging from outrage, sometimes genuine, sometimes feigned, to despair, sometimes genuine, sometimes feigned, on occasions veering from one reaction to the other and back again. At the same time the practitioner has to deal with police officers in the police station, from the station sergeant who has responsibilities for the welfare of the client to the investigating, interviewing officers, all with their own sometimes under estimated burdens. All these relationships have to be marked by calm, determined professionalism.

For these purposes the practitioner's grasp of the applicable legal principles must be entirely secure, and the response to each aspect of the situation must accurately reflect them. In the difficult atmosphere that can sometimes prevail even the most experienced practitioner may need to be able to make immediate reference to authoritative guidance; for the less experienced, the need to do so will inevitable.

This new handbook provides ready access to the relevant information. Anthony Edwards is one of the legal profession's foremost and respected criminal practitioners, authoritative and formidably clear in everything he writes, and he has been assisted by Matthew Hardcastle, who has had many recent encounters with the realities faced by a young solicitor at the police station with a client. The handbook is their joint work. It offers the practitioner practical, readily accessible information, which will prove to be immensely valuable as and when unexpected difficulties arise in the police station. In short, it admirably fulfils its purpose.

Igor Judge

Preface

There are many good texts assisting solicitors and their representatives in acquiring the necessary skills for police station work. However we also need to know the relevant law for the offences that are, or may be, under investigation, and the defences to those allegations. We have found it much more difficult to find a good but portable text. For some years the firm has been using the excellent handbook published annually for police officers by the Police National Legal Database.

With my authorship of the Blackstone's Magistrates' Court Handbook and my editorship of the Youth Court Handbook, it seemed timely to attempt to fill this gap and produce a handbook aimed at defence practitioners in the police station, as part of the same series.

The writing and design of this book has substantially been carried out by Matthew Hardcastle. I have reviewed all that has been produced.

We have been assisted in this task by a team of solicitors who work or have worked with us and began their careers as police station representatives. They have taken responsibility for different parts of the text. They are:

Gareth Hall
Jennifer Hill
Carlos Orjuela
Nalton Stembari
Duncan Watson

We are very grateful to them for their help and their considerable efforts. We are also very grateful to Lord Judge for his kind words of introduction.

This is a new work and we have had to make difficult decisions on what to include and what might be omitted. We could not include the PACE Codes in the space available but they are available at every police station. We have sought to refer to the relevant parts but to achieve this required a significant change in style to the remaining text. Where case law is cited we have strived to provide a neutral citation to assist practioners seeking to consider the relevant judgment in full. We include the youth gravity matrix in the sentencing section of all relevant offences with further guidance to be found in the Appendix **J3.1.1.** We have also worked on the basis that we will omit offences normally investigated with advance notice to the defence as these allow time for research before any attendance at the police station.

We very much welcome feedback on whether we have made the right decisions and all other suggestions to make the work more helpful to those advising daily in the police station.

As with any criminal work, the law is being changed as we write and the law of diversion from prosecution in particular is undergoing major reform. The PACE Codes of Practice, as referred to in this text, are the civilian Codes of Practice. Practioners will be mindful of the separate Service Police Codes of Practice, when dealing with an investigation undertaken by the Service Police. We have tried to state the law accurately as at 17 April 2015 and have included many of the new offences brought into force under the Criminal Justice and Courts Act 2015 and Serious Crime Act 2015 in Appendix J.

Acknowledgements

We are grateful to the College of Policing for permission to quote from their offence gravity matrix. It should be used in conjunction with legislation as set down by the Police and Criminal Evidence Act 1984 and the Legal Aid, Sentencing and Punishment of Offenders Act 2012 as per Crown Prosecution Service (CPS) legal guidance.

Contents

Part C General Defences

Part D Pre-Attendance

Part E Vulnerable Clients

Part F Ancillary Procedures

Part G Other Interviews

Part H Representations

Part I Out of Court Disposal Options

Part J Appendices

Icons List

The following icons are used throughout this book:

Sentencing

TO Trigger Offence

Cross Reference to *Blackstone's Criminal Practice*

Table of Cases

Table of Legislation

Statutes

Statutory Instruments

Other UK Instruments

European Directives

International Instruments

List of Abbreviations

ABH	actual bodily harm
DPP	Director of Public Prosecutions
GBH	grievous bodily harm
GM	genetically modified
PACE	Police and Criminal Evidence Act 1984
TIC	Taken into consideration

PART A
Routes to Criminality

A1 **Attempt**

Criminal Attempts Act 1981

s 1 'Attempting to commit an offence'

(1) If, with intent to commit an offence to which this section applies, a person does an act which is more than merely preparatory to the commission of the offence, he is guilty of attempting to commit the offence.

(2) A person may be guilty of attempting to commit an offence to which this section applies even though the facts are such that the commission of the offence is impossible.

. . .

(4) This section applies to any offence which, if it were completed, would be triable in England and Wales as an indictable offence, other than—

(a) conspiracy (at common law or under section 1 of the Criminal Law Act 1977 or any other enactment);

(b) aiding, abetting, counselling, procuring or suborning the commission of an offence;

(ba) an offence under section 2(1) of the Suicide Act 1961 (encouraging or assisting suicide);

(c) offences under section 4(1) (assisting offenders) or 5(1) (accepting or agreeing to accept consideration for not disclosing information about an arrestable offence) of the Criminal Law Act 1967.

NB Summary only offences are not triable on indictment and therefore do not fall within the purview of this Act.

In accordance with the terms of s 1(1) Criminal Attempts Act 1981 an offence is committed if, '*with intent to commit an offence…*'. This means that mere suspicion that an offence is to take or has taken place will not suffice *R v Pace and Rogers* [2014] EWCA Crim 186.

See *Blackstone's Criminal Practice* A5.69

A2 **Conspiracy**

Criminal Law Act 1977

s 1 'The offence of conspiracy'

(1) Subject to the following provisions of this Part of this Act, if a person agrees with any other person or persons that a course of conduct shall be pursued which, if the agreement is carried out in accordance with their intentions, either—

(a) will necessarily amount to or involve the commission of any offence or offences by one or more of the parties to the agreement, or

(b) would do so but for the existence of facts which render the commission of the offence or any of the offences impossible, he is guilty of conspiracy to commit the offence or offences in question.

(2) Where liability for any offence may be incurred without knowledge on the part of the person committing it of any particular fact or circumstance necessary for the commission of the offence, a person shall nevertheless not be guilty of conspiracy to commit that offence by virtue of subsection (1) above unless he and at least one other party to the agreement intend or know that that fact or circumstance shall or will exist at the time when the conduct constituting the offence is to take place.

. . .

(4) In this Part of this Act 'offence' means an offence triable in England and Wales.

s 2 'Exemptions from liability for conspiracy'

(1) A person shall not by virtue of section 1 above be guilty of conspiracy to commit any offence if he is an intended victim of that offence.

(2) A person shall not by virtue of section 1 above be guilty of conspiracy to commit any offence or offences if the only other person or persons with whom he agrees are (both initially and at all times during the currency of the agreement) persons of any one or more of the following descriptions, that is to say—

(a) his spouse or civil partner;

(b) a person under the age of criminal responsibility; and

(c) an intended victim of that offence or of each of those offences.

(3) A person is under the age of criminal responsibility for the purposes of subsection (2)(b) above so long as it is conclusively presumed, by virtue of section 50 of the Children and Young Persons Act 1933, that he cannot be guilty of any offence.

NB For the purposes of s 2(3) Criminal Law Act 1977 this would be a person under the age of 10.

It should be noted that s 2(2)(a) does not offer protection to a spouse where they enter the conspiracy in the knowledge that others, aside from their partner, are involved *R v Chrastny* [1992] 94 Cr App R 283.

See *Blackstone's Criminal Practice* A5.41

A3 Aid, Abet, Counsel, or Procure an Offence

Accessories and Abettors Act 1861

s (8) 'Abettors in misdemeanors'

Whosoever shall aid, abet, counsel, or procure the commission of any indictable offence, whether the same be an offence at common law or by virtue of any Act passed or to be passed, shall be liable to be tried, indicted, and punished as a principal offender.

The words in s 8 should be given their ordinary meaning *(Attorney General's Reference (No. 1 of 1975)* (1975) 61 Cr App R 118).

See *Blackstone's Criminal Practice* A5.3

A4 Joint Enterprise

- For a defendant to be liable as part of a joint enterprise there must be an act by the joint party towards facilitating the crime which is more than mere presence. Once this act has occurred, a party can be guilty by reason of joint enterprise if:
  1. They are a joint principal in the offence;
  2. They assist or encourage the principal offender; or
  3. They are guilty by reason of parasitic liability (below)
- Where a defendant is party to a joint enterprise it is sufficient (for the offence of murder) for a secondary party to have realized that the primary party might kill with intent to do so or with intent to cause grievous bodily harm. However, where the act(s) of the principal are unforeseen by the secondary those actions would fall outside the joint venture and the secondary party would not be guilty (*R v Powell* [1997] UKHL 45).
- Where the only unforeseen act is the use of a different, but equally dangerous, weapon to the one agreed this would not be sufficient for the secondary party to escape liability (*R v Powell* [1997] UKHL 45).
- Parasitic accessory liability arises where (i) D1 and D2 have a common intention to commit crime A; (ii) D1, as an incident of committing crime A, commits crime B; and (iii) D2 had foreseen the possibility that he might do so (*R v Gnango* [2011] UKSC 59). Therefore, if A anticipates that serious harm will be done during an assault and B kills the victim, A will be liable for murder.

See *Blackstone's Criminal Practice* **A4.10**

A5 Serious Crime Act 2007 Offences

Serious Crime Act 2007

s 44 'Intentionally encouraging or assisting an offence'

(1) A person commits an offence if—
   (a) he does an act capable of encouraging or assisting the commission of an offence; and
   (b) he intends to encourage or assist its commission.

(2) But he is not to be taken to have intended to encourage or assist the commission of an offence merely because such encouragement or assistance was a foreseeable consequence of his act.

s 45 'Encouraging or assisting an offence believing it will be committed'

A person commits an offence if—
   (a) he does an act capable of encouraging or assisting the commission of an offence; and
   (b) he believes—
      (i) that the offence will be committed; and
      (ii) that his act will encourage or assist its commission.

s 46 'Encouraging or assisting offences believing one or more will be committed'

(1) A person commits an offence if—
   (a) he does an act capable of encouraging or assisting the commission of one or more of a number of offences; and
   (b) he believes—
      (i) that one or more of those offences will be committed (but has no belief as to which); and
      (ii) that his act will encourage or assist the commission of one or more of them.

(2) It is immaterial for the purposes of subsection (1)(b)(ii) whether the person has any belief as to which offence will be encouraged or assisted.

(3) If a person is charged with an offence under subsection (1)—
   (a) the indictment must specify the offences alleged to be the 'number of offences' mentioned in paragraph (a) of that subsection; but
   (b) nothing in paragraph (a) requires all the offences potentially comprised in that number to be specified.

(4) In relation to an offence under this section, reference in this Part to the offences specified in the indictment is to the offences specified by virtue of subsection (3)(a).

A5.1 Interpretation of Serious Crime Act offences

Serious Crime Act 2007

s 47 'Proving an offence under this Part'

(1) Sections 44, 45 and 46 are to be read in accordance with this section.
(2) If it is alleged under section 44(1)(b) that a person (D) intended to encourage or assist the commission of an offence, it is sufficient to prove that he intended to encourage or assist the doing of an act which would amount to the commission of that offence.
(3) If it is alleged under section 45(b) that a person (D) believed that an offence would be committed and that his act would encourage or assist its commission, it is sufficient to prove that he believed—
   (a) that an act would be done which would amount to the commission of that offence; and
   (b) that his act would encourage or assist the doing of that act.
(4) If it is alleged under section 46(1)(b) that a person (D) believed that one or more of a number of offences would be committed and that his act would encourage or assist the commission of one or more of them, it is sufficient to prove that he believed—
   (a) that one or more of a number of acts would be done which would amount to the commission of one or more of those offences; and
   (b) that his act would encourage or assist the doing of one or more of those acts.
(5) In proving for the purposes of this section whether an act is one which, if done, would amount to the commission of an offence—
   (a) if the offence is one requiring proof of fault, it must be proved that—
      (i) D believed that, were the act to be done, it would be done with that fault;
      (ii) D was reckless as to whether or not it would be done with that fault; or
      (iii) D's state of mind was such that, were he to do it, it would be done with that fault; and
   (b) if the offence is one requiring proof of particular circumstances or consequences (or both), it must be proved that—
      (i) D believed that, were the act to be done, it would be done in those circumstances or with those consequences; or
      (ii) D was reckless as to whether or not it would be done in those circumstances or with those consequences.
(6) For the purposes of subsection (5)(a)(iii), D is to be assumed to be able to do the act in question.
(7) In the case of an offence under section 44—
   (a) subsection (5)(b)(i) is to be read as if the reference to 'D believed' were a reference to 'D intended or believed'; but
   (b) D is not to be taken to have intended that an act would be done in particular circumstances or with particular consequences merely because its being done in those circumstances or with those consequences was a foreseeable consequence of his act of encouragement or assistance.

(8) Reference in this section to the doing of an act includes reference to—
  (a) a failure to act;
  (b) the continuation of an act that has already begun;
  (c) an attempt to do an act (except an act amounting to the commission of the offence of attempting to commit another offence).
(9) In the remaining provisions of this Part (unless otherwise provided) a reference to the anticipated offence is—
  (a) in relation to an offence under section 44, a reference to the offence mentioned in subsection (2); and
  (b) in relation to an offence under section 45, a reference to the offence mentioned in subsection (3).

s 49 'Supplemental provisions'

(1) A person may commit an offence under this Part whether or not any offence capable of being encouraged or assisted by his act is committed.
(2) If a person's act is capable of encouraging or assisting the commission of a number of offences—
  (a) section 44 applies separately in relation to each offence that he intends to encourage or assist to be committed; and
  (b) section 45 applies separately in relation to each offence that he believes will be encouraged or assisted to be committed.
(3) A person may, in relation to the same act, commit an offence under more than one provision of this Part.
(4) In reckoning whether—
  (a) for the purposes of section 45, an act is capable of encouraging or assisting the commission of an offence; or
  (b) for the purposes of section 46, an act is capable of encouraging or assisting the commission of one or more of a number of offences;
offences under this Part and listed offences are to be disregarded.
(5) 'Listed offence' means—
  (a) in England and Wales, an offence listed in Part 1, 2 or 3 of Schedule 3

...

(7) For the purposes of sections 45(b)(i) and 46(1)(b)(i) it is sufficient for the person concerned to believe that the offence (or one or more of the offences) will be committed if certain conditions are met.

A5.2 Defences to Serious Crime Act offences

Serious Crime Act 2007

s 50 'Defence of acting reasonably'

(1) A person is not guilty of an offence under this Part if he proves—
  (a) that he knew certain circumstances existed; and
  (b) that it was reasonable for him to act as he did in those circumstances.
(2) A person is not guilty of an offence under this Part if he proves—
  (a) that he believed certain circumstances to exist;
  (b) that his belief was reasonable; and

(c) that it was reasonable for him to act as he did in the circumstances as he believed them to be.

(3) Factors to be considered in determining whether it was reasonable for a person to act as he did include—
(a) the seriousness of the anticipated offence (or, in the case of an offence under section 46, the offences specified in the indictment);
(b) any purpose for which he claims to have been acting;
(c) any authority by which he claims to have been acting.

s 51 'Protective offences: victims not liable'

(1) In the case of protective offences, a person does not commit an offence under this Part by reference to such an offence if—
(a) he falls within the protected category; and
(b) he is the person in respect of whom the protective offence was committed or would have been if it had been committed.

(2) 'Protective offence' means an offence that exists (wholly or in part) for the protection of a particular category of persons ('the protected category').

Thus in relation to a 'protected offence': D is a 12-year-old girl and encourages P, a 40-year-old man to have sex with her. P does not attempt to have sex with D. D cannot be guilty of encouraging or assisting child rape despite the fact it is her intent that P have sexual intercourse with a child under 13 (child rape) because she would be considered the 'victim' of that offence had it taken place and the offence of child rape was enacted to protect children under the age of 13 (Serious Crime Act 2007 Explanatory Notes).

Serious Crime Act 2007

s 51A 'Exceptions to section 44 for encouraging or assisting suicide'

Section 44 does not apply to an offence under section 2(1) of the Suicide Act 1961 . . .

Section 59 Serious Crime Act 2007 abolished the previous common law offences of incitement and commissioning.

See *Blackstone's Criminal Practice* **A5.3**

Part B
Offences

B1 **Offences Against the Person**

B1.1 **Defences to allegations of assault**

For there to be an assault there must be an unlawful act. An act will not be unlawful in the following circumstances:

1. A person acting in **defence of property**. However the act must be to ward off an act that would be unlawful or criminal (*DPP v Bayer* [2003] EWHC 2567 (Admin)) and the degree of force used must be reasonable in the circumstances as the defendant honestly, however mistakenly, believed them to be. This principle is demonstrated in a comparison between *Bayer* (above) and *R v Morris* [2013] EWCA Crim 436. In *Bayer* the act that gave rise to the defence of property was the planting of genetically modified crops. As the planting of GM crops is a lawful act the Court of Appeal held that the defence of property could not apply. Whereas, in *Morris*, a taxi driver mistakenly believed that his passenger was attempting to make off without payment; the driver, in an attempt to prevent the crime of making off without payment, drove dangerously. The Court of Appeal held that the taxi driver's honest but mistaken belief in these circumstances provided a defence.
2. Where there is **consent**. This applies particularly in sport and to medical procedures. The consent must be informed. The defence is normally limited to common assault and was not available (*R v Brown* [1992] UKHL 7) in sado-masochistic situations where ABH was caused. Exceptionally a wife may consent to be 'branded' *(R v Wilson* [1996] 2 Cr App R 241) as it was the equivalent of a tattoo.
3. **Lawful correction or chastisement** but subject to s 58 of the Children Act 2004 so that it is only available for common assault.

Children Act 2004

s 58 'Reasonable punishment'

(1) In relation to any offence specified in subsection (2), battery of a child cannot be justified on the ground that it constituted reasonable punishment.

(2) The offences referred to in subsection (1) are—

(a) an offence under section 18 or 20 of the Offences against the Person Act 1861 (wounding and causing grievous bodily harm);

(b) an offence under section 47 of that Act (assault occasioning actual bodily harm);

(c) an offence under section 1 of the Children and Young Persons Act 1933 (cruelty to persons under 16).

(3) Battery of a child causing actual bodily harm to the child cannot be justified in any civil proceedings on the ground that it constituted reasonable punishment.

(4) For the purposes of subsection (3) 'actual bodily harm' has the same meaning as it has for the purposes of section 47 of the Offences against the Person Act 1861.

s 65 'Interpretation'

(1) In this Act—

...

'child' means, subject to section 9, a person under the age of eighteen (and 'children' is to be construed accordingly).

s 9 'Care leavers and young persons with learning disabilities'

(2) Any reference to a child includes, in addition to a person under the age of 18, a person aged 18, 19 or 20 who—

(a) has been looked after by a local authority at any time after attaining the age of 16; or

(b) has a learning disability.

(3) For the purposes of subsection (2)—

a person is 'looked after by a local authority' if—

(a) for the purposes of the Children Act 1989, he is looked after by a local authority in England and Wales;

...

'learning disability' means a state of arrested or incomplete development of mind which induces significant impairment of intelligence and social functioning.

4. See General Defences in Part C especially **self-defence.**

B1.2 **Common assault/battery**

Criminal Justice Act 1988

s 39 'Common assault and battery to be summary offences'

Common assault and battery shall be summary offences and a person guilty of either of them shall be liable to a fine, to imprisonment for a term not exceeding six months, or to both.

B1.2.1 Breakdown

Offence	Elements of the Offence	Defence
s 39 Criminal Justice Act 1988 'Common assault and battery'	• Unlawfully • Assaulted • Another person • Intentionally or recklessly	• Negative any element of the offence • Consent *R v Wilson* **B1.1** • Mistake *R v Williams* (below) • Defences to allegations of assault **B1.1** • General Defences **C**

B1.2.2 Interpretation

- An 'assault' is to cause another to fear the intended use of unlawful force to another person (*R v Ireland* [1996] EWCA Crim 441).
- A battery involves the unlawful application of force by the defendant upon the victim (*R v Ireland* [1996] EWCA Crim 441).
- A mere omission to act cannot amount to an assault (*Fagan v Metropolitan Police Commissioner* (1968) 52 Cr App R 700).
- This is a crime of basic intent.

B1.2.3 Defences

- Where a defendant has been labouring under a mistake as to the facts, he must be judged according to his mistaken view of the facts (*R v Williams* [1983] EWCA Crim 4).
- See defences to assault **B1.1**.
- See General Defences **C**.

B1.2.4 Sentencing

s 39 Criminal Justice Act 1988

Summary Only: 6 months' imprisonment/a fine

Youth Gravity Matrix

OFFENCE	Gravity Score	Offence type	AGGRAVATING FACTORS	MITIGATING FACTORS
Common assault (s 39 Criminal Justice Act 1988)	2	S	• Deliberate aggression without provocation • Vulnerable victim • Weapon used • Premeditation • Domestic violence • Group action	• Trivial nature of action • Impulsive action • Injury very minor

See *Blackstone's Criminal Practice* **B2.1**

B1.3 **Threats to kill**

Offences against the Person Act 1861

s 16 'Threats to kill'

A person who without lawful excuse makes to another a threat, intending that that other would fear it would be carried out, to kill that other or a third person shall be guilty of an offence and liable on conviction on indictment to imprisonment for a term not exceeding ten years.

B1.3.1 **Breakdown**

Offence	Elements of the Offence	Defence
s 16 Offences against the Person Act 1981 'Threats to kill'	• 'A' without lawful excuse • Makes a threat to kill 'B' or a third party • Intending that 'B' would fear this threat to be carried out	• Negative any element of the offence. • Self-defence *R v Cousins* (below) • Defences to allegations of assault **B1.1** • General Defences **C**

B1.3.2 **Interpretation**

- As long as the sender acts intentionally with full knowledge of the contents of the letter and without lawful excuse, it is unnecessary to look for an ulterior evil motive when considering whether the act was malicious, an intentional act containing an implied threat is sufficient. The sender's motive is irrelevant save for sentencing (*R v Solanke* (1970) 54 Cr App R 30).

B1.3.3 Defences

- Self-defence can provide a lawful excuse when making a threat to kill (*R v Cousins* (1982) 74 Cr App R 363).
- See defences to assault **B1.1.**
- See General Defences **C.**

B1.3.4 Key points

- A foetus is not capable of being considered as 'another' for the purposes of this section (*R v Tait* (1990) 90 Cr App R 44).

B1.3.5 Sentencing

s 16 Offences against the Person Act 1861

Summary: 6 months' imprisonment/a fine

Indictment: 10 years' imprisonment

Youth Gravity Matrix

OFFENCE	Gravity Score	Offence type	AGGRAVATING FACTORS	MITIGATING FACTORS
Threats to kill (s16 OAP Act 1861)	3	E	• Calculated	• Threat made in heat of the moment

See *Blackstone's Criminal Practice* **B1.143**

B1.4 Assault occasioning actual bodily harm

Offences against the Person Act 1861

s 47 'Assault occasioning actual bodily harm'

(1) Whosever shall be convicted upon an indictment of any assault occasioning actual bodily harm [shall be guilty of an offence]

B1.4.1 Related offences

- Common assault/battery **B1.2.**
- GBH **B.1.5.**

B1.4.2 Breakdown

Offence	Elements of the Offence	Defence
s 47 Offences against the Person Act 1861 'Assault occasioning actual bodily harm'	• Unlawfully • Assaulted • Another person • Occasioning them actual bodily harm • Intentionally or recklessly	• Negative any element of the offence • Consent *R v Wilson* (below) • Defences to allegations of assault **B1.1** • General Defences **C**

B1.4.3 Interpretation

- 'Bodily harm' has its ordinary meaning and includes any hurt or injury calculated to interfere with the health or comfort of the [complainant]. Such hurt or injury need not be permanent, but must be more than merely transient and trifling (*R v Donovan* (1936) 25 Cr App R 1).
- Psychiatric injury is capable of amounting to bodily harm. However, such injury must be proved by expert evidence on behalf of the Crown and cannot be left to inference (*R v Chan-Fook* [1993] EWCA Crim 1).
- This is a crime of basic intent.

B1.4.4 Defences

- At the instigation of the complainant, with no aggressive intent by the defendant, consent may provide a defence to an assault that would otherwise have been legal in a different context, for example tattooing (*R v Wilson* [1996] 2 Cr App R 241). However, contrast this with:
- *R v Brown* [1992] UKHL 7 in which it was held that consent cannot be a defence to a charge of assault occasioning actual bodily harm or grievous bodily harm in the context of sado-masochism.
- See defences to assault **B1.1**.
- See General Defences **C**.

B1.4.5 Key points

- Where someone creates a danger and thereby exposes another to a reasonably foreseeable risk of injury which materializes, there is an evidential basis for the actus reus of an assault occasioning actual bodily harm. However, it remains necessary for the prosecution to prove an intention to assault or appropriate recklessness (*DPP v Santana-Bermudez* [2003] EWHC 2908 (Admin)).

- Cutting of a substantial part of the victim's hair may constitute an offence under this section (*DPP v Smith* [2006] EWHC 94 (Admin)).
- Silent phone calls may amount to a relevant act for the purposes of s 47. However, it is the making of the phone call not the words or silence that ensue that is relevant (*R v Ireland* [1996] EWCA Crim 441).

B1.4.6 Sentencing

s 47 Offences against the Person Act 1861

Summary: 6 months' imprisonment and or a fine

Indictment: 5 years' imprisonment

Youth Gravity Matrix

OFFENCE	Gravity Score	Offence type	AGGRAVATING FACTORS	MITIGATING FACTORS
ABH (s 47 OAP Act 1861)	3	E	• Weapon Used • More than one blow • Attacked while victim vulnerable or defenceless eg 'on floor' • Unprovoked attack • Nature of the injury (especially where serious / disfiguring injury) • Premeditation • Domestic violence • Group action	• Impulsive action • Provocation • Minor injury

See *Blackstone's Criminal Practice* **B2.27**

B1.5 Wounding, or inflicting grievous bodily harm

Offences Against the Person Act 1861

s 20 'Inflicting bodily injury, with or without weapon'

(1) Whosoever shall unlawfully and maliciously wound or inflict any grievous bodily harm upon any other person, either with or without any weapon or instrument shall be guilty of an offence ...

B1.5.1 Related offences

- s 18 Grievous bodily harm **B1.6**.
- s 47 Assault occasioning actual bodily harm **B1.4**.

B1.5.2 Breakdown

Offence	Elements of the Offence	Defence
s 20 Offences against the Person Act 1861 'Wounding or grievous bodily harm'	• Unlawfully • Maliciously • Intentionally or recklessly • Wounded or inflicted grievous bodily harm • Upon another person	• Negative any element of the offence • Defences to allegations of assault **B1.1** • General Defences **C**

B1.5.3 Interpretation

- 'Maliciously' includes the position where a defendant has the intention to commit the relevant action or where the defendant has foreseen that the particular kind of harm might be done and yet has gone on to take the risk of it (*R v Cunningham* (1957) 41 Cr App R 155).
- 'Grievous bodily harm' should be given its ordinary meaning and is 'serious harm' (*DPP v Smith* (1960) 44 Cr App R 261).
- 'Wound' means a break in the continuity of the skin (*R v Smith* (1837) 8 C&P 173 and *R v Waltham* (1849) 3 Cox 442). It does not include the rupturing of an internal blood vessel (*C (a minor) v Eisenhower* (1984) 78 Cr App R 48).
- This is a crime of basic intent.

B1.5.4 Defences

- See defences to assault **B1.1**.
- See General Defences **C**.

B1.5.5 Key points

- Bodily harm includes psychiatric injury: *R v Ireland; R v Burstow* [1998] AC 147, HL.
- Grievous bodily harm can be inflicted by infecting the victim with HIV through unprotected consensual sexual intercourse

where there is a person from whom the risk is concealed and who is not consenting to it (*R v Dica* [2004] EWCA Crim 1103).

B1.5.6 Sentencing

s 20 Offences against the Person Act 1861

Summary: 6 months' imprisonment and/or a fine

Indictment: 5 years' imprisonment

Youth Gravity Matrix

OFFENCE	Gravity Score	Offence type	AGGRAVATING FACTORS	MITIGATING FACTORS
GBH/Wounding (s 20 OAP Act 1861)	4	E	• Weapon used • More than one blow • Unprovoked attack • Group action • Domestic violence	• Impulsive action • Provocation • Minor injury

See *Blackstone's Criminal Practice* **B2.48**

B1.6 Wounding or grievous bodily harm with intent

Offences against the Person Act 1861

s 18 'Wounding or causing grievous bodily harm'

(1) Whosoever shall unlawfully and maliciously by any means whatsoever wound or cause any grievous bodily harm to any other person with intent to do some grievous bodily harm to any person, or with intent to resist or prevent the lawful apprehension or detainer of any person, shall be guilty of an offence.

B1.6.1 Related offences

- s 20 B1.5.

B1.6.2 Breakdown

Offence	Elements of the Offence	Defence
s 18 Offences against the Person Act 1861 'Wounding or grievous bodily harm with intent'	• Unlawfully and maliciously • Caused grievous bodily harm or wounded a person • With intent to • Do grievous bodily harm or • Resist/prevent lawful apprehension/detention of self or another	• Negative any element of the offence • Defences to allegations of assault **B1.1** • General Defences **C**

B1.6.3 Interpretation

- See s 20 OAP Act **B1.5**.

B1.6.4 Defences

- See defences to assault **B1.1**.
- See General Defences **C**.

B1.6.5 Key points

- Specific intention must be proven to establish an offence under this section. Proving that the defendant foresaw that serious harm was the likely result of his actions will not be enough to do this. He must intend to cause the harm (*R v Belfon* [1976] 63 Cr App R 59).
- This is a crime of specific intent.

B1.6.6 Sentencing

s 18 Offences against the Person Act 1861

Indictable only: life imprisonment

Youth Gravity Matrix

OFFENCE	Gravity Score	Offence type	AGGRAVATING FACTORS	MITIGATING FACTORS
GBH/Wounding with intent (s 18 OAP Act 1861)	4	I	Always refer to the CPS	

See *Blackstone's Criminal Practice* **B2.64**

B1.7 Attempted murder

- Where a defendant faces an allegation of attempted murder the actus reus remains the same as for murder but the prosecution must prove an intent to kill rather than to cause serious injury.
- See attempt **A1**.
- See murder **B1.8**.

See *Blackstone's Criminal Practice* A5.72.

B1.8 Murder

Contrary to Common Law

Where a person of sound mind and discretion unlawfully kills any reasonable creature in being and under the Queen's peace, with intent to kill or cause grievous bodily harm.

B1.8.1 Related offences

- Manslaughter **B1.9**.
- Infanticide **B4.3.1**.
- Attempted murder **B1.7**.

B1.8.2 Breakdown

Offence	Elements of the Offence	Defence
Murder—Contrary to common law	• A person of sound mind and discretion • Unlawfully • Does an act that is a substantial cause of someone else's death; and • Does that act with the intent to kill or cause serious harm	• Negative any element of the offence • Loss of control (below) **B1.8.4.1** • Diminished responsibility (below) **B1.8.4.3** • Suicide pact (below) **B1.8.4.4** • Defences to allegations of assault **B1.1** • General Defences **C**

B1.8.3 Interpretation

- A person will be considered to be of sound mind unless it is proved by the defendant that they were insane at the time of the act.
- An act need not be the sole or the principal cause of death—it is enough for it to be the substantial cause.
- Under the Queen's peace excludes acts of killing when committed in war.
- Murder requires only the intent to cause serious harm. It does not require an intent to kill.
- This is a crime of specific intent.

B1.8.4 Defences

B1.8.4.1 *Loss of control*

Coroners and Justice Act 2009

s 54 'Partial defence to murder: loss of control'

(1) Where a person ('D') kills or is a party to the killing of another ('V'), D is not to be convicted of murder if:
   (a) D's acts and omissions in doing or being party to the killing resulted from D's loss of self-control,
   (b) the loss of self control had a qualifying trigger, and
   (c) a person of D's sex and age, with a normal degree of tolerance and self-restraint and in the circumstances of D, might have reacted in the same or in a similar way to D.

(2) For the purposes of subsection (1)(a), it does not matter whether or not the loss of control was sudden.

(3) In subsection (1) (c) the reference to 'the circumstances of D' is a reference to all of D's circumstances other than those whose only relevance to D's conduct is that they bear on D's general capacity for tolerance or self-restraint.

(4) Subsection (1) does not apply if, in doing or being a party to the killing, D acted in a considered desire for revenge.

(5) On a charge of murder, if sufficient evidence is adduced to raise an issue with respect to the defence under subsection (1), the jury must assume that the defence is satisfied unless the prosecution proves beyond all reasonable doubt that it is not.

(6) For the purposes of subsection (5), sufficient evidence is adduced to raise an issue with respect to the defence if evidence is adduced on which, in the opinion of the trial judge, a jury, properly directed, could reasonably conclude that the defence might apply.

(7) A person who, but for this section, would be liable to be convicted of murder is liable instead to be convicted of manslaughter.
(8) The fact that one party to a killing is by virtue of this section not liable to be convicted of murder does not affect the question whether the killing amounted to murder in the case of any other party to it.

s 55 'Meaning of "qualifying trigger"'

(1) This section applies for the purposes of section 54.
(2) A loss of self-control had a qualifying trigger if subsection (3), (4) or (5) applies.
(3) This subsection applies if D's loss of self-control was attributable to D's fear of serious violence from V against D or another identified person.
(4) This subsection applies if D's loss of self-control was attributable to a thing or things done or said (or both) which—
    (a) constituted circumstances of an extremely grave character, and
    (b) caused D to have a justifiable sense of being seriously wronged.
(5) This subsection applies if D's loss of self-control was attributable to a combination of the matters mentioned in subsections (3) and (4).
(6) In determining whether a loss of self-control had a qualifying trigger—
    (a) D's fear of serious violence is to be disregarded to the extent that it was caused by a thing which D incited to be done or said for the purpose of providing an excuse to use violence;
    (b) a sense of being seriously wronged by a thing done or said is not justifiable if D incited the thing to be done or said for the purpose of providing an excuse to use violence;
    (c) the fact that a thing done or said constituted sexual infidelity is to be disregarded.
(7) In this section references to 'D' and 'V' are to be construed in accordance with section 54.

B1.8.4.2 *Summary*

This is a partial defence and is set out in sections 54 and 55 of the Coroners and Justice Act 2009. It can be summarized in the flow chart located at B1.8.7 below.

- For the purposes of this partial defence, sexual infidelity can be properly taken into account where it was integral to the circumstances and where it is one of a number of factors which caused the defendant to lose control (*R v Clinton* [2012] EWCA Crim 2).
- There was no general rule but the defence is not available because the defendant generated the conduct in issue (*Daniel v Trinidad and Tobago* [2014] UKPC 3). See also *Marsh v DPP* 2015 EWHC 1022.

- As this is a partial defence, if it succeeds a conviction for manslaughter will result.

B1.8.4.3 *Diminished responsibility*

This is a partial defence and is set out in section 2 of the Homicide Act 1957 as amended.

Homicide Act 1957

s 2 'Persons suffering from diminished responsibility'

(1) A person who kills or is a party to the killing of another is not to be convicted of murder if D was suffering from an abnormality of mental functioning which:
   (a) arose from a recognised medical condition
   (b) substantially impaired D's ability to do one or more things mentioned in subsection (1A), and
   (c) provides an explanation for D's acts or omissions in doing or being a party to the killing.

(1A) Those things are:
   (a) to understand the nature of D's conduct;
   (b) to form a rational judgment;
   (c) to exercise self-control.

(1B) For the purposes of subsection (1)(c), an abnormality of mental functioning provides an explanation for D's conduct if it causes, or is a significant contributory factor in causing, D to carry out that conduct.

- It is for the defence to prove diminished responsibility to the civil standard.
- As this is a partial defence, if it succeeds a conviction for manslaughter will result.
- Voluntary acute intoxication, from alcohol or other substance, is not capable of founding the partial defence of diminished responsibility (*R v Dowds* [2012] EWCA Crim 281).
- The effect of drink will not necessarily fall within the defence but it may be otherwise if there is an abnormality of mind based on alcohol dependency syndrome with associated cognitive impairment (*R v D Williams* [2013] EWCA Crim 2749).
- Consider the M'Naghten rules in appropriate cases.

B1.8.4.4 *Suicide pact*

Homicide Act 1957

s 4 'Suicide pact'

(1) It shall be manslaughter, and shall not be murder, for a person acting in pursuance of a suicide pact between him and another to kill the other or be a party to the other being killed by a third person.
(2) Where it is shown that a person charged with the murder of another killed the other or was a party to his being killed, it shall be for the defence to prove that the person charged was acting in pursuance of a suicide pact between him and the other.
(3) For the purposes of this section 'suicide pact' means a common agreement between two or more persons having for its object the death of all of them, whether or not each is to take his own life, but nothing done by a person who enters into a suicide pact shall be treated as done by him in pursuance of the pact unless it is done while he has the settled intention of dying in pursuance of the pact.

- This is a partial defence. If successful, a conviction for manslaughter will follow.
- The burden of proof lies with the defendant.

Consider the general defences in Part C; however duress is not available as a defence to murder.

B1.8.5 Key point

- Consider the various forms of liability A4.

B1.8.6 Sentencing

Murder

Indictable only: life imprisonment

See *Blackstone's Criminal Practice* B1.1–1.51

B1.8.7 Loss of control

Table A Loss of Control

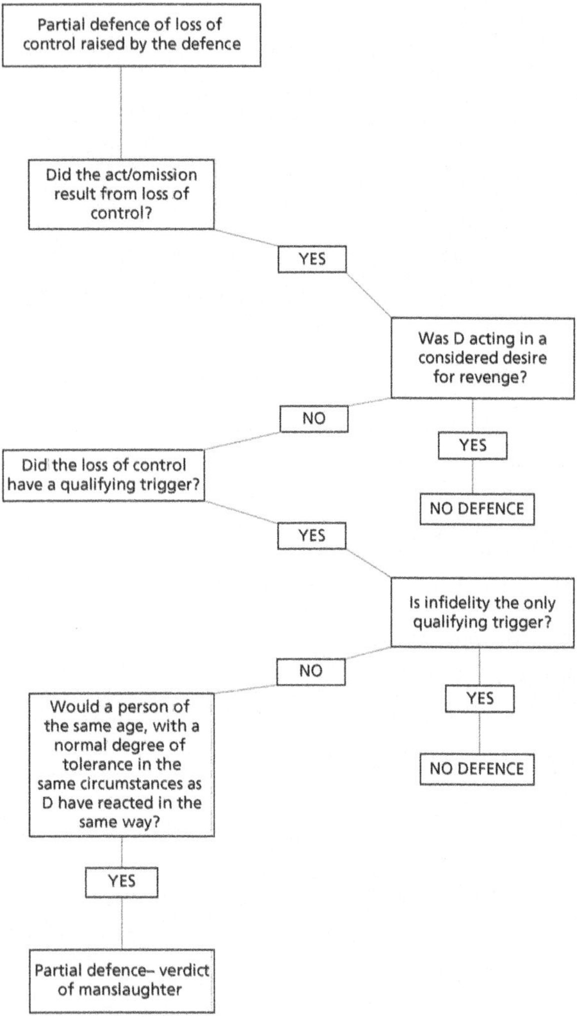

B1.9 **Manslaughter**

Common law

The unlawful killing of another human being

B1.9.1 **Related offences**

- Murder **B1.8**.

B1.9.2 **Breakdown**

Offence	Elements of the Offence	Defence
Manslaughter (By way of partial defence to murder)	• The elements of murder are made out **B1.8** • But there is an applicable partial defence **B1.8.4**	
Manslaughter (Unlawful Act)—common law	• 'A' commits an unlawful act • Which results in the death of another human being • The act was one that a would have lead a reasonable man to foresee some risk	• Negative any element of the offence • Defences to allegations of assault **B1.1** • General Defences **C**
Manslaughter (Gross Negligence) *R v Adomako* (1994) Cr App R 362	• A duty of care exists • The duty is breached • Resulting in death • The breach was so be as to be 'grossly negligent'	• Negative any element of the offence • Defences to allegations of assault **B1.1** • General Defences **C**

B1.9.3 **Interpretation**

- For unlawful act manslaughter there must be an act that resulted to the death of another. Where there is an omission, even a deliberate omission, a charge of manslaughter is not an inevitable consequence (*R v Lowe* (1973) 57 Cr App R 365).
- For cases of gross negligence manslaughter the jury will have to consider whether the extent to which the defendant's conduct departed from the proper standard to such an extent as for it to be judged criminal *(R v Adomako* (1994) Cr App R 362).
- For cases of gross negligence manslaughter, when a person has created or contributed to the creation of a state of affairs which he knows, or ought reasonably to know, has become life threatening, a consequent duty on him to act by taking reasonable steps to save the other's life will normally arise. In *R v Evans* [2009]

EWCA Crim 650 drug users who shared a familial bond were in the house and saw the victim take drugs and, to all appearances, overdose. The subsequent failure of those witnessing the overdose to call the police was held as sufficient to make out the offence of manslaughter.

- However, in cases involving the supply of drugs where the supplier has left after the drug has been ingested but before complications arise it was held that the drug is freely and voluntarily self-administered by the deceased; the deceased had a choice whether to inject himself or not. As this choice will be taken in the knowledge of what the deceased was doing it will be their act that causes death and not the supplier's (*R v Kennedy* [2007] UKHL 38).

B1.9.4 Defences

- See defences to assault **B1.1**.
- See the General Defences C.

B1.9.5 Sentencing

Indictable only: life imprisonment

See *Blackstone's Criminal Practice* **B1.52–B1.712**

B1.10 Assault/resist/impersonate and obstruct emergency workers

Emergency Workers (Obstructions) Act 2006

s 1 'Obstructing or hindering certain emergency workers responding to emergency circumstances'

(1) A person who without reasonable excuse obstructs or hinders another while that other person is, in a capacity mentioned in subsection (2) below, responding to emergency circumstances, commits an offence.

(2) The capacity referred to in subsection (1) above is—

(a) that of a person employed by a fire and rescue authority in England and Wales;

(b) in relation to England and Wales, that of a person (other than a person falling within paragraph (a)) whose duties as an employee or as a servant of the Crown involve—

(i) extinguishing fires; or

(ii) protecting life and property in the event of a fire;

(c) that of a person employed by a relevant NHS body in the provision of ambulance services (including air ambulance services), or of a person providing such services pursuant to arrangements made by, or at the request of, a relevant NHS body;
(d) that of a person providing services for the transport of organs, blood, equipment or personnel pursuant to arrangements made by, or at the request of, a relevant NHS body;
(e) that of a member of Her Majesty's Coastguard;
(f) that of a member of the crew of a vessel operated by—
   (i) the Royal National Lifeboat Institution, or
   (ii) any other person or organisation operating a vessel for the purpose of providing a rescue service,

   or a person who musters the crew of such a vessel or attends to its launch or recovery.

s 2 'Obstructing or hindering persons assisting emergency workers'

(1) A person who without reasonable excuse obstructs or hinders another in the circumstances described in subsection (2) below commits an offence.
(2) Those circumstances are where the person being obstructed or hindered is assisting another while that other person is, in a capacity mentioned in section 1(2) of this Act, responding to emergency circumstances.

B1.10.1 Breakdown

Offence	Elements of the Offence	Defence
s 1 Emergency Workers (Obstructions) Act 2006 'Obstruct/hinder an emergency worker'	• Without reasonable excuse • Obstruct or hinder • Another person • Being in a capacity as per s 1(2) • Going to, dealing with, or preparing to deal with • An emergency circumstance	• Negative any element of the offence • Reasonable excuse (below) **B1.10.4** • Defences to allegations of assault **B1.1** • General Defences **C**
s 2 Emergency Workers (Obstructions) Act 2006 'Obstruct/hinder another assisting'	• Without reasonable excuse • Obstruct or hinder • Another person who is assisting • An emergency worker as defined in capacity per s 1(2) • Who is going to, dealing with, or preparing to deal with • An emergency circumstance	• Negative any element of the offence • Reasonable excuse (below) **B1.10.4** • Defences to allegations of assault **B1.1** • General Defences **C**

B1.10.2 Interpretation

Emergency Workers (Obstructions) Act 2006

s 1 'Obstructing or hindering certain emergency workers responding to emergency circumstances'

(3) For the purposes of this section and section 2 of this Act, a person is responding to emergency circumstances if the person—
   (a) is going anywhere for the purpose of dealing with emergency circumstances occurring there; or
   (b) is dealing with emergency circumstances or preparing to do so.

(4) For the purposes of this Act, circumstances are 'emergency' circumstances if they are present or imminent and—
   (a) are causing or are likely to cause—
      (i) serious injury to or the serious illness (including mental illness) of a person;
      (ii) serious harm to the environment (including the life and health of plants and animals);
      (iii) serious harm to any building or other property; or
      (iv) a worsening of any such injury, illness or harm; or
   are likely to cause the death of a person.

B1.10.3 Defences

- See defences to assault **B1.1**.
- See General Defences **C**.
- Reasonable excuse.

B1.10.4 Key points

- 'Reasonable excuse' as a defence to s 1(1) covers incidents where obstruction or hindrance was inadvertent or unavoidable. The example offered by **the Home Office Circular 003/2007, issued 01/02/1997** is a person who is in a traffic jam who causes an obstruction because he cannot get out of the way.

B1.10.5 Sentencing

s 1 Emergency Workers (Obstructions) Act 2006

Summary: A fine

B1.11 Assault/resist/wilfully obstruct a constable in the execution of his duty

Police Act 1996

s 89 'Assaults on constables'

(1) Any person who assaults a constable in the execution of his duty, or a person assisting a constable in the execution of his duty, shall be guilty of an offence and liable on summary conviction to imprisonment for a term not exceeding six months or to an unlimited fine, or to both.

(2) Any person who resists or wilfully obstructs a constable in the execution of his duty, or a person assisting a constable in the execution or his duty, shall be guilty of an offence and liable on summary conviction to imprisonment for a term not exceeding one month or to a fine not exceeding level 3 on the standard scale, or to both.

B1.11.1 Related offences

- Common assault **B1.2**.
- Obstructing a drugs search.

Misuse of Drugs Act 1971

s 23 'Powers to search and obtain evidence'

(4) A person commits an offence if he—

(a) intentionally obstructs a person in the exercise of his powers under this section; or

(b) conceals from a person acting in the exercise of his powers under subsection (1) above any such books, documents, stocks or drugs as are mentioned in that subsection; or

(c) without reasonable excuse (proof of which shall lie on him) fails to produce any such books or documents as are so mentioned where their production is demanded by a person in the exercise of his power under that subsection.

- Assault with intent to resist arrest.

Offences against the Person Act 1861

s 38 'Assault with intent to commit felony, or on peace officers, &c.'

Whosoever .... shall assault any person with intent to resist or prevent the lawful apprehension or detainer of himself or of any other person for any offence, shall be guilty of a misdemeanour, and being convicted thereof shall be liable, at the discretion of the court, to be imprisoned for any term not exceeding two years ...

B1.11.2 Breakdown

Offence	Elements of the Offence	Defence
s 89(1) Police Act 1996 'Assault on constables'	• Assault • A constable, or • A person assisting a constable • In the execution of their duty	• Negative any element of the offence • Defences to allegations of assault **B1.1** • General Defences **C**
s 89(2) Police Act 1996 'Obstructing a police officer'	• Resist, or • Wilfully obstruct • A constable, or • A person assisting a constable • In the execution of their duty	• Negative any element of the offence • Defences to allegations of assault **B1.1** • General Defences **C**
s 38 Offences against the Person Act 1861 'Assault with the intent to resist arrest'	• Assault • Any person • With intent to resist, • Or with intent to prevent • Lawful apprehension or detention • Of himself or of another • In relation to an offence	• Negative any element of the offence • Defences to allegations of assault **B1.1** • General Defences **C**
s 23(4)(a) Misuse of Drugs Act 1971 'Obstruct a drugs search'	• Intentionally • Obstructs • A person acting in the exercise of his powers under s 1 Misuse of Drugs Act 1971	• Negative any element of the offence • Defences to allegations of assault **B1.1** • Reasonable excuse **B1.11.3** • General Defences **C**
s 23(4)(b) Misuse of Drugs Act 1971 'Concealment during a drugs search'	• Conceal an item listed in s 23(1) • Where production of any items mentioned above • Have been demanded • By a person acting in the exercise of his powers under s 1	• Negative any element of the offence • Defences to allegations of assault **B1.1** • Reasonable excuse **B1.11.3** • General Defences **C**
s 23(4)(c) Misuse od Drugs Act 1971 'Obstruct a drugs search—fail to product documents'	• Fail to produce any items listed in s 23(1) • Without reasonable excuse • Which have been demanded • By a person in the exercise of his power under s 1	• Negative any element of the offence • Defences to allegations of assault **B1.1** • Reasonable excuse **B1.11.3** • General Defences **C**

B1.11.3 Defences

- See defences to assault **B1.1**.
- See General Defences **C**.

Misuse of Drugs Act 1971

s 23 'Powers to search and obtain evidence'

(4) A person commits an offence if he—

...

(d) without reasonable excuse (proof of which shall lie on him) fails to produce any such books or documents as are so mentioned where their production is demanded by a person in the exercise of his power under that subsection.

B1.11.4 Key points

- The lawful execution of duty must continue throughout. Any lapse in legality at any point may render all subsequent dealings outside of the execution of a constable's duty (*DPP v Hawkins* [1988] 3 All ER 673).
- There is no requirement of knowledge on the part of the client that the officer was lawfully acting as such, or that they were acting in the execution of their duty (*Albert v Lanvin* [1981] 1 All ER 628).
- By virtue of s 8 of the Prisons Act 1952, prison officers whilst lawfully acting as such (within the execution of their duty) shall have all the powers, authority, protection, and privileges of a constable.
- Powers of arrest must be conferred upon the individual lawfully. Police officers have powers of arrest by virtue of statute. In respect of civilians and a citizen's arrest an offence must have been committed for a lawful power to arrest to exist (*R v Self* [1992] EWCA Crim 2).
- There is no power of detention short of arrest, save to carry out certain searches, and whilst ordinary contact is lawful, a touch beyond that will take an officer outside their duty (*R (Shah) v CCC* [2013] EWHC 1747 (Admin)).

B1.11.5 Sentencing

s 89(1) Police Act 1996

Summary: 6 months' imprisonment and/or a fine

s 89(2) Police Act 1996/s 23 Misuse of Drugs Act 1971

Summary: 1 month's imprisonment and/or a fine not exceeding level 3 on the standard scale

s 38 Offences Against the Person Act 1861

Summary: 6 months' imprisonment and/or fine

Indictment: 2 years' imprisonment

Youth Gravity Matrix

OFFENCE	Gravity Score	Offence type	AGGRAVATING FACTORS	MITIGATING FACTORS
Assault on police (s 51 Police Act 1996)	3	S	• Sustained assault • Attempt to prevent arrest of another • Premeditation • Any injuriescaused • Group action	None

See *Blackstone's Criminal Practice* **B2.37**

B1.12 **False imprisonment**

R v Rahman (1985) 81 Cr App R 349

False imprisonment is committed where the defendant unlawfully and intentionally or recklessly restrains the victim's freedom of movement from a particular place.

B1.12.1 **Related offences**

- Kidnapping **B1.13**.
- Child abduction (see **B4.4**).

B1.12.2 **Breakdown**

Offence	Elements of the Offence	Defence
False imprisonment (*R v Rahman* (1985) 81 Cr App R 349)	• Intentionally or recklessly • Restrain the freedom or movement of a person (A) • A does not consent to the restraint • Without lawful excuse	• Negative any element of the offence • Defences to allegations of assault **B1.1** • General Defences **C**

B1.12.3 Defences

- See General Defences C.

B1.12.4 Key points

- There is no need for physical restraint. Freedom of movement can be restrained through words alone, though if this is the case the victim must realize he is restrained for the offence to be committed (*Alderson v Booth* [1969] QB 216).
- The restraint of movement need only be momentary for the offence to take place (*Simpson v Hill* (1795) 1 Esp 431).
- A wrongly held belief, caused by self-induced intoxication, that the victim consented to the detention is no defence (*R v Hutchins* [1988] Crim LR 379).

B1.12.5 Sentencing

False imprisonment

Indictment: at large (life imprisonment)

Youth Gravity Matrix

OFFENCE	Gravity Score	Offence type	AGGRAVATING FACTORS	MITIGATING FACTORS
False imprisonment	4	1	Always refer to the CPS	

See *Blackstone's Criminal Practice* **B2.91**

B1.13 Kidnapping

R v D [1984] AC 778

The taking or carrying away of one person by another, by force or by fraud, without the consent of the person so taken or carried away, and without lawful excuse.

B1.13.1 Related offences

- Child abduction **B4.4**.
- False imprisonment **B1.12**.

B1.13.2 Breakdown

Offence	Elements of the Offence	Defence
Kidnapping (*R v D* [1984] AC 778)	• Taking or carrying away • Of one person (A) by another (B) • By force or by fraud • Without A's consent • Without lawful excuse	• Negative any element of the offence • Defences to allegations of assault **B1.1** • General Defences **C**

B1.13.3 Defences

- See General Defences C.

B1.13.4 Key points

- In a case where fraud is established it is very difficult to see a situation where the victim's consent could be a consideration *R v Cort* [2003] EWCA Crim 2149.
- It is necessary that the victim is deprived of their liberty (*R v Hendy-Freegard* [2007] EWCA Crim 1236, CA).
- Consent or compliance obtained through force or fear is not true consent (*R v G* [2001] EWCA Crim 1367).
- The *mens rea* for kidnapping is likely to be the same as that for false imprisonment (*R v Hutchins* [1988] Crim LR 379).

B1.13.5 Sentencing

Indictable only: At large (life imprisonment)

Youth Gravity Matrix

OFFENCE	Gravity Score	Offence type	AGGRAVATING FACTORS	MITIGATING FACTORS
Kidnapping	4	1	Always refer to the CPS	

See *Blackstone's Criminal Practice* **B2.97**

B2 **Drugs**

B2.1 **Production of a controlled drug**

Misuse of Drugs Act 1971

s 4 'Restriction of production and supply of controlled drugs'

(1) Subject to any regulations under section 7 of this Act for the time being in force, it shall not be lawful for a person—
    (a) to produce a controlled drug ...

(2) Subject to section 28 of this Act, it is an offence for a person—
    (a) to produce a controlled drug in contravention of subsection (1) ... or
    (b) to be concerned in the production of such a drug in contravention of that subsection by another.

B2.1.1 **Related offences**

- Cultivation of a controlled drug **B2.5.**
- Permitting premises to be used for drugs **B2.6.**
- Possession with intent to supply **B2.4.1.**

B2.1.2 **Breakdown**

Offence	Elements of the Offence	Defence
s 4(2)(a) Misuse of Drugs Act 1971 'Restriction of production and supply of controlled drugs'	• Produce • A controlled drug of Classes A, B, or C	• Negative any element of the offence • s 28 Misuse of Drugs Act 1971 **B2.1.4** • General Defences **C**
s 4(2)(b) Misuse of Drugs Act 1971 'Restriction of production and supply of controlled drugs'	• Be concerned • In the production of • A controlled drug of Classes A, B, or C • By another	• Negative any element of the offence • s 28 Misuse of Drugs Act 1971 **B2.1.4** • General Defences **C**

B2.1.3 Interpretation

Misuse of Drugs Act 1971

s 37 'Interpretation'

(1) ... 'produce', where the reference is to producing a controlled drug, means producing it by manufacture, cultivation or any other method, and 'production' has a corresponding meaning ...

- 'Be concerned in': The prosecution has to prove (1) the supply of a drug to another, or as the case may be, the making of an offer to supply a drug to another, in contravention of section 4(1) of the Act; (2) participation by the defendant in an enterprise involving such supply or, as the case may be, such offer to supply; and (3) knowledge by the defendant of the nature of the enterprise, ie that it involved supply of a drug or, as the case may be, offering to supply a drug (*R v Hughes* (1985) 81 Cr App R 344).

s 37 'Interpretation'

(1) ... 'controlled drug' has the meaning assigned by section 2 of this Act.

s 2 'Controlled drugs and their classification for purposes of this Act'

(1) In this Act—
   (a) the expression 'controlled drug' means any substance or product for the time being specified in Part I, II, or III of Schedule 2 to this Act; and.
   (b) the expressions 'Class A drug', 'Class B drug' and 'Class C drug' mean any of the substances and products for the time being specified respectively in Part I, Part II and Part III of that Schedule;

and the provisions of Part IV of that Schedule shall have effect with respect to the meanings of expressions used in that Schedule.

B2.1.4 Defences

- Statutory

Misuse of Drugs Act 1971

s 28 'Proof of lack of knowledge etc. to be a defence in proceedings for certain offences'

(3) Where in any proceedings for an offence to which this section applies it is necessary, if the accused is to be convicted of the offence charged, for the prosecution to prove that some substance or product involved in the alleged offence was the controlled drug which the prosecution alleges it to have been, and it is proved that the substance or product in question was that controlled drug, the accused—

(a) shall not be acquitted of the offence charged by reason only of proving that he neither knew nor suspected nor had reason to suspect that the substance or product in question was the particular controlled drug alleged; but
(b) shall be acquitted therefore—
   (i) if he proves that he neither believed nor suspected nor had reason to suspect that the substance or product in question was a controlled drug; or
   (ii) if he proves that he believed the substance or product in question to be a controlled drug, or a controlled drug of a description, such that, if it had in fact been that controlled drug or a controlled drug of that description, he would not at the material time have been committing any offence to which this section applies.

- See General Defences C.

B2.1.5 Key point

- An individual who allows the use of their premises in the knowledge that a controlled drug may be produced there is more likely to face charges under 'permitting premises to be used for drugs' **B2.6** than that of production. In such a circumstance the individual is deemed to have a passive presence, insufficient for an offence under s 4(2)(b). A degree of participation in the production is required, ie a positive act by the client towards the forming of the drug into a useable product (*R v Farr* [1982] Crim LR 745).

B2.1.6 Sentencing

s 8 Misuse of Drugs Act 1971

*Class A***

Summary: 6 months' imprisonment and/or fine

Indictment: life imprisonment and/or fine

Class B

Summary: 6 months' imprisonment and/or fine

Indictment: maximum 14 years' imprisonment and/or fine

Class C

Summary: 3 months' imprisonment and/or £2,500 fine

Indictment: maximum 14 years' imprisonment and/or fine

** Triable either way unless the defendant could receive the minimum sentence of seven years for a third drug trafficking offence under section 110 Powers of Criminal Courts (Sentencing) Act 2000 in which case the offence is triable only on indictment.

Youth Gravity Matrix

OFFENCE	Gravity Score	Offence type	AGGRAVATING FACTORS	MITIGATING FACTORS
CLASS 'A' DRUG Production	4	E	• Commercial cultivation • Large quantity	• Small quantities consistent with personal use
CLASS 'B' OR 'C' DRUG Production/ cultivation	4	E	• On school premises • Commercial scale • Supports organized crime	• Small quantities consistent with personal use

See Blackstone's Criminal Practice **B19.55**

B2.2 Supply of a controlled drug

Misuse of Drugs Act 1971

s 4 'Restriction of production and supply of controlled drugs'

(1) Subject to any regulations under section 7 of this Act for the time being in force, it shall not be lawful for a person—

...

(b) to supply or offer to supply a controlled drug to another.

(3) Subject to section 28 of this Act, it is an offence for a person—

(a) to supply or offer to supply a controlled drug to another in contravention of subsection (1) above; or

(b) to be concerned in the supplying of such a drug to another in contravention of that subsection; or

(c) to be concerned in the making to another in contravention of that subsection of an offer to supply such a drug.

B2.2.1 Related offences

- Possession with intent to supply **B2.5.1**.

B2.2.2 Breakdown

Offence	Elements of the Offence	Defence
s 4(3)(a) Misuse of Drugs Act 1971 'Supply/ offer to supply'	• Supply; or • Offer to supply • A controlled drug of Classes A, B, or C	• Negative any element of the offence • s 28 Misuse of Drugs Act 1971 **B2.1.4** • General Defences **C**
s 4(3)(b) Misuse of Drugs Act 1971 'Be concerned in the supply'	• Be concerned • In the supply of • A controlled drug of Classes A, B, or C • By another	• Negative any element of the offence • s 28 Misuse of Drugs Act 1971 **B2.1.4** • General Defences **C**
s 4(3)(b) Misuse of Drugs Act 1971 'Concerned in making an offer to supply'	• Be concerned in the making of an offer • To supply • A controlled drug of Classes A, B, or C	• Negative any element of the offence • s 28 Misuse of Drugs Act 1971 **B2.1.4** • General Defences **C**

B2.2.3 Interpretation

- 'To be concerned in' see **B2.1.3**.
- 'Supply'.

Misuse of Drugs Act 1971

s 37 'Interpretation'

(1) 'supplying' including distributing.

B2.2.4 Defences

- s 28 Misuse of Drugs Act 1971 **B2.1.4**.
- Consider the General Defences **C**.

B2.2.5 Key points

- An offer may be by words or conduct (*R v Mitchell* [1992] Crim LR 723).
- The necessary ingredient of the offence, apart from possession, was the intent to supply to another, that is sufficient for the offence to be made out (*R v Ibrahima* [2005] EWCA Crim 1436).
- An offence under s 4(3) is the offer of sale, not whether the defendant had, or had easy access to the controlled drug (*R v Mitchell* [1992] Crim LR 723).

- A person who prevents or wilfully obstructs a search under s 23 may commit a further offence under s 23(4) Misuse of Drugs Act 1971 **B1.11.1**.

B2.2.6 Sentencing

s 4(3)(a), (b), and (c) Misuse of Drugs Act 1971

*Class A***

Summary: 6 months' imprisonment and/or fine

Indictment: life imprisonment and/or fine

Class B

Summary: 6 months' imprisonment and/or fine

Indictment: maximum 14 years' imprisonment and/or fine

Class C

Summary: 3 months' imprisonment and/or £2,500 fine

Indictment: maximum 14 years' imprisonment and/or fine

** Triable either way unless the defendant could receive the minimum sentence of seven years for a third drug trafficking offence under section 110 Powers of Criminal Courts (Sentencing) Act 2000 in which case the offence is triable only on indictment.

Youth Gravity Matrix

OFFENCE	Gravity Score	Offence type	AGGRAVATING FACTORS	MITIGATING FACTORS
CLASS 'A' DRUG Supply/possession with intent to supply	4	E	• On school premises	
CLASS 'B' OR 'C' DRUG Supply/possession with intent to supply	4	E	• On school premises • Group of people pooling resources to buy a supply to share between them	• No profit made • Intimidated to commit offence on behalf of another

TO

See *Blackstone's Criminal Practice* **B19.37**

B2.3 Importation of a controlled drug

s 3 Misuse of Drugs Act 1971

s 170 Customs and Excise Management Act 1979

Misuse of Drugs Act 1971

s 3 'Restriction of importation and exportation of controlled drugs'

(1) Subject to subsection (2) below—
(a) the importation of a controlled drug; and
(b) the exportation of a controlled drug,
are hereby prohibited.

Customs and Excise Management Act 1979

s 170 'Penalty for fraudulent evasion of duty, etc'

(2) Without prejudice to any other provision of the Customs and Excise Acts 1979, if any person is, in relation to any goods, in any way knowingly concerned in any fraudulent evasion or attempt at evasion
...
(b) of any prohibition or restriction for the time being in force with respect to the goods under or by virtue of any enactment;
he shall be guilty of an offence under this section and may be arrested.

(3) Subject to subsection (4), (4A), (4B) or (4C) below, a person guilty of an offence under this section shall be liable—
(a) on summary conviction, to a £20,000 fine, or to imprisonment for a term not exceeding 6 months, or to both; or
(b) on conviction on indictment, to a fine, or to imprisonment for a term not exceeding 7 years, or to both.

(4) In the case of an offence under this section in connection with prohibition or restriction on importation or exportation having effect by virtue of section 3 of the Misuse of Drugs Act 1971, subsection (3) above shall have effect subject to the modifications specified in Schedule 1 to this Act.

B2.3.1 Breakdown

Offence	Elements of the Offence	Defence
s 3 Misuse of Drugs Act 1971 'Importation/exportation of a controlled drug'	• Importation/exportation • Of a controlled drug of Classes A, B, or C	• Negative any element of the offence • s 3 Misuse of Drugs Act 1971 **B2.3.3** • s 7 Misuse of Drugs Act 1971 **B2.3.3** • General Defences **C**

s 170 Customs and Excise Management Act 1979 'Evading the prohibition'	• Knowingly concerned in • Fraudulent evasion; or • An attempt at evasion • In contravention of any prohibition or restriction in force	• Negative any element of the offence • General Defences **C**

B2.3.2 Interpretation

Customs and Excise Management Act 1979

Schedule 1 'Controlled drugs: variation of punishments for certain offences under this Act'

(1) Section 50(4), 68(3) and 170(3) of this Act shall have effect in a case where the goods in respect of which the offence referred to in that subsection was committed were a Class A drug, Class B drug or a temporary class drug as if for the words from 'shall be liable' onwards there were substituted the following words, that is to say—

'shall be liable—

(a) on summary conviction, to a £20,000 fine, or to imprisonment for a term not exceeding 6 months, or to both;

(b) on conviction on indictment—

(i) where the goods were a Class A drug, to a fine, or to imprisonment for life, or to both; and

(ii) where they were a Class B drug or a temporary class drug, to a fine, or to imprisonment for a term not exceeding 14 years, or to both'.

(2) Section 50(4), 68(3) and 170(3) of this Act shall have effect in a case where the goods in respect of which the offence referred to in that subsection was committed were a Class C drug as if for the words from 'shall be liable' onwards there were substituted the following words, that is to say—

'shall be liable—

(a) on summary conviction, to a £20,000 fine, or to imprisonment for a term not exceeding 3 months, or to both;

(c) on conviction on indictment, to a fine, or to imprisonment for a term not exceeding 14 years, or to both'.

(3) In this Schedule 'Class A drug', 'Class B drug', 'Class C drug' and 'temporary class drug' have the same meanings as in the Misuse of Drugs Act 1971.

- 'Knowingly concerned': involves not merely knowledge of, but also participation in an operation calculated to evade a prohibition and knowledge that the substance in question is indeed prohibited (*R v Taaffe* (1984) 78 Cr App R 301).

- 'Fraudulent:' 'means dishonest conduct deliberately intended to evade the prohibition . There is no necessity for the prosecution to prove acts of deceit practised on a customs officer (*Attorney General's Reference (No 1 of 1981)* (1982) 75 Cr App R 45).

B2.3.3 Defences

Misuse of Drugs Act 1971

s 3 'Restriction of importation and exportation of controlled drugs'

(2) Subsection (1) above does not apply—
   (a) to the Secretary of State and in compliance with any conditions attached to the importation or exportation of a controlled drug which is for the time being excepted from paragraph (a) or, as the case may be, paragraph (b) of subsection (1) above by regulations under section 7 of this Act or by virtue of section 7A; or
   (b) to the importation or exportation of a controlled drug under and in accordance with the terms of a licence issued by the Secretary of State and in compliance with any conditions attached thereto.

s 7 'Authorisation of activities otherwise unlawful under foregoing provisions'

(1) The Secretary of State may by regulations—
   (a) except from section 3(1)(a) or (b), 4(1)(a) or (b) or 5(1) of this Act such controlled drugs as may be specified in the regulations; and
   (b) make such other provision as he thinks fit for the purpose of making it lawful for persons to do things which under any of the following provisions of this Act, that is to say sections 4(1), 5(1) and 6(1), it would otherwise be unlawful for them to do.

(2) Without prejudice to the generality of paragraph (b) of subsection (1) above, regulations under that subsection authorising the doing of any such thing as is mentioned in that paragraph may in particular provide for the doing of that thing to be lawful—
   (a) if it is done under and in accordance with the terms of a licence or other authority issued by the Secretary of State and in compliance with any conditions attached thereto; or
   (b) if it is done in compliance with such conditions as may be prescribed ...

- See General Defences C.

B2.3.4 Key points

- The suspect may be mistaken as to the nature of the substance being trafficked, and a belief, albeit mistaken, that that item was not at the time prohibited may provide a defence (*R v Taaffe* (1984) 78 Cr App R 301 and *R v Forbes* [2001] UKHL 40, by analogy).

- It is not necessary to prove that the suspect knew the precise category of what was being smuggled, simply that it was prohibited (*R v Hussain* (1969) 53 Cr App R 448).
- Where a charge is instead brought under the 1971 Act rather than the 1979 Act, a defence under s 28 of the 1971 Act may apply **B2.1.5**.

B2.3.5 Sentencing

s 3 Misuse of Drugs Act 1971

s 170 Customs and Excise Management Act 1979

*Class A***

Summary: 6 months' imprisonment and/or fine

Indictment: life imprisonment

Class B

Summary: 6 months' imprisonment and/or fine

Indictment: 14 years' imprisonment

Class C

Summary: 3 months' imprisonment and/or band fine

Indictment: 14 years' imprisonment

** Triable either way unless the suspect could receive the minimum sentence of seven years for a third drug trafficking offence under section 110 Powers of Criminal Courts (Sentencing) Act 2000 in which case the offence is triable only on indictment.

See *Blackstone's Criminal Practice* **B19.61**

B2.4 Possession with intent to supply a controlled drug

Misuse of Drugs Act 1971

s 5 'Restriction of possession of controlled drugs'

(3) Subject to section 28 of this Act, it is an offence for a person to have a controlled drug in his possession, whether lawfully or not, with intent to supply it to another in contravention of section 4(1) of this Act.

s 4 'Restriction of production and supply of controlled drugs'

(1) Subject to any regulations under section 7 of this Act for the time being in force, it shall not be lawful for a person—
  (a) to produce a controlled drug; or
  (b) to supply or offer to supply a controlled drug to another.

B2.4.1 Related offences

- Supply of a controlled drug **see B2.2.**

Misuse of Drugs Act 1971

s 5 'Restriction of possession of controlled drugs'

(1) Subject to any regulations under section 7 of this Act for the time being in force, it shall not be lawful for a person to have a controlled drug in his possession.

(2) Subject to section 28 of this Act and to subsection (4) below, it is an offence for a person to have a controlled drug in his possession in contravention of subsection (1) above.

(2A) Subsections (1) and (2) do not apply in relation to a temporary class drug.

B2.4.2 Breakdown

Offence	Elements of the Offence	Defence
s 5(3) Misuse of Drugs Act 1971 'Possession with intent to supply'	• Possession • Of a controlled drug of Classes, A, B, or C • With the intention • To supply/provide the controlled drug • To another	• Negative any element of the offence • s 28 Misuse of Drugs Act 1971 **B2.1.4** • General Defences **C**
s 5 Misuse of Drugs Act 1971 'Possession of a controlled drug'	• Possession • Of a controlled drug of Classes A, B, or C	• Negative any element of the offence • s 28 Misuse of Drugs Act 1971 **B2.1.4** • s 5 Misuse of Drugs Act 1971 **B2.4.4** • General Defences **C**

B2.4.3 Interpretation

- 'Possession'.

Misuse of Drugs Act 1971

s 37 'Interpretation'

(3) For the purposes of this Act the things which a person has in his possession shall be taken to include any thing subject to his control which is in the custody of another.

- 'Possession' is read in its ordinary use: one has in one's possession whatever is, to one's own knowledge, physically in one's custody or under one's physical control (*DPP v Brooks* (1974) 59 Cr App R 185).
- 'Supply'.

Misuse of Drugs Act 1971

s 37 'Interpretation'

(1) ... 'supplying' including distributing

...

(3) For the purposes of this Act the things which a person has in his possession shall be taken to include any thing subject to his control which is in the custody of another.

B2.4.4 Defences

Misuse of Drugs Act 1971

s 28 'Proof of lack of knowledge etc. to be a defence in proceedings for certain offences'

(3) Where in any proceedings for an offence to which this section applies it is necessary, if the accused is to be convicted of the offence charged, for the prosecution to prove that some substance or product involved in the alleged offence was the controlled drug which the prosecution alleges it to have been, and it is proved that the substance or product in question was that controlled drug, the accused—

...

(a) shall not be acquitted of the offence charged by reason only of proving that he neither knew nor suspected nor had reason to suspect that the substance or product in question was the particular controlled drug alleged; but

(b) shall be acquitted therefore—

...

(i) if he proves that he neither believed nor suspected nor had reason to suspect that the substance or product in question was a controlled drug.

s 5 'Restriction of possession of controlled drugs'

(4) In any proceedings for an offence under subsection (2) above in which it is proved that the accused had a controlled drug in his possession, it shall be a defence for him to prove—

(a) that, knowing or suspecting it to be a controlled drug, he took possession of it for the purpose of preventing another from committing or continuing to commit an offence in connection with that drug and that as soon as possible after taking possession of it he took all such steps as were reasonably open to him to destroy the drug or to deliver it into the custody of a person lawfully entitled to take custody of it; or

(b) that, knowing or suspecting it to be a controlled drug, he took possession of it for the purpose of delivering it into the custody of a person lawfully entitled to take custody of it and that as soon as possible after taking possession of it he took all such steps as were reasonably open to him to deliver it into the custody of such a person.

- See General Defences **C**.

B2.4.5 Key points

- Where a person is in unlawful possession of a controlled drug which has been deposited with him for safe keeping; he has the intent to supply that drug to another if his intention is to return the drug to the person who deposited it with him (*R v Maginnis* [1987] UKHL 4).
- The necessary ingredient of the offence, apart from possession, was the intent to supply to another. That would be sufficient to make out the offence (*R v Ibrahima* [2005] EWCA Crim 1436).
- The mental element involves proof of knowledge that the thing exists and that it is in his possession. Proof of knowledge that the thing is an article of a particular kind, quality, or description is not required (*R v Lambert* [2001] UKHL 37).
- Using restricted drugs (eg cannabis) for medicinal purposes does not make possession lawful (*AG's Reference (No 2 of 2004)* [2005] EWCA Crim 1415).
- The power to search for a controlled drug is contained with s 23 Misuse of Drugs Act 1971, which allows for a search of person, property, vehicle, or vessel. A person who prevents or wilfully obstructs a search may commit a further offence under s 23(4) Misuse of Drugs Act 1971 **B1.11.1**. PACE Code A also allows the search of a person found within a premises for which a search power has been authorized (PACE Code A, para 2.27(b)).

- Section 23 Misuse of Drugs Act 1971 is still subject to the provisions of s 2 Police and Criminal Evidence Act 1984 which if not adhered to may render any evidence obtained inadmissible. Ensure the search provisions of the 1971 Act are in accordance with the lawful search of an individual under PACE, in particular in respect of intimate searches (PACE Code A, NfG para 6).
- Powers governing searches under the 1971 Act are contained within PACE Code A.
- The Home Secretary has the power under Misuse of Drugs Act 1971 to designate a substance or product as temporarily akin to a Class B drug. A Temporary Class Drug Order (TCDO) will attract the same levels of punishment as those drugs specified as within Class B.

B2.4.6 Sentencing

s 5(3) possession with intent to supply a controlled drug

Class A

Summary: 6 months' imprisonment and/or a fine

Indictment: life imprisonment and/or unlimited fine

Class B

Summary: 6 months' imprisonment and/or a fine

Indictment: 14 years' custody and/or fine

Class C

Summary: 3 months' imprisonment and/or a fine not exceeding level 4 on the standard scale

Indictment: 14 years' custody and/or fine

Youth Gravity Matrix

OFFENCE	Gravity Score	Offence type	AGGRAVATING FACTORS	MITIGATING FACTORS
CLASS 'A' DRUG Supply/possession with intent to supply	4	E	• On school premises	
CLASS 'B' OR 'C' DRUG Supply/possession with intent to supply	4	E	• On school premises • Group of people pooling resources to buy a supply to share between them	• No profit made • Intimidated to commit offence on behalf of another

TO

s 5(1) and (2) possession of a controlled drug

Class A

Summary: 6 months' imprisonment and/or a fine

Indictment: 7 years' imprisonment and/or fine

Class B

Summary: 3 months' imprisonment and/or a fine not exceeding level 4 on the standard scale

Indictment: 5 years' imprisonment and/or fine

Class C

Summary: 3 months' imprisonment and/or a fine not exceeding level 3 on the standard scale

Indictment: 2 years' imprisonment and/or fine

Youth Gravity Matrix

OFFENCE	Gravity Score	Offence type	AGGRAVATING FACTORS	MITIGATING FACTORS
CLASS 'A' DRUG Possession	3	E	• On school premises • In prison establishment • Large quantity	• Small quantities consistent with personal use
CLASS 'B' OR 'C' DRUG Possession	2	E	• On school premises • In prison establishment • Large quantity	• Small quantities consistent with personal use

TO

B2.4.7 Diversion

The **ACPO Guidance on Cannabis/Khat Possession for Personal Use, January 2009** gives a three-stage escalation framework for adult defendants and guidance regarding youth defendants. Adult defendants may first receive a pre-arrest caution/warning, followed by a PND and as a final strike may be liable to arrest and charge.

Case law gives guidance on the administration of a caution for the possession of cannabis/khat.

B2.4.8 PND for cannabis/khat Class B

Possession of cannabis under s5(3) can now be dealt with by way of a PND instant penalty provided that the suspect is aged 16 or over.

For possession with intent to supply see *Blackstone's Criminal Practice* **B19.48**.

For possession of a controlled drug see *Blackstone's Criminal Practice* **B19.19**.

B2.5 Cultivation of a controlled drug

Misuse of Drugs Act 1971

s 6 'Restriction of cultivation of cannabis plant'

(1) Subject to any regulations under section 7 of this Act for the time being in force, it shall not be lawful for a person to cultivate any plant of the genus Cannabis.

(2) Subject to section 28 of this Act, it is an offence to cultivate any such plant in contravention subsection (1) above.

B2.5.1 Related offences

- Produce a controlled drug **B2.1**.
- Permitting premises to be used for drugs **B2.6**.

B2.5.2 Breakdown

Offence	Elements of the Offence	Defence
s 6 Misuse of Drugs Act 1971 'Cultivation of Cannabis Plant'	• Cultivate • Cannabis plant(s)	• Negative any element of the offence • s 28 Misuse of Drugs Act 1971 **B2.1.4** • General Defences **C**

B2.5.3 Interpretation

- Cultivate

Misuse of Drugs Act 1971

s 37 'Interpretation'

(1) ... 'produce', where the reference is to producing a controlled drug, means producing it by manufacture, cultivation or any other method, and 'production' has a corresponding meaning;

...

'cannabis' (except in the expression 'cannabis resin') means any plant of the genus Cannabis or any part of any such plant (by whatever name designated) except that it does not include cannabis resin or any of the following products after separation from the rest of the plant, namely—

(a) mature stalk of any such plant,
(b) fibre produced from mature stalk of any such plant, and
(c) seed of any such plant.

B2.5.4 Defences

- s 28 Misuse of Drugs Act **B2.1.4**.
- See General Defences **C**.

B2.5.5 Key point

- A simple act such as placing a plant in a protected environment (eg a bedroom where it is shielded from the elements) or watering the soil is a positive act encouraging growth (*Taylor v Chief Constable of Kent* (1981) 72 Cr App R 318).

B2.5.6 Sentencing

s 6 Misuse of Drugs Act 1971

Summary: 6 months' imprisonment and/or fine

Indictment: 14 years' imprisonment and/or a fine

Youth Gravity Matrix

OFFENCE	Gravity Score	Offence type	AGGRAVATING FACTORS	MITIGATING FACTORS
CLASS 'B' OR 'C' DRUG Production/ cultivation	4	E	• On school premises • Commercial scale • Supports organized crime	• Small quantities consistent with personal use

See *Blackstone's Criminal Practice* **B19.62**

B2.6 Permitting premises to be used for drugs

B2.6.1 Permitting premises to be used for drugs

Misuse of Drugs Act 1971

s 8 'Occupiers etc. of premises to be punishable for permitting certain activities to take place there'

A person commits an offence if, being the occupier or concerned in the management of any premises, he knowingly permits or suffers any of the following activities to take place on those premises, that is to say—

(a) producing or attempting to produce a controlled drug in contravention of section 4(1) of this Act;

(b) supplying or attempting to supply a controlled drug to another in contravention of section 4(1) of this Act, or offering to supply a controlled drug to another in contravention of section 4(1);

(c) preparing opium for smoking;

(d) smoking cannabis, cannabis resin or prepared opium.

B2.6.2 Related offences

- Produce a controlled drug **B2.1**.
- Supply of a controlled drug **B2.1**.
- Possession with intent to supply **B2.4**.
- Cultivation of a controlled drug **B2.5**.

B2.6.3 Breakdown

Offence	Elements of the Offence	Defence
s 8(a) Misuse of Drugs Act 1971 'Occupiers etc. of premises to be punishable for permitting certain activities to take place there'	• Occupier or being concerned in the management of premises • Knowingly • Permits/suffers • On the premises • Production/attempts to produce, • Of a controlled drug of Classes A, B, or C	• Negative any element of the offence • General Defences **C**

Offence	Elements of the Offence	Defence
s 8(b) Misuse of Drugs Act 1971 'Occupiers etc. of premises to be punishable for permitting certain activities to take place there'	• Occupier or being concerned in the management of premises • Knowingly • Permits/suffers • On the premises • Supply/attempts to supply/offering to supply • Of a controlled drug of Classes A, B, or C • To another	• Negative any element of the offence • General Defences **C**
s 8(c) Misuse of Drugs Act 1971 'Occupiers etc. of premises to be punishable for permitting certain activities to take place there'	• Occupier or being concerned in the management of premises • Knowingly • Permits/suffers • On the premises • Preparing opium for smoking	• Negative any element of the offence • General Defences **C**
s 8(d) Misuse of Drugs Act 1971 'Occupiers etc. of premises to be punishable for permitting certain activities to take place there'	• Occupier or being concerned in the management of premises • Knowingly permits/suffers • On the premises • Smoking cannabis, cannabis resin, or smoking prepared opium.	• Negative any element of the offence • General Defences **C**

B2.6.4 Interpretation

- 'Occupier': should be given its ordinary meaning and includes anyone who is by licence entitled to exclusive possession, eg a tenant under a lease (*R v Tao* (1976) 63 Cr App R 163).
- 'Knowingly': actual knowledge or knowledge of circumstances existing (*R v Souter* [1971] 2 All ER 1151). Knowledge may be inferred.
- 'Producing': **B2.1.4**.
- 'Supplying': **B2.4.3**.
- 'Controlled drug': **B2.1.4**.

B2.6.5 Defences

- s 28 Misuse of Drugs Act **B2.1.4**.
- See General Defences **C**.

B2.6.6 Key points

- Suspicion is not knowledge but where there is wilful blindness this may be sufficient (*R v Thomas* (1976) 63 Cr App R 65; *Sweet v Parsley* [1970] AC 132).
- What the prosecution must prove to establish the offence of permitting under s 8(b) is (i) knowledge, actual or by closing eyes to the obvious, that [drug] dealing is taking place; and (ii) unwillingness to prevent it, which can be inferred from failure to take reasonable steps readily available to prevent it (*R v Brock and Wyner* [2000] EWCA Crim 85).

B2.6.7 Sentencing

s 8 Misuse of Drugs Act 1971

*Class A***

Summary: 6 months' imprisonment and/or fine

Indictment: 14 years' imprisonment

Class B

Summary: 6 months' imprisonment and/or band A fine

Indictment: 14 years' imprisonment

Class C

Summary: 3 months' imprisonment and/or band A fine

Indictment: 14 years' imprisonment

** Triable either way unless the defendant could receive the minimum sentence of seven years for a third drug trafficking offence under section 110 Powers of Criminal Courts (Sentencing) Act 2000 in which case the offence is triable only on indictment.

Youth Gravity Matrix

OFFENCE	Gravity Score	Offence type	AGGRAVATING FACTORS	MITIGATING FACTORS
Permit use of premises for smoking cannabis or cannabis resin	2	E	• On commercial basis • Evidence of widespread use	• Vulnerable offender

See *Blackstone's Criminal Practice* **B19.78**

B3 **Sexual Offences**

B3.1 **Interpretation for sexual offences**

Sexual Offences Act 2003

s 21 'Positions of trust'

(1) For the purposes of sections 16 to 19, a person (A) is in a position of trust in relation to another person (B) if—
   (a) any of the following subsections applies, or
   (b) any condition specified in an order made by the Secretary of State is met.

(2) This subsection applies if A looks after persons under 18 who are detained in an institution by virtue of a court order or under an enactment, and B is so detained in that institution.

(3) This subsection applies if A looks after persons under 18 who are resident in a home or other place in which—
   (a) accommodation and maintenance are provided by an authority in accordance with section 22C(6) of the Children Act 1989, or
   (b) accommodation is provided by a voluntary organisation under section 59(1) of that Act,

   and B is resident, and is so provided with accommodation and maintenance or accommodation, in that place.

(4) This subsection applies if A looks after persons under 18 who are accommodated and cared for in one of the following institutions—
   (a) a hospital,
   (b) in Wales, an independent clinic,
   (c) a care home,
   (d) a community home, voluntary home or children's home, or
   (e) a home provided under section 82(5) of the Children Act 1989,

   and B is accommodated and cared for in that institution.

(5) This subsection applies if A looks after persons under 18 who are receiving education at an educational institution and B is receiving, and A is not receiving, education at that institution.

...

(7) This subsection applies if A is engaged in the provision of services under, or pursuant to anything done under—
   (a) sections 8 to 10 of the Employment and Training Act 1973, or
   (b) section 68, 70(1)(b) or 74 of the Education and Skills Act 2008,

   and, in that capacity, looks after B on an individual basis.

(8) This subsection applies if A regularly has unsupervised contact with B (whether face to face or by any other means)—
   (a) in the exercise of functions of a local authority under section 20 or 21 of the Children Act 1989,

(9) This subsection applies if A, as a person who is to report to the court under section 7 of the Children Act 1989 on matters relating to the

welfare of B, regularly has unsupervised contact with B (whether face to face or by any other means).

(10) This subsection applies if A is a personal adviser appointed for B under—
   (a) section 23B(2) of, or paragraph 19C of Schedule 2 to, the Children Act 1989,

   and, in that capacity, looks after B on an individual basis.

(11) This subsection applies if—
   (a) B is subject to a care order, a supervision order or an education supervision order, and
   (b) in the exercise of functions conferred by virtue of the order on an authorised person or the authority designated by the order, A looks after B on an individual basis.

(12) This subsection applies if A—
   (a) is an officer of the Service or Welsh family proceedings officer (within the meaning given by section 35 of the Children Act 2004) appointed for B under section 41(1) of the Children Act 1989,
   (b) is appointed a children's guardian of B under rule 6 or rule 18 of the Adoption Rules 1984 (S.I. 1984/265),
   (c) is appointed to be the guardian ad litem of B under rule 9.5 of the Family Proceedings Rules 1991 (S.I. 1991/1247), or
   (d) is appointed to be the children's guardian of B under rule 59 of the Family Procedure (Adoption) Rules 2005 (S.I. 2005/2795) or rule 16.3(1)(ii) or rule 16.4 of the Family Procedure Rules 2010 (S.I. 2010/2955),

   and, in that capacity, regularly has unsupervised contact with B (whether face to face or by any other means).

(13) This subsection applies if—
   (a) B is subject to requirements imposed by or under an enactment on his release from detention for a criminal offence, or is subject to requirements imposed by a court order made in criminal proceedings, and
   (b) A looks after B on an individual basis in pursuance of the requirements.

s 22 'Positions of trust interpretation'

(1) The following provisions apply for the purposes of section 21.

(2) Subject to subsection (3), a person looks after persons under 18 if he is regularly involved in caring for, training, supervising or being in sole charge of such persons.

(3) A person (A) looks after another person (B) on an individual basis if—
   (a) A is regularly involved in caring for, training or supervising B, and
   (b) in the course of his involvement, A regularly has unsupervised contact with B (whether face to face or by any other means).

(4) A person receives education at an educational institution if—
   (a) he is registered or otherwise enrolled as a pupil or student at the institution, or
   (b) he receives education at the institution under arrangements with another educational institution at which he is so registered or otherwise enrolled.

(5) In section 21—

   'authority'—
      (a) in relation to England and Wales, means a local authority;

'care home' means an establishment which is a care home for the purposes of the Care Standards Act 2000;

'care order' has—

(a) in relation to England and Wales, the same meaning as in the Children Act 1989,

'children's home' has—

(a) in relation to England and Wales, the meaning given by section 1 of the Care Standards Act 2000,'community home' has the meaning given by section 53 of the Children Act 1989;

'education supervision order' has—

(a) in relation to England and Wales, the meaning given by section 36 of the Children Act 1989,

'hospital' means—

(a) a hospital as defined by section 275 of the National Health Service Act 2006, or section 206 of the National Health Service (Wales) Act 2006; or

(b) any other establishment—

(i) in England, in which any of the services listed in subsection (6) are provided; and

(ii) in Wales, which is a hospital within the meaning given by section 2(3) of the Care Standards Act 2000;

'independent clinic' has—

(a) the meaning given by section 2 of the Care Standards Act 2000;

'supervision order' has—

(a) in relation to England and Wales, the meaning given by section 31(11) of the Children Act 1989,

'voluntary home' has—

(a) in relation to England and Wales, the meaning given by section 60(3) of the Children Act 1989,

(6) The services referred to in paragraph (b)(i) of the definition of 'hospital' are as follows—

(a) medical treatment under anaesthesia or intravenously administered sedation;

(b) dental treatment under general anaesthesia;

(c) obstetric services and, in connection with childbirth, medical services;

(d) termination of pregnancies;

(e) cosmetic surgery, other than—

(i) ear and body piercing;

(ii) tattooing;

(iii) the subcutaneous injection of a substance or substances into the skin for cosmetic purposes; or

(iv) the removal of hair roots or small blemishes on the skin by the application of heat using an electric current.

s 68 'Voyeurism interpretation'

(1) For the purposes of section 67, a person is doing a private act if the person is in a place which, in the circumstances, would reasonably be expected to provide privacy, and—

(a) the person's genitals, buttocks or breasts are exposed or covered only with underwear,

(b) the person is using a lavatory, or
(c) the person is doing a sexual act that is not of a kind ordinarily done in public.

(2) In section 67, 'structure' includes a tent, vehicle or vessel or other temporary or movable structure.

s 74 'Consent'

For the purposes of this Part, a person consents if he agrees by choice, and has the freedom and capacity to make that choice.

s 75 'Evidential presumptions about consent'

(1) If in proceedings for an offence to which this section applies it is proved—
(a) that the defendant did the relevant act,
(b) that any of the circumstances specified in subsection (2) existed, and
(c) that the defendant knew that those circumstances existed, the complainant is to be taken not to have consented to the relevant act unless sufficient evidence is adduced to raise an issue as to whether he consented, and the defendant is to be taken not to have reasonably believed that the complainant consented unless sufficient evidence is adduced to raise an issue as to whether he reasonably believed it.

(2) The circumstances are that—
(a) any person was, at the time of the relevant act or immediately before it began, using violence against the complainant or causing the complainant to fear that immediate violence would be used against him;
(b) any person was, at the time of the relevant act or immediately before it began, causing the complainant to fear that violence was being used, or that immediate violence would be used, against another person;
(c) the complainant was, and the defendant was not, unlawfully detained at the time of the relevant act;
(d) the complainant was asleep or otherwise unconscious at the time of the relevant act;
(e) because of the complainant's physical disability, the complainant would not have been able at the time of the relevant act to communicate to the defendant whether the complainant consented;
(f) any person had administered to or caused to be taken by the complainant, without the complainant's consent, a substance which, having regard to when it was administered or taken, was capable of causing or enabling the complainant to be stupefied or overpowered at the time of the relevant act.

(3) In subsection (2)(a) and (b), the reference to the time immediately before the relevant act began is, in the case of an act which is one of a continuous series of sexual activities, a reference to the time immediately before the first sexual activity began.

s 76 'Conclusive presumptions about consent'

(1) If in proceedings for an offence to which this section applies it is proved that the defendant did the relevant act and that any of the circumstances specified in subsection (2) existed, it is to be conclusively presumed—
(a) that the complainant did not consent to the relevant act, and

(b) that the defendant did not believe that the complainant consented to the relevant act.

(2) The circumstances are that—

(a) the defendant intentionally deceived the complainant as to the nature or purpose of the relevant act;

(b) the defendant intentionally induced the complainant to consent to the relevant act by impersonating a person known personally to the complainant.

s 77 'Sections 75 and 76: relevant acts'

In relation to an offence to which sections 75 and 76 apply, references in those sections to the relevant act and to the complainant are to be read as follows—

Offence	Relevant Act
An offence under section 1 (rape).	The defendant intentionally penetrating, with his penis, the vagina, anus, or mouth of another person ('the complainant').
An offence under section 2 (assault by penetration).	The defendant intentionally penetrating, with a part of his body or anything else, the vagina or anus of another person ('the complainant'), where the penetration is sexual.
An offence under section 3 (sexual assault).	The defendant intentionally touching another person ('the complainant'), where the touching is sexual.
An offence under section 4 (causing a person to engage in sexual activity without consent).	The defendant intentionally causing another person ('the complainant') to engage in an activity, where the activity is sexual.

s 78 'Sexual'

For the purposes of this Part (except section 71), penetration, touching or any other activity is sexual if a reasonable person would consider that—

(a) whatever its circumstances or any person's purpose in relation to it, it is because of its nature sexual, or

(b) because of its nature it may be sexual and because of its circumstances or the purpose of any person in relation to it (or both) it is sexual.

s 79 'General interpretation'

(1) The following apply for the purposes of this Part.

(2) Penetration is a continuing act from entry to withdrawal.

(3) References to a part of the body include references to a part surgically constructed (in particular, through gender reassignment surgery).

(4) 'Image' means a moving or still image and includes an image produced by any means and, where the context permits, a three-dimensional image.

(5) References to an image of a person include references to an image of an imaginary person.

(6) 'Mental disorder' has the meaning given by section 1 of the Mental Health Act 1983.
(7) References to observation (however expressed) are to observation whether direct or by looking at an image.
(8) Touching includes touching—
(a) with any part of the body,
(b) with anything else,
(c) through anything,
and in particular includes touching amounting to penetration.
(9) 'Vagina' includes vulva.
(10) In relation to an animal, references to the vagina or anus include references to any similar part.

B3.1.1 Common law interpretation

- The correct approach to be taken when applying s 78(b) is to treat it in two parts: (1) whether that, because of its nature, the touching *could* be sexual, and if so, (2) whether, in view of the circumstances and/or the purpose of any person in relation to the touching, the touching was in *fact* sexual (*R v H* [2005] EWCA Crim 732).
- The word 'breasts' in s 68(1)(a) Sexual Offences Act 2003 does not extend to the exposed male chest (*R v Bassett* [2008] EWCA Crim 1174).
- Where (B) consents to sexual intercourse on the proviso that (A) wear a condom, should (A) have sexual intercourse with (B) without a condom this would amount to rape (*Assange v Swedish Prosecution Authority* [2011] EWHC 2849 (Admin)).

B3.1.2 Notification requirements

Those offences for which a Sexual Offences Notification Requirement is required ('Qualifying Offence') will be identified in the respective offence. A conviction for any Qualifying Offence will automatically trigger the notification requirement.

For some offences a specific order (see Schedule 3 Sexual Offences Act 2003) is required before the notification provisions apply; for the purposes of this book these are:

Sexual Assault by Touching **B3.6**	Sexual Assault by Touching a Child Under 13 **B3.17**	Arranging or Facilitating a Child Sex Offence **B3.23**	Abuse of Position of Trust: Sexual Activity with a Child **B3.20**

Abuse of Position of Trust: Causing or Inciting a Child to Engage in Sexual Activity **B3.21**	Commit an Offence with Intent to Commit a Sexual Offence **B3.12**	Exposure **B3.9**	Voyeurism **B3.8**

B3.1.2.1 *Notification requirements (adult)*

Description of Relevant Offender	Notification Period
A person who has been sentenced to a term of imprisonment of 30 months or more	Indefinite
A person who has been admitted to a hospital subject to a restriction order	Indefinite
A person who has been sentenced to a term of imprisonment of more than 6 months but less than 30 months	10 years
A person who has been sentenced to a term of imprisonment of 6 months or less	7 years
A person who has been admitted to a hospital without a restriction order	7 years
A person subject to a caution	2 years
A person subject to a conditional discharge	The period of the conditional discharge
A person of any other description (fine/ community order etc)	5 years

B3.1.2.2 *Notification requirements (youth)*

Where a person is under the age of 18 at the time of the offence, the notification requirements are significantly different.

For a person aged under 18 the automatic notification requirement is only triggered for the following offences:

Rape (**B3.4**)	Assault by Penetration (**B3.5**)	Causing or Inciting a Child to Engage in Sexual Activity (**B3.22**)	Rape of a Child Under 13 (**B3.15**)
Assault of a Child Under 13 by Penetration (**B3.16**)	Causing or Inciting a Child Under 13 to Engage in Sexual Activity (**B3.22**)	Offences Against a Person with a Mental Disorder (ss 30–37)	Administering a Substance with Intending to Commit a Sexual Offence (**B3.11**)

For those under the age of 18 at the time of the offence, the notification period is half of that for an adult (s 82(2) Sexual Offences Act 2003):

Description of Relevant Offender	Notification Period
A person who has been sentenced to a term of imprisonment of 30 months or more	Indefinite
A person who has been admitted to a hospital subject to a restriction order	Indefinite
A person who has been sentenced to a term of imprisonment of more than 6 months but less than 30 months	5 years
A person who has been sentenced to a term of imprisonment of 6 months or less	3½ years
A person who has been admitted to a hospital without a restriction order	3 ½ years
A person subject to a youth caution/youth conditional caution	1 year
A person subject to a conditional discharge	The period of the conditional discharge
A person of any other description (fine/ community order etc)	2½ years

B3.2 Defences for sexual offences

Sexual Offences Act 2003

s 23 'Sections 16 to 19: exception for spouses and civil partners'

(1) Conduct by a person (A) which would otherwise be an offence under any of sections 16 to 19 against another person (B) is not an offence under that section if at the time—
   (a) B is 16 or over, and
   (b) A and B are lawfully married [or civil partners of each other].

(2) In proceedings for such an offence it is for the defendant to prove that A and B [were at the time lawfully married or civil partners of each other].

s 24 'Sections 16 to 19: sexual relationships which pre-date position of trust'

(1) Conduct by a person (A) which would otherwise be an offence under any of sections 16 to 19 against another person (B) is not an offence under that section if, immediately before the position of trust arose, a sexual relationship existed between A and B.

(2) Subsection (1) does not apply if at that time sexual intercourse between A and B would have been unlawful.

(3) In proceedings for an offence under any of sections 16 to 19 it is for the defendant to prove that such a relationship existed at that time.

B3.3 **Historic sexual offences**

The Sexual Offences Act 2003 ('SOA 2003') came into force on **1 May 2004** and applies to any relevant offence which occurs on, or after, this date. Where an offence occurred before 1 May 2004

Offence	Elements SOA 2003	Elements SOA 1956	Key Changes
Rape (s 1 SOA 2003) (s 1 SOA 1956)	• A penetrates the vagina, anus, or mouth of B • Using his penis • B does not consent to the penetration • A does not reasonably believe B consents	• A has vaginal or anal sexual intercourse • With a person who does not consent to it (B) • At the time, A knows, or is reckless to the fact, that B does not consent to it	• Rape cannot occur orally under the SOA 1956 • Reasonable belief in consent is not a consideration for offences of rape under SOA 1956
Sexual Assault/ Indecent Assault (s 2 SOA 2003—by penetration) (s 3 SOA 2003—by touching) (s 14 SOA 1956—female) (s 15 SOA 1956—Male)	• A intentionally penetrates the vagina or anus of B • Using a part of his body or anything else • The penetration is sexual • B does not consent to the penetration • A does not reasonably believe B consents *Or* • Intentional touching of a person (B) by another person (A) • B is aged 13 or older • The touching was sexual in nature • A did not reasonably believe that B consented	• A person makes an indecent assault • On a woman • A girl who is under 16 cannot consent • A woman who is a defective cannot consent *Or* • A person makes an indecent assault • On a man • A boy who is under 16 cannot consent • A man who is a defective cannot consent	• Under SOA 1956 the offences are split by gender • There is the defence of marriage for an indecent assault on a woman • It is a defence under SOA 1956—where the female victim is under 16—for the defendant to have an honest belief that the victim was over 16 (*R v K* [2001] UKHL 41)

Offence	Elements SOA 2003	Elements SOA 1956	Key Changes
Buggery (s 12 SOA 1956)	N/A	• A commits buggery with another person or animal • It is a defence if the act takes place between two people who have attained the age of 16; and • The act takes place in private	N/A

the SOA 2003 does not reach back and apply. There are important differences between the SOA 2003 and the Sexual Offences Act 1956 ('SOA 1956') and these as demonstrated below:

- See notification requirements **B3.1.2**.

B3.4 Rape

Sexual Offences Act 2003

s 1 'Rape'

(1) A person (A) commits an offence if—
- (a) He intentionally penetrates the vagina, anus, or mouth of another person (B) with the penis,
- (b) B does not consent to the penetration, and
- (c) A does not reasonably believe B consents.

B3.4.1 Related offences

See also:

- Historic rape **B3.3**.
- Rape of a child under 13 years old **B3.15**.
- Sexual assault by penetration **B3.5**.
- Sexual assault by penetration of a child under 13 years old **B3.16**.
- Sexual activity with a child **B3.19**.
- Arranging/facilitating the commission of a child sex offence **B3.23**.

B3.4.2 Breakdown

Offence	Elements of the Offence	Defence
s 1 Sexual Offences Act 2003 'Rape'	• A penetrates the vagina, anus, or mouth of B • Using his penis • B does not consent to the penetration • A does not reasonably believe that B consents	• Negative any element of the offence • *R v Bree* **B3.4.4** • Defences for sexual offences **B3.2** • General Defences **C**

B3.4.3 Interpretation

See interpretation for sexual offences **B3.1**.

> **Sexual Offences Act 2003**
>
> **s 1 'Rape'**
>
> (2) Whether the belief is reasonable is to be determined having regard to all the circumstances, including any steps A has taken to ascertain whether B consents.

B3.4.4 Defences

- See General Defences **C**.
- If, through drink (or for any other reason) the complainant has temporarily lost capacity to choose whether to have intercourse on the relevant occasion, there is no consent. However, where the complainant has voluntarily consumed even substantial quantities of alcohol, but nevertheless remains capable of choosing whether or not to have intercourse, and in drink agrees to do so, this would not be rape (*R v Bree* [2007] EWCA Crim 804).

B3.4.5 Key points

- The scope of any consent can be limited; in *R (on the application of F) v DPP* [2013] EWHC 945 (Admin) it was held that where the complainant consented to sexual intercourse on the condition that ejaculation would not occur within the vagina, any intention by the defendant to ejaculate within the vagina would vitiate this consent and make out the offence of rape. It is important to note that as penetration is a continuing act (s 79(2) Sexual Offences Act 2003) and as such it is not necessary for the defendant to have formed an intention to do any act outside of the scope of the complainant's consent before sexual intercourse began.

- Where (B) consents to sexual intercourse on the proviso that (A) wear a condom, should (A) have sexual intercourse with (B) without a condom this would amount to rape *Assange v Swedish Prosecution Authority* [2011] EWHC 2849 (Admin).

B3.4.6 Sentencing

s 1 Sexual Offences Act 2003

Indictment: life imprisonment

See notification requirements **B3.1.2**.

Youth Gravity Matrix

OFFENCE	Gravity Score	Offence type	AGGRAVATING FACTORS	MITIGATING FACTORS
Rape (s 1)	4	I	Defer Decision to CPS	

See *Blackstone's Criminal Practice* **B3.6**

B3.5 Sexual assault by penetration

Sexual Offences Act 2003

s 2 'Assault by Penetration'

(1) A person (A) commits an offence if—
   (a) he intentionally penetrates the vagina or anus of another person (B) with a part of his body or anything else,
   (b) the penetration is sexual,
   (c) B does not consent to the penetration, and
   (d) A does not reasonably believe that B consents.

(2) Whether a belief is reasonable is to be determined having regard to all the circumstances, including any steps A has taken to ascertain whether B consents.

(3) Sections 75 and 76 apply to an offence under this section.

B3.5.1 Related offences

See also:

- Sexual assault by penetration of a child under 13 years old **B3.15**.

- Rape **B3.4**.
- Rape of a child under 13 years old **B3.15**.

B3.5.2 Breakdown

Offence	Elements of the Offence	Defence
s 2 Sexual Offences Act 2003 'Sexual assault by penetration'	• A penetrates the vagina or anus of B • Using a part of his body or anything else • The penetration is sexual • B does not consent to the penetration • A does not reasonably believe that B consents	• Negative any element of the offence • Defences for sexual offences **B3.2** • General Defences **C**

B3.5.3 Interpretation

- See interpretation for sexual offences **B3.1**.

B3.5.4 Defences

- See General Defences **C**.

B3.5.5 Key points

- As with rape, penetration of the vagina includes penetration of a surgically reconstructed vagina (s 79(3) Sexual Offences Act 2003).
- Penetration is a continuing act from entry to withdrawal (s 79(2) Sexual Offences Act 2003).

B3.5.6 Sentencing

An offender convicted of these offences is automatically subject to notification.

s 2 Sexual Offences Act 2003

Indictment: life imprisonment

See notification requirements **B3.1.2**.

Youth Gravity Matrix

OFFENCE	Gravity Score	Offence type	AGGRAVATING FACTORS	MITIGATING FACTORS
Assault by penetration (s 2)	4	I	Defer Decision to CPS	

See *Blackstone's Criminal Practice* **B3.43**

B3.6 **Sexual assault by touching**

Sexual Offences Act 2003

s 3 'Sexual Assault'

(1) A person (A) commits an offence if—
- (a) he intentionally touches another person (B),
- (b) the touching is sexual,
- (c) B does not consent to the touching, and
- (d) A does not reasonably believe that B consents.

(2) Whether a belief is reasonable is to be determined having regard to all the circumstances, including any steps A has taken to ascertain whether B consents.

(3) Sections 75 and 76 apply to an offence under this section.

B3.6.1 **Breakdown**

Offence	Elements of the Offence	Defence
s 3 Sexual Offences Act 2003 'Sexual assault by touching'	• Intentional touching of a person (B) by another person (A) • B is aged 13 or older • A does not reasonably believe that B consents	• Negative any element of the offence • Defences for sexual offences **B3.2** • General Defences **C**

B3.6.2 **Defences**

- See General Defences C.

B3.6.3 Key points

- See s 79(8) **B3.1** for the definition of touching.
- In *R v H* [2005] 1 WLR 2005 the grabbing of a female's tracksuit bottoms, without touching any part of her body, in an attempt to pull her towards the male was deemed to satisfy the offence under

s 3 but note that the defendant did not give evidence in this trial and an inference was drawn.

- The question of whether touching is sexual should be considered objectively through s 78 **B3.1**.
- The touching must be deliberate and recklessness is insufficient. This is a crime of basic intent so that voluntary intoxication will not provide a defence to intentional touching but a drunken accident is still an accident (*R v Heard* [2007] EWCA Crim 125).

B3.6.4 Sentencing

s 3(1)–(3) Sexual Offences Act 2003

Summary: fine and/or 6 months' imprisonment

Indictment: 10 years' imprisonment

See notification requirements **B3.1.2**.

Youth Gravity Matrix

OFFENCE	Gravity Score	Offence type	AGGRAVATING FACTORS	MITIGATING FACTORS
Sexual assault (s 3)	3	E	• Force used • Elderly/younger victim • Group action • **Abuse of position**	

See *Blackstone's Criminal Practice* **B3.52**

B3.7 Causing a person to engage in sexual activity without consent

Sexual Offences Act 2003

s 4 'Causing a person to engage in sexual activity without consent'

(1) A person (A) commits an offence if—
   (a) he intentionally causes another person (B) to engage in an activity,
   (b) the activity is sexual,
   (c) B does not consent to engaging in the activity, and
   (d) A does not reasonably believe that B consents.

(2) Whether a belief is reasonable is to be determined having regard to all the circumstances, including any steps A has taken to ascertain whether B consents.

(3) Sections 75 and 76 apply to an offence under this section.

(4) A person is guilty of an offence under this section, if the activity caused involved—
   (a) penetration of B's anus or vagina,
   (b) penetration of B's mouth with a person's penis,
   (c) penetration of a person's anus or vagina with a part of B's body or by B with anything else, or
   (d) penetration of a person's mouth with B's penis,

   is liable, on conviction on indictment, to imprisonment for life.

(5) Unless subsection (4) applies, a person guilty of an offence under this section is liable—
   (a) on summary conviction, to imprisonment for a term not exceeding 6 months or to a fine or both;
   (b) on conviction on indictment, to imprisonment for a term not exceeding 10 years.

B3.7.1 Breakdown

Offence	Elements of the Offence	Defence
s 4 Sexual Offences Act 2003 'Causing a person to engage in sexual activity without consent'	• (A) Intentionally causes another (B) to engage in an activity • The activity is sexual • B does not consent to engaging in the activity • A does not reasonably believe that B consents	• Negative any element of the offence • Defences for sexual offences **B3.2** • General Defences **C**

B3.7.2 Defences

- See General Defences **C**.

B3.7.3 Key points

- Sections 75–76 Sexual Offences Act 2003 (**B3.1**) apply to this section.

B3.7.4 Sentencing

s 4(5) Sexual Offences Act 2003

Summary: a fine and/or 6 months' imprisonment

Indictment: 10 years' imprisonment; or

(If s 4(4) **B3.7.1** applies) indictment: life

See notification requirements **B3.1.2**.

Youth Gravity Matrix

OFFENCE	Gravity Score	Offence type	AGGRAVATING FACTORS	MITIGATING FACTORS
Causing person to engage in sexual activity without consent (s 4)			Defer decision to CPS	
With penetration	4	I		
Without penetration	3	E		

See *Blackstone's Criminal Practice* **B3.60**

B3.8 **Voyeurism**

Sexual Offences Act 2003

s 67 'Voyeurism'

(1) A person commits an offence if—
  (a) for the purpose of sexual gratification, he observes another person doing a private act, and
  (b) he knows that the other person does not consent to being observed for his sexual gratification.

(2) A person commits an offence if—
  (a) he operates equipment with the intention of enabling another person to observe, for the purpose of obtaining sexual gratification, a third person (B) doing a private act, and
  (b) he knows that B does not consent to his operating equipment with that intention.

(3) A person commits an offence if—
  (a) he records another person (B) doing a private act,
  (b) he does so with the intention that he or a third person will, for the purpose of obtaining sexual gratification, look at an image of B doing the act, and
  (c) he knows that B does not consent to his recording the act with that intention.

(4) A person commits an offence if he installs equipment, or constructs or adapts a structure or part of a structure, with the intention of enabling himself or another person to commit an offence under subsection (1).

B3.8.1 Breakdown

Offence	Elements of the Offence	Defence
s 67(1) Sexual Offences Act 2003 'Voyeurism'	• For the purposes of sexual gratification • Observes another person doing a private act • The private act occurred in a place that would, in the circumstances, reasonably be expected to provide privacy • Knows the other person does not consent to being observed for his sexual gratification	• Negative any element of the offence • Defences for sexual offences **B3.2** • General Defences **C**
s 67(2) Sexual Offences Act 2003 'Voyeurism'	• Operates equipment • With the intention of enabling another person (A) to observe a third person (B) doing a private act • For the purposes of sexual gratification • Knows A does not consent to being observed for the purposes of sexual gratification	• Negative any element of the offence • Defences for sexual offences **B3.2** • General Defences **C**
s 67(3) Sexual Offences Act 2003 'Voyeurism'	• Records another person (B) doing a private act • Intending that he or a third person will view the image recorded of B for the purposes of sexual gratification • Knows B does not consent to being recorded for the purposes of sexual gratification	• Negative any element of the offence • Defences for sexual offences **B3.2** • General Defences **C**
s 67(4) Sexual Offences Act 2003 'Voyeurism'	• Installs equipment, or constructs or adapts a structure or part thereof • Intending to commit an offence under s 67(1) Sexual Offences Act 2003	• Negative any element of the offence • Defences for sexual offences **B3.2** • General Defences **C**

B3.8.2 Interpretation

See interpretation section **B3.1**.

- The interpretation of breasts does not include the male chest (*R v Bassett* [2008] EWCA Crim 1174).
- Reasonable expectation of privacy is a matter for the jury to decide (*R v Bassett* [2008] EWCA Crim 1174).

- Swimwear is unlikely to be considered underwear for the purposes of s 68(1) as held in the Northern Ireland case of (*PSNI v MacRitchie* [2008] NICA 26).

B3.8.3 Defences

- See General Defences **C**.

B3.8.4 Sentencing

s 67 Sexual Offences Act 2003

Summary: 6 months' imprisonment and/or a fine

Indictment: 2 years' imprisonment

See notification requirements **B3.1.2**.

Youth Gravity Matrix

OFFENCE	Gravity Score	Offence type	AGGRAVATING FACTORS	MITIGATING FACTORS
Voyeurism (s 67)	2	E	• Victim distressed • Victim observed in person • Repeat performances	• Single event

B3.9 Exposure/Outraging public decency

Sexual Offences Act 2003

s 66(1)

(1) A person commits an offence if—
  (a) he intentionally exposes his genitals, and
  (b) he intends that someone will see them and be caused alarm or distress

B3.9.1 Related offences

- Outraging public decency: *R v Mayling* (1963) 47 Cr App R 102.

B3.9.2 Breakdown

Offence	Elements of the Offence	Defence
s 66(1) Sexual Offences Act 2003 'Exposure'	• Intentional • Exposure of genitals • Intending that someone (B) else will see them; and • Intending B will be caused alarm or distress	• Negative any element of the offence • Defences for sexual offences **B3.2** • General Defences **C**
R v Mayling **(1963) 47 Cr App R 102 'Outraging public decency'**	• In public • Commits an act of lewd, obscene, or disgusting character • To outrage public decency • Seen by at least one person; and • The act was capable of being seen by more than one person	• Negative any element of the offence • Defences for sexual offences **B3.2** • General Defences **C**

B3.9.3 Defences

- See General Defences **C**.

B3.9.4 Key points

- The offence is gender neutral.
- For the offence of outraging public decency evidence of disgust need not be proved, it is sufficient that the act is merely capable of causing disgust (*R v Mayling* (1963) 47 Cr App R 102).

B3.9.5 Sentencing

s 66(1) Sexual Offences Act 2003

Summary: A fine/6 months' imprisonment

Indictment: 2 years' imprisonment

See notification requirements **B3.1.2**.

Youth Gravity Matrix

OFFENCE	Gravity Score	Offence type	AGGRAVATING FACTORS	MITIGATING FACTORS
Exposure (s 66)	2	E	• Victim put in fear • Repeat performances	

See *Blackstone's Criminal Practice* **B3.330**

B3.10 Sexual activity in a public lavatory

Sexual Offences Act 2003

s 71 'Sexual activity in a public lavatory'

(1) A person commits an offence if—
  (a) he is in a lavatory to which the public or a section of the public has or is permitted to have access, whether on payment or otherwise,
  (b) he intentionally engages in an activity, and,
  (c) the activity is sexual.

B3.10.1 Breakdown

Offence	Elements of the Offence	Defence
s 71 Sexual Offences Act 2003 'Sexual activity in a public lavatory'	• In a lavatory • To which the public has access (whether on payment or otherwise) • Intentionally engages in sexual activity	• Negative any element of the offence • Defences for sexual offences **B3.2** • General Defences **C**

B3.10.2 Interpretation

Sexual Offences Act 2003

s 71 'Sexual activity in a public lavatory'

(2) For the purposes of this section, an activity is sexual if a reasonable person would, in all the circumstances but regardless of any person's purpose, consider it to be sexual.

B3.10.3 Defences

• See General Defences C.

B3.10.4 Sentencing

s 71 Sexual Offences Act 2003

Summary: a fine and/or 6 months' imprisonment

Youth Gravity Matrix

OFFENCE	Gravity Score	Offence type	AGGRAVATING FACTORS	MITIGATING FACTORS
Sexual activity in public lavatory (s 71)	2	S	• Genuine chance of public witnessing the offence • Youth victim	• Consenting victim and offender over age of legal consent

B3.11 Administer a substance intending to commit a sexual offence

Sexual Offences Act 2003

s 61 'Administering a Substance with Intent'

(1) A person commits an offence if he intentionally administers a substance to, or causes a substance to be taken by, another person (B)—
  (a) knowing that B does not consent, and
  (b) with the intention of stupefying or overpowering B, so as to enable any person to engage in a sexual activity that involves B.

B3.11.1 Related offences

See also:

- Commit an offence with intent to commit a sexual offence **B3.12**.
- Rape **B3.4**.
- Sexual assault by penetration **B3.5**/touching **B3.6**.

B3.11.2 Breakdown

Offence	Elements of the Offence	Defence
s 61 Sexual Offences Act 2003 'Administering a substance with intent'	• A, intentionally administers/causes a substance to be taken by B • Intending to stupefy or overpower B • So that A or another is able to engage in sexual activity with B • A knows that B does not consent to the taking the substance	• Negative any element of the offence • Defences for sexual offences **B3.2** • General Defences **C**

B3.11.3 Interpretation

See the section on general interpretation for sexual offences **B3.1** for the meanings of:

- 'sexual' (s 78 SOA 2003); see both the statutory and common law interpretation.
- 'consent' (s 74 SOA 2003).

B3.11.4 Defences

- See General Defences C.

B3.11.5 Key points

- There is no need for any sexual activity to take place for the offence to be made out.
- The absence of consent relates to the administration or taking of the substance, not to any sexual activity that may take place.

B3.11.6 Sentencing

s 61 Sexual Offences Act 2003

Summary: a fine and/or 6 months' imprisonment

Indictment: 10 years' imprisonment

See notification requirements **B3.1.2**.

Youth Gravity Matrix

OFFENCE	Gravity Score	Offence type	AGGRAVATING FACTORS	MITIGATING FACTORS
Administering substance with intent to commit sexual offence (s 61)	3	E	None	

See *Blackstone's Criminal Practice* **B3.257**

B3.12 Commit an offence with intent to commit a sexual offence

Sexual Offences Act 2003

s 62 'Committing an offence with intent to commit a sexual offence'

(1) A person commits an offence under this section if he commits any offence with the intention of committing a relevant sexual offence.

(2) In this section, 'relevant sexual offence' means any offence under this Part (including an offence of aiding, abetting, counselling or procuring such an offence).

B3.12.1 Breakdown

Offence	Elements of the Offence	Defence
s 62 Sexual Offences Act 2003 'Committing an offence with intent to commit a sexual offence'	• Commit any offence • With the intention • Of committing a relevant sexual offence	• Negative any element of the offence • Defences for sexual offences **B3.2** • General Defences **C**

B3.12.2 Defences

- See General Defences C.

B3.12.3 Key points

- A relevant sexual offence is any offence in Part 1 of the SOA 2003; Part 1 incorporates ss 1–79 of the 2003 Act.

B3.12.4 Sentencing

An offender convicted of this offence is automatically subject to notification requirements.

s 62 Sexual Offences Act 2003

Summary: a fine and/or 6 months' imprisonment

Indictment: 10 years' imprisonment (not involving kidnapping or false imprisonment).

Indictment: life imprisonment (where an offence of kidnapping or false imprisonment is involved).

See notification requirements **B3.1.2**.

Youth Gravity Matrix

OFFENCE	Gravity Score	Offence type	AGGRAVATING FACTORS	MITIGATING FACTORS
Commit offence with intent to commit sexual offence (s 62)	3	E	Defer Decision to CPS	
For kidnapping/ false imprisonment offences only	4	I		

See *Blackstone's Criminal Practice* **B3.257**

B3.13 Soliciting to obtain the services of a prostitute

Sexual Offences Act 2003

s 51A 'Soliciting'

(1) It is an offence for a person in a street or public place to solicit another (B) for the purpose of obtaining B's sexual services as a prostitute.

B3.13.1 Related offences

Street Offences Act 1959

s 1 'Loitering or soliciting for purposes of prostitution'

(1) It shall be an offence for a person aged 18 or over (whether male or female) persistently to loiter or solicit in a street or public place for the purpose of prostitution.

B3.13.2 Breakdown

Offence	Elements of the Offence	Defence
s 51A Sexual Offences Act 2003 'Soliciting'	• In a street of public place • Solicits another (B) • For the purpose of obtaining B's sexual services as a prostitute	• Negative any element of the offence • Defences for sexual offences **B3.2** • General Defences **C**

Offence	Elements of the Offence	Defence
s 1 Street Offences Act 1959 'Loitering or soliciting for purposes of prostitution'	• Persistently loiter/solicit • In a street/public place • For the purposes of prostitution	• Negative any element of the offence • Defences for sexual offences **B3.2** • General Defences **C**

B3.13.3 Interpretation

Sexual Offences Act 2003

s 51A 'Soliciting'

(2) The reference to a person in a street or public place includes a person in a vehicle in a street or public place.

...

(4) In this section 'street' has the meaning given by section 1(4) of the Street Offences Act 1959.

s 54 'Sections 51A to 53A: Interpretation'

(1) In sections 52, 53 and 53A, 'gain' means—
  (a) any financial advantage, including the discharge of an obligation to pay or the provision of goods or services (including sexual services) gratuitously or at a discount; or
  (b) the goodwill of any person which is or appears likely, in time, to bring financial advantage.

(2) In sections 51A, 52, 53 and 53A 'prostitute' and 'prostitution' have the meaning given by section 51(2).

(3) In section 53A 'payment' has the meaning given by section 51(3).

s 51 'Sections 48 to 50: Interpretation'

(2) In those sections 'prostitute' means a person (A) who, on at least one occasion and whether or not compelled to do so, offers or provides sexual services to another person in return for payment or a promise of payment to A or a third person; and 'prostitution' is to be interpreted accordingly.

(3) In subsection (2), 'payment' means any financial advantage, including the discharge of an obligation to pay or the provision of goods or services (including sexual services) gratuitously or at a discount.

Street Offences Act 1959

s 1 'Loitering or soliciting for purposes of prostitution'

(4) For the purposes of this section—
  (a) conduct is persistent if it takes place on two or more occasions in any period of three months;

(b) any reference to a person loitering or soliciting for the purposes of prostitution is a reference to a person loitering or soliciting for the purposes of offering services as a prostitute;
(c) 'street' includes any bridge, road, lane, footway, subway, square, court, alley or passage, whether a thoroughfare or not, which is for the time being open to the public; and the doorways and entrances of premises abutting on a street (as hereinbefore defined), and any ground adjoining and open to a street, shall be treated as forming part of the street.

B3.13.4 Defences

- See General Defences C.

B3.13.5 Key points

- *Behrendt v Burridge* [1976] 3 All ER 285: A prostitute sitting on a stool in a window under a light is soliciting.

B3.13.6 Sentencing

s 51A Sexual Offences Act 2003

Summary only: fine not exceeding level 3 on the standard scale

s 1 Street Offences Act 1959

Summary only: fine not exceeding level 2 on the standard scale (after a previous conviction: level 3)

See *Blackstone's Criminal Practice* B3.203

B3.14 Paying for sexual services of a prostitute subject to exploitation

Sexual Offences Act 2003

s 53A 'Paying for sexual services of a prostitute subjected to force etc.'

(1) A person (A) commits an offence if—
(a) A makes or promises payment for the sexual services of a prostitute (B),

(b) A third person (C) has engaged in exploitative conduct of a kind likely to induce or encourage B to provide the sexual services for which A has made or promised payment, and
(c) C engaged in that conduct for or in the expectation of gain for C or another person (apart from A or B).

B3.14.1 Related offences

- Persistently loitering **B3.13.1**.
- Soliciting to obtain services of a prostitute **B3.13**.

B3.14.2 Breakdown

Offence	Elements of the Offence	Defence
s 53A Sexual Offences Act 2003 'Paying for sexual services of a prostitute subject to exploitation'	• (A) Made or promised payment • For sexual services of a prostitute (B) • B is/was subject to exploitative conduct by (C) of a kind likely to induce/encourage B to provide sexual services for A • C is engaged in the exploitative conduct for the expectation of gain for C or another (except A or B)	• Negative any element of the offence • Defences for sexual offences **B3.2** • General Defences **C**

B3.14.3 Interpretation

Sexual Offences Act 2003

s 53A 'Paying for sexual services of a prostitute subjected to force etc.'

(2) The following are irrelevant—
(a) where in the world the sexual services are to be provided and whether those services are provided,
(b) whether A is, or ought to be, aware that C has engaged in exploitative conduct.
(3) C engages in exploitative conduct if—
(a) C uses force, threats (whether or not relating to violence) or any other form of coercion, or

(b) C practises any form of deception.
(4) A person guilty of an offence under this section is liable on summary conviction to a fine not exceeding level 3 on the standard scale.

s 54 [Section 53A] 'Interpretation'

(1) In [sections 53A], *'gain'* means—
(a) any financial advantage, including the discharge of an obligation to pay or the provision of goods or services (including sexual services) gratuitously or at a discount; or
(b) the goodwill of any person which is or appears likely, in time, to bring financial advantage.
(2) In [section 53A] *'prostitute'* and *'prostitution'* have the meaning given by section 51(2).
(3) In section 53A *'payment'* has the meaning given by section 51(3).

s 51 'Sections 48 to 50: interpretation'

(2) In those sections 'prostitute' means a person (A) who, on at least one occasion and whether or not compelled to do so, offers or provides sexual services to another person in return for payment or a promise of payment to A or a third person; and 'prostitution' is to be interpreted accordingly.
(3) In subsection (2), 'payment' means any financial advantage, including the discharge of an obligation to pay or the provision of goods or services (including sexual services) gratuitously or at a discount.

B3.14.4 Defences

- See General Defences C.

B3.14.5 Key points

- This is a strict liability offence.

B3.14.6 Sentencing

s 53A Sexual Offences Act 2003

Summary only: a fine not exceeding level 3 on the standard scale

B3.15 Rape of a child under 13

Sexual Offences Act 2003

s 5 'Rape of a child under 13'

(1) A person commits an offence if—
(a) he intentionally penetrates the vagina, anus or mouth of another person with his penis, and
(b) the other person is under 13.

B3.15.1 Related offences

See also:

- Sexual assault by penetration of a child under 13 years old **B3.16**.
- Sexual activity with a child **B3.19**.
- Arranging/facilitating the commission of a child sex offence **B3.23**.

B3.15.2 Breakdown

Offence	Elements of the Offence	Defence
s 5 Sexual Offences Act 2003 'Rape of child under 13'	• (A) penetrates the vagina, anus or mouth of (B) • Using his penis • B is under 13 years old at the time of penetration	• Negative any element of the offence • Defences for sexual offences **B3.2** • General Defences **C**

B3.15.3 Interpretation

- See interpretation for sexual offences **3.1**.

B3.15.4 Defences

- See General Defences C.

B3.15.5 Key points

- This is an offence of strict liability; it is no defence that the suspect believed the victim was aged 16 or over.
- The section on the rape of an adult under s 1 Sexual Offences Act 2003 **B3.4** provides further important information relevant to this part.

B3.15.6 Sentencing

s 5 Sexual Offences Act 2003

Indictment: life imprisonment

See notification requirements **B3.1.2**.

Youth Gravity Matrix

OFFENCE	Gravity Score	Offence type	AGGRAVATING FACTORS	MITIGATING FACTORS
Rape of child under 13 (s 5)	4	I	Defer Decision to CPS	

See *Blackstone's Criminal Practice* **B3.68**

B3.16 **Sexual assault by penetration of a child under 13**

Sexual Offences Act 2003

s 6 'Assault of a child under 13 by penetration'

(1) A person commits an offence if—
- (a) he intentionally penetrates the vagina or anus of another person with a part of his body or anything else,
- (b) the penetration is sexual, and
- (c) the other person is under 13.

B3.16.1 **Related offences**

- Rape of a child under 13 **B3.15**.
- Sexual assault by touching a child under 13 **B3.17**.
- Sexual assault by penetration **B3.5**.

B3.16.2 **Breakdown**

Offence	Elements of the Offence	Defence
s 6 Sexual Offences Act 2003 'Assault of a child under 13 by penetration'	• (A) intentionally penetrates the vagina or anus of (B) • Using a part of his body or anything else • The penetration is sexual • B is under 13 years old	• Negative any element of the offence • Defences for sexual offences **B3.2** • General Defences **C**

B3.16.3 **Interpretation**

- See the section on general interpretation for sexual offences **B3.1** for the meaning of 'sexual'; see both the statutory and common law interpretation.

B3.16.4 Defences

- See General Defences C.

B3.16.5 Key points

- As with rape, penetration of the vagina includes penetration of a surgically reconstructed vagina (s 79(3) Sexual Offences Act 2003).
- There is no defence for a mistaken belief the victim was aged 13 or older.

B3.16.6 Sentencing

An offender convicted of these offences is automatically subject to notification.

s 6 Sexual Offences Act 2003

Indictment: life imprisonment

See notification requirements **B3.1.2**.

Youth Gravity Matrix

OFFENCE	Gravity Score	Offence type	AGGRAVATING FACTORS	MITIGATING FACTORS
Assault of child under 13 by penetration (s 6)	4	I	Defer Decision to CPS	

See *Blackstone's Criminal Practice* **B3.92**

B3.17 Sexual assault by touching a child under 13

Sexual Offences Act 2003

s 7 'Sexual assault of a child under 13'

(1) A person commits an offence if—

(a) he intentionally touches another person,

(b) the touching is sexual, and

(c) the other person is under 13.

B3.17.1 Breakdown

Offence	Elements of the Offence	Defence
s 7 Sexual Offences Act 2003 'Sexual assault by touching on a child under 13'	• (A) Intentionally touches another person (B) • B is aged under 13 • The touching is sexual in nature	• Negative any element of the offence • Defences for sexual offences **B3.2** • General Defences **C**

B3.17.2 Interpretation

- See interpretation for sexual offences **B3.1**.

B3.17.3 Defences

- See General Defences **C**.

B3.17.4 Sentencing

An offender convicted of these offences is automatically subject to notification.

s 7 Sexual Offences Act 2003

Summary: a fine and/or 6 months' imprisonment

Indictment: 14 years' imprisonment

See notification requirements **B3.1.2**.

Youth Gravity Matrix

OFFENCE	Gravity Score	Offence type	AGGRAVATING FACTORS	MITIGATING FACTORS
Sexual assault of child under 13 (s7)	3	E	• Facilitated by drugs/alcohol • Force used • Group action	• Offender and victim of similar age and no element of coercion or corruption present

See *Blackstone's Criminal Practice* **B3.92**

B3.18 Causing or inciting a child under 13 to engage in sexual activity

Sexual Offences Act 2003

s 8 'Causing or inciting a child under 13 to engage in sexual activity'

(1) A person (A) commits an offence if—
- (a) he intentionally causes another person (B) to engage in an activity,
- (b) the activity is sexual, and
- (c) B is under 13

(2) A person guilty of an offence under this section, if the activity caused involved—
- (a) penetration of B's anus or vagina,
- (b) penetration of B's mouth with a person's penis,
- (c) penetration of a person's anus or vagina with a part of B's body or by B with anything else, or
- (d) penetration of a person's mouth with B's penis, is liable, on conviction on indictment, to imprisonment for life.

(3) Unless subsection (2) applies, a person guilty of an offence under this section is liable—
- (a) on summary conviction, to imprisonment for a term not exceeding 6 months or to a fine or both;
- (b) on conviction on indictment, to imprisonment for a term not exceeding 14 years.

B3.18.1 Breakdown

Offence	Elements of the Offence	Defence
s 8 Sexual Offences Act 2003 'Causing or inciting a child under 13 to engage in sexual activity'	• (A) Intentionally causes another (B) to engage in an activity • B is under 13 • The activity is sexual	• Negative any element of the offence • Defences for sexual offences **B3.2** • General Defences C

B3.18.2 Defences

- See General Defences C.

B3.18.3 Key points

- Section 8(1) creates two basic offences. The first is where a defendant intentionally causes a child (B) to engage in 'sexual activity'.

The second is where a defendant intentionally incites a child (B) to engage in 'sexual activity'. In the latter case the essence of the offence is the intentional 'incitement', that is the intentional seeking to bring about something by encouragement or persuasion, by the defendant (*R v Walker (Simon John)* [2006] EWCA Crim 1907).

- 'The causing or inciting must be intentional ... [and] [i]f the offence charged is that of intentional incitement the prosecution does not have to prove that defendant intended that the actual sexual activity should take place, because the essence of the offence is the intentional incitement of the person under 13 to engage in sexual activity' (*R v Grout* [2011] EWCA Crim 299).
- Section 8 creates four different offences, each of which must be carried out intentionally. The first is causing penetrative sexual activity; the second is inciting such activity; the third is causing non-penetrative sexual activity and the fourth is inciting such activity (*R v Grout* [2011] EWCA Crim 299).

B3.18.4 Sentencing

s 4(5) Sexual Offences Act 2003

Summary: A fine and/or 6 months' imprisonment

Indictment: 14 years' imprisonment; or

(If s 8(2) **B3.18.1** applies) indictment: life

See notification requirements **B3.1.2**.

Youth Gravity Matrix

OFFENCE	Gravity Score	Offence type	AGGRAVATING FACTORS	MITIGATING FACTORS
Causing/Inciting child under 13 to engage in sexual activity without consent (s 8)	4	I	Defer decision to CPS	
With penetration			• Facilitated by drugs/alcohol • Force used Group action	
Without penetration	3	E		

See *Blackstone's Criminal Practice* **B3.87**

B3.19 Sexual activity with a child

Sexual Offences Act 2003

s 9 'Sexual Activity with a Child'

(1) A person aged 18 or over (A) commits an offence if—
  (a) he intentionally touches another person (B),
  (b) the touching is sexual, and
  (c) either—
    (i) B is under 16 and A does not reasonably believe that B is 16 or over, or
    (ii) B is under 13.

B3.19.1 Related offences

See also:

- Sexual assault by touching **B3.6**.
- Sexual assault by touching a child under 13 **B3.17**.
- Sexual assault by penetration **B3.5**.
- Sexual assault by penetration of a child under 13 years old **B3.16**.

B3.19.2 Breakdown

Offence	Elements of the Offence	Defence
s 9 Sexual Offences Act 2003 'Sexual activity with a child'	• (A), aged 18 or over, intentionally touches (B) • The touching is sexual; and • Either: • B is under 16 and A does not reasonably believe B is 16 or over; or • B is under 13	• Negative any element of the offence • Defences for sexual offences **B3.2** • General Defences **C**

B3.19.3 Interpretation

- See interpretation for sexual offences **B3.1**.

B3.19.4 Defences

- See General Defences **C**.
- Where the child in question is aged over 13 it is a defence if the suspect reasonably believed that the child was over 16 (s 9(1)(c)(i) Sexual Offences Act 2003).

B3.19.5 Key points

- See **B3.1** for 'touching'.

B3.19.6 Sentencing

An offender convicted of these offences is automatically subject to notification requirements.

Sexual Offences Act 2003

s 9 'Sexual Activity with a Child'

(2) A person guilty of an offence under this section, if the touching involved—
  (a) penetration of B's anus or vagina with a part of A's body or anything else,
  (b) penetration of B's mouth with A's penis,
  (c) penetration of A's anus or vagina with a part of B's body, or
  (d) penetration of A's mouth with B's penis,
  is liable, on conviction on indictment, to imprisonment for a term not exceeding 14 years.
(3) Unless subsection (2) applies, a person guilty of an offence under this section is liable—
  (a) on summary conviction, to imprisonment for a term not exceeding 6 months or to a fine not exceeding the statutory maximum or both;
  (b) on conviction on indictment, to imprisonment for a term not exceeding 14 years.

Summary: a fine and/or 6 months' imprisonment

Indictment: 14 years' imprisonment

Where the suspect is aged under 18 the maximum penalty is 5 years' imprisonment.

See notification requirements **B3.1.2**.

Youth Gravity Matrix

OFFENCE	Gravity Score	Offence type	AGGRAVATING FACTORS	MITIGATING FACTORS
Sexual activity with child (s 9)			• Facilitated by drugs/alcohol • Force used • Group action	• Offender and victim of similar age and no element of coercion or corruption present
Victim under 13	3	I		
Victim under 16	2	E		

See *Blackstone's Criminal Practice* **B3.92**

B3.20 Abuse of position of trust: sexual activity with a child

Sexual Offences Act 2003

s 16 'Abuse of position of trust: sexual activity with a child'

(1) A person aged 18 or over (A) commits an offence if—
- (a) he intentionally touches another person (B),
- (b) the touching is sexual,
- (c) A is in a position of trust in relation to B,
- (d) where subsection (2) applies, A knows or could reasonably be expected to know of the circumstances by virtue of which he is in a position of trust in relation to B, and
- (e) either—
  - (i) B is under 18 and A does not reasonably believe that B is 18 or over, or
  - (ii) B is under 13.

(2) This subsection applies where A—
- (a) is in a position of trust in relation to B by virtue of circumstances within section 21(2), (3), (4) or (5), and
- (b) is not in such a position of trust by virtue of other circumstances.

B3.20.1 Related offences

- Sexual activity with a child **B3.19**.

B3.20.2 Breakdown

Offence	Elements of the Offence	Defence
s 16 Sexual Offences Act 2003 'Abuse of a position of trust: sexual activity with a child'	• (A) intentionally touched (b) • The touching was sexual • A is in a position of trust in relation to B; and either: • B is under 18 and A does not believe B is over 18; or • B is under 13	• Negative any element of the offence • Defences for sexual offences **B3.2** • General Defences **C**

B3.20.3 Interpretation

Sexual Offences Act 2003

s 16 'Abuse of position of trust: sexual activity with a child'

(3) Where in proceedings for an offence under this section it is proved that the other person was under 18, the defendant is to be taken not to have reasonably believed that that person was 18 or over unless sufficient evidence is adduced to raise an issue as to whether he reasonably believed it.

(4) Where in proceedings for an offence under this section—
   (a) it is proved that the defendant was in a position of trust in relation to the other person by virtue of circumstances within section 21(2), (3), (4) or (5), and
   (b) it is not proved that he was in such a position of trust by virtue of other circumstances,

it is to be taken that the defendant knew or could reasonably have been expected to know of the circumstances by virtue of which he was in such a position of trust unless sufficient evidence is adduced to raise an issue as to whether he knew or could reasonably have been expected to know of those circumstances.

- See interpretation for sexual offences **B3.1**.

B3.20.4 Defences

- See General Defences **C**.
- See defences to sexual offences **B3.2**.

B3.20.5 Key points

- Whilst the key elements are the same for the offence under s 9 SOA 2003, with the addition of a position of trust, it is important to note that a child for the purposes of this section is anyone under the age of 18.
- Section 16(3) imposes a rebuttable presumption that the accused knew the victim was under 18 if indeed it is proved that they were under 18 at the time of the sexual activity.
- Section 16(4) imposes a rebuttable presumption that the accused knew or could have been reasonably expected to know he was in a position of trust, if in fact it is proved he was in a position of trust by virtue of circumstances described in s 21(2)–(5), unless:
  - the accused proves on the balance of probabilities that the position of trust arose in other circumstances, or

- the accused adduces sufficient evidence to raise an issue as to whether he could have been expected to know of the circumstances giving rise to the position of trust.

B3.20.6 Sentencing

s 16 Sexual Offences Act

Summary: a fine and/or 6 months' imprisonment

Indictment: 5 years' imprisonment

See notification requirements **B3.1.2**.

See *Blackstone's Criminal Practice* **B3.128**

B3.21 Abuse of position of trust: causing or inciting a child to engage in sexual activity

Sexual Offences Act 2003

s 17 'Abuse of position of trust: causing or inciting a child to engage in sexual activity'

(1) A person aged 18 or over (A) commits an offence if—
  (a) he intentionally causes or incites another person (B) to engage in an activity,
  (b) the activity is sexual,
  (c) A is in a position of trust in relation to B,
  (d) where subsection (2) applies, A knows or could reasonably be expected to know of the circumstances by virtue of which he is in a position of trust in relation to B, and
  (e) either—
    (i) B is under 18 and A does not reasonably believe that B is 18 or over, or
    (ii) B is under 13.

(2) This subsection applies where A—
  (a) is in a position of trust in relation to B by virtue of circumstances within section 21(2), (3), (4) or (5), and
  (b) is not in such a position of trust by virtue of other circumstances.

B3.21.1 Breakdown

Offence	Elements of the Offence	Defence
s 17 Sexual Offences Act 2003 'Abuse of position of trust: causing or inciting a child to engage in sexual activity'	• (A), aged over 18, intentionally • Causes or incites (B) to engage in an activity • This activity is sexual; and • A is in a position of trust in relation to B; and either • B is under 18 and A does not believe that B is over 18; or • B is under 13	• Negative any element of the offence • Defences for sexual offences **B3.2** • General Defences **C**

B3.21.2 Interpretation

Sexual Offences Act 2003

s 17 'Abuse of position of trust: causing or inciting a child to engage in sexual activity'

(3) Where in proceedings for an offence under this section it is proved that the other person was under 18, the defendant is to be taken not to have reasonably believed that that person was 18 or over unless sufficient evidence is adduced to raise an issue as to whether he reasonably believed it.

(4) Where in proceedings for an offence under this section—

(a) it is proved that the defendant was in a position of trust in relation to the other person by virtue of circumstances within section 21(2), (3), (4) or (5), and

(b) it is not proved that he was in such a position of trust by virtue of other circumstances,

it is to be taken that the defendant knew or could reasonably have been expected to know of the circumstances by virtue of which he was in such a position of trust unless sufficient evidence is adduced to raise an issue as to whether he knew or could reasonably have been expected to know of those circumstances.

B3.21.3 Defences

- See General Defences **C**.
- See defences to sexual offences **B3.2**.

B3.21.4 Key points

- Whilst the key elements are the same for the offence under s 10 SOA 2003, with the addition of a position of trust, it is important to note that a child for the purposes of this section is anyone under the age of 18.

- Section 17(3) imposes a rebuttable presumption that the accused knew the victim was under 18 if indeed it is proved that they were under 18 at the time of the sexual activity.
- Section 17(4) imposes a rebuttable presumption that the accused knew or could have been reasonably expected to know he was in a position of trust, if in fact it is proved he was in a position of trust by virtue of circumstances described in s 21(2)–(5), unless:
  - the accused proves on the balance of probabilities that the position of trust arose in other circumstances, or
  - the accused adduces sufficient evidence to raise an issue as to whether he could have been expected to know of the circumstances giving rise to the position of trust.

B3.21.5 Sentencing

s 17 Sexual Offences Act 2003

Summary: a fine and/or 6 months' imprisonment

Indictment: 5 years' imprisonment

See notification requirements **B3.1.2**.

See *Blackstone's Criminal Practice* **B3.128**

B3.22 Causing or inciting a child to engage in sexual activity

Sexual Offences Act 2003

s 10 'Causing or inciting a child to engage in sexual activity'

(1) A person (a) aged 18 or over commits an offence if—
  (a) He intentionally causes or incites another person (b) to engage in an activity
  (b) the activity is sexual, and
  (c) either—
    (i) B is under 16 and A does not reasonably believe B is over 16, or
    (i) B is under 13.

B3.22.1 Related offences

See also:

- Arranging/facilitating the commission of a child sex offence **B3.23**.
- Sexual activity with a child **B3.19**.

B3.22.2 Breakdown

Offence	Elements of the Offence	Defence
s 10 Sexual Offences Act 2003 'Causing a child to engage in sexual activity'	• (A), aged over 18, intentionally • Causes or incites (B) to engage in an activity • This activity is sexual; and either: • B is under 16 and A does not reasonable believe B is over 16; or • B is under 13	• Negative any element of the offence • Defences for sexual offences **B3.2** • General Defences **C**

B3.22.3 Interpretation

- See interpretation for sexual offences **B3.1**.
- It is important to note that consent is not in issue here; it is the act of incitement or encouragement to engage in sexual activity that is relevant, not the willingness or ability to consent of B.
- No sexual activity actually need take place; it is sufficient for there to be intentional incitement only.

B3.22.4 Defences

- Consider the General Defences C.

B3.22.5 Key points

- It does not matter whether a particular child can be identified as the subject of the incitement for the offence to be made out (*R v Jones* [2007] EWCA Crim 1118).

B3.22.6 Sentencing

s 10 Sexual Offences Act 2003

Summary: a fine and/or 6 months' imprisonment

Indictment: 14 years' imprisonment

Unless s 10(2) applies:

Sexual Offences Act 2003

s 10 'Causing or inciting a child to engage in sexual activity'

(2) A person guilty under this section, if the activity caused or incited involved—
- (a) penetration of B's anus or vagina,
- (b) penetration of B's mouth with a person's penis,
- (c) the penetration of a person's anus or vagina with a part of B's body or by B with anything else, or
- (d) penetration of a person's mouth with B's penis

is liable, on conviction on indictment, to imprisonment for a term not exceeding 14 years.

Indictment: 14 years' imprisonment

For either offence, where the suspect is aged under 18 the maximum penalty is 5 years' imprisonment.

See notification requirements **B3.1.2**.

Youth Gravity Matrix

OFFENCE	Gravity Score	Offence type	AGGRAVATING FACTORS	MITIGATING FACTORS
Causing/inciting child to engage in sexual activity (s 10) Victim under 13 Victim under 16	3 2	I E	• Facilitated by drugs/alcohol • Force used • Group action	None

See *Blackstone's Criminal Practice* **B3.92**

B3.23 Arranging or facilitating a child sex offence

Sexual Offences Act 2003

s 14 'Arranging or facilitating commission of a child sex offence'

(1) A person commits an offence if—
- (a) he intentionally arranges or facilitates something that he intends to do, intends another person to do, or believes that another person will do, in any part of the world, and

(b) doing it will involve the commission of an offence under any of sections 9 to 13.

(2) A person does not commit an offence under this section if—
(a) he arranges or facilitates something that he believes another person will do, but that he does not intend to do or intend another person to do, and
(b) any offence within subsection (1)(b) would be an offence against a child for whose protection he acts.

(3) For the purposes of subsection (2), a person acts for the protection of a child if he acts for the purpose of—
(a) protecting the child from sexually transmitted infection,
(b) protecting the physical safety of the child,
(c) preventing the child from becoming pregnant, or
(d) promoting the child's emotional well-being by the giving of advice,
and not for the purpose of obtaining sexual gratification or for the purpose of causing or encouraging the activity constituting the offence within subsection (1)(b) or the child's participation in it.

B3.23.1 Related offences

See also:

- Sexual activity with a child **B3.19**.
- Causing or inciting a child to engage in sexual activity **B3.22**.

B3.23.2 Breakdown

Offence	Elements of the Offence	Defence
s 14 Sexual Offences Act 2003 'Arranging or facilitating the commission of a child sex offence'	• (A) intentionally arranges/ facilitates something • That A: • Intends to do themselves; or • Intends someone else to do; or • Believes someone else will do • That which is arranged constitutes an offence under ss 9–13 of this Act	• Negative any element of the offence • s 14 Sexual Offences Act 2003 **B3.23.4** • Defences for sexual offences **B3.2** • General Defences **C**

B3.23.3 Interpretation

- See interpretation for sexual offences **B3.1**.

B3.23.4 Defences

Sexual Offences Act 2003

s 14 'Arranging or facilitating commission of a child sex offence'

(2) A person does not commit an offence under this section if—
  (a) he arranges or facilitates something that he believes another person will do, but that he does not intend to do or intend another person to do, and
  (b) any offence within subsection (1)(b) would be an offence against a child for whose protection he acts.

(3) For the purposes of subsection (2), a person acts for the protection of a child if he acts for the purpose of—
  (a) protecting the child from sexually transmitted infection,
  (b) protecting the physical safety of the child,
  (c) preventing the child from becoming pregnant, or
  (d) promoting the child's emotional well-being by the giving of advice,

and not for the purpose of obtaining sexual gratification or for the purpose of causing or encouraging the activity constituting the offence within subsection (1)(b) or the child's participation in it.

- See General Defences **C**.

B3.23.5 Sentencing

s 14 Sexual Offences Act 2003

Summary: a fine and/or 6 months' imprisonment

Indictment: 14 years' imprisonment

See notification requirements **B3.1.2**.

B3.24 Meeting a child following sexual grooming

Sexual Offences Act 2003

s 15 'Meeting a child following sexual grooming'

(1) A person aged 18 or over (A) commits an offence if—
  (a) A has met or communicated with another person (B) on one or more occasions and subsequently—
    (i) A intentionally meets B,

(ii) A travels with the intention of meeting B in any part of the world or arranges to meet B in any part of the world, or
(iii) B travels with the intention of meeting A in any part of the world,
(b) A intends to do anything to or in respect of B, during or after the meeting mentioned in paragraph (a)(i) to (iii) and in any part of the world, which if done will involve the commission by A of a relevant offence,
(c) B is under 16, and
(d) A does not reasonably believe that B is 16 or over.
(2) In subsection (1)—
(a) the reference to A having met or communicated with B is a reference to A having met B in any part of the world or having communicated with B by any means from, to or in any part of the world;
(b) 'relevant offence' means—
(i) an offence under this Part,
....
(iii) anything done outside England and Wales which is not an offence within sub-paragraph (i) but would be an offence within sub-paragraph (i) if done in England and Wales.

B3.24.1 Related offences

See also:

- Arranging or facilitating a child sex offence **B3.23.**
- Causing or inciting a child to engage in sexual activity **B3.22.**
- Sexual activity with a child **B3.19.**

B3.24.2 Breakdown

Offence	Elements of the Offence	Defence

s 15 Sexual Offences Act 2003 'Meeting a child following sexual grooming'	• (A) is aged 18 or over
	• (B) is aged 16 years or younger; and
	• A does not reasonably believe B is 16 or over
	• A has communicated or met with B on one or more occasions in the past
	• Subsequently; either
	  • A arranges to meet with B; or
	  • A travels with the intention to meet B; or
	  • A intentionally meets B; or
	  • B travels with the intention of meeting A
		• Negative any element of the offence
		• Defences for sexual offences **B3.2**
		• General Defences **C**

Offence	Elements of the Offence	Defence
	• A's intention during or after the meeting (or arranged/attempted meeting) is to do something in respect of B that, if it were carried out in England & Wales would constitute an offence under ss 1–79 of this Act.	

B3.24.3 Interpretation

- See interpretation for sexual offences **B3.1**.

B3.24.4 Defences

- See General Defences **C**.

B3.24.5 Criminal Justice and Courts Act 2014

- In a case in which person A met or communicated with person B only once before the event mentioned in section 15(1)(a)(i) to (iii) of the Sexual Offences Act 2003, an offence under that section is committed only if the meeting or communication took place after 13 April 2015.

B3.24.6 Sentencing

s 15 Sexual Offences Act 2003

Summary: a fine and/or 6 months' imprisonment

Indictment: 10 years' imprisonment

See notification requirements **B3.1.2**.

B3.25 Indecent photographs of children

Protection of Children Act 1978

s 1 'Indecent Photographs of Children'

(1) It is an offence for a person—

(a) to take, or permit to be taken or to make, any indecent photograph or pseudo-photograph of a child; or

(b) to distribute or show such indecent photographs or pseudo-photographs; or

(c) to have in his possession such indecent photographs or pseudo-photographs, with a view to their being distributed or shown by himself or others; or
(d) to publish or cause to be published any advertisement likely to be understood as conveying that the advertiser distributes or shows such indecent photographs or pseudo-photographs, or intends to do so.

B3.25.1 Related offences

- Possession of indecent images.

Criminal Justice Act 1988

s 160 'Summary offence of possession of indecent photograph of child'

(1) Subject to section 160A, it is an offence for a person to have any indecent photograph or pseudo-photograph of a child in his possession.

B3.25.2 Breakdown

Offence	Elements of the Offence	Defence
s 1(a) Protection of Children Act 1978 'Indecent photographs of children'	• Takes, makes, or permits to be taken • Indecent photographs or pseudo-photographs	• Negative any element of the offence • Defences for sexual offences **B3.2** • s 1 Protection of Children Act 1978 **B3.25.4** • General Defences **C**
s 1(b) Protection of Children Act 1978 'Indecent photographs of children'	• Distributes or shows to another person • Indecent photographs or pseudo-photographs	• Negative any element of the offence • Defences for sexual offences **B3.2** • s 1 Protection of Children Act 1978 **B3.25.4** • General Defences **C**
s 1(c) Protection of Children Act 1978 'Indecent photographs of children'	• Possess • Indecent photographs or pseudo-photographs • With the view to them being distributed or shown • By himself or others	• Negative any element of the offence • Defences for sexual offences **B3.2** • s 1 Protection of Children Act 1978 **B3.25.4** • General Defences **C**
s 1(d) Protection of Children Act 1978 'Indecent photographs of children'	• Publish or cause to be published • An advertisement • Likely to be understood as conveying the advertiser does distribute, or intends to distribute • Indecent photographs or pseudo-photographs	• Negative any element of the offence • Defences for sexual offences **B3.2** • s 1 Protection of Children Act 1978 **B3.25.4** • General Defences **C**

Offence	Elements of the Offence	Defence
s 160 Criminal Justice Act 1988 'Possession of indecent photograph of child'	• Possess • Indecent photograph/ pseudo-photograph of a child	• Negative any element of the offence • Defences for sexual offences **B3.2** • s 160 Criminal Justice Act 1988 **B3.25.4** • s 160A Criminal Justice Act 1988 **B3.25.4** • General Defences **C**

B3.25.3 Interpretation

Protection of Children Act 1978

s 1 'Indecent photographs of children'

(2) For purposes of this Act, a person is to be regarded as distributing an indecent photograph or pseudo-photograph if he parts with possession of it to, or exposes or offers it for acquisition by, another person.

s 7 'Interpretation'

...

(2) References to an indecent photograph include an indecent film, a copy of an indecent photograph or film, and an indecent photograph comprised in a film.

(3) Photographs (including those comprised in a film) shall, if they show children and are indecent, be treated for all purposes of this Act as indecent photographs of children and so as respects pseudo-photographs.

(4) References to a photograph include—
- (a) the negative as well as the positive version; and
- (b) data stored on a computer disc or by other electronic means which is capable of conversion into a photograph.

(4A) References to a photograph also include—
- (a) a tracing or other image, whether made by electronic or other means (of whatever nature)—
  - (i) which is not itself a photograph or pseudo-photograph, but
  - (ii) which is derived from the whole or part of a photograph or pseudo-photograph (or a combination of either or both); and
- (b) data stored on a computer disc or by other electronic means which is capable of conversion into an image within paragraph (a);

and subsection (8) applies in relation to such an image as it applies in relation to a pseudo-photograph.

(5) 'Film' includes any form of video-recording.

(6) 'Child', subject to subsection (8), means a person under the age of 18.

(7) 'Pseudo-photograph' means an image, whether made by computer-graphics or otherwise howsoever, which appears to be a photograph.

(8) If the impression conveyed by a pseudo-photograph is that the person shown is a child, the pseudo-photograph shall be treated for all purposes of this Act as showing a child and so shall a pseudo-photograph where the predominant impression conveyed is that the person shown is a child

notwithstanding that some of the physical characteristics shown are those of an adult.

(9) References to an indecent pseudo-photograph include—
 (a) a copy of an indecent pseudo-photograph; and
 (b) data stored on a computer disc or by other electronic means which is capable of conversion into a pseudo-photograph.

- While 'making' includes intentional copying, it does not include unintentional copying (*Atkins v DPP* [2000] EWHC Admin 302).
- Based on a defendant's previous use of particular sites, there may be an evidential basis for a jury to conclude that illegal, 'pop-up' activity would occur and the defendant would thereby make indecent images (*R v Harrison* [2007] EWCA Crim 2976).
- The provision of a password allowing another to access a computer so that an indecent images can be viewed will constitute 'showing' for the purposes of s 1 Protection of Children Act 1978—(*R v Fellows and Arnold* [1997] 1 Cr App R 244).
- The meaning of 'photograph' and 'pseudo-photograph' in s 7 Protection of Children Act 1978 applies to s 160 Criminal Justice Act 1988.
- There are three categories of images (from the Sentencing Guidelines):

	Possession	**Distribution***	**Production****
Category A	Possession of images involving penetrative sexual activity. Possession of images involving sexual activity with an animal or sadism.	Sharing images involving penetrative sexual activity. Sharing images involving sexual activity with an animal or sadism.	Creating images involving penetrative sexual activity. Creating images involving sexual activity with an animal or sadism.
Category B	Possession of images involving non-penetrative sexual activity.	Sharing of images involving non-penetrative sexual activity.	Creating images involving non-penetrative sexual activity.
Category C	Possession of other indecent images not falling within categories A or B.	Sharing of other indecent images not falling within categories A or B.	Creating other indecent images not falling within categories A or B.

* Distribution includes possession with a view to distributing or sharing images.

** Production includes the taking or making of any image at source, for instance the original image.

Making an image by simple downloading should be treated as possession for the purposes of sentencing.

B3.25.4 Defences

Protection of Children Act 1978

s 1 'Indecent photographs of children'

(4) Where a person is charged with an offence under subsection (1)(b) or (c), it shall be a defence for him to prove—
  - (a) that he had a legitimate reason for distributing or showing the photographs or pseudo-photographs or (as the case may be) having them in his possession; or
  - (b) that he had not himself seen the photographs or pseudo-photographs and did not know, nor had any cause to suspect, them to be indecent.

Criminal Justice Act 1988

s 160 'Summary offence of possession of indecent photograph of child

(2) Where a person is charged with an offence under subsection (1) above, it shall be a defence for him to prove—
  - (a) that he had a legitimate reason for having the photograph or pseudo-photograph in his possession; or
  - (b) that he had not himself seen the photograph or pseudo-photograph and did not know, nor had any cause to suspect, it to be indecent; or
  - (c) that the photograph or pseudo-photograph was sent to him without any prior request made by him or on his behalf and that he did not keep it for an unreasonable time.

s 160A 'Marriage and other relationships'

(1) This section applies where, in proceedings for an offence under section 160 relating to an indecent photograph or pseudo-photograph of a child, the defendant proves that the photograph or pseudo-photograph was of the child aged 16 or over, and that at the time of the offence charged the child and he—
  - (a) were married or civil partners of each other, or
  - (b) lived together as partners in an enduring family relationship.

(2) This section also applies where, in proceedings for an offence under section 160 relating to an indecent photograph or pseudo-photograph of a child, the defendant proves that the photograph or pseudo-photograph was of the child aged 16 or over, and that at the time when he obtained it the child and he—
  - (a) were married or civil partners of each other, or
  - (b) lived together as partners in an enduring family relationship.

(3) This section applies whether the photograph or pseudo-photograph showed the child alone or with the defendant, but not if it showed any other person.

(4) If sufficient evidence is adduced to raise an issue as to whether the child consented to the photograph or pseudo-photograph being in the defendant's possession, or as to whether the defendant reasonably believed that the child so consented, the defendant is not guilty of the offence unless it is proved that the child did not so consent and that the defendant did not reasonably believe that the child so consented.

- Knowledge is an essential element in the offence of possession under s 160 so that an accused cannot be convicted where he cannot be shown to be aware of the existence of photographs (*Atkins v DPP* EWHC Admin 302).
- The question of what constitutes 'a legitimate reason' (for the purposes of both s 160(2)(a) of the CJA and s 1(4)(a) of the PCA) is a pure question of fact in each case (*Atkins v DPP* EWHC Admin 302).
- In the special case of deleted computer images, if a person cannot retrieve or gain access to an image he no longer has custody or control of it as he has put it beyond his reach. However, it will be a matter for the jury to decide whether images on a hard disk drive are within the control of the defendant, and to do so having regard to all the circumstances of the case (*R v Porter* [2006] EWCA Crim 560).
- See General Defences **C**.

B3.25.5 Sentencing

An offender convicted of this offence is automatically subject to notification requirements.

s 1 Protection of Children Act 1978

Summary: a fine and/or 6 months' imprisonment

Indictment: 10 years' imprisonment

s 160 Criminal Justice Act 1988

Summary: a fine and/or 6 months' imprisonment

Indictment: 5 years' imprisonment

See notification requirements **B3.1.2**.

Youth Gravity Matrix

OFFENCE	Gravity Score	Offence type	AGGRAVATING FACTORS	MITIGATING FACTORS
Where a youth is in possession of pornographic images the involvement of any adult should be fully investigated, as the youth may be the victim of abuse or grooming. In such cases referral to social services may be more appropriate than criminal justice action				
Possession of indecent photograph/ pseudo photograph of a child (s 160 Criminal Justice Act 1998)	3	E	• Child under 13 • Large number of images • Images are level 3 or above	

OFFENCE	Gravity Score	Offence type	AGGRAVATING FACTORS	MITIGATING FACTORS
Making an indecent photograph/pseudo photograph of a child (s 1(1) Protection of Children Act 1978	3	E	• Child under 13 • Large number of images • Images are level 3 or above • Images distributed • Damage caused	

See *Blackstone's Criminal Practice* **B3.306**

B4 Offences Against Children

B4.1 Child cruelty

Children and Young Persons Act 1933

s 1 'Cruelty to persons under sixteen'

(1) If any person who has attained the age of sixteen years and has responsibility for any child or young person under that age, wilfully assaults, ill treats, (whether physically or otherwise) neglects, abandons, or exposes him, or causes or procures him to be assaulted, ill-treated (whether physically or otherwise), neglected, abandoned, or exposed, in a manner likely to cause him unnecessary suffering or injury to health (whether the suffering or injury is of a physical or psychological nature) that person shall be guilty of an offence.

(2A) The reference in subsection (2)(b) to the infant being 'in bed' with another ('the adult') includes a reference to the infant lying next to the adult in or on any kind of furniture or surface being used by the adult for the purpose of sleeping (and the reference to the time when the adult 'went to bed' is to be read accordingly).

(2B) A drug is a prohibited drug for the purposes of subsection (2)(b) in relation to a person if the person's possession of the drug immediately before taking it constituted an offence under section 5(2) of the Misuse of Drugs Act 1971.

B4.1.1 Related offences

- Grievous bodily harm **B1.6.**
- Actual bodily harm **B1.4.**
- Death of a child **B4.3.**

B4.1.2 Breakdown

Offence	Elements of the Offence	Defence
s 1(1) Children and Young Persons Act 1933 'Cruelty to persons under sixteen'	• Being a person 16 years or over • Having responsibility • For a child/young person • Wilfully assault/ill-treat/neglect/abandon/expose • The child/young person; or • Cause/procure the child/young person • To be assaulted/ill treated • In a manner likely to cause • Unnecessary suffering/injury to health	• Negative any element of the offence • General Defences **C**

B4.1.3 Interpretation

Children and Young Persons Act 1933

s 1 'Cruelty to persons under sixteen'

(2) For the purposes of this section—
(a) a parent or other person legally liable to maintain a child or young person, or the legal guardian of a child or young person, shall be deemed to have neglected him in a manner likely to cause injury to his health if he has failed to provide adequate food, clothing, medical aid or lodging for him, or if, having been unable otherwise to provide such food, clothing, medical aid or lodging, he has failed to take steps to procure it to be provided under the enactments applicable in that behalf;
(b) where it is proved that the death of an infant under three years of age was caused by suffocation (not being suffocation caused by disease or the presence of any foreign body in the throat or air passages of the infant) while the infant was in bed with some other person who has attained the age of sixteen years, that other person shall, if he was, when he went to bed, under the influence of drink, be deemed to have neglected the infant in a manner likely to cause injury to its health.

(3) A person may be convicted of an offence under this section—
(a) notwithstanding that actual suffering or injury to health, or the likelihood of actual suffering or injury to health, was obviated by the action of another person;
(b) notwithstanding the death of the child or young person in question.

s 17 'Interpretation of Part 1'

(1) For the purposes of this Part of this Act, the following shall be presumed to have responsibility for a child or young person—
(a) any person who—
(i) has parental responsibility for him (within the meaning of the Children Act 1989); or
(ii) is otherwise legally liable to maintain him; and
(b) any person who has care of him.

(2) A person who is presumed to be responsible for a child or young person by virtue of subsection (1)(a) shall not be taken to have ceased to be responsible for him by reason only that he does not have care of him.

Children Act 1989

s 3 'Meaning of "parental responsibility"'

(1) In this Act 'parental responsibility' means all the rights, duties, powers, responsibilities and authority which by law a parent of a child has in relation to the child and his property.

B4.1.4 Defences

- See General Defences C.

B4.1.5 Sentencing

s 1(1) Children and Young Persons Act 1933

Summary: 6 months' imprisonment an/or a fine

Indictment: 10 years' imprisonment and/or a fine

See *Blackstone's Criminal Practice* **B2.137**

B4.2 Drunk while in charge of a child

Licensing Act 1902

s 2 'Penalty for being drunk while in charge of child'

(2) If any person is found drunk in any highway or other public place, whether a building or not, or on any licensed premises, while having the charge of a child apparently under the age of seven years, he shall, if the child is under that age, be liable on summary conviction, to a fine not exceeding level 2 on the standard scale, or to imprisonment for any period not exceeding one month.

B4.2.1 Related offences

- Drunk and disorderly **B7.10**.
- Child cruelty **B4.1**.

B4.2.2 Breakdown

Offence	Elements of the Offence	Defence
s 2 Licensing Act 1902 'Drunk in charge of a child'	• Found drunk • In a highway or public place • In charge of a child • Under the age of seven years	• Negative any element of the offence • General Defences **C**

B4.2.3 Interpretation

Licensing Act 1902

s 2 'Penalty for being drunk while in charge of child'

(2) If the child appears to the court to be under the age of seven, the child shall, for the purposes of this section, be deemed to be under that age unless the contrary is proved.

s 8 'Interpretation of "public place"'

For the purposes ... sections one and two of this Act, the expression 'public place' shall include any place to which the public have access, whether on payment or otherwise.

s 8A 'Interpretation of "licensed premises"'

... 'licensed premises' includes—

(a) any licensed premises within the meaning of section 193 of the Licensing Act 2003, and
(b) any premises which may be used for a permitted temporary activity by virtue of Part 5 of that Act.

- Drunk—a person is described as drunk when he is affected by alcohol and appears to be incapable of taking care of himself—s 1 Licensing Act 1902.

B4.2.4 Defences

- See General Defences C.

B4.2.5 Key points

- This is a strict liability offence.

s 2 Licensing Act 1902

Summary only: 1 month's imprisonment and/or a fine not exceeding level 2 on the standard scale

B4.3 Death of a child or vulnerable adult

Domestic Violence, Crime and Victims Act 2004

s 5 'The offence'

(1) a person (D) is guilty of an offence if—
(a) a child or vulnerable adult (V) dies as a result of the unlawful act of a person who—
(i) was a member of the same household as V, and
(ii) had frequent contact with him,
(b) D was such a person at the time of that act,
(c) At that time there was a significant risk of serious physical harm being caused to V by the unlawful act of such a person, and
(d) Either was the person whose act caused V's death or—
(i) D was, or thought to have been, aware of the risk mentioned in paragraph (c),

(ii) D failed to take such steps as he could reasonably have been expected to take to protect V from the risk, and
(iii) The act occurred in circumstances of the kind that D foresaw or ought to have foreseen.

(2) The prosecution does not have to prove whether it is the first alternative in subsection (1)(d) or the second (sub-paragraphs (i) to (iii)) that applies.

B4.3.1 Related offences

- Murder **B1.8**.
- Manslaughter **B1.9**.

Infanticide Act 1938

s 1 'Offence of infanticide'

(1) Where a woman by any wilful act or omission causes the death of her child being a child under the age of twelve months, but at the time of the act or omission the balance of her mind was disturbed by reason of her not having fully recovered from the effect of giving birth to the child or by reason of the effect of lactation consequent upon the birth of the child, then, if the circumstances were such that but for this Act the offence would have amounted to murder or manslaughter, she shall be guilty of felony, to wit of infanticide, and may for such offence be dealt with and punished as if she had been guilty of the offence of manslaughter of the child.

(2) Where upon the trial of a woman for the murder of her child, being a child under the age of twelve months, the jury are of opinion that she by any wilful act or omission caused its death, but that at the time of the act or omission the balance of her mind was disturbed by reason of her not having fully recovered from the effect of giving birth to the child or by reason of the effect of lactation consequent upon the birth of the child, then the jury may, if the circumstances were such that but for the provisions of this Act they might have returned a verdict of murder or manslaughter, return in lieu thereof a verdict of infanticide.

Infant Life (Preservation) Act 1929

s 1 'Punishment for child destruction'

(1) Subject as hereinafter in this subsection provided, any person who, with intent to destroy the life of a child capable of being born alive, by any wilful act causes a child to die before it has an existence independent of its mother, shall be guilty of felony, to wit, of child destruction, and shall be liable on conviction thereof on indictment to penal servitude for life:

Provided that no person shall be found guilty of an offence under this section unless it is proved that the act which caused the death of the child was not done in good faith for the purpose only of preserving the life of the mother.

B4.3.2 Breakdown

Offence	Elements of the Offence	Defence
s 5 Domestic Violence, Crime and Victims Act 2004 'Death of a child'	• Being a member of the same household; and • Having frequent contact with a person who was, at that time, a child/vulnerable adult • Caused that person's death; or • Was/ought to have been aware that there was a significant risk of serious physical harm being caused to that person • By an unlawful act by a member of their household • Which occurred in circumstances of the kind that the defendant foresaw or ought to have foreseen; and • The defendant failed to take such steps as they could reasonably have been expected to take to protect them from that risk	• Negative any element of the offence • s 5 Domestic Violence, Crime and Victims Act 2004 **B4.3.4** • General Defences **C**
s 1 Infanticide Act 1938 'Infanticide'	• A woman • Acts/omits to act • Wilfully • Thereby causing the death of a child under 12 months of age • At the time having a disturbed balance of mind; and • This disturbance was caused by: • Reason of her not having fully recovered from the effect of giving birth to the child; or • Reason of the effect of lactation consequent upon the birth of the child • And: • The circumstances were such that but for this Act the offence would have amounted to murder	• Negative any element of the offence • General Defences **C**

Offence	Elements of the Offence	Defence
s 1 Infant Life (Preservation) Act 1929 'Child destruction'	• A wilful act • With the intent to destroy life capable of being born alive • Causing a child to die before it has an existence independent of its mother	• Negative any element of the offence • s 1 Infant Life (Preservation) Act 1929 **B4.3.4** • General Defences **C**

B4.3.3 Interpretation

Domestic Violence, Crime and Victims Act 2004

s 5 'The offence'

(4) For the purposes of this section—

(a) a person is to be regarded as a 'member' of a particular household, even if he does not live in that household, if he visits it so often and for such periods of time that it is reasonable to regard him as a member of it;

(b) where V lived in different households at different times, 'the same household as V'refers to the household in which V was living at the time of the act that caused the death or serious physical harm.

(5) For the purposes of this section an 'unlawful' act is one that—

(a) constitutes an offence, or

(b) would constitute an offence but for being the act of—

(i) a person under the age of ten, or

(ii) a person entitled to rely on a defence of insanity.

Paragraph (b) does not apply to an act of D.

(6) In this section—

'act' includes a course of conduct and also includes omission;

'child' means a person under the age of 16;

'serious' harm means harm that amounts to grievous bodily harm for the purposes of the Offences against the Person Act 1861 (c. 100);

'vulnerable adult' means a person aged 16 or over whose ability to protect himself from violence, abuse or neglect is significantly impaired through physical or mental disability or illness, through old age or otherwise.

Infant Life (Preservation) Act 1929

s 1 'Punishment for child destruction'.

(2) For the purposes of this Act, evidence that a woman had at any material time been pregnant for a period of twenty-eight weeks or more shall be prima facie proof that she was at that time pregnant of a child capable of being born alive.

B4.3.4 Defences

- See General Defences C.

Domestic Violence, Crime and Victims Act 2004

s 5 'The offence'

(3) If D was not the mother or father of V—

(a) D may not be charged with an offence under this section if he was under the age of 16 at the time of the act that caused the death or serious physical harm.

Infant Life (Preservation) Act 1929

s 1 'Punishment for child destruction'

(1) ... No person shall be found guilty of [child destruction]... unless it is proved that the act which caused the death of the child was not done in good faith for the purpose only of preserving the life of the mother.

B4.3.5 Key points

- Where the identity of the person responsible for causing the death is never established, the defendants are to be sentenced on the basis that they allowed the perpetrator to act as he did (*R v Ikram & Parveen* [2008] EWCA Crim 586).
- The word significant should be given its ordinary meaning (*R v Stephens* [2007] EWCA Crim 1249).
- For s 5(1) the defendant cannot be convicted unless *he or she* failed to take the steps which could reasonably have been expected. This pre-condition requires close analysis of the defendant's personal position (*R v Khan* [2009] EWCA Crim 2).
- The *mens rea* for the offence of infanticide is contained explicitly in the first few words of section 1(1), namely the prosecution must prove that the defendant acted or omitted to act wilfully. There is no reference to any intention to kill or cause serious bodily harm (*R v Gore* [2007] EWCA Crim 2789).

B4.3.6 Sentencing

s 5 Domestic Violence, Crime and Victims Act 2004

Indictable only: 14 years' imprisonment and/or a fine

s 1 Infanticide Act 1938

Indictable only: life imprisonment

s 1 Infant Life (Preservation) Act 1929

Indictable only: life imprisonment

Youth Gravity Matrix

OFFENCE	Gravity Score	Offence type	AGGRAVATING FACTORS	MITIGATING FACTORS
Causing or allowing the death of a child or vulnerable adult (s 5 Domestic Violence, Crime and Victims Act 2004)	4	I	Always refer to the CPS	
Infanticide	4	I	Always refer to the CPS	
Child destruction	4	I	Always refer to the CPS	

See *Blackstone's Criminal Practice* **B1.73–B1.131**

B4.4 **Child abduction**

Child Abduction Act 1984

s 1 'Offence of abduction of child by parent, etc'

(1) Subject to subsections (5) and (8) below, a person connected with a child under the age of 16 commits an offence if he takes or sends the child out of the United Kingdom without the appropriate consent.

B 4.4.1 **Related offences**

Child Abduction Act 1984

s (2) 'Offence of abduction of child by other persons'

(1) Subject to subsection (3) below, a person, other than one mentioned in subsection (2) below, commits an offence if, without lawful authority or reasonable excuse, he takes or detains a child under the age of sixteen—
   (a) so as to remove him from the lawful control of any person having lawful control of the child; or
   (b) so as to keep him out of the lawful control of any person entitled to lawful control of the child.

See also:

- Kidnapping **B1.13**.
- False Imprisonment **B 1.12**.

B 4.4.2 Breakdown

Offence	Elements of the Offence	Defence
s 1 Child Abduction Act 1984 'Child abduction by parent'	• Being a parent of; or • Being a person connected with • A child under 16 years of age • Took or sent the child • Out of the United Kingdom • Without the appropriate consent	• Negative any element of the offence • s 1 Child Abduction Act 1984 **B4.4.4** • General Defences **C**
s 2 Child Abduction Act 1984 'Child abduction by other persons'	• Without lawful authority/ reasonable excuse • Not being a parent/person connected with the child • Detained or took • A child under 16 years of age • So as to remove/keep him/ her • From/out of the lawful control • Of a person having/entitled to lawful control • Of that child	• Negative any element of the offence • s 2 Child Abduction Act **B4.4.4** • General Defences **C**

B4.4.3 Interpretation

Child Abduction Act 1984

s 1 'Offence of abduction of child by parent, etc'

(2) A person is connected with the child for the purposes of this section if—

(a) he is a parent of the child; or

(b) in the case of a child whose parents were not married to each other at the time of birth, there are reasonable grounds for believing that he is the father of the child; or

(c) he is a guardian of the child; or

(ca) He is a special guardian of the child; or

(d) he is named in a child arrangements order as a person with whom the child is to live; or

(e) he has custody of the child

(3) In this section 'the appropriate consent', in relation to a child, means—

(a) the consent of each of the following—
  (i) The child's mother;
  (ii) The child's father, if he has parental responsibility for him;
  (iii) Any guardian of the child;
  (iv) Any person in whose favour a residence order is in force with respect to the child; or
  (v) Any person who has custody of the child; or
(b) by leave of the court granted under or by virtue of any provision of Part II of the Children Act 1989; or
(c) if any person has custody of the child, the leave of the court which awarded custody to him ...

(7) For the purposes of this section—
  (a) `guardian of a child', 'special guardian', residence order' and `parental responsibility' have the same meaning as in the Children Act 1989; and
  (b) a person shall be treated as having custody of a child if there is in force an order of a court in the United Kingdom awarding him (whether solely or jointly with another person) custody, legal custody or care and control of the child.

(8) This section shall have effect subject to the provisions of the Schedule to this Act in relation to a child who is in the care of a local authority detained in a place of safety, remanded otherwise than on bail or the subject of proceedings or an order relating to adoption.

s 2 'Offence of abduction of child by other persons'

(2) The persons are—
  (a) where the father and mother of the child in question were married to each other at the time of his birth, the child's father and mother;
  (b) where the father and mother of the child in question were not married to each other at the time of his birth, the child's mother; and
  (c) any other person mentioned in section 1(2)(c) to (e) above.

s 3 'Construction of references to taking, sending and detaining'

For the purposes of this Part of this Act—
  (a) a person shall be regarded as taking a child if he causes or induces the child to accompany him or any other person or causes the child to be taken;
  (b) a person shall be regarded as sending a child if he causes the child to be sent;
  (c) a person shall be regarded as detaining a child if he causes the child to be detained or induces the child to remain with him or any other person; and
  (d) references to a child's parents and to a child whose parents were (or were not) married to each other at the time of his birth shall be construed in accordance with section 1 of the Family Law Reform Act 1987 (which extends their meaning).

B4.4.4 Defences

Child Abduction Act 1984

s 1 'Offence of abduction of child by parent, etc'

(4) A person does not commit an offence under this section by taking or sending a child out of the United Kingdom without obtaining the appropriate consent if—

He is a person in whose favour there is a residence order in force with respect to the child, and he takes or sends the child out of the United Kingdom for a period of less than one month; or

He is a special guardian of the child and he takes or sends the child out of the United Kingdom for a period of less than three months.

(4A) Subsection 4 above does not apply if the person taking or sending the child out of the United Kingdom does so in breach of an order under Part 2 of the Children Act 1989.

(5) A person does not commit an offence under this section by doing anything without the consent of another person whose consent is required under the foregoing provisions if—

He does it in the belief that the other person—

Has consented; or

(ia) Who is a special guardian of the child; or

Would consent if he was aware of all the relevant circumstances; or

He has taken all reasonable steps to communicate with the other person but has been unable to communicate with him; or

The other person has unreasonably refused to consent.

(5A) Subsection (5)(c) above does not apply if—

The person who refused to consent is a person—

In whose favour there is a residence order with respect to the child; or

Who has custody of the child; or

The person taking or sending the child out of the United Kingdom is, by so acting, in breach of an order made by a court in the United Kingdom.

(6) Where, in proceedings for an offence under this section, there is sufficient evidence to raise an issue as to the application of subsection (5) above, it shall be for the prosecution to prove that that subsection does not apply.

s 2 'Offence of abduction of child by other persons'

(3) In proceedings against any person for an offence under this section, it shall be a defence for that person to prove—
   (a) where the father and mother of the child in question were not married to each other at the time of his birth—
      (i) that he is the child's father; or

(ii) that, at the time of the alleged offence, he believed, on reasonable grounds, that he was the child's father; or

(b) that, at the time of the alleged offence, he believed that the child had attained the age of sixteen.

B 4.4.5 Key points

- The s 1 offence deals with people connected, as defined, to the child. Any other persons will fall within the ambit of the s 2 offence.
- It is for the prosecution to rebut the defence of consent (s 5 Child Abduction Act 1984).
- Removal is a specific event rather than a continuing activity (*R (Nicolaou) v Redbridge Magistrates Court* [2012] EWHC 1647 (Admin)).
- Section 1 Family Reform Act 1987 provides authority on a child's parents; this includes civil partnerships, adoption, and any other circumstance otherwise treated in law as legitimate.

B4.4.6 Sentencing

s 1/s 2 Child Abduction Act 1984

Summary: 6 months' imprisonment and/or a fine

Indictment: 7 years' imprisonment

See *Blackstone's Criminal Practice* **B2.104**

B5 Theft Act Offences

B5.1 The *Ghosh* Test

Where an offence requires an element of dishonesty the same test of dishonesty applies for each. The leading authority is *R v Ghosh* [1982] EWCA Crim 2 and the test is colloquially known as the *Ghosh* Test.

There are two steps to dishonesty; the objective and the subjective.

STEP ONE

Were the accused's actions dishonest according to the ordinary standards of reasonable and honest people?

STEP TWO

If so, did the accused know that those actions were dishonest according to the ordinary standards of reasonable and honest people?

If step one is not satisfied, the prosecution fails and there is no need to consider step two.

B5.2 Theft

Theft Act 1968

s 1 'Basic definition of theft'

(1) A person is guilty of theft if he dishonestly appropriates property belonging to another with the intention of permanently depriving the other of it; and
'thief' and 'steal' shall be construed accordingly.

(2) It is immaterial whether the appropriation is made with a view to gain, or is made for the thief's own benefit.

B5.2.1 Breakdown

Offence	Elements of the Offence	Defence
s 1 Theft Act 1968 'Theft'	• Dishonest • Appropriation of • Property • Belonging to another • With intention to permanently deprive the other of it	• Negative any element of the offence • s 2 Theft Act 1968 **B5.2.3** • *R v Skivington* **B5.2.3** • General Defences **C**

B5.2.2 Interpretation

- Dishonesty—The *Ghosh* Test **B5.1**.

Theft Act 1968

s 3 'Appropriates'

(1) Any assumption by a person of the rights of an owner amounts to an appropriation, and this includes, where he has come by the property (innocently or not) without stealing it, any later assumption of a right to it by keeping or dealing with it as owner.

(2) Where property or a right or interest in property is or purports to be transferred for value to a person acting in good faith, no later assumption by him of rights which he believed himself to be acquiring shall, by reason of any defect in the transferor's title amount to theft of the property.

s 4 'Property'

(1) 'Property' includes money and all other property, real or personal, including things in action and other intangible property.

(2) A person cannot steal land, or things forming part of land and severed from it by him or by his directions, except in the following cases, that is to say—

(a) when he is a trustee or personal representative, or is authorised by power of attorney, or as liquidator of a company, or otherwise, to sell or dispose of land belonging to another, and he appropriates the land or anything forming part of it by dealing with it in breach of the confidence reposed in him; or

(b) when he is not in possession of the land and appropriates anything forming part of the land by severing it or causing it to be severed, or after it has been severed; or

(c) when, being in possession of the land under a tenancy, he appropriates the whole or part of any fixture or structure let to be used with the land.

For purposes of this subsection 'land' does not include incorporeal hereditaments; 'tenancy' means a tenancy for years or any less period and includes an agreement for such a tenancy, but a person who after the end of a tenancy remains in possession as statutory tenant or otherwise is to be treated as having possession under the tenancy, and 'let' shall be construed accordingly.

...

(3) A person who picks mushrooms growing wild on any land, or who picks flowers, fruit or foliage from a plant growing wild on any land, does not (although not in possession of the land) steal what he picks, unless he does it for reward or for sale or other commercial purpose.

For purposes of this subsection 'mushroom' includes any fungus, and 'plant' includes any shrub or tree.

(4) Wild creatures, tamed or untamed, shall be regarded as property; but a person cannot steal a wild creature not tamed nor ordinarily kept in captivity, or the carcase of any such creature, unless either it has been reduced into possession by or on behalf of another person and possession

of it has not since been lost or abandoned, or another person is in course of reducing it into possession.

s 5 'Belonging to another'

(1) Property shall be regarded as belonging to any person having possession or control of it, or having in it any proprietary right or interest (not being an equitable interest arising only from an agreement to transfer or grant an interest).

(2) Where property is subject to a trust, the persons to whom it belongs shall be regarded as including any person having a right to enforce the trust, and an intention to defeat the trust shall be regarded accordingly as an intention to deprive of the property any person having that right.

(3) where a person receives property from or on account of another, and is under an obligation to the other to retain and deal with that property or its proceeds in a particular way, the property or proceeds shall be regarded (as against him) as belonging to another.

(4) where a person gets property by another's mistake, and is under an obligation to make restoration (in whole or in part) of the property or its proceeds or of the value thereof, then to the extent of that obligation the property or the proceeds shall be regarded (as against him) as belonging to the person entitled to restoration, and an intention not to make restoration shall be regarded accordingly as an intention to deprive that person of the property or proceeds.

(5) property of a corporation sole shall be regarded as belonging to the corporation notwithstanding a vacancy in the corporation.

s 6 'With the intention of permanently depriving the other of it'

(1) A person appropriating property belonging to another without meaning the other permanently to lose the thing itself is nevertheless to be regarded as having the intention of permanently depriving the other of it if his intention is to treat the thing as his own to dispose of regardless of the other's rights; and a borrowing or lending may amount to so treating it if, but only if, the borrowing or lending is for a period and in circumstances making it equivalent to an outright taking or disposal.

(2) Without prejudice to the generality of subsection (1) above, where a person, having possession or control (lawfully or not) of property belonging to another, parts with the property under a condition as to its return which he may not be able to perform, this (if done for purposes of his own and without the other's authority) amounts to treating the property as his own to dispose of regardless of the other's rights.

B5.2.3 Defences

Theft Act 1968

s 2 'Dishonestly'

(1) A person's appropriation of property belonging to another is not to be regarded as dishonest:

(a) if he appropriates the property in the belief that he has in law the right to deprive the other of it, on behalf of himself or a third person; or
(b) if he appropriates the property in the belief that he would have had the other's consent if the other new of the appropriation and the circumstances of it; or
(c) (except where the property came to him as trustee or personal representative) if he appropriates the property in the belief that the person to whom the property belongs cannot be discovered by taking reasonable steps.

(2) A person's appropriation of property belonging to another may be dishonest notwithstanding that he is willing to pay for the property.

- An honest belief of a lawful claim, even if mistaken, can provide a defence (*R v Skivington* (1967) 51 Cr App R 167).

B5.2.4 Key points

- 'Appropriation' means the assumption of any rights of an owner (*DPP v Gomez* [1992] UKHL 4).
- 'Appropriation' (s 3) can occur even if the owner consents (*Lawrence v Metropolitan Police Commissioner* (1971) UKHL 2).
- Where an item is left, intended as a gift (ie donations to a charity shop) the item is not abandoned and the would-be donor would retain ownership of the items until the intended recipient took possession (*R (on the application of Ricketts) v Basildon* MC [2010] EWHC 2358 (Admin)).
- A person in possession or control of another's property, who dishonestly and for their own purpose, deals with it in a manner which they know its risking its loss may be regarded as having the intention to permanently deprive (*R v Fernandes* [1996] 1 Cr App R 175).
- An item that would otherwise constitute or be regarded as 'property' for the purposes of the Theft Act does not cease to be so because its possession or control is, for whatever reason, unlawful or illegal or prohibited (*R v Smith & Others* [2011] EWCA Crim 66).
- Confidential information (such as answers to an exam) cannot be considered property for the purposes of this Act (*Oxford v Moss* (1979) 68 Cr App R 183).

B5.2.5 Sentencing

s 1 Theft Act 1968

Summary: 6 months' imprisonment and/or a fine

Indictment: 7 years' imprisonment and/or a fine

Youth Gravity Matrix

OFFENCE	Gravity Score	Offence type	AGGRAVATING FACTORS	MITIGATING FACTORS
Theft – up to £100 in value – over £100 (approx) Theft (shoplifting) Value £100 (Home office), £200 (max)	 2 3	E	• Planned • Sophistication • Organized team • Adult involving children • Significant related damage • Unrecovered property of considerable value	• Theft for reasons of poverty/ personal need • Coercion from others in group in reluctant offender

See *Blackstone's Criminal Practice* **B4.1**

B5.3 **Handling stolen goods**

Theft Act 1968

s 22 'Handling Stolen Goods'

(1) A person handles stolen goods if (otherwise than in the course of the stealing) knowing or believing them to be stolen goods he dishonestly receives the goods, or dishonestly undertakes or assists in their retention, removal, disposal or realisation by or for the benefit of another person, or if he arranges to do so.

B5.3.1 **Related offences**

- Theft **B5.2**.
- Burglary **B5.12**.
- Money laundering **B6.7**.

B5.3.2 **Breakdown**

Offence	Elements of the Offence	Defence
s 22 Theft Act 1968 'Handling stolen goods'	• Otherwise than in the course of stealing • Knowing/believing goods to be stolen • Dishonestly received them or • Dishonestly undertook/assisted • In the retention/removal/ disposal/realization of them or • Arranged to do so by/for the benefit of another	• Negative any element of the offence • General Defences **C**

B5.3.3 Interpretation

Theft Act 1968

s 24 'Scope of offences relating to stolen goods'

(1) The provisions of this Act relating to goods which have been stolen shall apply whether the stealing occurred in England or Wales or elsewhere, and whether it occurred before or after the commencement of this Act, provided that the stealing (if not an offence under this Act) amounted to an offence where and at the time when the goods were stolen; and references to stolen goods shall be construed accordingly.

(2) For purposes of those provisions references to stolen goods shall include, in addition to the goods originally stolen and parts of them (whether in their original state or not)—
   (a) any other goods which directly or indirectly represent or have at any time represented the stolen goods in the hands of the thief as being the proceeds of any disposal or realisation of the whole or part of the goods stolen or of goods so representing the stolen goods; and
   (b) any other goods which directly or indirectly represent or have at any time represented the stolen goods in the hands of a handler of the stolen goods or any part of them as being the proceeds of any disposal or realisation of the whole or part of the stolen goods handled by him or of goods so representing them.

(3) But no goods shall be regarded as having continued to be stolen goods after they have been restored to the person from whom they were stolen or to other lawful possession or custody, or after that person and any other person claiming through him have otherwise ceased as regards those goods to have any right to restitution in respect of the theft.

(4) For purposes of the provisions of this Act relating to goods which have been stolen (including subsections (1) to (3) above) goods obtained in England or Wales or elsewhere either by blackmail or [subject to subsection (5) below, by fraud (within the meaning of the Fraud Act 2006)] shall be regarded as stolen; and 'steal', 'theft' and 'thief'shall be construed accordingly.

(5) Subsection (1) above applies in relation to goods obtained by fraud as if—
   (a) the reference to the commencement of this Act were a reference to the commencement of the Fraud Act 2006, and
   (b) the reference to an offence under this Act were a reference to an offence under section 1 of that Act.

B5.3.4 Defences

- See General Defences C.

B5.3.5 Key points

- In *R v Hall* (1985) 81 Cr App R 260 it was held that 'A man may be said to know that goods are stolen when he is told by someone with first hand knowledge … that such is the case. Belief, of course, is something short of knowledge. It may be said to be the state of mind of a person who says to himself: "I cannot say I know for certain that these goods are stolen, but there can be no other reasonable conclusion in the light of all the circumstances, in the light of all that I have heard and seen."'

- Belief requires more than suspicion.
- Failing to tell the police the location of stolen goods is not in itself assisting in their retention however it is strong evidence of assisting (*R v Brown* (1969) 53 Cr App R 527).
- In proceedings for handling stolen goods s 27(4) provides two extra routes for the admission of a defendant's previous convictions for handling stolen goods and theft.

B5.3.6 Sentencing

s 22 Theft Act 1968

Summary: 6 months' imprisonment and/or a fine

Indictment: 14 years' imprisonment

Youth Gravity Matrix

OFFENCE	Gravity Score	Offence type	AGGRAVATING FACTORS	MITIGATING FACTORS
Handling stolen property	3	E	• Property stolen to order • Professional receiver • Youth coercing children • Property of high value	• Received under pressure from another • Very low value

See *Blackstone's Criminal Practice* B4.160

B5.4 Advertising rewards for return of goods stolen or lost

Theft Act 1968

s 23 'Advertising rewards for return of goods stolen or lost'

Where any public advertisement of a reward for the return of any goods which have been stolen or lost uses any words to the effect that no questions will be asked, or that the person producing the goods will be safe from apprehension or inquiry, or that any money paid for the purchase of the goods or advanced by way of loan on them will be repaid, the person advertising the reward and any person who prints or publishes the advertisement shall (be guilty of an offence) on summary conviction be liable to a fine not exceeding level 3 on the standard scale.

B5.4.1 Breakdown

Offence	Elements of the Offence	Defence
s 23 Theft Act 1968 'Advertising rewards for the return of good stolen or lost'	• A person advertises or prints or publishes • A public advertisement for the return of goods stolen or lost • Using words to the effect that no questions will be asked/or that the person producing the goods will be safe from apprehension/that any money paid or loaned for the purchase will be repaid	• Negative any element of the offence • General Defences **C**

B5.4.2 Interpretation

Theft Act 1968

s 34 'Interpretation'

(2) For purposes of this Act—

...

(b) 'goods', except in so far as the context otherwise requires, includes money and every other description of property except land, and includes things severed from the land by stealing.

B5.4.3 Defences

- See General Defences C.

B5.4.4 Key points

- This is an offence of strict liability *(Denham v Scott* (1984) 77 Cr App R 210).
- The offence is to combine an offer of a reward with a promise that no questions will be asked etc. It does not matter if the advertiser is uncertain whether the goods were lost or stolen.

B5.4.5 Sentencing

s 23 Theft Act 1968

Summary only: level 3 fine

TO

B5.5 Robbery

Theft Act 1968

s 8(1) 'Robbery'

A person is guilty of robbery if he steals, and immediately before or at the time of doing so, he uses force on any person or puts or seeks to put any person in fear of being then and there subjected to force.

B5.5.1 Related offences

- Theft **B5.2**.
- Assault with intent to rob **B5.6**.

B5.5.2 Breakdown

Offence	Elements of the Offence	Defence
s 8 Theft Act 1968 'Robbery'	• Stole property • Immediately before/at the time of doing so • And in order to do so • Used force on a person or put/sought to put person in fear of immediate force	• Negative any element of the offence • *R v Skivington* **B5.5.3** • General Defences **C**

B5.5.3 Defences

- A claim of right is a defence to robbery or any aggravated form of robbery (*R v Skivington* [1967] 1 All ER 483, CA).
- See General Defences **C**.

B5.5.4 Key points

- Appropriation is a continuing act and if force is used then, subject to the other elements of the offence being present, a robbery will have been committed (*R v Hale* (1979) 68 Cr App R 415).
- An item that would otherwise constitute or be regarded as 'property' for the purposes of the Theft Act does not cease to be so because its possession or control is, for whatever reason, unlawful or illegal or prohibited (*R v Smith & Others* [2011] EWCA Crim 66).
- Whether force was used in order to steal is a matter for the jury (*R v Dawson* (1977) 64 Cr App R 170).

B5.5.5 Sentencing

s 8 Theft Act 1968

Indictable only: life imprisonment

Youth Gravity Matrix

OFFENCE	Gravity Score	Offence type	AGGRAVATING FACTORS	MITIGATING FACTORS
Robbery/assault with intent to rob	4	I	Always refer to the CPS	

TO

See *Blackstone's Criminal Practice* **B4.66**

B5.6 Assault with intent to rob

Theft Act 1968

s 8 'Robbery'

(2) A person guilty of robbery, or an assault with intent to rob [is guilty of an offence].

B5.6.1 Related offences

- Robbery **B5.5**.
- Offences against the person **B1**.

B5.6.2 Breakdown

Offence	Elements of the Offence	Defence
s 8(2) Theft Act 1968 'Assault with the intent to rob'	• Assault • With the intent to rob	• Negative any element of the offence • *R v Skivington* **B5.5.3** • General Defences **C**

B5.6.3 Defences

- See General Defences C.

B5.6.4 Sentencing

s 8(2) Theft Act 1968

Indictable only: life imprisonment

Youth Gravity Matrix

OFFENCE	Gravity Score	Offence type	AGGRAVATING FACTORS	MITIGATING FACTORS
Robbery/assault with intent to rob	4	I	Always refer to the CPS	

See *Blackstone's Criminal Practice* **B4.66**

B5.7 Making off without payment

Theft Act 1978

s 3 'Making off without payment'

(1) Subject to subsection (3) below, a person who, knowing that payment on the spot for any goods supplied or service done is required or expected from him, dishonestly makes off without having paid as required or expected and with intent to avoid payment of the amount due shall be guilty of an offence.

(2) For purposes of this section 'payment on the spot' includes payment at the time of collecting goods on which work has been done or in respect of which service has been provided.

(3) Subsection (1) above shall not apply where the supply of the goods or the doing of the service is contrary to law, or where the service done is such that payment is not legally enforceable.

B5.7.1 Related offences

- Theft B5.2.

B5.7.2 Breakdown

Offence	Elements of the Offence	Defence
s 3 Theft Act 1978 'Making off without payment'	• Knowing immediate payment is required/expected • For goods supplied/ service done • Dishonestly • Made off • Without having paid as required/expected • With intent to avoid payment of amount due	• Negative any element of the offence • s 3 Theft Act 1978 **B5.7.4** • General Defences **C**

B5.7.3 Interpretation

Theft Act 1978

s 3 'Making off without payment'

(2) For purposes of this section 'payment on the spot' includes payment at the time of collecting goods on which work has been done or in respect of which service has been provided.

- Dishonesty, see *R v Ghosh* **B5.1**.
- Making off involves a departure from the spot where payment was required and 'dishonestly makes off' should be given its ordinary natural meaning (*R v Brooks* (1983) 76 Cr App R 66, CA).
- The following must be proved to secure a conviction under s 3 Theft Act 1978:
  (a) the defendant made off without making a payment on the spot;
  (b) knowledge that payment on the spot was required or expected;
  (c) dishonesty; and
  (d) an intent to permanently avoid the amount due (*R v Allen* (1984) 79 Cr App R 265).

B5.7.4 Defences

Theft Act 1978

s 3 'Making off without payment'

(3) Subsection (1) above shall not apply where the supply of the goods or the doing of the service is contrary to law, or where the service done is such that payment is not legally enforceable.

- See General Defences C.

B5.7.5 Sentencing

s 3 Theft Act 1978

Summary: 6 months' imprisonment and/or a fine

Indictment: 2 years' imprisonment

TO

See *Blackstone's Criminal Practice* B5.34

B5.8 Dishonestly retain a wrongful credit

Theft Act 1968

s 24A(1) 'Dishonestly retaining a wrongful credit'

A person is guilty of an offence if—

(a) A wrongful credit has been made to an account kept by him or in respect of which he has any right or interest;

(b) He knows or believes that the credit is wrongful; and

(c) He dishonestly fails to take such steps as are reasonable in the circumstances to secure that the credit is cancelled.

B5.8.1 Breakdown

Offence	Elements of the Offence	Defence
s 24A Theft Act 1968 'Dishonestly retain a wrongful credit'	• Knowing/believing • A wrongful credit made to an account • Kept by them/in which they have a right or interest • Dishonestly • Fails to take reasonable steps to cancel the credit	• Negative any element of the offence • General Defences **C**

B5.8.2 Interpretation

Theft Act 1968

s 24A 'Dishonestly retaining a wrongful credit'

(2) References to a credit are to a credit of an amount of money.

(2A) A credit to an account is wrongful to the extent that it derives from—
- (a) theft;
- (b) blackmail;
- (c) fraud (contrary to section 1 of the Fraud Act 2006); or
- (d) stolen goods.

...

(5) In determining whether a credit to an account is wrongful, it is immaterial (in particular) whether the account is overdrawn before or after the credit is made.

...

(8) References to stolen goods include money which is dishonestly withdrawn from an account to which a wrongful credit has been made, but only to the extent that the money derives from the credit.

(9) 'Account' means an account kept with—
- (a) a bank;
- (b) a person carrying on a business which falls within subsection (10) below; or
- (c) a person falling within any of paragraphs (a) to (j) of the definition of 'electronic money issuer' in regulation 2(1) of the Electronic Money Regulations 2011.

(10) A business falls within s.24A(9)(b) if—
- (a) in the course of the business money received by way of deposit is lent to others; or
- (b) any other activity of the business is financed, wholly or to any material extent, out of the capital of or the interest on money received by way of deposit.

- The word 'cancelled', means cancelling the original credit so as to achieve the same effect as if it had not been made in the first place (*R v Lee* [2006] EWCA Crim 156).

B5.8.3 Defences

- See General Defences **C**.

B5.8.4 Sentencing

s 24A Theft Act 1968

Summary: 6 months' imprisonment and/or a fine

Indictment: 10 years' imprisonment

B5.9 Abstract electricity

Theft Act 1968

s 13 'Abstracting of electricity'

A person who dishonestly uses without due authority, or dishonestly causes to be wasted or diverted, any electricity [commits an offence].

B5.9.1 Related offences

- Theft **B5.2**.

B5.9.2 Breakdown

Offence	Elements of the Offence	Defence
s 13 Theft Act 1968 'Abstract electricity'	• Dishonestly/Uses without due authority/causes to be wasted/ diverted • Any electricity	• Negative any element of the offence • General Defences **C**

B5.9.3 Interpretation

- Dishonesty **B5.1**.

B5.9.4 Defences

- See General Defences **C**.

B5.9.5 Key points

- No proactive step is required by a defendant; it is sufficient that electricity is dishonestly used with no intention of paying for it (*R v McCreadie and Tume* [1993] 96 Cr App R 143).

B5.9.6 Sentencing

s 13 Theft Act 1968

Summary: 6 months' imprisonment and/or a fine

Indictment: 5 years' imprisonment

Youth Gravity Matrix

OFFENCE	Gravity Score	Offence type	AGGRAVATING FACTORS	MITIGATING FACTORS
Abstracting electricity	2	E	• Special equipment • High usage • Prolonged period • Commercial gain such as cannabis farms	• Poverty/ personal need • Coercion by others

TO

See *Blackstone's Criminal Practice* B4.141

B5.10 Removal of articles from places open to the public

Theft Act 1968

s 11 'Removal of Articles from Places Open to the Public'

(1) Subject to subsections (2) and (3) below, where the public have access to a building in order to view the building or part of it, or a collection or part of a collection housed in it, any person who without lawful authority removes from the building or its grounds the whole or part of any article displayed or kept for display to the public in the building or that part of it or in its grounds shall be guilty of an offence.

(2) It is immaterial for purposes of subsection (1) above, that the public's access to a building is limited to a particular period or particular occasion; but where anything removed from a building or its grounds is there otherwise than as forming part of, or being on loan for exhibition with,

a collection intended for permanent exhibition to the public, the person removing it does not thereby commit an offence under this section unless he removes it on a day when the public have access to the building as mentioned in subsection (1) above.

B5.10.1 Related offences

- Theft **B5.2**.

B5.10.2 Breakdown

Offence	Elements of the Offence	Defence
s 11 Theft Act 1968 'Removal of articles from places open to the public'	• Without lawful authority • Removes from a building an article displayed or kept for display • Public has access to the building or part to view the building or a collection	• Negative any element of the offence • s 11 Theft Act 1968 **B5.10.4** • General Defences **C**

B5.10.3 Interpretation

Theft Act 1968

s 11 'Removal of articles from places open to the public'

(1) ...

For this purpose 'collection' includes a collection got together for a temporary purpose, but references in this section to a collection do not apply to a collection made or exhibited for the purpose of effecting sales or other commercial dealings.

B5.10.4 Defences

Theft Act 1968

s 11 'Removal of articles from places open to the public'

(3) A person does not commit an offence under this section if he believes that he has lawful authority for the removal of the thing in question or that he would have it if the person entitled to give it knew of the removal and the circumstances of it.

- See General Defences **C**.

B5.10.5 Key point

- Once the defence have raised the issue of lawful excuse it will be for the Crown to disprove it.

B5.10.6 Sentencing

s 11 Theft Act 1968

Summary: 6 months' imprisonment/fine

Indictment: 5 years' imprisonment

B5.11 Going equipped to steal

Theft Act 1968

s 25 'Going equipped for stealing, etc'

(1) A person shall be guilty of an offence if, when not at his place of abode, he has with him any article for use in the course of or in connection with any burglary or theft.

B5.11.1 Related offences

- Burglary **B5.12**.

B5.11.2 Breakdown

Offence	Elements of the Offence	Defence
s 25 Theft Act 1968 'Going equipped for stealing'	• Not at place of abode • Has with him • Article(s) for use in course of/in connection with • A burglary/theft	• Negative any element of the offence • General Defences **C**

B5.11.3 Interpretation

- A 'place of abode' is construed with two elements: the element of a site and the element of an intention to abide. In (*R v Bundy* (1977) 65 Cr App R 239) the defendant slept rough in his car and it was held that this vehicle could not be said to be a 'place of abode' while in transit.

B5.11.4 Defences

- See General Defences **C**.

B5.11.5 Key points

- A theft need not be committed for this offence to be made out (*R v Minor* (1988) 86 Cr App R 378).
- The article need not be intended for immediate use but it must be intended for future use (*R v Ellames* [1974] 1 WLR 1391).
- Proof of intent is required and not mere contemplation of an offence (*R v Hargreaves* [1985] Crim LR 243).

B5.11.6 Sentencing

s 25 Theft Act 1968

Summary: 6 months' imprisonment and/or a fine

Indictment: 3 years' imprisonment

Youth Gravity Matrix

OFFENCE	Gravity Score	Offence type	AGGRAVATING FACTORS	MITIGATING FACTORS
Going equipped to steal	2	E		

TO

See *Blackstone's Criminal Practice* **B4.151**

B5.12 Burglary

Theft Act 1968

s 9 'Burglary'

(1) A person is guilty of burglary if—

(a) he enters any building or part of a building as a trespasser and with intent to commit any such offence as is mentioned in subsection (2) below; or

(b) having entered any building or part of a building as a trespasser he steals or attempts to steal anything in the building or that part of it or inflicts or attempts to inflict on any person therein any grievous bodily harm.

(2) The offences referred to in subsection (1)(a) above are offences of stealing anything in the building or part of a building in question, of inflicting on any person therein any grievous bodily harm therein, and of doing unlawful damage to the building or anything therein.

B5.12.1 Related offences

- Aggravated burglary **B5.14**.

B5.12.2 Breakdown

Offence	Elements of the Offence	Defence
s 9(1)(a) Theft Act 1968 'Burglary'	• Entered a building/part of a building • As a trespasser • With intent • To steal property therein/ inflict grievous bodily harm on person therein/ do unlawful damage to the building or anything therein.	• Negative any element of the offence • General Defences **C**
s 9(1)(b) Theft Act 1968 'Burglary'	• Having entered a building/ part of a building • As a trespasser • Stole or attempted to steal anything therein/inflicted or attempted to inflict grievous bodily harm on any person therein.	• Negative any element of the offence • General Defences **C**

B5.12.3 Interpretation

- Entry must be effective and substantial (*R v Collins* [1972] EWCA Crim 1).

B5.12.4 Defences

- See General Defences **C**.

B5.12.5 Key points

- See 'third strike burglary' **B5.13**.
- If a defendant enters a building as a trespasser with an intention to steal it is immaterial that there are subsequently no goods worth stealing (*R v Walkington* (1979) 68 Cr App R 427).

B5.12.6 Sentencing

s 9(1) Theft Act 1968

Summary: 6 months' imprisonment and/or a fine

Indictment: 10 years' imprisonment (dwelling 14 years' imprisonment)

- See 'third strike burglary' B5.13.

Youth Gravity Matrix

OFFENCE	Gravity Score	Offence type	AGGRAVATING FACTORS	MITIGATING FACTORS
Burglary dwelling—with use (or threat) of force against victim	4	E		
Burglary dwelling Burglary non-dwelling Burglary with intent to steal/criminal damage	4 3 3	E	• Deliberate targeting of victim/ vulnerable victim • Excessive trauma experienced by victim • Night time occupier present • Use or threat of force against victim • Soiling/ransacking/ vandalism of premises • Pre-meditated or professionally planned • Group offence • 'Ram-raiding' or tools carried for offence • High economic or sentimental value of property stolen/ damaged • Excessive damage, eg boiler removal and water leaks	• Vacant premises • Low value • Coercion from others in group or reluctant offender • Committed on impulse • Genuine regret or remorse • Property recovered and returned to owner

B5.13 Third strike burglary

Powers of the Criminal Courts (Sentencing) Act 2000

s 111 'Minimum of three years for third domestic burglary'

(1) This section applies where—
  (a) A person is convicted of a domestic burglary committed after 30th November 1999;

(b) At the time when that burglary was committed, he was 18 or over and had two relevant domestic burglary convictions; and
(c) One of those other burglaries was committed after he had been convicted of the other and both of them were committed after the relevant date.

(2) The court shall impose an appropriate custodial sentence for a term of at least three years except where the court is of the opinion that there are particular circumstances which—
(a) Relate to any of the offences or to the offender; and
(b) Would make it unjust to do so in all the circumstances

(2A) For the purposes of subsection (1)—
(a) A 'relevant domestic burglary convection' means—
(i) A conviction in England and Wales of a domestic burglary, or
(ii) A conviction in any other part of the United Kingdom or any other member State of an offence which would, if done in England and Wales at the time of the conviction, have constituted domestic burglary;
(b) 'the relevant date', in relation to a relevant domestic burglary conviction, means—
(i) In respect of a conviction in England and Wales, 30 November 1999, and
(ii) In any other case, the day on which this subsection comes into force.

(4) ... Where—
(a) A person is charged with a domestic burglary which, apart from this subsection, would be triable either way, and
(b) The circumstances are such that, if he were convicted of the burglary, he could be sentenced for it under subsection (2) above; the burglary shall be triable only on indictment.

(5) In this section 'domestic burglary' means a burglary committed in respect of a building or part of a building which is a dwelling.

See *Blackstone's Criminal Practice* B4.75

B5.14 **Aggravated burglary**

Theft Act 1968

s 10 'Aggravated burglary'

(1) A person is guilty of aggravated burglary if he commits any burglary and at the time has with him any firearm or imitation firearm, any weapon of offence, or any explosive.

B5.14.1 Related offences

- Burglary **B5.12**.

B5.14.2 Breakdown

Offence	Elements of the Offence	Defence
s 10 Theft Act 1968 'Aggravated burglary'	• Committed burglary • Had with them • Firearm/imitation firearm/weapon of offence/explosive	• Negative any element of the offence • General Defences **C**

B5.14.3 Interpretation

Theft Act 1968

s 10 'Aggravated burglary'

(1) ...(a) 'firearm' includes an airgun or air pistol, and 'imitation firearm' means anything which has the appearance of being a firearm, whether capable of being discharged or not; and

(b) 'weapon of offence' means any article made or adapted for use for causing injury to or incapacitating a person, or intended by the person having it with him for such use; and

(c) 'explosive' means any article manufactured for the purpose of producing a practical effect by explosion, or intended by the person having it with him for that purpose.

- See Burglary **B5.12**.

B5.14.4 Defences

- See General Defences **C**.

B5.14.5 Key points

- In dealing with a 'weapon of offence' it is an intention to use any such weapon at the time of the offence that is the relevant consideration (*R v Kelly* (1993) 97 Cr App R 245).
- Section 10 should be read purposively and an accomplice holding a weapon outside a property would not be sufficient to constitute an offence under this section (*R v Klass* [1997] EWCA Crim 3072).
- The phrase 'has with him' should be read as '***knowingly*** has with him' (*R v Cugullere* (1961) 45 Cr App R 108).

B5.14.6 **Sentencing**

s 10 Theft Act 1968
Indictable: life imprisonment

Youth Gravity Matrix

OFFENCE	Gravity Score	Offence type	AGGRAVATING FACTORS	MITIGATING FACTORS
Aggravated burglary	4	I	Defer decision to CPS	

See *Blackstone's Criminal Practice* **B4.97**

B5.15 **Blackmail**

Theft Act 1968

s 21 'Blackmail'

(1) A person is guilty of blackmail if, with a view to gain for himself or another or with intent to cause loss to another, he makes any unwarranted demand with menaces and for this purpose a demand with menaces is unwarranted unless the person making it does so in the belief—
(a) That he has reasonable grounds for making the demands; and
(b) That the use of the menaces is a proper means of reinforcing the demands.

B5.15.1 **Breakdown**

Offence	Elements of the Offence	Defence
s 21 Theft Act 1968 'Blackmail'	• With view to gain for self/another or intent to cause loss to another • Made unwarranted demand with menaces	• Negative any element of the offence • General Defences **C**

B5.15.2 Interpretation

Theft Act 1968

s 21 'Blackmail

(1) ... a demand with menaces is unwarranted unless the person making it does so in the belief—
  (a) that he has reasonable grounds for making the demand; and
  (b) that the use of the menaces is a proper means of reinforcing the demand.

(2) The nature of the act or omission demanded is immaterial, and it is also immaterial whether the menaces relate to action to be taken by the person making the demand.

- *Menaces* should be taken at its ordinary meaning (*R v Garwood* (1987) 85 Cr App R 85).

B5.15.3 Defences

- See General Defences C.

B5.15.4 Sentencing

s 21 Theft Act 1968

Indictable only: 14 years' imprisonment

Youth Gravity Matrix

OFFENCE	Gravity Score	Offence type	AGGRAVATING FACTORS	MITIGATING FACTORS
Blackmail	4	I	Always refer to the CPS	Blackmail

TO

See *Blackstone's Criminal Practice* **B5.43**

B6 Fraud and Money Laundering Offences

B6.1 Fraud

Fraud Act 2006

s 1 'Fraud'

(1) A person is guilty of fraud if he is in breach of any of the sections listed in subsection (2) (which provide for different ways of committing the offence).

(2) The sections are—
- (a) section 2 (fraud by false representation),
- (b) section 3 (fraud by failing to disclose information), and
- (c) section 4 (fraud by abuse of position).

s 2 'Fraud by false representation'

(1) A person is in breach of this section if he—
- (a) dishonestly makes a false representation, and
- (b) intends, by making the representation—
  - (i) to make a gain for himself or another, or
  - (ii) to cause loss to another or to expose another to a risk of loss.

s 3 'Fraud by failing to disclose information'

(1) A person is in breach of this section if he—
- (a) dishonestly fails to disclose to another person information which he is under a legal duty to disclose, and
- (b) intends, by failing to disclose the information—
  - (i) to make a gain for himself or another, or
  - (ii) to cause loss to another or to expose another to a risk of loss.

s 4 'Fraud by abuse of position'

(1) A person is in breach of this section if he—
- (a) occupies a position in which he is expected to safeguard, or not to act against, the financial interests of another person,
- (b) dishonestly abuses that position, and
- (c) intends, by means of the abuse of that position—
  - (i) to make a gain for himself or another, or
  - (ii) to cause loss to another or to expose another to a risk of loss.

(2) A person may be regarded as having abused his position even though his conduct consisted of an omission rather than an act.

B6.1.1 Related offences

Fraud Act 2006

s 6 'Possession etc of articles for use in frauds'

(1) A person is guilty of an offence if he has in his possession or under his control any article for use in the course of or in connection with any fraud.

s 7 'Making or supplying articles for use in frauds'

(1) A person is guilty of an offence if he makes, adapts, supplies or offers to supply any article—
   (a) knowing that it is designed or adapted for use in the course of or in connection with fraud, or
   (b) intending it to be used to commit, or assist in the commission of, fraud.

s 11 'Obtaining services dishonestly'

(1) A person is guilty of an offence under this section if he obtains services for himself or another—
   (a) by a dishonest act, and
   (b) in breach of subsection (2).
(2) A person obtains services in breach of this subsection if—
   (a) they are made available on the basis that payment has been, is being or will be made for or in respect of them,
   (b) he obtains them without any payment having been made for or in respect of them or without payment having been made in full, and
   (c) when he obtains them, he knows—
      (i) that they are being made available on the basis described in paragraph (a), or
      (ii) that they might be, but intends that payment will not be made, or will not be made in full.

- Consideration should be given to alternative offences under the Theft Act **B5**.

B6.1.2 Breakdown

Offence	Elements of the Offence	Defence
s 1 Fraud Act 2006 'Fraud'	• A person is guilty of fraud if he is in breach of the following sections: • s 2—Fraud by false representation; or • s 3—Fraud by failing to disclose information; or • Fraud by abuse of position	

Offence	Elements of the Offence	Defence
s 2 Fraud Act 2006 'Fraud by false representation'	• Dishonestly • Make a false representation • Intending • To make a gain for himself/to cause another loss/expose another to risk of loss	• Negative any element of the offence • General Defences **C**
s 3 Fraud Act 2006 'Fraud by failing to disclose information'	• Dishonestly • Fail to disclose to another person • Information which he is under a legal duty to disclose • Intending • To make a gain for himself/to cause another loss/expose another to risk of loss	• Negative any element of the offence • General Defences **C**
s 4 Fraud Act 2006 'Fraud by abuse of position'	• Occupy a position in which you are expected to safeguard/not act against the financial interests of another person; and • Dishonestly abuse that position • Intending • To make a gain for himself/to cause another loss/expose another to risk of loss • The conduct of this offence can be made out by an act or omission	• Negative any element of the offence • General Defences **C**
s 6 Fraud Act 2006 'Possession of articles for use in fraud'	• Have in possession/control • Any article • For use in/connection with • Any fraud	• Negative any element of the offence • General Defences **C**
s 7 Fraud Act 2006 'Making or supplying articles for use in frauds'	• Make/adapt/supply/offer to supply • Any article • Knowing that it is designed/adapted for use in the course of/connection with fraud; or • Intending it to be used to commit/assist in the commission of fraud	• Negative any element of the offence • General Defences **C**

Offence	Elements of the Offence	Defence
s 11 Fraud Act 2006 'Obtaining services dishonestly'	• Obtain services for himself/another • By a dishonest act; and • Services are made available on the basis that payment has been/is being/will be made; and • Services are obtained without payment/payment in full; and • When services are obtained he knows • That the services are being made available on the basis that payment has been/is being/will be made; or • That the services might be being made available on the basis that payment has been/is being/will be made and that payment will not be made/made in full	• Negative any element of the offence • General Defences **C**

B6.1.3 Interpretation

Fraud Act 2006

s 2 'Representation'

(2) A representation is false if—
  (a) it is untrue or misleading, and
  (b) the person making it knows that it is, or might be, untrue or misleading.

(3) 'Representation' means any representation as to fact or law, including a representation as to the state of mind of—
  (a) the person making the representation, or
  (b) any other person.

(4) A representation may be express or implied.

(5) For the purposes of this section a representation may be regarded as made if it (or anything implying it) is submitted in any form to any system or device designed to receive, convey or respond to communications (with or without human intervention).

s 5 'Gain' and 'loss'

(1) The references to gain and loss in sections 2 to 4 are to be read in accordance with this section.

(2) 'Gain' and 'loss'—
  (a) extend only to gain or loss in money or other property;
  (b) include any such gain or loss whether temporary or permanent; and 'property' means any property whether real or personal (including things in action and other intangible property).

(3) 'Gain' includes a gain by keeping what one has, as well as a gain by getting what one does not have.

(4) 'Loss' includes a loss by not getting what one might get, as well as a loss by parting with what one has.

s 8 'Article'

(1) For the purposes of—
  (a) sections 6 and 7, and
  (b) the provisions listed in subsection (2), so far as they relate to articles for use in the course of or in connection with fraud, 'article' includes any program or data held in electronic form.

- Dishonesty—see *Ghosh* Test **B5.1**.

B6.1.4 Defences

- See General Defences **C**.

B6.1.5 Key points

- It is necessary to prove intention to make out offences under ss 1–4 Fraud Act 2006.
- If an offence is committed with the consent/connivance of a director/manager/secretary/similar officer of a body corporate or a person purporting to act in that capacity he *and* the body corporate are liable to proceedings: s 12 Fraud Act 2006.
- Gain or loss does not have to occur. It is an intention to cause a gain or loss that is required.
- A representation can be made in any manner.
- When considering whether a person is under a 'legal duty' consideration should be given to implied duties (Sale of Goods Act etc) as well as to explicit duties.
- Abuse (s 4) is not defined and should be read widely.
- Section 6 does not require the holder of the article to be the person intending to commit the fraud; it is sufficient that he is aware that the article in his possession will be used in the course of/connection with a fraud.
- Section 11 requires a dishonest act; an omission alone is insufficient.

B6.1.6 Sentencing

s 1 Fraud Act 2006

Summary: a fine/6 months' imprisonment

Indictment: 10 years' imprisonment

s 2 Fraud Act 2006

Summary: a fine/6 months' imprisonment

Indictment: 10 years' imprisonment

s 3 Fraud Act 2006

Summary: a fine/6 months' imprisonment

Indictment: 10 years' imprisonment

s 4 Fraud Act 2006

Summary: a 5 fine/6 months' imprisonment

Indictment: 10 years' imprisonment

s 6 Fraud Act 2006

Summary: a 5 fine/6 months' imprisonment

Indictment: 5 years' imprisonment

s 7 Fraud Act 2006

Summary: a fine/6 months' imprisonment

Indictment: 10 years' imprisonment

s 11 Fraud Act 2006

Summary: a fine/6 months' imprisonment

Indictment: 5 years' imprisonment

Youth Gravity Matrix

OFFENCE	Gravity Score	Offence type	AGGRAVATING FACTORS	MITIGATING FACTORS
Fraud by false representation (ss 1 and 2 Fraud Act 2006)	2	E	• Sophistication • Two or more involved • Committed over lengthy period • Unrecovered property of considerable value • Value £200+ (approx)	• Poverty/ personal need • Coercion from others in group/ reluctant offender • Value £50 or less
Possession of articles for use in frauds (s 6 of the Fraud Act 2006)	2	E		
Obtaining services dishonestly (s 11 Fraud Act 2006)	2	E	• Sophistication • Organised team • Unrecovered property of considerable value • Value £200+ (approx.)	• Poverty/ personal need • Coercion from others in group/ reluctant offender • Value £50 or less

TO

See *Blackstone's Criminal Practice* B5.4

B6.2 **Dishonest benefit fraud**

Social Security Administration Act 1992

s 111A 'Dishonest representations for obtaining benefit etc'

(1) If a person dishonestly—

(a) makes a false statement or representation ...

with a view to obtaining any benefit or other payment or advantage under the relevant social security legislation (whether for himself or for some other person), he shall be guilty of an offence.

Dishonestly producing or furnishing a false document/information or knowingly causing or allowing a false document/information to be produced or furnished

Social Security Administration Act 1992

s 111A 'Dishonest representations for obtaining benefit etc'

(1) If a person dishonestly—

...

(b) produces or furnishes, or causes or allows to be produced or furnished, any document or information which is false in a material particular

with a view to obtaining any benefit or other payment or advantage under the relevant social security legislation (whether for himself or for some other person), he shall be guilty of an offence.

Dishonestly failing to notify a change in circumstances

Social Security Administration Act 1992

s 111A 'Dishonest representations for obtaining benefit etc'

(1A) A person shall be guilty of an offence if—

(a) there has been a change of circumstances affecting any entitlement of his to any benefit or other payment or advantage under any provision of the relevant social security legislation;

(b) the change is not a change that is excluded by regulations from the changes that are required to be notified;
(c) he knows that the change affects an entitlement of his to such a benefit or other payment or advantange; and
(d) he dishonestly fails to give a prompt notification of that change in the prescribed manner to the prescribed person.

Dishonestly causing or allowing a person to fail to notify a change in circumstances

Social Security Administration Act 1992

s 111A 'Dishonest representations for obtaining benefit etc'

(1B) a person shall be guilty of an offence if—
(a) there has been a change of circumstances affecting any entitlement of another person to any benefit or other payment or advantage under any provison of the relevant social security legislation;
(b) the change is not a change that is excluded by regulations from the changes that are required to be notified;
(c) he knows that the change affects an entitlement of that person to such a benefit or other payment or advantage; and
(d) he dishonestly causes or allows that other person to fail to give a prompt notification of that change in the prescribed manner to the prescribed person.

Benefit recipient dishonestly failing to promptly notify a change in circumstances

Social Security Administration Act 1992

s 111A 'Dishonest representations for obtaining benefit etc'

(1D) In a case where subsection (1C) above applies, the recipient is guilty of an offence if—
(a) he knows that the change affects an entitlement of the claimant to a benefit or other payment or advantage under a provision of the relevant social security legislation;
(b) the entitlement is one in respect of which he has a right to receive payments to which the claimant has, or (but for the arrangements under which they are payable to the recipient) would have, an entitlement; and
(c) he dishonestly fails to give a prompt notification of that change in the prescribed manner to the prescribed person.

A person other than the benefit recipient dishonestly causing or allowing the benefit recipient to fail to promptly notify a change in circumstances

Social Security Administration Act 1992

s 111A 'Dishonest representations for obtaining benefit etc'

(1E) In a case where that subsection applies, a person other than the recipient is guilty of an offence if—

(a) he knows that the change affects an entitlement of the claimant to a benefit or other payment or advantage under a provision of the relevant social security legislation;

(b) the entitlement is one in respect of which the recipient has a right to receive payments to which the claimant has, or (but for the arrangements under which they are payable to the recipient) would have, an entitlement; and

(c) he dishonestly causes or allows the recipient to fail to give a prompt notification of that change in the prescribed manner to the prescribed person.

B6.2.1 Breakdown

Offence	Elements of the Offence	Defence
s 111A(1)(a) Social Security and Administration Act 1992 'Dishonestly making a false representation'	• (A) made a representation for the purpose of obtaining benefit • The representation was false; and • A acted dishonestly	• Negative any element of the offence • General Defences **C**
s 111A(1)(b) Social Security and Administration Act 1992 'Dishonestly producing or furnishing a false document/information or knowingly causing or allowing a false document/information to be produced or furnished'	• (A) furnished or produced a document for the purpose of obtaining benefit • The information or document was false in a material particular; and • A acted dishonestly; or • A allowed a document to be produced/that information to be furnished • A knew that the information/document was false in a material particular; and • A acted dishonestly	• Negative any element of the offence • General Defences **C**

Offence	Elements of the Offence	Defence
s 111A(1A) Social Security and Administration Act 1992 'Dishonestly failing to notify a change in circumstances'	• (A) was claiming a benefit • There was a change in circumstances • The change of circumstances affected A' entitlement to the benefit • A knew the change would affect his entitlement to benefit • A failed to give a prompt notification of that change in the prescribed manner to the prescribed person; and • A acted dishonestly	• Negative any element of the offence • *R v Zorlu* **B6.2.2** • General Defences **C**
s 111A(1B) Social Security and Administration Act 1992 'Dishonestly causing or allowing a person to fail to notify a change in circumstances'	• (A) knew (B) was claiming a benefit • There was change in circumstances; and • The change in circumstances affected B's entitlement to the benefit; and • A knew that the change would affect B's entitlement to the benefit • A dishonestly caused or allowed X to fail to notify the change promptly in the prescribed manner to the prescribed person	• Negative any element of the offence • *R v Tilley* **B6.2.2** • General Defences **C**
s 111A(1D) Social Security and Administration Act 1992 'Benefit recipient dishonestly failing to promptly notify a change in circumstances'	• (A) was receiving a benefit for (B) • There was a change in B's circumstances • A knew that the change in circumstances affected claimant B's entitlement to benefit • A dishonestly failed to give a prompt notification of the change in circumstances in the prescribed manner to the prescribed person	• Negative any element of the offence • General Defences **C**

Offence	Elements of the Offence	Defence
s 111A(1E) Social Security and Administration Act 1992 'A person other than the benefit recipient dishonestly causing or allowing the benefit recipient to fail to promptly notify a change in circumstances'	• (A) knows (B) receives a benefit • There was a change in B's circumstances • A knew that the change in circumstances affected B's benefit entitlement • A dishonestly caused or allowed the benefit recipient to fail to promptly notify a change in circumstances in the prescribed manner to the prescribed person	• Negative any element of the offence • General Defences **C**

B6.2.2 **Defences**

- In *R v Zorlu* [2009] EWCA Crim 589 Lord Justice Aikens noted in obiter that 'it is hard to see how [living together] would be a relevant "change of circumstance" unless the partner coming to live with the recipient of income support was going in some way to assist financially that recipient. Merely because a partner is living in the same house does not, of course, prove that fact at all.'
- There must be a positive act for 'allowing' under s 111A(1B) (*R v Tilley* [2009] EWCA Crim 1426).
- See General Defences C.

B6.2.3 **Sentencing**

s 111 Social Security Administration Act 1992

Summary: 6 months' imprisonment/a fine/both

Indictment: 7 years' imprisonment/a fine/both

- See alternatives to prosecution for benefit fraud **B6.4**.

B6.3 **Benefit fraud**

NB For these offences it only needs to be shown that the defendant acted knowingly.

Social Security Administration Act 1992

s 112 'False representations for obtaining benefit etc'

(1) If a person for the purposes of obtaining benefit or other payment under the relevant social security legislation whether for himself or some other person, or for any other purpose connected with that legislation—
(a) Makes a statement or representation which he knows to be false,
he shall be guilty of an offence.

s 112 'False representations for obtaining benefit etc'

(1) If a person for the purposes of obtaining benefit or other payment under the relevant social security legislation whether for himself or some other person, or for any other purpose connected with that legislation—
...
(b) Produces or furnishes, or knowingly causes of knowingly allows to be produced or furnished, any document or information which he knows to be false in a material particular, he shall be guilty of an offence.

s 112 'False representations for obtaining benefit etc'

(1A) A person shall be guilty of an offence if—
(a) there has been a change of circumstances affecting any entitlement of his to any benefit or other payment or advantage under any provision of the relevant social security legislation;
(b) the change is not a change that is excluded by regulations from the changes that are required to be notified;
(c) he knows that the change affects an entitlement of his to such a benefit or other payment or advantage; and
(d) he fails to give a prompt notification of that change in the prescribed manner to the prescribed person.

s 112 'False representations for obtaining benefit etc'

(1B) A person is guilty of an offence under this section if—
(a) there has been a change of circumstances affecting any entitlement of another person to any benefit or other payment or advantage under any provision of the relevant social security legislation;
(b) the change is not a change that is excluded by regulations from the changes that are required to be notified;
(c) he knows that the change affects an entitlement of that other person to such a benefit or other payment or advantage; and
(d) he causes or allows that other person to fail to give a prompt notification of that change in the prescribed manner to the prescribed person.

s 112 'False representations for obtaining benefit etc'

(1C) In a case where subsection (1C) of section 111A above applies, the recipient is guilty of an offence if—
(a) he knows that the change affects an entitlement of the claimant to a benefit or other payment or advantage under a provision of the relevant social security legislation;
(b) the entitlement is one in respect of which he has a right to receive payments to which the claimant has, or (but for the arrangements

under which they are payable to the recipient) would have, an entitlement; and

(c) he fails to give a prompt notification of that change in the prescribed manner to the prescribed person.

s 112 'False representations for obtaining benefit etc'

(1D) In a case where that subsection applies, a person other than the recipient is guilty of an offence if—

(a) he knows that the change affects an entitlement of the claimant to a benefit or other payment or advantage under a provision of the relevant social security legislation;

(b) the entitlement is one in respect of which the recipient has a right to receive payments to which the claimant has, or (but for the arrangements under which they are payable to the recipient) would have, an entitlement; and

(c) he causes or allows the recipient to fail to give a prompt notification of that change in the prescribed manner to the prescribed person.

B6.3.1 Breakdown

Offence	Elements of the Offence	Defence
s 112(1)(a) Social Security and Administration Act 1992 'Knowingly making a false representation'	• A representation was made for the purpose of obtaining benefit • (A) made the representation • The representation was false • A knew that the representation was false	• Negative any element of the offence • *Flintshire CC v Reynolds* **B6.3.2** • General Defences **C**
s 112(1)(b) Social Security and Administration Act 1992 'Knowingly producing or furnishing false document/information or knowingly causing or allowing a false document/information to be produced or furnished'	• (A) furnished or produced a document or information for the purposes of obtaining benefit • The information or document was false in a material particular; or • A knowingly allowed that document to be produced or that information to be furnished; and • A knew that the document/information was false in a material particular	• Negative any element of the offence • *Flintshire CC v Reynolds* **B6.3.2** • General Defences **C**

s 112(1A) Social Security and Administration Act 1992 'Knowingly failing to notify a change in circumstances'	• (A) was claiming a benefit • There was a change in circumstances • The change of circumstances affected A's entitlement to benefit • A knew the change would affect his entitlement to benefit • A failed to give prompt notification of that change in the prescribed manner to the prescribed person	• Negative any element of the offence • *Coventry City Council v Vassell* **B6.3.2** • General Defences **C**
s 112(1B) Social Security and Administration Act 1992 'Knowingly causing or allowing a person to fail to notify a change in circumstances'	• (A) was claiming a benefit • (B) knew that A was claiming the benefit • There was a change in circumstances that affected A's entitlement to benefit • B caused or allowed A to fail to notify the change promptly in the prescribed manner to the prescribed person	• Negative any element of the offence • General Defences **C**
s 112(1C) Social Security and Administration Act 1992 'Benefit recipient knowingly failing to promptly notify a change in circumstances'	• (A) was receiving a benefit • There was a change in circumstances which affected A's circumstances • A knew that the change in circumstances affected his entitlement to benefit • A knowingly failed to give prompt notification of the change in circumstances in the prescribed manner to the prescribed person	• Negative any element of the offence • General Defences **C**
s 112(1D) Social Security and Administration Act 1992 'A person other than the benefit recipient knowingly causes or allows the benefit recipient to fail to promptly notify a change in circumstances'	• (A) was receiving benefits • There was a change of circumstances that affected A's benefit entitlement • (B) knew that the change of circumstances affected benefit claimant A's benefit entitlement • B knowingly caused or allowed the benefit recipient to fail to give a prompt notification of the change in circumstances in the prescribed manner to the prescribed person	• Negative any element of the offence • General Defences **C**

B6.3.2 Defences

- For offences under s 112(1) constructive knowledge is not sufficient for an offence to be made out and actual knowledge is required (*Flintshire CC v Reynolds* [2006] EWHC 195 (Admin)).
- For the s 112(1A) offence a claimant must *know* that a change has affected his entitlement to a benefit for a criminal offence to have been committed (*Coventry City Council v Vassell* [2011] EWHC 1542 (Admin)).
- See General Defences C.

B6.3.3 Sentencing

s 112 Social Security and Administration Act 1992
Summary only: 3 months' imprisonment/a fine

B6.4 Alternatives to prosecution for benefit fraud

The following applies to the offences listed in Parts **B6.2** and **B6.3**:

1.	No Charge (No Further Action ('NFA')	The matter is closed and there is no criminal record.
2.	Loss of Benefit Provision	A sanction in the form of a fixed 13-week benefit disqualification period. This is where a person is convicted of benefit fraud in two separate proceedings, which have been committed within a five year period. There is also a 4-week loss of benefit sanction available for all offences of benefit fraud which result in a criminal sanction (convictions, administrative penalties, and cautions). Benefits can be withdrawn, or reduced by 20 or 40 per cent during the disqualification period.
3.	Administrative Penalty (*s 115 Social Security and Administration Act 1992)*	Where the suspect agrees to pay a financial penalty. The amount of the penalty is currently stipulated at 30 per cent of the amount of the gross overpayment. The standard maximum for an administrative penalty is £5,000 but this is not a fixed maximum and greater overpayment can, on occasion, be dealt with by an administrative penalty.

4.	Caution	When investigated by a local authority, this is not a criminal caution. The matter is at an end. The caution is held on file by the local authority.
5.	Charge	The matter is charged and will proceed to court. This is likely to be by summons.

Where a client seeks disposal by an administrative penalty or caution a full and frank admission of guilt is required.

If the matter is being investigated by the DWP Fraud Investigation Service a caution is not available for offences committed on or after 1 April 2012, but the CPS may direct that a caution shall be administered if the case is referred to them.

B6.4.1 Sanctions

Where a client is convicted of 'benefit fraud' their benefits may be sanctioned. A sanction can be either a reduction in the amount of benefit received or the cessation of benefit payments.

Benefits that can be stopped or reduced if convicted of benefit fraud:

- Carer's Allowance
- Employment & Support Allowance
- Housing/Council Tax Benefit
- Incapacity Benefit
- Income Support
- Industrial Death Benefit
- Industrial Injuries Disablement Benefit
- Industrial Injuries Reduced Earnings Allowance
- Industrial Injuries Retirement Allowance
- Industrial Injuries Unemployment Support
- Jobseeker's Allowance
- Severe Disablement Allowance
- Pension Credit
- Severe Disablement Allowance
- Universal Credit
- War Disablement Pension
- War Widow's Pension
- War Pension Unemployment Supplement
- War Pension Allowance for Lower Standard of Occupation
- Widowed Mother's/Parent Allowance
- Widow's Pension/Bereavement Allowance
- Working Tax Credit

The above benefits can also be sanctioned if convicted of benefit fraud for:

• Attendance Allowance • Bereavement Payment • Child Benefit • Child Tax Credit • Christmas Bonus • Council Tax Allowance • Disability Living Allowance • Graduated Retirement Benefit • Guardian's Allowance	• Industrial Injuries Constant Attendance Allowance (where a Disablement Pension is payable) • Industrial Injuries Exceptionally Severe Disablement Allowance (where a Disablement Pension is payable) • Personal Independence Payment • Social Fund Payments • State Pension • War Pension Constant Support Allowance • War Pension Exceptionally Severe Disablement Allowance • War Pension Mobility Supplement

The following benefits cannot be stopped or reduced for benefit fraud:

• Diffuse Mesothelioma Scheme (2008) • Health in Pregnancy Grant • Maternity Allowance • Pneumoconiosis (Workers' Compensation) 1979	• Statutory Adoption Pay • Statutory Maternity Pay • Statutory Paternity Pay • Statutory Sick Pay

B6.5 **Money laundering**

Concealing etc

Proceeds of Crime Act 2002

s 327 'Concealing etc'

(1) A person commits an offence if he—
- (a) conceals criminal property;
- (b) disguises criminal property;
- (c) converts criminal property;
- (d) transfers criminal property;
- (e) removes criminal property from England and Wales or from Scotland or from Northern Ireland.

Arrangements

Proceeds of Crime Act 2002

s 328 'Arrangements'

(1) A person commits an offence if he enters into or becomes concerned in an arrangement which he knows or suspects facilitates (by whatever means) the acquisition, retention, use or control of criminal property by or on behalf of another person.

Acquisition, use, and possession

Proceeds of Crime Act 2002

s 329 'Acquisition, use and possession'

(1) A person commits an offence if he—
- (a) acquires criminal property;
- (b) uses criminal property;
- (c) has possession of criminal property.

B6.5.1 Breakdown

Offence	Elements of the Offence	Defence
s 327 Proceeds of Crime Act 2002 'Concealing etc'	• Conceal/disguise/convert/transfer; or • Remove from England/Wales/Scotland/Northern Ireland • Criminal property	• Negative any element of the offence • s. 327 Proceeds of Crime Act 2002 **B6.5.3** • General Defences **C**
s 328 Proceeds of Crime Act 2002 'Arragements'	• Enter/become concerned in an arrangement • Known or suspected • To facilitate the acquisition/retention/use/control of criminal property • By or on behalf of another	• Negative any element of the offence • s 328 Proceeds of Crime Act 2002 **B6.5.3** • General Defences **C**
s 327 Proceeds of Crime Act 2002 'Acquisition, use and possession'	• Acquire/use/possesses • Criminal property	• Negative any element of the offence • s 329 Proceeds of Crime Act 2002 **B6.5.3** • General Defences **C**

B6.5.2 Interpretation

Proceeds of Crime Act 2002

s 329 'Acquisition, use and possession'

(3) For the purposes of this section—
- (a) a person acquires property for inadequate consideration if the value of the consideration is significantly less than the value of the property;
- (b) a person uses or has possession of property for inadequate consideration if the value of the consideration is significantly less than the value of the use or possession;
- (c) the provision by a person of goods or services which he knows or suspects may help another to carry out criminal conduct.

s 340 'Interpretation'

(2) Criminal conduct is conduct which—
- (a) constitutes an offence in any part of the United Kingdom, or
- (b) would constitute an offence in any part of the United Kingdom if it occurred there.

(3) Property is criminal property if—
- (a) it constitutes a person's benefit from criminal conduct or it represents such a benefit (in whole or part and whether directly or indirectly), and
- (b) the alleged offender knows or suspects that it constitutes or represents such a benefit.

(4) It is immaterial—
- (a) who carried out the conduct;
- (b) who benefited from it;
- (c) whether the conduct occurred before or after the passing of this Act.

...

Explanatory notes

Money laundering

6. Money laundering is the process by which the proceeds of crime are converted into assets which appear to have a legitimate origin, so that they can be retained permanently or recycled into further criminal enterprises.

B6.5.3 Defences

Proceeds of Crime Act 2002

s 327 'Concealing etc'

(2) But a person does not commit such an offence if—
- (a) he makes an authorised disclosure under section 338 and (if the disclosure is made before he does the act mentioned in subsection (1)) he has the appropriate consent;
- (b) he intended to make such a disclosure but had a reasonable excuse for not doing so;
- (c) the act he does is done in carrying out a function he has relating to the enforcement of any provision of this Act or of any other enactment relating to criminal conduct or benefit from criminal conduct.

(2A) Nor does a person commit an offence under subsection (1) if—
- (a) he knows, or believes on reasonable grounds, that the relevant criminal conduct occurred in a particular country or territory outside the United Kingdom, and
- (b) the relevant criminal conduct—
  - (i) was not, at the time it occurred, unlawful under the criminal law then applying in that country or territory, and
  - (ii) is not of a description prescribed by an order made by the Secretary of State.

(2B) In subsection (2A) 'the relevant criminal conduct' is the criminal conduct by reference to which the property concerned is criminal property.

(2C) A deposit-taking body that does an act mentioned in paragraph (c) or (d) of subsection (1) does not commit an offence under that subsection if—
- (a) it does the act in operating an account maintained with it, and
- (b) the value of the criminal property concerned is less than the threshold amount determined under section 339A for the act.

(3) Concealing or disguising criminal property includes concealing or disguising its nature, source, location, disposition, movement or ownership or any rights with respect to it.

s 328 'Arrangements'

(2) But a person does not commit such an offence if—
- (a) he makes an authorised disclosure under section 338 and (if the disclosure is made before he does the act mentioned in subsection (1)) he has the appropriate consent;
- (b) he intended to make such a disclosure but had a reasonable excuse for not doing so;
- (c) the act he does is done in carrying out a function he has relating to the enforcement of any provision of this Act or of any other enactment relating to criminal conduct or benefit from criminal conduct.

(3) Nor does a person commit an offence under subsection (1) if—
- (a) he knows, or believes on reasonable grounds, that the relevant criminal conduct occurred in a particular country or territory outside the United Kingdom, and
- (b) the relevant criminal conduct—
  - (i) was not, at the time it occurred, unlawful under the criminal law then applying in that country or territory, and
  - (ii) is not of a description prescribed by an order made by the Secretary of State.

(4) In subsection (3) 'the relevant criminal conduct' is the criminal conduct by reference to which the property concerned is criminal property.

s 329 'Acquisition, use and possession'

(2) But a person does not commit such an offence if—
- (a) he makes an authorised disclosure under section 338 and (if the disclosure is made before he does the act mentioned in subsection (1)) he has the appropriate consent;
- (b) he intended to make such a disclosure but had a reasonable excuse for not doing so;
- (c) he acquired or used or had possession of the property for adequate consideration;

(d) the act he does is done in carrying out a function he has relating to the enforcement of any provision of this Act or of any other enactment relating to criminal conduct or benefit from criminal conduct.

(2A) Nor does a person commit an offence under subsection (1) if—

(a) he knows, or believes on reasonable grounds, that the relevant criminal conduct occurred in a particular country or territory outside the United Kingdom, and

(b) the relevant criminal conduct—

(i) was not, at the time it occurred, unlawful under the criminal law then applying in that country or territory, and

(ii) is not of a description prescribed by an order made by the Secretary of State.

(2B) In subsection (2A) 'the relevant criminal conduct' is the criminal conduct by reference to which the property concerned is criminal property.

s 388 'Authorised disclosure'

(1) For the purposes of this Part a disclosure is authorised if—

(a) it is a disclosure to a constable, a customs officer or a nominated officer by the alleged offender that property is criminal property, and

...

(c) the first, second or third condition set out below is satisfied.

(2) The first condition is that the disclosure is made before the alleged offender does the prohibited act.

(2A) The second condition is that—

(a) the disclosure is made while the alleged offender is doing the prohibited act,

(b) he began to do the act at a time when, because he did not then know or suspect that the property constituted or represented a person's benefit from criminal conduct, the act was not a prohibited act, and

(c) the disclosure is made on his own initiative and as soon as is practicable after he first knows or suspects that the property constitutes or represents a person's benefit from criminal conduct.

(3) The third condition is that—

(a) the disclosure is made after the alleged offender does the prohibited act,

(b) [he has a reasonable excuse] for his failure to make the disclosure before he did the act, and

(c) the disclosure is made on his own initiative and as soon as it is practicable for him to make it.

(4) An authorised disclosure is not to be taken to breach any restriction on the disclosure of information (however imposed).

(5) A disclosure to a nominated officer is a disclosure which—

(a) is made to a person nominated by the alleged offender's employer to receive authorised disclosures, and

(b) is made in the course of the alleged offender's employment.

- See General Defences C.

B6.5.4 Key points

- For there to be criminal property, there must be an intent or a suspicion that there is a benefit from criminal conduct.
- In *Wilkinson v DPP* [2006] EWHC 3012 (Admin), the court discouraged the use of this offence (with its requirement only for suspicion rather than belief) when a handling charge would adequately have reflected the seriousness of the offence.
- For there to be an offence there must be actual criminal conduct and the proceeds must already be the product of that crime (*R v Gabriel* [2006] EWCA Crim 229).
- There are two ways in which the Crown can prove that the property derives from crime. Either:
  1. by showing that it derives from criminal conduct of a specific kind; or
  2. by proving that the circumstances in which it was handled create an irresistible inference that it can only have derived from crime (*R v Anwoir* [2008] EWCA Crim 1354).
- Consideration must be given to the nature of the property at the time it was received by the defendant. Should the defendant receive property that is not yet criminal in nature the offence will not be made out (*R v Geary* [2010] EWCA Crim 1925). It was for a jury to decide whether payments which were of "clean" money had changed their nature and become criminal property because it was obtained by fraud (*R v GH* [2015] UKSC 24).

B6.5.5 Sentencing

ss 327–329 Proceeds of Crime Act 2002

Summary: 6 months' imprisonment and/or a fine

Indictment: 14 years' imprisonment

See *Blackstone's Criminal Practice* **B21**

B6.6 Conspiracy to defraud

Scott v Commissioner of the Police of the Metropolis [1974] UKHL 4

An agreement by two or more persons by dishonesty (a) to deprive a person of something which is his or to which he is or might be entitled; or (b) to injure some proprietary right of his.

B6.6.1 Related offences

- Statutory conspiracies particularly under the Fraud Act 2006 **B6.1**.
- Inchoate offences under Serious Crime Act 2007 **A5**.

B6.6.2 Breakdown

Offence	Elements of the Offence	Defence
Conspiracy to defraud (*Scott v Commissioner of the Police of the Metropolis* [1974] UKHL 4)	• An agreement by two or more people • Dishonestly • Intending to defraud being aware that the successful implementation of the scheme will result in the complainant (c) being defrauded; and either • Depriving (c) of something which is his or to which he is or might be entitled; or • By injuring some proprietary right of (c)	• Negative any element of the offence • General Defences **C**

B6.6.3 Defences

- See General Defences C.

B6.6.4 Key points

- To defraud means to deprive dishonestly a person of something which is his or of something to which he is or would or might but for the perpetration of the fraud, be entitled *(Scott v Commissioner of the Police of the Metropolis* [1974] UKHL 4).
- There must be an intent to cause to dishonestly cause some economic or financial loss.
- Or, where the Crown relies on economic prejudice a dishonest agreement is not sufficient unless there is a proprietary right or interest of the complainant that is or may actually be prejudiced and the conspiracy must contain some unlawfulness. It is not an offence under this head to seek to achieve a lawful objective by a lawful means (*Serious Fraud Office v Evans & Others* [2014] EWHC 3803 (QB)).
- Others than the defendants may benefit from the fraud (*R v Hollinshead* [1985] AC 975).

B6.6.5 Sentencing

Indictable only: 10 years and/or a fine

See *Blackstone's Criminal Practice* **A5.61**

B7 **Public Order Offences**

B7.1 **Riot**

Public Order Act 1986

s 1 'Riot'

(1) Where 12 or more persons who are present together use or threaten unlawful violence for a common purpose and the conduct of them (taken together) is such as would cause a person of reasonable firmness present at the scene to fear for his personal safety, each of the persons using unlawful violence for the common purpose is guilty of riot.

B7.1.1 **Related offences**

- Violent disorder **B7.2**.

B7.1.2 **Breakdown**

Offence	Elements of the Offence	Defence
s 1 Public Order Act 1986 'Riot'	• 12 or more persons • Present together • Use/threaten unlawful violence • For a common purpose • As would cause a person of reasonable firmness present at the scene to fear for his personal safety	• Negative any element of the offence • s 6 Public Order Act 1986 **B7.1.4** • General Defences **C**

B7.1.3 **Interpretation**

Public Order Act 1986

s 1 'Riot'

(2) It is immaterial whether or not the 12 or more use or threaten unlawful violence simultaneously.

(3) The common purpose may be inferred from conduct.

(4) No person of reasonable firmness need actually be, or be likely to be, present at the scene.

(5) Riot may be committed in private as well as in public places.

s 7 'Procedure'

(1) No prosecution for an offence of riot or incitement to riot may be instituted except by or with the consent of the Director of Public Prosecutions.

s 8 'Interpretation'

In this Part—

...

'violence' means any violent conduct, so that—

(a) except in the context of affray, it includes violent conduct towards property as well as violent conduct towards persons, and

(b) it is not restricted to conduct causing or intended to cause injury or damage but includes any other violent conduct (for example, throwing at or towards a person a missile of a kind capable of causing injury which does not hit or falls short).

B7.1.4 Defences

Public Order Act 1986

s 6 'Mental element: miscellaneous'

(1) A person is guilty of riot only if he intends to use violence or is aware that his conduct may be violent.

...

(5) For the purposes of this section a person whose awareness is impaired by intoxication shall be taken to be aware of that of which he would be aware if not intoxicated, unless he shows either that his intoxication was not self-induced or that it was caused solely by the taking or administration of a substance in the course of medical treatment.

(6) In subsection (5) 'intoxication' means any intoxication, whether caused by drink, drugs or other means, or by a combination of means.

(7) Subsections (1)...[does] not affect the determination for the purposes of riot or violent disorder of the number of persons who use or threaten violence.

- See General Defences **C**.

B7.1.5 Key points

- Section 7(1) No prosecution for an offence of riot or incitement to riot may be instituted except by or with the consent of the Director of Public Prosecutions ('DPP').
- Section 1(7) Prosecution of Offences Act 1985 c 23 applies; accordingly, for a riot charge, a step taken (or consent given) by a Crown prosecutor will be treated as taken by the DPP.

B7.1.6 Sentencing

s 1 Public Order Act 1986

Indictment: 10 years' imprisonment/a fine/both

Youth Gravity Matrix

OFFENCE	Gravity Score	Offence type	AGGRAVATING FACTORS	MITIGATING FACTORS
Riot (s 1)	4	I	Always refer to the CPS	

See *Blackstone's Criminal Practice* **B11.15**

B7.2 Violent disorder

Public Order Act 1986

s 2 'Violent disorder'

(1) Where 3 or more persons who are present together use or threaten unlawful violence and the conduct of them (taken together) is such as would cause a person of reasonable firmness present at the scene to fear for his personal safety, each of the persons using or threatening unlawful violence is guilty of violent disorder.

B7.2.1 Related offences

- Riot **B7.1**.
- Affray **B7.3**.

B7.2.2 Breakdown

Offence	Elements of the Offence	Defence
s 2 Public Order Act 1986 'Violent disorder'	• 3 or more persons • Present together • Use/threaten unlawful violence • As would cause a person of reasonable firmness present at the scene to fear for his personal safety	• Negative any element of the offence • s 6 Public Order Act 1986 **B7.1.4** • General Defences **C**

B7.2.3 Interpretation

Public Order Act 1986

s 2 'Violent disorder'

(2) It is immaterial whether or not the 3 or more use or threaten unlawful violence simultaneously.

(3) No person of reasonable firmness need actually be, or be likely to be, present at the scene.
(4) Violent disorder may be committed in private as well as in public places.

s 7 'Procedure'

(3) If on the trial on indictment of a person charged with violent disorder or affray the jury find him not guilty of the offence charged, they may (without prejudice to section 6(3) of the Criminal Law Act 1967) find him guilty of an offence under section 4.

s 8 'Interpretation'

In this Part—

...

'violence' means any violent conduct, so that—

(a) except in the context of affray, it includes violent conduct towards property as well as violent conduct towards persons, and
(b) it is not restricted to conduct causing or intended to cause injury or damage but includes any other violent conduct (for example, throwing at or towards a person a missile of a kind capable of causing injury which does not hit or falls short).

B7.2.4 Defences

- See **B7.1.4** on the issue of intoxication.
- See General Defences **C**.

B7.2.5 Key points

- 'Present together' should be given its ordinary meaning and does not require a common purpose (*R v NW* [2010] EWCA Crim 404).
- If a jury acquits any person relied upon by the Crown to make up one of the three or more persons involved then the Crown cannot rely upon that acquitted person to fulfil the actus reus of the offence (*R v Mechen* [2004] EWCA Crim 388).
- Consideration should be given to whether the conduct/violence was unlawful.

B7.2.6 Sentencing

s 2 Public Order Act 1986

Summary: 6 months' imprisonment/a fine not exceeding the statutory maximum/both

Indictment: 5 years' imprisonment/a fine/both

Youth Gravity Matrix

OFFENCE	Gravity Score	Offence type	AGGRAVATING FACTORS	MITIGATING FACTORS
Violent disorder (s 2)	3	E	Planned action Premeditated action Use of weapons People put in fear Damage caused Busy public place Large group	

See *Blackstone's Criminal Practice* **B11.28**

B7.3 **Affray**

Public Order Act 1986

s 3 'Affray'

(1) A person is guilty of affray if he uses or threatens unlawful violence towards another and his conduct is such as would cause a person of reasonable firmness present at the scene to fear for his personal safety.

B7.3.1 **Related offences**

- s 4 Public Order Act **B7.4.**
- s 4A Public Order Act **B7.5.**
- s 5 Public Order Act **B7.6.**

B7.3.2 **Breakdown**

Offence	Elements of the Offence	Defence
s 3 Public Order Act 1986 'Affray'	• Use/threat of unlawful violence • Towards another; and • The conduct is such as would cause a person of reasonable firmness present at the scene to fear for his personal safety	• Negative any element of the offence • s 6 Public Order Act 1986 **B7.1.4** • General Defences **C**

B7.3.3 Interpretation

Public Order Act 1986

s 3 'Affray'

(2) Where 2 or more persons use or threaten the unlawful violence, it is the conduct of them taken together that must be considered for the purposes of subsection (1).
(3) For the purposes of this section a threat cannot be made by the use of words alone.
(4) No person of reasonable firmness need actually be, or be likely to be, present at the scene.
(5) Affray may be committed in private as well as in public places.

B7.3.4 Defences

- See **B7.1.4** on the issue of intoxication,
- See General Defences C.

B7.3.5 Key points

- A third person need not actually be present for this offence to be made out.
- Affray may be committed in private as well as in public places. However, where there is no realistic possibility of a third party entering, there will be difficulty proving a public order offence (*Leeson v Director of Public Prosecutions* [2010] EWHC 994 (Admin)).
- The fear or otherwise of a third party who is actually present at the scene may be of assistance in considering whether the offence is made out (*R v Blinkhorn* [2006] EWCA Crim 1416).
- Where an incident is between two people with the opportunity for a hypothetical third person to distance themselves, affray is an inappropriate charge (*R v Sanchez* 1996 WL 1090244).
- The use, or threat, of unlawful violence must be directed at a person present at the scene for the offence of affray to be made out (*I v DPP* [2001] UKHL 10).

B7.3.6 Sentencing

s 3 Public Order Act 1986

Summary: A fine /6 months' imprisonment

Indictment: 3 years' imprisonment

Youth Gravity Matrix

OFFENCE	Gravity Score	Offence type	AGGRAVATING FACTORS	MITIGATING FACTORS
Affray (s 3)	3	E	• Use of weapons • People put in fear • Damage caused • Busy public place • Group action	

See *Blackstone's Criminal Practice* **B11.37**

B7.4 **Fear or provocation of violence**

Public Order Act 1986

s 4 'Fear or provocation of violence'

(1) A person is guilty of an offence if he—
  (a) uses towards another person threatening, abusive or insulting words or behaviour, or
  (b) distributes or displays to another person any writing, sign or other visible representation which is threatening, abusive or insulting,

with intent to cause that person to believe that immediate unlawful violence will be used against him or another by any person, or to provoke the immediate use of unlawful violence by that person or another, or whereby that person is likely to believe that such violence will be used or it is likely that such violence will be provoked.

(2) An offence under this section may be committed in a public or a private place, except that no offence is committed where the words or behaviour are used, or the writing, sign or other visible representation is distributed or displayed, by a person inside a dwelling and the other person is also inside that or another dwelling.

B7.4.1 **Related offences**

- s 4A **B7.5**.
- s 5 **B7.6**.

B7.4.2 Breakdown

Offence	Elements of the Offence	Defence
s 4(1)(a) Public Order Act 1986 'Fear or provocation of violence'	• Use of threatening, abusive or insulting • Words or behaviour • Towards another person (B) • With intention: i. To cause B to believe immediate unlawful violence would be caused against B or another, by him or any another person; or ii. To provoke the immediate use of unlawful violence by B or another; or iii. That B would likely believe that violence would be used; or iv. That B would likely believe that violence would be provoked.	• Negative any element of the offence • s 6 Public Order Act 1986 **B7.4.4** • General Defences **C**
s 4(1)(b) Public Order Act 1986 'Fear or provocation of violence'	• Distribution or display • To another person (B) • Writing, a sign or other visible representation • Which was threatening, abusive or insulting • With intention: i. To cause B to believe immediate unlawful violence would be caused against B or another, by him or any another person; or ii. To provoke the immediate use of unlawful violence by B or another; or iii. That B would likely believe that violence would be used; or iv. That B would likely believe that violence would be provoked.	• Negative any element of the offence • s 6 Public Order Act 1986 **B7.4.4** • General Defences **C**

B7.4.3 Interpretation

Public Order Act 1986

s 8 'Interpretation'

In this Part—

'dwelling' means any structure or part of a structure occupied as a person's home or as other living accommodation (whether the occupation is separate

or shared with others) but does not include any part not so occupied, and for this purpose *'structure'* includes a tent, caravan, vehicle, vessel or other temporary or movable structure;

'violence' means any violent conduct, so that—

(a) except in the context of affray, it includes violent conduct towards property as well as violent conduct towards persons, and

(b) it is not restricted to conduct causing or intended to cause injury or damage but includes any other violent conduct (for example, throwing at or towards a person a missile of a kind capable of causing injury which does not hit or falls short).

B7.4.4 Defences

Public Order Act 1986

s 6 'Mental element: miscellaneous'

(3) A person is guilty of an offence under section 4 only if he intends his words or behaviour, or the writing, sign or other visible representation, to be threatening, abusive or insulting, or is aware that it may be threatening, abusive or insulting.

. . .

(5) For the purposes of this section a person whose awareness is impaired by intoxication shall be taken to be aware of that of which he would be aware if not intoxicated, unless he shows either that his intoxication was not self-induced or that it was caused solely by the taking or administration of a substance in the course of medical treatment.

(6) In subsection (5) *'intoxication'* means any intoxication, whether caused by drink, drugs or other means, or by a combination of means.

B7.4.5 Key points

- The offence can be racially aggravated in nature, with reference to the provisions of the Crime and Disorder Act 1998, s 31 **B7.7**. The offence, initially summary only, becomes triable either way if an element of racial aggravation is suspected.
- 'Insulting' should be given its ordinary usual meaning (*Brutus v Cozens* [1972] UKHL 6).
- For the conduct to be used towards another, that other must be physically present (*Atkin v DPP* (1989) 89 Cr App R 199).

B7.4.6 Sentencing

s 4 Public Order Act 1986

Summary: 6 months' imprisonment and/or fine

NB The offence, initially summary only, becomes triable either way if a racially or religiously aggravated element is suspected **B7.7**.

Youth Gravity Matrix

OFFENCE	Gravity Score	Offence type	AGGRAVATING FACTORS	MITIGATING FACTORS
Threatening, abusive or insulting words or behaviour intended to cause fear of violence or to provoke violence (s 4)	2	S	• Use of weapons • Group action • People put in fear • Risk of escalation • Busy public place	• No risk of escalation

See *Blackstone's Criminal Practice* **B11.47**

B7.5 Intentional harassment, alarm, or distress

Public Order Act 1986

s 4A 'Intentional harassment, alarm or distress'

(1) A person is guilty of an offence if, with intent to cause a person harassment, alarm or distress, he—
 (a) uses threatening, abusive or insulting words or behaviour, or disorderly behaviour, or
 (b) displays any writing, sign or other visible representation which is threatening, abusive or insulting,

thereby causing that or another person harassment, alarm or distress.

(2) An offence under this section may be committed in a public or a private place, except that no offence is committed where the words or behaviour are used, or the writing, sign or other visible representation is displayed, by a person inside a dwelling and the person who is harassed, alarmed or distressed is also inside that or another dwelling.

B7.5.1 Related offences

- s 4 **B7.4**.
- s 5 **B7.6**.

B7.5.2 Breakdown

Offence	Elements of the Offence	Defence
s 4A(1)(a) Public Order Act 1986 'Intentional harassment, alarm or distress'	• Intending • To cause harassment, alarm or distress • To another person • Uses threatening, abusive or insulting words or behaviour; or • Disorderly behaviour • Causing that person or another harassment, alarm or distress.	• Negative any element of the offence • s 4A(3) Public Order Act 1986 **B7.5.3** • General Defences **C**
s 4A(1)(b) Public Order Act 1986 'Intentional harassment, alarm or distress'	• Intending • To cause harassment, alarm or distress • To another person • Displays writing, a sign or other visible representation • Which is threatening, abusive or insulting • Causing that person or another harassment, alarm or distress.	• Negative any element of the offence • s 4A(3) Public Order Act 1986 **B7.5.3** • General Defences **C**

B7.5.3 Defences

Public Order Act 1986

s 4A 'Intentional harassment, alarm or distress'

(3) It is a defence for the accused to prove—
 (a) that he was inside a dwelling and had no reason to believe that the words or behaviour used, or the writing, sign or other visible representation displayed, would be heard or seen by a person outside that or any other dwelling, or
 (b) that his conduct was reasonable.

- See General Defences **C**.

B7.5.4 Key points

- The offence can be racially aggravated in nature, with reference to the provisions of the Crime and Disorder Act 1998, s 31 **B7.7**. The offence, initially summary only, becomes triable either way if an element of racial aggravation is suspected.

B7.5.5 Sentencing

Public Order Act 1986, s4A

Summary: 6 months' imprisonment and/or fine

NB The offence, initially summary only, becomes triable either way if a racially or religiously aggravated element is suspected B7.7.

Youth Gravity Matrix

OFFENCE	Gravity Score	Offence type	AGGRAVATING FACTORS	MITIGATING FACTORS
Intentionally causing harassment, alarm or distress through threatening abusive or insulting words or behaviour or display (s 4A)	3	S	• Racial overtones • Risk of escalation • Group action	• No risk of escalation

See *Blackstone's Criminal Practice* B11.60

B7.6 Harassment, alarm, or distress

Public Order Act 1986

s 5

(1) A person is guilty of an offence if he—

(a) uses threatening or abusive words or behaviour, or disorderly behaviour, or

(b) displays any writing, sign or other visible representation which is threatening or abusive within the hearing or sight of a person likely to be caused harassment, alarm or distress thereby.

(2) An offence under this section may be committed in a public or a private place, except that no offence is committed where the words or behaviour are used, or the writing, sign or other visible representation is displayed, by a person inside a dwelling and the other person is also inside that or another dwelling.

B7.6.1 Related offences

- s 4 B7.4.
- s 4A B7.5.

B7.6.2 Breakdown

Offence	Elements of the Offence	Defence
s 5(1)(a) Public Order Act 1986 'Harassment, alarm or distress'	• Use of threatening or abusive • Words; or • Disorderly behaviour • Within the hearing or sight • Of a person likely to be caused harassment, alarm or distress thereby	• Negative any element of the offence • s 5 Public Order Act 1986 **B7.6.4** • General Defences **C**
s 5(1)(b) Public Order Act 1986 'Harassment, alarm or distress'	• Display and writing, a sign or other visible representation • Which is threatening or abusive • Within the hearing or sight • Of a person likely to be caused harassment, alarm or distress thereby	• Negative any element of the offence • s 5 Public Order Act 1986 **B7.6.4** • General Defences **C**

B7.6.3 Interpretation

Dwelling

Public Order Act 1986

s 8 'Interpretation'

In this Part—

'dwelling' means any structure or part of a structure occupied as a person's home or as other living accommodation (whether the occupation is separate or shared with others) but does not include any part not so occupied, and for this purpose *'structure'* includes a tent, caravan, vehicle, vessel or other temporary or movable structure...

B7.6.4 Defences

Public Order Act 1986

s 5 'Harassment, alarm or distress'

(3) It is a defence for the accused to prove—

(a) that he had no reason to believe that there was any person within hearing or sight who was likely to be caused harassment, alarm or distress, or

(b) that he was inside a dwelling and had no reason to believe that the words or behaviour used, or the writing, sign or other visible representation displayed, would be heard or seen by a person outside that or any other dwelling, or

(c) that his conduct was reasonable.

s 6 'Mental element: miscellaneous'

(4) A person is guilty of an offence under section 5 only if he intends his words or behaviour, or the writing, sign or other visible representation, to be threatening, abusive or insulting, or is aware that it may be threatening, abusive or insulting or (as the case may be) he intends his behaviour to be or is aware that it may be disorderly.

(5) For the purposes of this section a person whose awareness is impaired by intoxication shall be taken to be aware of that of which he would be aware if not intoxicated, unless he shows either that his intoxication was not self-induced or that it was caused solely by the taking or administration of a substance in the course of medical treatment.

(6) In subsection (5) 'intoxication' means any intoxication, whether caused by drink, drugs or other means, or by a combination of means.

- See General Defences **C**.

B7.6.5 Key points

- The offence can be racially aggravated in nature, with reference to the provisions of the Crime and Disorder Act 1998, s 31 **B7.7**. The offence under s 5 is summary only but with a higher maximum penalty where racial aggravation is shown.
- There must be persons present in the vicinity at the time, and it is those persons who are likely to be caused harassment by the offending behaviour. It is insufficient that there may have been someone in the vicinity who, if they were present, were likely to be caused harassment (*Holloway v DPP* [2004] EWHC 2621 (Admin)).
- 'It is wrong to infer in the absence of evidence [to the contrary] that a group of young people who [are] in the vicinity would obviously have experienced alarm or distress at hearing [...] commonplace swear words' (*Harvey v DPP* [2011] EWHC B1(Admin)).

B7.6.6 Sentencing

s 5 Public Order Act 1986

Summary: A fine not exceeding level 3 on the standard scale

NB The offence remains summarily tried where an element of racial aggravation is suspected **B7.7** however the penalty increases to a fine not exceeding level 4 on the standard scale.

Youth Gravity Matrix

OFFENCE	Gravity Score	Offence type	AGGRAVATING FACTORS	MITIGATING FACTORS
Threatening, abusive or insulting words or behaviour likely to cause harassment, alarm or distress (s 5)	2	S	• Risk of escalation • Group action	• Isolated incident

See *Blackstone's Criminal Practice* **B11.69**

B7.7 Racially aggravated public order offences

Crime and Disorder Act 1998

s 31

(1) A person is guilty of an offence under this section if he commits—
(a) an offence under section 4 of the Public Order Act 1986 (fear or provocation of violence);
(b) an offence under section 4A of that Act (intentional harassment, alarm or distress); or
(c) an offence under section 5 of that Act (harassment, alarm or distress),
which is racially or religiously aggravated for the purposes of this section.

s 29

(1) A person is guilty of an offence under this section if he commits—
(a) an offence under section 20 of the Offences Against the Person Act 1861(malicious wounding or grievous bodily harm);
(b) an offence under section 47 of that Act (actual bodily harm); or
(c) common assault,
which is racially or religiously aggravated for the purposes of this section.

s 30

(1) A person is guilty of an offence under this section if he commits an offence under section 1(1) of the Criminal Damage Act 1971 (destroying or damaging property belonging to another) which is racially or religiously aggravated for the purposes of this section.

...

(3) For the purposes of this section, section 28(1)(a) above shall have effect as if the person to whom the property belongs or is treated as belonging for the purposes of that Act were the victim of the offence.

s 32

(1) A person is guilty of an offence under this section if he commits—
  (a) an offence under section 2 or 2A of the Protection from Harassment Act 1997 (offence of harassment and stalking); or
  (b) an offence under section 4 or 4A of that Act (putting people in fear of violence and stalking involving fear of violence or serious alarm or distress),

which is racially or religiously aggravated for the purposes of this section.

B7.7.1 Interpretation

Racially or religiously aggravated

Crime and Disorder Act 1998

s 28

(1) An offence is racially or religiously aggravated for the purposes of sections 29 to 32 below if—
  (a) at the time of committing the offence, or immediately before or after doing so, the offender demonstrates towards the victim of the offence hostility based on the victim's membership (or presumed membership) of a racial or religious group; or
  (b) the offence is motivated (wholly or partly) by hostility towards members of a racial or religious group based on their membership of that group.

(2) In subsection (1)(a) above—

'membership', in relation to a racial or religious group, includes association with members of that group;
'presumed' means presumed by the offender.

(3) It is immaterial for the purposes of paragraph (a) or (b) of subsection (1) above whether or not the offender's hostility is also based, to any extent, on any other factor not mentioned in that paragraph.

(4) In this section *'racial group'* means a group of persons defined by reference to race, colour, nationality (including citizenship) or ethnic or national origins.

(5) In this section *'religious group'* means a group of persons defined by reference to religious belief or lack of religious belief.

B7.7.2 Key points

- The definition of 'racial group' in s 28(1)(c) is specifically constructed to be wide. Reference to individuals as 'bloody foreigners' or an 'immigrant' may be sufficient (*R v Rogers* [2007] UKHL 8 and *Attorney General's Reference (No. 4 of 2004)* [2005] EWCA Crim 889 respectively).

- Regard has to be given to the circumstances in which a reference to an individual's perceived racial group or religious group may have been made. The hostility may be given a wider scope (even if not immediately preceding, immediately after, or at the time of; s 28(1)(b)) if a previous incident was 'capable of colouring the behaviour of the appellant throughout [the] subsequent events' (*DPP v M* [2004] EWHC 1453 (Admin) and *R v Babbs* [2007] ECWA Crim 2732).
- For s 28(1)(a) it is an objective test to the intent of the defendant; *DPP v Greene* [2004] EWHC 1225 and *Jones v DPP* [2010] EWHC 523 (Admin).
- For s 28(1)(b), by contrast, the motivation has to be proved with reference to the outcome sought (*Jones v DPP* [2010] EWHC 523 (Admin)).

B7.7.3 Sentencing

s 29 Crime and Disorder Act 1998/s 20 and s 47 Offences Against the Person Act 1861

Summary: 6 months' imprisonment and/or a fine

Indictment: 7 years' imprisonment and/or a fine

s 39 Offences Against the Person Act 1861

Summary: 6 months' imprisonment and/or a fine

Indictment: 2 years' imprisonment and/or a fine

s 30 Crime and Disorder Act 1998/s 1 Criminal Damage Act 1971

Summary: 6 months' imprisonment and/or a fine

Indictment: 14 years' imprisonment and/or a fine

s 31 Crime and Disorder Act 1998/s 4 and s 4A Public Order Act 1986

Summary: 6 months' imprisonment and/or a fine

Indictment: 2 years' imprisonment and/or a fine

s 5 Public Order Act 1986

Summary: A fine not exceeding level 4 on the standard scale.

s 32 Crime and Disorder Act 1998/s 2 Protection From Harassment Act 1997

Summary: 6 months' imprisonment and/or fine

Indictment: 2 years' imprisonment and/or a fine

s 4 Protection From Harassment Act 1997

Summary: 6 months' imprisonment and/or fine

Indictment: 7 years' imprisonment and/or a fine

See *Blackstone's Criminal Practice* **B11.149**

B7.8 Breach of anti-social behaviour order

Crime and Disorder Act 1998

s 1 'Anti-social behaviour orders'

(10) If without reasonable excuse a person does anything which he is prohibited from doing by an anti-social behaviour order, he is guilty of an offence…

B7.8.1 Breach of criminal behaviour order

Anti-social Behaviour, Crime and Policing Act 2014

s 30 'Breach of order'

(1) A person who without reasonable excuse—
   (a) does anything he or she is prohibited from doing by a criminal behaviour order, or
   (b) fails to do anything he or she is required to do by a criminal behaviour order,
   commits an offence.

(2) A person guilty of an offence under this section is liable—
   (a) on summary conviction, to imprisonment for a period not exceeding 6 months or to a fine, or to both;
   (b) on conviction on indictment, to imprisonment for a period not exceeding 5 years or to a fine, or to both.

(3) If a person is convicted of an offence under this section, it is not open to the court by or before which the person is convicted to make an order under subsection (1)(b) of section 12 of the Powers of Criminal Courts (Sentencing) Act 2000 (conditional discharge).

B7.8.2 Breakdown

Offence	Elements of the Offence	Defence
s 1 Crime and Disorder Act 1998 'Breach of anti-social behaviour order'	• Without reasonable excuse • Commits an act • Which is prohibited by way of a valid ASBO	• Negative any element of the offence • s 1 Crime and Disorder Act 1998 **B7.8.3** • *R v Charles* **B7.8.4** • General Defences **C**
s 30 Anti-Social Behaviour, Crime and Policing Act 2014 'Breach of criminal behaviour order'	• Without reasonable excuse • Does anything prohibited by a criminal behaviour order; or • Fails to do anything required by a criminal behaviour order	• Negative any element of the offence • s 30 Anti-social Behaviour, Crime and Policing Act 2014 **B7.8.3** • *R v Charles* **B7.8.4** • General Defences **C**

B7.8.3 Defences

Crime and Disorder Act 1998

s 1 'Anti-social behaviour orders'

(10) If without reasonable excuse a person does anything which he is prohibited from doing by an anti-social behaviour order, he is guilty of an offence . . .

Anti-social Behaviour, Crime and Policing Act 2014

s 30 'Breach of order'

(1) A person who without reasonable excuse—

- See General Defences **C**.

B7.8.4 Key points

- The precise terms and duration of the ASBO/CBO should be checked.
- Breach of an interim Order is also an offence

- Ignorance, forgetfulness, or misunderstanding of the terms of an ASBO/CBO may constitute a reasonable excuse. What is a reasonable excuse is a matter for consideration by a jury given all the facts of the case, including a suspect's state of mind (*R v Nicholson* [2006] EWCA Crim 1518) and (*JB v DPP* [2012] EWHC 72 (Admin)).
- It is for the prosecution to disprove, to the criminal standard, a lack of reasonable excuse once the issue has been raised (*R v Charles* [2009] EWCA Crim 1570).

B7.8.5 Sentencing

s 1 Crime and Disorder Act 1998

Summary:6months'imprisonmentand/orafineIndictment: 5 years' imprisonment and/or a fine

s 30 Anti-social Behaviour, Crime and Policing Act 2014

Summary: 6 months' imprisonment and/or a fine or both

Indictment: 5 years' imprisonment and/or a fine or both

Youth Gravity Matrix

OFFENCE	Gravity Score	Offence type	AGGRAVATING FACTORS	MITIGATING FACTORS
Breach of ASBO	3	E	• Flagrant or repeated breach	• Consequence of breach not understood

B7.9 Squatting

Legal Aid, Sentencing and Punishment of Offenders Act 2012

s 144 'Offence of squatting in a residential building'

(1) A person commits an offence if

(a) the person is in a residential building as a trespasser having entered it as a trespasser,

(b) the person knows or ought to know that he or she is a trespasser, and

(c) the person is living in the building or intends to live there for any period.

B7.9.1 Breakdown

Offence	Elements of the Offence	Defence
s 144 Legal Aid, Sentencing and Punishment of Offenders Act 2012 'Squatting'	• Enters as a trespasser • Into a residential building • Knew or ought to know they are a trespasser; and • Living or intending to live in the building	• Negative any element of the offence • General Defences **C**

B7.9.2 Interpretation

'Building'

> **Legal Aid, Sentencing and Punishment of Offenders Act 2012**
>
> **s 144 'Offence of squatting in a residential building'**
>
> (3) For the purposes of this section—
> (a) 'building' includes any structure or part of a structure (including a temporary or moveable structure), and
> (b) a building is 'residential' if it is designed or adapted, before the time of entry, for use as a place to live.

- A trespasser is a person who deliberately enters a building with the knowledge (or recklessness) that they are a trespasser *R v Collins* [1972] EWCA Crim 1.

B7.9.3 Defences

- See General Defences C.

B7.9.4 Key points

- Section 144(7) provides that the offence applies regardless of whether the trespasser entered the property before or after commencement of the Act. An individual who may have been living in the premises prior to commencement will be guilty of an offence if after commencement of the 2012 Act they satisfy the particulars of s 144(1).
- The offence only captures individuals whose initial entry and occupation of a building was unlawful from the start. A tenant who initially enters a property with the permission of the landlord,

but who falls behind with rent payments or decides to withhold rent does not become a trespasser.

- An individual who holds over at the end of a lease and so remains in temporary occupation does not become a trespasser; s 144(2).
- An individual who derives title from a trespasser, or has the permission of a trespasser to enter the property, may be similarly treated as such if they do not have the initial permission of the owner or lawful occupier; s 144(4).
- An individual who enters non-residential property with the intention of living there will not be guilty of a criminal offence under the 2012 Act. They may only be guilty of an offence if other crimes are committed when entering or staying in a property, for example, criminal damage.

B7.9.5 Sentencing

s 144 Legal Aid, Sentencing and Punishment of Offenders Act 2012

Summary: 6 months' imprisonment and/or a fine

B7.10 Drunk and disorderly

Criminal Justice Act 1967

s 91

(1) Any person who in any public place is guilty, while drunk, of disorderly behaviour shall be liable on summary conviction to a fine not exceeding level 3 on the standard scale.

B7.10.1 Breakdown

Offence	Elements of the Offence	Defence
s 91 Criminal Justice Act 1967 'Drunk and disorderly'	• In any public place • Whilst drunk • Displays disorderly behaviour	• Negative any element of the offence • General Defences **C**

B7.10.2 Interpretation

- 'Public place'

Criminal Justice Act 1967

s 91

(4) In this section *'public place'* includes any highway and any other premises or place to which at the material time the public have or are permitted to have access, whether on payment or otherwise.

- 'Drunk'

The word 'drunk' should be given its ordinary and natural meaning. Whether a defendant was drunk is a simple question of fact in each case (*Neale v RMJE (A Minor)* (1985) 80 Cr App R 20).

- 'Disorderly behaviour'

The words 'disorderly behaviour' should be given their ordinary and natural meaning. Whether a defendant was drunk is a simple question of fact in each case (*Carroll v DPP* [2009] EWHC 554 (Admin)).

B7.10.3 Defences

- See General Defences C.

B7.10.4 Key points

- 'Drunk' is limited to consumption of alcohol and not other substances (*Neale v RMJE (A Minor)* (1985) 80 Cr App R 20).
- It is the choice to consume alcohol which makes out this element of the offence if it results in drunkenness (*Neale v RMJE* as above).
- There is no requirement of specific intent to act in a disorderly way. Behaviour whether disorderly or not is given an objective standard (*Carroll v DPP* [2009] EWHC 554 (Admin)).

B7.10.5 Sentencing

s 91 Criminal Justice Act 1967

Summary: A fine not exceeding level 3 on the standard scale

Youth Gravity Matrix

OFFENCE	Gravity Score	Offence type	AGGRAVATING FACTORS	MITIGATING FACTORS
Drunk and disorderly	1	S	• Risk of escalation • Busy public place • Offensive language or behaviour • Threatening	• Only witnessed by a police officer • Little inconvenience to the public • Non-threatening (consider supportive interventions)

B7.10.6 Diversion

Drunkenness in a public place may be dealt with by an upper-tier PND instant penalty provided that the suspect is an adult,

See *Blackstone's Criminal Practice* **B11.202**

B8 Communications Offences

B8.1 Harassment

Protection from Harassment Act 1997

s 1 'Prohibition of harassment'

(1) A person must not pursue a course of conduct—
  (a) which amounts to harassment of another, and
  (b) which he knows or ought to know amounts to harassment of the other.

(1A) A person must not pursue a course of conduct—
  (a) which involves harassment of two or more persons, and
  (b) which he knows or ought to know involves harassment of those persons, and
  (c) by which he intends to persuade any person (whether or not one of those mentioned above)—
    (i) not to do something that he is entitled or required to do, or
    (ii) to do something that he is not under any obligation to do.

(2) For the purposes of this section or section 2A(2)(c), the person whose course of conduct is in question ought to know that it amounts to [or involves] harassment of another if a reasonable person in possession of the same information would think the course of conduct amounted to or involved harassment of the other.

s 2 'Offence of harassment'

(1) A person who pursues a course of conduct in breach of section 1(1) or (1A) is guilty of an offence.

s 4 'Putting people in fear of violence'

(1) A person whose course of conduct causes another to fear, on at least two occasions, that violence will be used against him is guilty of an offence if he knows or ought to know that his course of conduct will cause the other so to fear on each of those occasions.

(2) For the purposes of this section, the person whose course of conduct is in question ought to know that it will cause another to fear that violence will be used against him on any occasion if a reasonable person in possession of the same information would think the course of conduct would cause the other so to fear on that occasion.

B8.1.1 Related offences

Protection From Harassment Act 1997

s 2A

(1) A person is guilty of an offence if—

(a) the person pursues a course of conduct in breach of section 1(1), and
(b) the course of conduct amounts to stalking.

(2) For the purposes of subsection (1)(b) (and section 4A(1)(a)) a person's course of conduct amounts to stalking of another person if—
(a) it amounts to harassment of that person,
(b) the acts or omissions involved are ones associated with stalking, and
(c) the person whose course of conduct it is knows or ought to know that the course of conduct amounts to harassment of the other person.

(3) The following are examples of acts or omissions which, in particular circumstances, are ones associated with stalking—
(a) following a person,
(b) contacting, or attempting to contact, a person by any means,
(c) publishing any statement or other material—
(i) relating or purporting to relate to a person, or
(ii) purporting to originate from a person,
(d) monitoring the use by a person of the internet, email or any other form of electronic communication,
(e) loitering in any place (whether public or private),
(f) interfering with any property in the possession of a person,
(g) watching or spying on a person.

s 4A

(1) A person ('A') whose course of conduct—
(a) amounts to stalking, and
(b) either—
(i) causes another ('B') to fear, on at least two occasions, that violence will be used against B, or
(ii) causes B serious alarm or distress which has a substantial adverse effect on B's usual day-to-day activities,

is guilty of an offence if A knows or ought to know that A's course of conduct will cause B so to fear on each of those occasions or (as the case may be) will cause such alarm or distress.

(2) For the purposes of this section A ought to know that A's course of conduct will cause B to fear that violence will be used against B on any occasion if a reasonable person in possession of the same information would think the course of conduct would cause B so to fear on that occasion.

(3) For the purposes of this section A ought to know that A's course of conduct will cause B serious alarm or distress which has a substantial adverse effect on B's usual day-to-day activities if a reasonable person in possession of the same information would think the course of conduct would cause B such alarm or distress.

B8.1.2 Breakdown

Offence	Elements of the Offence	Defence
s 1 Protection From Harassment Act 1997 'Harassment—non violent'	• By pursuing a course of conduct of two or more incidents • Which caused harassment • Knew/ought to know conduct amounted to harassment	• Negative any element of the offence • s 1 Protection of Harassment Act 1997 **B8.1.4** • General Defences **C**
s 4 Protection From Harassment Act 1997 'Harassment—fear of violence'	• By pursuing a course of conduct of two or more incidents • Caused fear of violence • Knew/ought to know conduct would cause fear of violence on each incident	• Negative any element of the offence • s 4 Protection of Harassment Act 1997 **B8.1.4** • General Defences **C**
s 2A Protection From Harassment Act 1997 'Stalking—non violent'	• Pursuing a course of conduct in breach of section 1(1) • Which amounts to stalking • Amounting to harassment • The acts/omissions are ones associated with stalking, and • The person following the course of conduct knows or ought to know the conduct amounts to harassment of the other person	• Negative any element of the offence • General Defences **C**
s 4A Protection From Harassment Act 1997 'Stalking—fear of violence'	• By pursuing a course of conduct amounting to stalking, either • Causes to another (X) • A fear that on at least two occasions violent would be used towards X • Knowing/ought to know conduct would cause fear of violence on each incident; or • Causes to another (X) • Serious alarm or distress • Which has a serious substantial effect on X's day-today activities • Knowing/ought to know conduct would cause such alarm and distress	• Negative any element of the offence • s 4A Protection of Harassment Act 1997 **B8.1.4** • General Defences **C**

B8.1.3 Interpretation

- 'Harassing'.

Protection from Harassment Act 1997

s 7 'Interpretation of this group of sections'

(2) References to harassing a person include alarming the person or causing the person distress.

- 'Course of conduct'.

Protection from Harassment Act 1997

s 7 'Interpretation of this group of sections'

(3) A *'course of conduct'* must involve—
  (a) in the case of conduct in relation to a single person (see section 1(1)), conduct on at least two occasions in relation to that person, or
  (b) in the case of conduct in relation to two or more persons (see section 1(1A)), conduct on at least one occasion in relation to each of those persons.

(3A) A person's conduct on any occasion shall be taken, if aided, abetted, counselled or procured by another—
  (a) to be conduct on that occasion of the other (as well as conduct of the person whose conduct it is); and
  (b) to be conduct in relation to which the other's knowledge and purpose, and what he ought to have known, are the same as they were in relation to what was contemplated or reasonably foreseeable at the time of the aiding, abetting, counselling or procuring.

(4) *'Conduct'* includes speech.

- 'Person'.

Protection from Harassment Act 1997

s 7 'Interpretation of this group of sections'

(5) References to a person, in the context of the harassment of a person, are references to a person who is an individual.

B8.1.4 Defences

- Non-violent harassment only.

Protection from Harassment Act 1997

s 1 'Prohibition of harassment'

(3) Subsection (1) or (1A) does not apply to a course of conduct if the person who pursued it shows—
  (a) that it was pursued for the purpose of preventing or detecting crime,

(b) that it was pursued under any enactment or rule of law or to comply with any condition or requirement imposed by any person under any enactment, or
(c) that in the particular circumstances the pursuit of the course of conduct was reasonable.

- Fear of violence only applicable to an offence under s 4.

Protection from Harassment Act 1997

s 4 'Putting people in fear of violence'

(3) It is a defence for a person charged with an offence under this section to show that—
  (a) his course of conduct was pursued for the purpose of preventing or detecting crime,
  (b) his course of conduct was pursued under any enactment or rule of law or to comply with any condition or requirement imposed by any person under any enactment, or
  (c) the pursuit of his course of conduct was reasonable for the protection of himself or another or for the protection of his or another's property.

- Stalking with fear of violence or serious alarm or distress only under s 4A.

Protection From Harassment Act 1997

s 4A

(4) It is a defence for A to show that—
  (a) A's course of conduct was pursued for the purpose of preventing or detecting crime,
  (b) A's course of conduct was pursued under any enactment or rule of law or to comply with any condition or requirement imposed by any person under any enactment, or
  (c) the pursuit of A's course of conduct was reasonable for the protection of A or another or for the protection of A's or another's property.

- See General Defences **C**.

B8.1.5 Key points

- The offence can be racially aggravated in nature, with reference to the provisions of the Crime and Disorder Act 1998, s 32 **B7.7**.
- A harassing course of conduct may continue intermittently over a long period of time and is only complete when the last act

occurred. The last incident considered as part of the course of conduct must be within the limitation period before the complaint is made, currently within 6 months as per Magistrates' Courts Act 1980, s 127 (*DPP v Baker* [2004] EWHC 2782 (Admin)).

- An individual may be prevented from pursuing a course of conduct by virtue of civil injunction. Such an individual cannot be convicted of a criminal offence where contempt of court proceedings have been initiated in respect of the same conduct (Protection From Harassment Act 1997, s 3).
- Under s 1(2), the test is entirely objective. The reasonable man cannot possess similar features to the individual such as a mental illness which, for example, manifests in obsessive behaviour. Mental illness is therefore not available as a defence (*R v C (Sean Peter)* [2001] EWCA Crim 1251).
- Under s 1(3)(a), an individual must show that the dominant 'purpose' of the course of conduct was the prevention or detection of crime and it was the purpose of the course of conduct itself that mattered. In this context this is a subjective state of mind, however the defendant must have acted rationally and the assessment of rationality is an objective test (*Hayes v Willoughby* [2013] UKSC 17).
- There is no statutory defence to an offence under s 2A (non-violent stalking).

B8.1.6 Sentencing

s 2 Protection from Harassment Act

Summary: 6 months' imprisonment and/or a fine

s 4 Protection from Harassment Act

Summary: 6 months' imprisonment and/or a fine

Indictable: 5 years' imprisonment and/or a fine

s 2A Protection from Harassment Act

Summary: 6 months' imprisonment and/or a fine

s 4A Protection from Harassment Act

Summary: 6 months' imprisonment and/or a fine

Indictable: 5 years' imprisonment and/or a fine

Youth Gravity Matrix

OFFENCE	Gravity Score	Offence type	AGGRAVATING FACTORS	MITIGATING FACTORS
Stalking Stalking includes (a) following a person, (b) contacting, or attempting to contact, a person by any means, (c) publishing any statement or other material relating or purporting to relate to a person, or purporting to originate from a person, (d) monitoring the use by a person of the internet, email or any other form of electronic communication, (e) loitering in any place (whether public or private), (f) interfering with any property in the possession of a person, (g) watching or spying on a person. Harassment (Section 2 of the Protection from Harassment Act 1997 Enacted Nov 2012	2 Consider YCC if conditions are suitable to prevent further contact If a restraining order is believed necessary then consider charge	E	• Views of the victim	
Stalking involving putting someone in fear of violence (Section 4A of the Protection from Harassment Act 1997) must occur on at least 2 occasions Enacted Nov 2012	3 Consider YCC if conditions are suitable to prevent further harassment If a restraining order is believed necessary then consider charge	E	• Level of violence • View of victim	

See *Blackstone's Criminal Practice* **B2.165**

B8.2 Offensive/false messages

Malicious Communications Act 1988

s 1 'Offence of sending letters etc. with intent to cause distress or anxiety'

(1) Any person who sends to another person—
 (a) a letter, electronic communication or article of any description which conveys—
  (i) a message which is indecent or grossly offensive;
  (ii) a threat; or
  (iii) information which is false and known or believed to be false by the sender; or
 (b) any article or electronic communication which is, in whole or part, of an indecent or grossly offensive nature,
is guilty of an offence if his purpose, or one of his purposes, in sending it is that it should, so far as falling within paragraph (a) or (b) above, cause distress or anxiety to the recipient or to any other person to whom he intends that it or its contents or nature should be communicated.

B8.2.1 Related offences

- Improper use of electronic public communications network **B8.3**.

B8.2.2 Breakdown

Offence	Elements of the Offence	Defence
s 1(1)(a) Malicious Communications Act 1988 'Malicious communications'	• Sends to another • A letter, electronic communication, or article of any description • Which conveys • A message which is indecent or grossly offensive; or • A threat; or • False information which is known or believed to be as such and known or believed to be false by the sender • With the purpose of causing distress or anxiety • To the recipient or another other person to whom it is intended that the item or its content is communicated	• Negative any element of the offence • s 1 Malicious Communications Act 1988 **B8.2.4** • General Defences **C**

Offence	Elements of the Offence	Defence
s 1(1)(b) Malicious Communications Act 1988 'Malicious communications'	• Send to another • Any article or electronic communication • In whole or part of an indecent or grossly offensive nature • With the purpose of causing distress or anxiety • To the recipient or another other person to whom it is intended the item or content is communicated	• Negative any element of the offence • s 1 Malicious Communications Act 1988 **B8.2.4** • General Defences **C**

B8.2.3 Interpretation

- Electronic communication.

> **Malicious Communications Act 1988**
>
> **s 1 'Offence of sending letters etc. with intent to cause distress or anxiety'**
>
> (2A) In this section 'electronic communication' includes—
> (a) any oral or other communication by means of an electronic communications network; and
> (b) any communication (however sent) that is in electronic form.
>
> (3) In this section references to sending include references to delivering or transmitting and to causing to be sent delivered or transmitted and 'sender' shall be construed accordingly.

B8.2.4 Defences

> **Malicious Communications Act 1988**
>
> **s 1 'Offence of sending letters etc. with intent to cause distress or anxiety'**
>
> (2) A person is not guilty of an offence by virtue of subsection (1)(a)(ii) above if he shows—
> (a) that the threat was used to reinforce a demand made by him on reasonable grounds; and
> (b) that he believed and had reasonable grounds for believing that the use of the threat was a proper means of reinforcing the demand.

- See General Defences **C**.

B8.2.5 Key points

- There is no requirement for the article to actually reach the intended recipient. The offence is made out if the item is intended to be 'sent', the encompassing definition is seen in s 1(3).
- 'Indecent or grossly offensive' are to be given their ordinary meaning. The true identifier is the intention of the sender to cause distress or anxiety by sending the item. Political or educational materials are not excluded by the Act, where the intention remains (*Connolly v DPP* [2007] EWHC 237 (Admin)).

B8.2.6 Sentencing

s 1 Malicious Communications Act 1988

Summary: 6 months' imprisonment and/or a fine

On indictment: 2 years and/or a fine

Youth Gravity Matrix

OFFENCE	Gravity Score	Offence type	AGGRAVATING FACTORS	MITIGATING FACTORS
Sending malicious communication (s 1 Malicious Communication Act 1988)	2	S	• Persistency	• Obvious to recipient that a hoax

B8.3 Improper use of electronic public communications network

Communications Act 2003

s 127 'Improper use of public electronic communications network'

(1) A person is guilty of an offence if he—

(a) sends by means of a public electronic communications network a message or other matter that is grossly offensive or of an indecent, obscene or menacing character; or

(b) causes any such message or matter to be so sent.

s 127 'Improper use of public electronic communications network'

(2) A person is guilty of an offence if, for the purpose of causing annoyance, inconvenience or needless anxiety to another, he—

(a) sends by means of a public electronic communications network, a message that he knows to be false,
(b) causes such a message to be sent; or
(c) persistently makes use of a public electronic communications network.

B8.3.1 Related offences

- Offensive/false messages **B8.2**.
- Bomb hoax **B8.4**.

B8.3.2 Breakdown

Offence	Elements of the Offence	Defence
s 127(1) Communications Act 2003 'Improper use of electronic public communications network'	• Sends • A message or other matter • That is grossly offensive or of an indecent, obscene or menacing character; or • Causes any such message or matter to be so sent • By means of a public electronic communications network	• Negative any element of the offence • General Defences **C**
s 127(2) Communications Act 2003 'Improper use of electronic public communications network'	• For the purpose of causing annoyance, inconvenience or needless anxiety to another • Sends a message • By a public electronic communications network • Knowing the message to be false; or • Causes such a message to be sent; or • Persistently makes use of a public electronic communications network	• Negative any element of the offence • General Defences **C**

B8.3.3 Defences

- See General Defences **C**.

B8.3.4 Key points

- Section 127(1) of the Act does not require intent. The test for 'grossly offensive' under this section is whether reasonable persons in our society would find the message grossly offensive, regardless of whether they are the recipient of the message or not (*DPP v Collins* [2006] UKHL 40).

- A message which does not create fear or apprehension in those to whom it was communicated, or who might reasonably be expected to see it (eg a joke and understood as a joke by those reading it) lacks the menace required for s 127(1)(a) (*Chambers v DPP* [2012] EWHC 2157 (Admin)).
- It is necessary to look at the cumulative effect of the conduct as to whether a public nuisance is caused, rather than looking at each instance in isolation (*R v Johnson* [1996] 2 Cr App R 434).
- Consider the possibility of an offence under s 47 Offences Against the Person Act 1861 **B1.4** if a recognizable psychiatric illness is suffered by a victim as a result of the individual's conduct (*R v Ireland; R v Burstow* [1997] UKHL 34).

B8.3.5 Sentencing

s 127 Communications Act 2003

Summary: 6 months' imprisonment and/or a fine

Youth Gravity Matrix

OFFENCE	Gravity Score	Offence type	AGGRAVATING FACTORS	MITIGATING FACTORS
Grossly offensive or indecent, obscene or menacing use of public electronic communications network (s 127(1) Communications Act 2003)	2	S	• Persistency • Discriminatory/ or sadistic in nature	• Obvious to recipient that a hoax
Sending false messages via public electronic communications network to cause annoyance, anxiety or inconvenience (s 127(2) Communications Act 2003)	2	S	• Persistency • Caused dangerous or large scale evacuation • Diversion of emergency services from genuine call • Serious financial loss	• Obvious to recipient that a hoax

B8.3.6 Diversion

- s 127(2)

Offences under s 127(2) may be dealt with by way of a PND instant penalty. Section 127(1) has no options for diversion by way of a PND.

The CPS provides guidance on the following guidance on four categories of communications offences:

> 1. Communications which may constitute credible threats of violence to the person or damage to property.
> 2. Communications which specifically target an individual or individuals and which may constitute harassment or stalking within the meaning of the Protection from Harassment Act 1997.
> 3. Communications which may amount to a breach of a court order. This can include offences under the Contempt of Court Act 1981, section 5 of the Sexual Offences (Amendment) Act 1992, breaches of a restraining order or breaches of bail. Cases where there has been an offence alleged to have been committed under the Contempt of Court Act 1981 or section 5 of the Sexual Offences (Amendment) Act 1992 should be referred to the Attorney General and via the Principal Legal Advisor's team where necessary.
> 4. Communications which do not fall into any of the categories above and fall to be considered separately (see below): i.e. those which may be considered grossly offensive, indecent, obscene or false.
>
> As a general approach, cases falling within paragraphs 12 (1), (2) or (3) should be prosecuted robustly where they satisfy the test set out in the Code for Crown Prosecutors. On the other hand, cases which fall within paragraph 12(4) will be subject to a high threshold and in many cases a prosecution is unlikely to be in the public interest.

Further guidance can be found on the CPS webpage:

<http://www.cps.gov.uk/legal/a_to_c/communications_sent_via_social_media/>

B8.4 Bomb hoaxes

Criminal Law Act 1977

s 51 'Bomb hoaxes'

(1) A person who
  (a) places any article in any place whatever; or
  (b) dispatches any article by post, rail or any other means whatever of sending things from one place to another

with the intention (in either case) of inducing in some other person a belief that it is likely to explode or ignite and thereby cause personal injury or damage to property is guilty of an offence.

(2) A person who communicates any information which he knows or believes to be false to another person with the intention of inducing in him or any other person a false belief that a bomb or other thing liable to explode or ignite is present in any place or location whatever is guilty of an offence.
(3) For a person to be guilty of an offence under subsection (1) or (2) above it is not necessary for him to have any particular person in mind as the person in whom he intends to induce the belief mentioned in that subsection.

B8.4.1 Breakdown

Offence	Elements of the Offence	Defence
s 51(1) Criminal Law Act 1977 'Bomb hoax'	• Places in any place; or • Dispatches by post, rail or any other means whatever of sending things from one place to another • Any article • With intention of inducing a belief that it is likely to explode or ignite; and • Thereby cause personal injury or damage to property	• Negative any element of the offence • General Defences **C**
s 51(2) Criminal Law Act 1977 'Bomb hoax'	• Communicates to another person • Any information • Known or believed to be false • With the intention of inducing in that other person • A false belief that a bomb or other thing liable to explode or ignite is present in any place or location	• Negative any element of the offence • General Defences **C**

B8.4.2 Interpretation

Criminal Law Act 1977

s 51 'Bomb hoaxes'

In this subsection *'article'* means substance.

B8.4.3 Defences

- See General Defences C.

B8.4.4 Key point

- There is no requirement that the person communicating the false information should specify a 'place or location' (*R v Webb* The Times, 19 June 1995).

B8.4.5 Sentencing

s 51 Criminal Law Act 1977

Summary: 6 months' imprisonment and/or a fine

Indictment: Imprisonment for a term not exceeding 7 years

Youth Gravity Matrix

OFFENCE	Gravity Score	Offence type	AGGRAVATING FACTORS	MITIGATING FACTORS
Bomb hoax (s 51 Criminal Law Act 1977)	3	S	• 'Copy-cat' scenario • Existing climate of fear • Caused dangerous or large scale evacuation, ie hospital, large sporting event • Serious financial loss	• Obvious to recipient that a hoax

See *Blackstone's Criminal Practice* B11.96

B8.5 False alarms of fire

Fire & Rescue Services Act 2004

s 49 'False alarms of fire'

(1) A person commits an offence if he knowingly gives or causes to be given a false alarm of fire to a person acting on behalf of a fire and rescue authority.

B8.5.1 Breakdown

Offence	Elements of the Offence	Defence
s 49 Fire & Rescue Services Act 2004 'False alarms of fire'	• Knowingly • Gives or causes to be given a false alarm of fire • To a person acting on behalf of a fire and rescue authority	• Negative any element of the offence • General Defences **C**

B8.5.2 Defences

- See General Defences C.

B8.5.3 Key point

- This offence under s 49 and that of bomb hoax **B8.4** are charged in preference to offences of wasting police time, where appropriate.

B8.5.4 Sentencing

s 49 Fire & Rescue Services Act 2004

Summary: 3 months' imprisonment and/or a fine not exceeding level 4

Youth Gravity Matrix

OFFENCE	Gravity Score	Offence type	AGGRAVATING FACTORS	MITIGATING FACTORS
False alarms to emergency services (Fire & Rescue Services Act 2004)	3	S	• Persistency	• Obvious to recipient that a hoax

B8.5.5 Diversion

Offences under s 49 can be dealt with by way of a PND instant penalty where the suspect is aged 18 years and over.

B9 Weapons Offences

Firearms Act 1968

s 57 'Interpretation'

(1) In this Act, the expression 'firearm' means a lethal barrelled weapon of any description from which any shot, bullet or other missile can be discharged and includes—

(a) any prohibited weapon, whether it is such a lethal weapon as aforesaid or not; and

(b) any component part of such a lethal or prohibited weapon; and

(c) any accessory to any such weapon designed or adapted to diminish the noise or flash caused by firing the weapon;

and so much of section 1 of this Act as excludes any description of firearm from the category of firearms to which that section applies shall be construed as also excluding component parts of, and accessories to, firearms of that description.

(2) In this Act, the expression 'ammunition' means ammunition for any firearm and includes grenades, bombs and other like missiles, whether capable of use with a firearm or not, and also includes prohibited ammunition.

(2A) In this Act 'self-loading' and 'pump-action' in relation to any weapon mean respectively that it is designed or adapted (otherwise than as mentioned in section 5(1)(a)) so that it is automatically reloaded or that it is so designed or adapted that it is re-loaded by the manual operation of the fore-end or forestock of the weapon.

(2B) In this Act 'revolver', in relation to a smooth-bore gun, means a gun containing a series of chambers which revolve when the gun is fired.

(3) For purposes of sections 45, 46, 50, 51(4) and 52 of this Act, the offences under this Act relating specifically to air weapons are those under sections 22(4), 22(5), 23(1), 24(4) and 24ZA(1).

(4) In this Act—

'acquire' means hire, accept as a gift or borrow and 'acquisition' shall be construed accordingly;

'air weapon' has the meaning assigned to it by section 1(3)(b) of this Act;

'another member State' means a member State other than the United Kingdom, and 'other member States' shall be construed accordingly;

'area' means a police area;

'Article 7 authority' means a document issued by virtue of section 32A(1)(b) or (2) of this Act;

'certificate' (except in a context relating to the registration of firearms dealers) and 'certificate under this Act' mean a firearm certificate or a shot gun certificate and—

(a) 'firearm certificate' means a certificate granted by a chief officer of police under this Act in respect of any firearm or ammunition to which section 1 of this Act applies and includes a certificate granted in Northern Ireland under section 1 of the Firearms Act 1920 or under an enactment of the Parliament of Northern Ireland amending or substituted for that section; and

(b) 'shot gun certificate' means a certificate granted by a chief officer of police under this Act and authorising a person to possess shot guns;

'civilian officer' means—

(a) as respects England and Wales—
   (i) a person employed by a chief constable established under section 2 of the Police Reform and Social Responsibility Act 2011,
   (ii) a person employed by the Commissioner of Police of the Metropolis, or
   (iii) a person employed by the Corporation of the City of London who is under the direction and control of the Commissioner of Police for the City of London;

. . .

'European firearms pass' means a document to which the holder of a certificate under this Act is entitled by virtue of section 32A(1)(a) of this Act; 'European weapons directive' means the directive of the Council of the European Communities No. 91/477/EEC (directive on the control of the acquisition and possession of weapons);

'firearms dealer' means a person who, by way of trade or business—

(a) manufactures, sells, transfers, repairs, tests or proves firearms or ammunition to which section 1 of this Act applies or shot guns; or
(b) sells or transfers air weapons;

'imitation firearm' means any thing which has the appearance of being a firearm (other than such a weapon as is mentioned in section 5(1)(b) of this Act) whether or not it is capable of discharging any shot, bullet or other missile.

'premises' includes any land;

'prescribed' means prescribed by rules made by the Secretary of State under section 53 of this Act;

'prohibited weapon' and 'prohibited ammunition' have the meanings assigned to them by section 5(2) of this Act;

'public place' includes any highway and any other premises or place to which at the material time the public have or are permitted to have access, whether on payment or otherwise;

'registered', in relation to a firearms dealer, means registered either—

(a) in Great Britain, under section 33 of this Act, or
(b) in Northern Ireland, under section 8 of the Firearms Act 1920 or any enactment of the Parliament of Northern Ireland amending or substituted for that section,

and references to 'the register', 'registration' and a 'certificate of registration' shall be construed accordingly, except in section 40;

'rifle' includes carbine;

'shot gun' has the meaning assigned to it by section 1(3)(a) of this Act and, in sections 3(1) and 45(2) of this Act and in the definition of 'firearms dealer', includes any component part of a shot gun and any accessory to a shot gun designed or adapted to diminish the noise or flash caused by firing the gun;

'slaughtering instrument' means a firearm which is specially designed or adapted for the instantaneous slaughter of animals or for the instantaneous stunning of animals with a view to slaughtering them; and

'transfer' includes let on hire, give, lend and part with possession, and 'transferee' and 'transferee' shall be construed accordingly.

(4A) For the purposes of any reference in this Act to the use of any firearm or ammunition for a purpose not authorised by the European weapons directive, the directive shall be taken to authorise the use of a firearm or ammunition as or with a slaughtering instrument and the use of a firearm and ammunition—

(a) for sporting purposes;

(b) for the shooting of vermin, or, in the course of carrying on activities in connection with the management of any estate, of other wildlife; and

(c) for competition purposes and target shooting outside competitions.

(5) The definitions in subsections (1) to (3) above apply to the provisions of this Act except where the context otherwise requires.

(6) For purposes of this Act—

(a) the length of the barrel of a firearm shall be measured from the muzzle to the point at which the charge is exploded on firing; and

(b) a shot gun or an air weapon shall be deemed to be loaded if there is ammunition in the chamber or barrel or in any magazine or other device which is in such a position that the ammunition can be fed into the chamber or barrel by the manual or automatic operation of some part of the gun or weapon.

B9.1 Section 1 firearms

Firearms Act 1968

s 1 'Requirement of firearms certificate'

(1) Subject to any exemption under this Act, it is an offence for a person—

(a) to have in his possession, or to purchase or acquire, a firearm to which this section applies without holding a firearm certificate in force at the time, or otherwise than as authorised by such a certificate;

(b) to have in his possession, or to purchase or acquire, any ammunition to which this section applies without holding a firearm certificate in force at the time, or otherwise than as authorised by such a certificate, or in quantities in excess of those so authorised.

B9.1.1 Related offences

Firearms Act 1968

s 1 'Requirement of firearms certificate'

(2) It is an offence for a person to fail to comply with a condition subject to which a firearm certificate is held by him.

- s 5 Firearms **B9.3**.

B9.1.2 Breakdown

Offence	Elements of the Offence	Defence
s 1(1)(a) Firearms Act 1968 'Requirement of firearms certificate'	• Possess/Purchase/Acquire • A firearm to which this section applies • Without holding a firearms certificate in force at that time/ otherwise in accordance with a firearms certificate	• Negative any element of the offence • General Defences **C**
s 1(1)(b) Firearms Act 1968 'Requirement of firearms certificate'	• Possess/Acquire/Purchase • Any ammunition to which this section applies • Without holding a firearms certificate in force at that time/otherwise in accordance with a firearms certificate/in quantities in excess of those so authorised	• Negative any element of the offence • General Defences **C**
s 1(2) Firearms Act 1968 'Fail to comply with a condition of a firearms certificate'	• Holding a firearms certificate • Fails to comply with any condition of said certificate	• Negative any element of the offence • General Defences **C**

B9.1.3 Interpretation

Firearms Act 1968

s 1 'Requirement of firearms certificate'

(3) This section applies to every firearm except—
   (a) a shot gun within the meaning of this Act, that is to say a smooth-bore gun (not being an air gun) which—
      (i) has a barrel not less than 24 inches in length and does not have any barrel with a bore exceeding 2 inches in diameter;

(ii) either has no magazine or has a non-detachable magazine incapable of holding more than two cartridges; and

(iii) is not a revolver gun; and

(b) an air weapon (that is to say, an air rifle, air gun or air pistol which does not fall within section 5(1) and which is not of a type declared by rules made by the Secretary of State under section 53 of this Act to be specially dangerous).

(3A) A gun which has been adapted to have such a magazine as is mentioned in subsection (3)(a)(ii) above shall not be regarded as falling within that provision unless the magazine bears a mark approved by the Secretary of State for denoting that fact and that mark has been made, and the adaptation has been certified in writing as having been carried out in a manner approved by him, either by one of the two companies mentioned in section 58(1) of this Act or by such other person as may be approved by him for that purpose.

(4) This section applies to any ammunition for a firearm, except the following articles, namely:—

(a) cartridges containing five or more shot, none of which exceeds .36 inch in diameter;

(b) ammunition for an air gun, air rifle or air pistol; and

(c) blank cartridges not more than one inch in diameter measured immediately in front of the rim or cannelure of the base of the cartridge.

B9.1.4 Defences

- The defence of duress of necessity ('Chapter C') is open for offences under this section but a person 'must desist from committing the crime as soon as he reasonably can' (*R v Pommell* [1995] EWCA Crim 7) and in any event this defence will be considered in a strictly limited ambit and on the facts of the individual case (*R v Gregory* [2011] EWCA Crim 1712).
- See General Defences C.

B9.1.5 Key points

- This is a strict liability offence. However ss 7–13 Firearms Act 1968 provide specific exemptions for areas such as lawful sport, auctioneers, and police offices among others.
- This offence can be made out even if a defendant is unaware that the item they possess would constitute a firearm under s 1 (*R v Hussain* (1981) 72 Cr App R 143).
- A person may be in 'possession' of a firearm without it being within his physical control at the material time (*Sullivan v Earl of Caithness* (1976) 62 Cr App R 105).
- The Crown are not required to go further than showing that the defendant had a firearm with him either at the time of his committing or being arrested for an offence and it would be for the

defendant to show lawful possession (*R v North* [2001] EWCA Crim 544).

- Section 1 is to be construed strictly and it is no defence to have a mistaken but honestly held belief that a firearm is an antique (*R v Howells* (1977) 65 Cr App R 86).
- Whether a firearm is an antique is a question of fact and degree in each case (*Richards v Curwen* (1977) 65 Cr App R 95).

B9.1.6 Sentencing

s 1 Firearms Act 1968

Summary: 6 months' imprisonment/a fine or both

Indictment: 5 years' imprisonment/a fine or both

NB If an offence is aggravated under s 4(4) Firearms Act 1968 (conversion of firearms/shortening of shotguns) then the maximum sentence on indictment is extended to 7 years.

s 1(2) Firearms Act 1968

Summary only: 6 months' imprisonment/a fine or both

Youth Gravity Matrix

OFFENCE	Gravity Score	Offence type	AGGRAVATING FACTORS	MITIGATING FACTORS
Possession of firearm/shotgun without certificate (s 1(1) and 2(1) Firearms Act 1968) (a) No certificate ever held (b) Following non-renewal	 3 2	E	• Any form of usage • Possession in public • Type/construction of weapons (eg prohibited) • History of lethargic renewal • Deliberate avoidance of renewal procedure	

See *Blackstone's Criminal Practice* **B12.102**

B9.2 Section 2 firearms

Firearms Act 1968

s 2 'Requirement of certificate for possession of shot guns'

(1) Subject to any exemption under this Act, it is an offence for a person to have in his possession, or to purchase or acquire, a shot gun without holding a certificate under this Act authorising him to possess shot guns.

B9.2.1 Related offences

- s 1 Firearms **B9.2.**
- s 5 Firearms **B9.3.**
- Firearms with intent **B9.4.**

B9.2.2 Breakdown

Offence	Elements of the Offence	Defence
s 2 Firearms Act 1968 'Possession of a shotgun without holding a shotgun certificate'	• Possess/Purchase/Acquire • A shotgun • Without holding a shotgun certificate	• Negative any element of the offence • s 11 Firearms Act 1968 **B9.2.4** • General Defences **C**

B9.2.3 Interpretation

Firearms Act 1968

s 1 'Requirement of a firearms certificate'

(3) . . .

(a) a shot gun within the meaning of this Act, that is to say a smooth-bore gun (not being an air gun) which—

(i) has a barrel not less than 24 inches in length and does not have any barrel with a bore exceeding 2 inches in diameter;

(ii) either has no magazine or has a non-detachable magazine incapable of holding more than two cartridges; and

(iii) is not a revolver gun . . .

- See Firearms Interpretation **B9.**

B9.2.4 Defences

Firearms Act 1968

s 11 'Sports, athletics and other approved activities'

(1) A person carrying a firearm or ammunition belonging to another person holding a certificate under this Act may, without himself holding such a certificate, have in his possession that firearm or ammunition under instructions from, and for the use of, that other person for sporting purposes only; but where the person carrying the firearm or ammunition is under the age of eighteen, this subsection applies only if the other person is of or over the age of eighteen.

. . .

(5) A person may, without holding a shot gun certificate, borrow a shot gun from the occupier of private premises and use it on those premises in the occupier's presence; but where the person borrowing the shot gun is under the age of eighteen, this subsection applies only if the occupier is of or over the age of eighteen.

- The limited defences for s 1 firearms offences also apply to this section **B9.1.4**.
- See General Defences **C**.

B9.2.5 Key point

- Where person A, holding a shotgun licence, passes the shotgun to person B, who does not, for the purposes of retention and/or cleaning. Person B will be held to have 'custodial possession' of the shotgun and commit an offence under s 2(1) Firearms Act 1968 (*Hall v Cotton* (1986) 83 Cr App R 257).

B9.2.6 Sentencing

s 2(1) Firearms Act 1968

Summary: 6 months' imprisonment/a fine or both

Indictment: 5 years' imprisonment/a fine or both

s 2(2) Firearms Act 1968

Summary only: 6 months' imprisonment/a fine or both

Youth Gravity Matrix

OFFENCE	Gravity Score	Offence type	AGGRAVATING FACTORS	MITIGATING FACTORS
Firearm—failure to comply with condition of certificate in relation to security of weapons (ss 1(2) and 2(2) Firearms Act 1968)	2	S	• Degree of carelessness/ insecurity • Previous history of insecurity • Certificate held for period of time—therefore knew of the requirement	

See *Blackstone's Criminal Practice* **B12.102**

B9.3 Prohibited weapons and ammunitions

Firearms Act 1968

s 5 'Weapons subject to general prohibition'

(1) A person commits an offence if, without the authority of the Defence Council, he has in his possession, or purchases or acquires, or manufactures, sells or transfers—

(a) Any firearms which is so designed or adapted that two or more missiles can be successively discharged without repeated pressure on the trigger;

(ab) any self-loading or pump-action rifled gun other than one which is chambered for .22 rimfire cartridges;

(aba) any firearm which either has a barrel les than 30 centimetres in length or is less than 60 centimetres in length overall, other than an air weapon, a muzzle loading gun or a firearm designed as signalling apparatus;

(ac) any self-loading or pump action smooth-bore gun which is not an air weapon or chambered for .22 rim-fire cartridges and either has a barrel less than 24 inches in length or is less than 40 inches in length overall;

(ad) any smooth-bore revolver gun other than one which is chambered for 9mm rim-fire cartridges or a muzzle-loading gun;

(ae) any rocket launcher, or any mortar, for projecting a stabilised missile, other than a launcher or mortar designed for mine-throwing or pyrotechnic purposes or as signalling apparatus;

(af) any air rifle, air gun or air pistol which uses, or is designed or adapted for use with, a self-contained gas cartridge system;

(b) Any weapon of whatever description designed or adapted for the discharge of any noxious liquid, gas or other thing; and

(c) Any cartridge with a bullet designed to explode on or immediately before impact, any ammunition containing or designed or adapted to contain any such noxious thing as is mentioned in paragraph (b) above and, if capable of being used with a firearm of any description, any grenade, bomb (or like missile), or rocket or shell designed to explode as aforesaid.

(1A) Subject to section 5A of this Act, a person commits an offence if, without the authority of the Secretary of State, he has in his possession, or purchases or acquires, or sells or transfers—

(a) Any firearm which is disguised as another object;

(b) Any rocket or ammunition not falling within paragraph (c) of subsection (1) of this section which consists or incorporates a missile designed to explode on or immediately before impact and is for military use;

(c) Any launcher or other projecting apparatus not falling within paragraph (ae) of that subsection which is designed to be used with any rocket or ammunition falling within paragraph (b) above or with ammunition which would fall within that paragraph but for its being ammunition falling within paragraph (c) of that subsection;

(d) Any ammunition for military use which consists in or incorporates a missile designed so that a substance contained in the missile will ignite in or immediately before impact;

(e) Any ammunition for military use which consists in or incorporates a missile designed, on account of its having a jacket and hard-core, to penetrate armour plating, armour screening or body armour;

(f) Any ammunition which incorporates a missile, designed or adapted to expand on impact;

(g) Anything which is designed to be projected as a missile from any weapon and is designed to be, or has been, incorporated in—
   (i) Any ammunition falling within any of the preceding paragraphs; or
   (ii) Any ammunition which would fall within any of those paragraphs but for its being specified in subsection (1) of this section.

B9.3.1 Breakdown

Offence	Elements of the Offence	Defence
s 5 Firearms Act 1968 'Weapons subject to general prohibition'	• The defendant • Without the authority of the Defence Council • Had in his possession/acquires/manufactured/sold/transferred • Any weapon or ammunition prohibited by section 5/section 5A	• Negative any element of the offence • See exemptions listed at **B9.3.2** • General Defences **C**

B9.3.2 Defences

- **Special exemptions from the prohibition of small firearms contained in s 5(1)(aba)—these are contained in the 1997 Act**
  - Slaughtering instruments—section 2
  - Firearms used for humane killing of animals—section 3
  - Shot pistols used for killing vermin—section 4
  - Races at athletic meetings—section 5
  - Trophies of war—section 6
  - Firearms of historic interest—section 7
  - Weapons and ammunition used for treating animals—section 8

All the above exemptions are subject to the person in possession to be authorized by a firearm certificate.

- **Exemptions from requirement of authority under s 5—contained in the 1968 Act**
  - Collectors (section 5A(1), (2), and (3))
  - For use in connection with—
    - The lawful shooting of deer
    - The shooting of vermin
    - The humane killing of animals
    - The shooting of animals for the protection of other animals or humans (see section 5A(4))
  - Slaughtering instruments (see section 5A(5))
  - Arms dealers (see section 5A(7))
- **Special exemptions from s 5—contained in the 1968 Act**
  - Police permit (section 7)
  - Authorized dealing with firearms (section 8)
  - Carriers and auctioneers (section 9)
  - Slaughter of animals (section 10)
  - Sports, athletics, and other approved activities (section 11)
  - Theatre and cinema (section 12)
  - Equipment for ships and aircraft (section 13)
- See General Defences **C**.

B9.3.3 Key point

- These are offences of strict liability.

B9.3.4 Sentencing

Offences contrary to section 5(1)(a), (ab), (aba), (ac), (ad), (ae), (af), and (c) and section 5(1A)(a) of the Firearms Act 1968

Indictable only: range 5–10 years

NB Offences under this section are caught by the minimum sentence provisions in section 51A. If convicted of one of these offences, a minimum sentence of 5 years' imprisonment will therefore apply unless there are in law exceptional circumstances

Offences contrary to section 5(1)(b) and section 5(1A)(b)–(g)

Summary: 6 months' or a fine or both

Indictment: 10 years' imprisonment, or a fine, or both

Youth Gravity Matrix

OFFENCE	Gravity Score	Offence type	AGGRAVATING FACTORS	MITIGATING FACTORS
Possession/supply etc of prohibited weapon or ammunition; ss 5 (1) (a), (ab), (aba), (ac), (ad), (ae), (af), (c), and 5(1A) (a) of 1968 Act	4	E		
Possession/supply etc of prohibited weapon (CS spray/stun gun; ss 5(1A) (b), (c),(d), (e), (f), and (g) and 5(1)(b) of 1968 Act	3	E	• Any form of usage or possession in public	

See *Blackstone's Criminal Practice* **B12.102**

B9.4 Firearms offences with intent

Firearms Act 1968

s 16 'Possession of a firearm with intent to injure'

(1) It is an offence for a person to have in his possession any firearm or ammunition with intent by means thereof to endanger life, or to enable another person by means thereof to endanger life, whether any injury has been caused or not.

B9.4.1 Related offences

Firearms Act 1968

s 16A 'Possession of firearm with intent to cause fear of violence'

It is an offence for a person to have in his possession any firearm or imitation firearm with intent—

(a) by means thereof to cause, or

(b) to enable another person by means thereof to cause,

any person to believe that unlawful violence will be used against him or another person.

s 17 'Use of firearm to resist arrest'

(1) It is an offence for a person to make or attempt to make any use whatsoever of a firearm or imitation firearm with intent to resist or prevent the lawful arrest or detention of himself or another person.

(2) If a person, at the time of his committing or being arrested for an offence specified in Schedule 1 to this Act, has in his possession a firearm or imitation firearm, he shall be guilty of an offence under this subsection unless he shows that he had it in his possession for a lawful object.

s 18 'Carrying firearm with criminal intent'

(1) It is an offence for a person to have with him a firearm or imitation firearm with intent to commit an indictable offence, or to resist arrest or prevent the arrest of another, in either case while he has the firearm or imitation firearm with him.

B9.4.2 Breakdown

Offence	Elements of the Offence	Defence
s 16 Firearms Act 1968 'Possession of a firearm with intent to injure'	• Possess • Any firearms/ammunition • With intent by means thereof • To endanger life/enable another to endanger life	• Negative any element of the offence • *R v Georgiades* **B9.4.4** • General Defences **C**
s 16A Firearms Act 1968 'Possession of firearm with intent to cause fear of violence'	• Possess • Any firearm/imitation firearm • With intent by means thereof • To cause any person to believe that unlawful violence will be used against him or another/ enable another to cause any person to believe that unlawful violence will be used against him or another	• Negative any element of the offence • General Defences **C**
s 17(1) Firearms Act 1968 'Use of firearm to resist arrest'	• Make/attempt to make use • Of a firearm/imitation firearm • With intent • To resist or prevent the lawful arrest or detention of himself or another	• Negative any element of the offence • General Defences **C**
s 17(2) Firearms Act 1968 'Use of firearm to resist arrest'	• At the time of being arrested for an offence in Schedule 1 of this act • Possesses a firearm/imitation firearm • Without lawful excuse	• Negative any element of the offence • General Defences **C**

Offence	Elements of the Offence	Defence
s 18 Firearms Act 1968 'Carrying firearm with criminal intent'.	• Have with you • A firearm/imitation firearm • With intent to cause an indictable offence; or • Have with you • A firearm/imitation firearm • To resist/prevent the arrest • Of another	• Negative any element of the offence • General Defences **C**

B9.4.3 Interpretation

- See Firearms Interpretation **B9.**
- s 16
  - If a defendant possesses a firearm only with the intent to take his own life then the s 16 offence will not be made out (*R v Norton* [1977] Crim LR 478).
- s 17.

Firearms Act 1968

s 17 'Use of firearm to resist arrest'

(4) For purposes of this section, the definition of 'firearm' in section 57(1) of this Act shall apply without paragraphs (b) and (c) of that subsection, and 'imitation firearm' shall be construed accordingly.

- 'Having possession' does not require the Crown to go further and to show that the defendant had the firearm with him at the time of his committing or being arrested for a Schedule 1 offence (*R v North* [2001] EWCA Crim 544).

Firearms Act 1968—Schedule 1				
Para 1 Offences under section 1 of the Criminal Damage Act 1971	**Para 2** Offences under any of the following provisions of the Offences Against the Person Act 1861:— sections 20 to 22 section 32 section 38 section 47	**Para 2A** Offences under Part I of the Child Abduction Act 1984 (abduction of children)	**Para 4** Theft, robbery, burglary, blackmail and any offence under section 12(1) (taking of motor vehicle or other conveyance without owner's consent) of the Theft Act 1968	**Para 5** Offences under section 89(1) of the Police Act 1996

Firearms Act 1968—Schedule 1				
Para 5A An offence under section 90(1) of the Criminal Justice Act 1991 (assaulting prisoner custody officer)	**Para 5B** An offence under section 13(1) of the Criminal Justice and Public Order Act 1994 (assaulting secure training centre custody officer)	**Para 6** Offences under any of the following provisions of the Sexual Offences Act 2003— (a) section 1 (b) section 2 (c) section 4 where the activity caused involved penetration within subsection (4)(a) to (d) of that section; (d) section 5 (e) section 6 (f) section 8 where an activity involving penetration within subsection (3)(a) to (d) of that section was caused; (g) section 30 where the touching involved penetration within subsection (3)(a) to (d) of that section; (h) section 31 where an activity involving penetration within subsection (3)(a) to (d) of that section was caused	**Para 8** Aiding or abetting the commission of any offence specified in paragraphs 1 to 6 of this Schedule	**Para 9** Attempting to commit any offence so specified

NB Para 3 relates only to Scotland and para 7 has been repealed.

- s 18

Firearms Act 1968

s 18 'Carrying firearm with criminal intent'

(2) In proceedings for an offence under this section proof that the accused had a firearm or imitation firearm with him and intended to commit an offence, or to resist or prevent arrest, is evidence that he intended to have it with him while doing so.

The ingredients of the offence under Section 18(1) are made out if it is proved:

(a) that the defendant had with him a firearm;
(b) that *he intended* to have it with him; and
(c) that *at the same time he had the intention* to commit an indictable offence or to resist or prevent arrest (emphasis added) (*R v Duhaney & Anor* [1997] EWCA Crim 2826).

B9.4.4 Defences

- See General Defences C.
- It a defence to s 16 if the possession with intent was for the purpose of self-defence when faced with an immediate attack, however these cases will be very rare (*R v Georgiades* (1989) 89 Cr App R 206).

B9.4.5 Key point

- It is immaterial for s 16 that the defendant intended to endanger life abroad (*R v Abdeikbir El-Hakkaoui* (1974) 60 Cr App R 281).

B9.4.6 Sentencing

s 16 Firearms Act 1968

Indictable only: life imprisonment/a fine or both

s 16A Firearms Act 1968

Indictable only: 10 years' imprisonment/a fine or both

s 17(1) Firearms Act 1968

Indictable only: life imprisonment/a fine or both

s 17(2) Firearms Act 1968

Indictable only: life imprisonment/a fine or both

s 18(1) Firearms Act 1968

Indictable only: life imprisonment/a fine or both

Youth Gravity Matrix

OFFENCE	Gravity Score	Offence type	AGGRAVATING FACTORS	MITIGATING FACTORS
Use firearm to resist arrest	4	I	Always refer to the CPS	
Possession of firearm with intent to endanger life/ injure property (s 16 Firearms Act 1968)	4	I	Always refer to the CPS	
Possession of firearm/imitation firearm with intent to cause fear of injury (s 16A, Firearms Act 1968)	4	I	Always refer to the CPS	
Possession of firearm whilst committing offence or with intent to commit offence (ss 17 and 18 Firearms Act 1968)	4	I	Always refer to the CPS	

See *Blackstone's Criminal Practice* **B12.85**

B9.5 Offensive weapons

Prevention of Crime Act 1953

s 1 'Prohibition of the carrying of offensive weapons without lawful authority or reasonable excuse'

(1) Any person who without lawful authority or reasonable excuse, the proof whereof shall lie on him, has with him in any public place any offensive weapon shall be guilty of an offence...

B9.5.1 Related offences

Criminal Justice Act 1988

s 139A 'Offence of having article with blade or point (or offensive weapon) on school premises'

(2) Any person who has an offensive weapon within the meaning of section 1 of the Prevention of Crime Act 1953 with him on school premises shall be guilty of an offence.

Prevention of Crime Act 1953

s 1A 'Offence of threatening with offensive weapon in public'

(1) A person is guilty of an offence if that person
 (a) has an offensive weapon with him or her in a public place,
 (b) unlawfully and intentionally threatens another person with the weapon, and
 (c) does so in such a way that there is an immediate risk of serious physical harm to that other person.

- On school premises.

Criminal Justice Act 1988

s 139AA 'Offence of threatening with article with blade or point or offensive weapon'

(1) A person is guilty of an offence if that person—
 (a) has an article to which this section applies with him or her in a public place or on school premises,
 (b) unlawfully and intentionally threatens another person with the article, and
 (c) does so in such a way that there is an immediate risk of serious physical harm to that other person.

(3) In relation to school premises this section applies to each of these—
 (a) an article to which section 139 applies; .
 (b) an offensive weapon within the meaning of section 1 of the Prevention of Crime Act 1953.

- Pointed/bladed article **B9.6**.

B9.5.2 Breakdown

Offence	Elements of the Offence	Defence
s 1 Prevention of Crime Act 1953 'Prohibition of the carrying of offensive weapons without lawful authority or reasonable excuse'	• Have with you • An offensive weapon • In a public place • Without lawful authority or reasonable excuse	• Negative any element of the offence • General Defences **C**
s 139A Criminal Justice Act 1988 'Prohibition of the carrying of offensive weapons without lawful authority or reasonable excuse—On School Premises'	• Have an offensive weapon • On school premises • Without good reason or lawful authority	• Negative any element of the offence • s 139A Criminal Justice Act 1988 **B9.5.4** • General Defences **C**
s 1A Prevention of Crime Act 1953 'Offence of threatening with offensive weapon in public'	• Have an offensive weapon • In a public place • Unlawfully and intentionally • Threaten • Another person with the weapon; and • There is an immediate risk of serious physical harm to that other person	• Negative any element of the offence • General Defences **C**
s 139AA Criminal Justice Act 1988 'Offence of threatening with offensive weapon in public—on school premises'	• Have an offensive weapon • On school premises • Unlawfully and intentionally • Threaten • Another person with the weapon; and • There is an immediate risk of serious physical harm to that other person	• Negative any element of the offence • General Defences **C**

B9.5.3 Interpretation

Prevention of Crime Act 1953

s 1 'Prohibition of the carrying of offensive weapons without lawful authority or reasonable excuse'

(4) In this section '*public place*' includes any highway and any other premises or place to which at the material time the public have or are permitted to have access, whether on payment or otherwise . . .

Criminal Justice Act 1988

s 139A 'Offence of having article with blade or point (or offensive weapon) on school premises'

(6) In this section and section 139B, '*school premises*' means land used for the purposes of a school excluding any land occupied solely as a dwelling by a person employed at the school; and '*school*' has the meaning given by section 4 of the Education Act 1996.

Education Act 1996

s 4 'Schools: general'

(1) In this Act 'school' means an educational institution which is outside the further education sector and the higher education sector and is an institution for providing—
(a) primary education,
(b) secondary education, or
(c) both primary and secondary education,
whether or not the institution also provides part-time education suitable to the requirements of junior pupils or further education.

Prevention of Crime Act 1953

s 1A

(2) For the purposes of this section physical harm is serious if it amounts to grievous bodily harm for the purposes of the Offences against the Person Act 1861.

Criminal Justice Act 1988

s 139AA 'Offence of threatening with article with blade or point or offensive weapon'

(4) For the purposes of this section physical harm is serious if it amounts to grievous bodily harm for the purposes of the Offences against the Person Act 1861.

B9.5.4 Defences

Criminal Justice Act 1988

s 139A 'Offence of having article with blade or point (or offensive weapon) on school premises'

(3) It shall be a defence for a person charged with an offence under subsection (1) or (2) above to prove that he had good reason or lawful authority for having the article or weapon with him on the premises in question.

s 139A 'Offence of having article with blade or point (or offensive weapon) on school premises'

(4) Without prejudice to the generality of subsection (3) above, it shall be a defence for a person charged with an offence under subsection (1) or (2) above to prove that he had the article or weapon in question with him—
 (a) for use at work,
 (b) for educational purposes,
 (c) for religious reasons, or
 (d) as part of any national costume.

- See General Defences **C**.

B9.5.5 Key points

- There are three categories of offensive weapons (*R v Simpson* (1984) 78 Cr App R 115)
  (1) Weapons made for causing injury to a person, ie *offensive* per se;
  (2) those adapted for to cause injury;
  (3) those not so made or adapted, but carried with the intention of causing injury.
- See key points in bladed/pointed article **B9.6**.
- Examples of weapons that are offensive per se may be found in the Criminal Justice Act 1988 (Offensive Weapons) Order 1988 and the subsequent Amendment Orders. Examples include a knuckle-duster, a butterfly knife, any disguised or concealed knife, a truncheon, or a samurai sword.
- Examples of weapons 'adapted' may include a broken bottle (*R v Simpson* (1984) as above).
- Where a person has possession of an article with lawful reason or reasonable excuse and does something with that article that is unlawful (causes injury) the article does not necessarily become offensive at that point. To be offensive the intention to have the article in a public place, or make an article with which to cause injury must be formed before the use of violence itself (*R v Jura* (1954) 38 Cr App R 53; *Ohlson v Hylton* [1975] 1 WLR 724; *Bates v Bulman* (1979) 68 Cr App R 21).

B9.5.6 Sentencing

s 1 Prevention of Crime Act 1953

Summary: 6 months' imprisonment and/or a fine

Indictable: 4 years' imprisonment and/or a fine

s 1A Prevention of Crime Act 1953

Summary: 12 months' imprisonment and/or a fine

Indictable: 4 years' imprisonment and/or a fine

s 139AA Criminal Justice Act 1988

Summary: 6 months' imprisonment and/or a fine

Indictable: 4 years' imprisonment and/or a fine

B9.5.7 Diversion

For all youths, consider the **ACPO Youth Offender Case Disposal Gravity Matrix 2013** which states:

> It is recommended that forces follow a national agreement to interpret
>
> Knife-Crime offences as follows:
>
> - The first arrest of a youth of any age for possession of an Offensive Weapon or Sharp Pointed blade, with aggravating factors, will result in the first instance with a charge.
> - The first arrest of a youth under 16 for simple possession of an Offensive Weapon or Sharp Pointed Blade, with no aggravating factors, will result in the first instance with a youth conditional caution. This must be supported by an appropriate YOT intervention, preferably with elements focussed on anti-knife crime education. A youth aged 16 or over will normally be charged.
> - The second arrest of a youth under 16 for simple possession of an Offensive Weapon or Sharp Pointed Blade will result in a charge (unless, in exceptional circumstances, 2 years have passed and it is considered appropriate to give another youth conditional caution).
> - The new offence of threatening a person in public or on school premises will result in a youth aged 16 or over going straight to charge, as this offence carries a minimum sentence of a 4 months detention and training order and therefore should not be dealt with using an out of court disposal.

Youth Gravity Matrix

OFFENCE	Gravity Score	Offence type	AGGRAVATING FACTORS	MITIGATING FACTORS
Possession of offensive weapon **for 16 and 17-year-olds**	4	E	• Method of use • Concern caused to member(s) of public • Degree of danger	
Possession of offensive weapon **for 10 to 15-year-olds**	**3** Second offence 4 charge	E	• Circumstances of possession • Concern caused to member(s) of public • Degree of danger	
Threatening with article with blade or point or offensive weapon in public or on school premises s 142 LASPO Act 2012 **Age 16 and 17-year-olds**	4	E	• **Minimum 4 months DTO so must charge**	
Threatening with article with blade or point or offensive weapon in public or on school premises s 142 LASPO Act 2012 **Age 10 to 15-year-olds**	4	E		

See *Blackstone's Criminal Practice* B12.138

B9.6 **Bladed/pointed article**

Criminal Justice Act 1988

s 139 'Offence of having an article with a blade or point in a public place'

(1) Subject to subsections (4) and (5) below, any person who has an article to which this section applies with him in a public place shall be guilty of an offence.

(2) Subject to subsection (3) below, this section applies to any article which has a blade or is sharply pointed except a folding pocketknife.
(3) This section applies to a folding pocketknife if the cutting edge of its blade exceeds 3 inches.

B9.6.1 Related offences

Criminal Justice Act 1988

s 139A 'Offence of having an article with a blade or point (or offensive weapon) on school premises'

(1) Any person who has an article to which section 139 of this Act applies with him on school premises shall be guilty of an offence.

s 139AA 'Offence of threatening with article with blade or point or offensive weapon'

(1) A person is guilty of an offence if that person—
  (a) has an article to which this section applies with him or her in a public place or on school premises,
  (b) unlawfully and intentionally threatens another person with the article, and
  (c) does so in such a way that there is an immediate risk of serious physical harm to that other person.
(2) In relation to a public place this section applies to an article to which section 139 applies.
(3) In relation to school premises this section applies to each of these—
  (a) an article to which section 139 applies;
  (b) an offensive weapon within the meaning of section 1 of the Prevention of Crime Act 1953.

- Offensive weapon **B9.5**.

B9.6.2 Breakdown

Offence	Elements of the Offence	Defence
s 139 Criminal Justice Act 1988 'Offence of having an article with a blade or point in a public place'	• Has either • An article with a blade; or • A sharply pointed object; or • A folding pocket knife where the cutting edge of the blade exceeds 3 inches/7.62cm • In a public place • Without good reason or lawful authority	• Negative any element of the offence • s 139 Criminal Justice Act 1988 **B9.6.4** • General Defences **C**

Offence	Elements of the Offence	Defence
s 139A Criminal Justice Act 1988 'Offence of having an article with a blade or point (or offensive weapon) on school premises'	• Has either • An article with a blade; or • A sharply pointed object; or • A folding pocket knife where the cutting edge of the blade exceeds 3 inches/7.62cm • On school premises • Without good reason or lawful authority	• Negative any element of the offence • s 139A Criminal Justice Act 1988 **B9.6.4** • General Defences **C**
s 139AA Criminal Justice Act 1988 'Offence of threatening with article with blade or point or offensive weapon'	• Has either • An article with a blade; or • A sharply pointed object; or • A folding pocket knife where the cutting edge of the blade exceeds 3 inches/7.62cm • In a public place; or • On school premises • Unlawfully and intentionally • Threatens • Another person with the article; and • There is an immediate risk of serious physical harm to that other person.	• Negative any element of the offence • General Defences **C**

B9.6.3 Interpretation

Criminal Justice Act 1988

s 139 'Offence of having an article with a blade or point in a public place'

(7) In this section 'public place' includes any place to which at the material time the public have or are permitted access, whether on payment or otherwise.

s 139A 'Offence of having article with blade or point (or offensive weapon) on school premises'

(6) In this section and section 139B, 'school premises' means land used for the purposes of a school excluding any land occupied solely as a dwelling by a person employed at the school; and 'school' has the meaning given by section 4 of the Education Act 1996.

Education Act 1996

s 4 'Schools: general'

(1) In this Act 'school' means an educational institution which is outside the further education sector and the higher education sector and is an institution for providing—
(a) primary education,

(b) secondary education, or
(c) both primary and secondary education,
whether or not the institution also provides part-time education suitable to the requirements of junior pupils or further education.

Criminal Justice Act 1988

s 139AA 'Offence of threatening with article with blade or point or offensive weapon'

(4) For the purposes of this section physical harm is serious if it amounts to grievous bodily harm for the purposes of the Offences against the Person Act 1861.

B9.6.4 Defences

Criminal Justice Act 1988

s 139 'Offence of having an article with a blade or point in a public place'

(4) It shall be a defence for a person charged with an offence under this section to prove that he had good reason or lawful authority for having the article with him in a public place
(5) Without prejudice to the generality of subsection (4) above, it shall be a defence for a person charged with an offence under this section to prove that he had the article with him—
(a) for use at work;
(b) for religious reasons; or
(c) as part of any national costume.

s 139A 'Offence of having article with blade or point (or offensive weapon) on school premises'

(3) It shall be a defence for a person charged with an offence under subsection (1) or (2) above to prove that he had good reason or lawful authority for having the article or weapon with him on the premises in question.
(4) Without prejudice to the generality of subsection (3) above, it shall be a defence for a person charged with an offence under subsection (1) or (2) above to prove that he had the article or weapon in question with him—
(a) for use at work,
(b) for educational purposes,
(c) for religious reasons, or
(d) as part of any national costume.

- See General Defences C.

B9.6.5 Key points

- A screwdriver is not a bladed or sharply pointed article for the purposes of s 139(2) (*R v Davis* [1998] EWCA Crim 681).
- Whether a blade is sharp, or otherwise, is not a material averment of the offence (*Brooker v DPP* [2005] EWHC 1132 (Admin)).
- 'Folding' in its ordinary meaning [and] means 'foldable' at all times without the intervention of some further process, namely the pressing of a button or release of a catch (*R v Deegan* [1998] EWCA Crim 385).
- A demarcated area does not automatically become public if there is no means of obstructing those who try to access it (gate, fence etc). It may however be considered public if it is proved that members of the public do in fact have access to it by going onto it in their capacity as members of the public *(Harriot v DPP* [2005] EWHC 965 (Admin)).
- A private place adjacent to public land does not become public by virtue of being able to reach into it to inflict injury (*R v Roberts* [2003] EWCA Crim 2753).
- 'Has with him in a public place' means 'knowingly has with him in any public place', it being for the prosecution to prove the individual's knowledge (*R v Cugullere* (1961) 45 Cr App R 108).
- Forgetfulness alone cannot amount to a good reason for having a bladed/pointed article 'with him' (*R v McCalla* (1988) 87 Cr App R 372). However forgetfulness coupled with other factors preventing the individual from ridding himself of the offending article may be sufficient to amount to a good reason (*R v Jolie* [2003] EWCA Crim 1543).
- Having an item simply out of habit is not a 'good reason'. A multi-tool with numerous other innocuous tools does not legitimize a blade thereon if the blade/point is within the description of s 139(2) (*R v Giles* [2003] EWCA Crim 1287).
- It is a matter for the jury having regard to the individual's state of mind and their perceived imminence of an attack whether a 'reasonable excuse' is made out by carrying a bladed/pointed article for protection. It is on the individual to show on the balance of probabilities that he fears an imminent attack (*R v McAuley* [2009] EWCA Crim 2130; *R v Clancy* [2012] EWCA Crim 8).
- Religious reasons (under s 139(5)(b)) will only discharge the defendant's burden, of showing good reason for possession, where the defendant had a settled intention to practise on the day in question (*R v Wang* [2003] EWCA Crim 3228).

B9.6.6 Sentencing

s 139 Criminal Justice Act 1988

Summary: 6 months. imprisonment and/or a fine

Indictable: 4 years' imprisonment and/or a fine

s 139A Criminal Justice Act 1988

Summary: 6 months' imprisonment and/or a fine

Indictable: 4 years' imprisonment and/or a fine

s 139AA Criminal Justice Act 1988

Summary: 6 months' imprisonment and/or a fine

Indictable: 4 years' imprisonment and/or a fine

Criminal Justice Act 1988

s 139A 'Offence of having article with blade or point (or offensive weapon) on school premises'

(7) Where a person aged 16 or over is convicted of an offence under this section, the court must impose an appropriate custodial sentence (with or without a fine) unless the court is of the opinion that there are particular circumstances which—
  - (a) relate to the offence or to the offender, and
  - (b) would make it unjust to do so in all the circumstances.

(8) In this section 'appropriate custodial sentence' means—
  - (a) in the case of a person who is aged 18 or over when convicted, a sentence of imprisonment for a term of at least 6 months;
  - (b) in the case of a person who is aged at least 16 but under 18 when convicted, a detention and training order of at least 4 months.

B9.6.7 Diversion

For all youths, consider the **ACPO Youth Offender Case Disposal Gravity Matrix 2013**. See **B9.5.7**.

Youth Gravity Matrix

OFFENCE	Gravity Score	Offence type	AGGRAVATING FACTORS	MITIGATING FACTORS
Possession of sharp pointed blade **for 16 and 17-year-olds**	4	E		
Possession of sharp pointed blade **for 10 to 15-year-olds**	3	E	• Circumstances of possession • Concern caused to member(s) of public	

See *Blackstone's Criminal Practice* B12.138

B10 **Road Traffic Offences**

B10.1 **Road traffic interpretation**

Road Traffic Act 1988

s 3ZA 'Meaning of careless, or inconsiderate, driving'

(1) This section has effect for the purposes of sections 2B and 3 above and section 3A below.

(2) A person is to be regarded as driving without due care and attention if (and only if) the way he drives falls below what would be expected of a competent and careful driver.

(3) In determining for the purposes of subsection (2) above what would be expected of a careful and competent driver in a particular case, regard shall be had not only to the circumstances of which he could be expected to be aware but also to any circumstances shown to have been within the knowledge of the accused.

(4) A person is to be regarded as driving without reasonable consideration for other persons only if those persons are inconvenienced by his driving.

s 11 'Interpretation of sections 4 to 10 [Road Traffic Act 1988]'

(1) The following provisions apply for the interpretation of sections 3A to 10 of this Act.

(2) In those sections—

'drug' includes any intoxicant other than alcohol,

'fail' includes refuse,

'hospital' means an institution which provides medical or surgical treatment for in-patients or out-patients,

'the prescribed limit' means, as the case may require—

(a) 35 microgrammes of alcohol in 100 millilitres of breath,
(b) 80 milligrammes of alcohol in 100 millilitres of blood, or
(c) 107 milligrammes of alcohol in 100 millilitres of urine,

or such other proportion as may be prescribed by regulations.

'registered health care professional' means a person (other than a medical practitioner) who is—

(a) a registered nurse; or
(b) a registered member of a health care profession which is designated for the purposes of this paragraph by an order made by the Secretary of State.

(3) A person does not co-operate with a preliminary test or provide a specimen of breath for analysis unless his co-operation or the specimen—

(a) is sufficient to enable the test or the analysis to be carried out, and
(b) is provided in such a way as to enable the objective of the test or analysis to be satisfactorily achieved.

(4) A person provides a specimen of blood if and only if—
(a) he consents to the taking of such a specimen from him; and
(b) the specimen is taken from him by a medical practitioner or, if it is taken in a police station, either by a medical practitioner or by a registered health care professional.

s 185 'Meaning of "motor vehicle" and other expressions relating to vehicles'

(1) In this Act—

...

'motor car' means a mechanically propelled vehicle, not being a motor cycle or an invalid carriage, which is constructed itself to carry a load or passengers and the weight of which unladen—
(a) if it is constructed solely for the carriage of passengers and their effects, is adapted to carry not more than seven passengers exclusive of the driver and is fitted with tyres of such type as may be specified in regulations made by the Secretary of State, does not exceed 3050 kilograms,
(b) if it is constructed or adapted for use for the conveyance of goods or burden of any description, does not exceed 3050 kilograms, or 3500 kilograms if the vehicle carries a container or containers for holding for the purposes of its propulsion any fuel which is wholly gaseous at 17.5 degrees Celsius under a pressure of 1.013 bar or plant and materials for producing such fuel,
(c) does not exceed 2540 kilograms in a case not falling within sub-paragraph (a) or (b) above,

'motor cycle' means a mechanically propelled vehicle, not being an invalid carriage, with less than four wheels and the weight of which unladen does not exceed 410 kilograms,

'motor vehicle' means, subject to section 20 of the Chronically Sick and Disabled Persons Act 1970 (which makes special provision about invalid carriages, within the meaning of that Act), a mechanically propelled vehicle intended or adapted for use on roads, and

'trailer' means a vehicle drawn by a motor vehicle.

s 192 'General interpretation of Act'

(1) In this Act—

'bridleway' means a way over which the public have the following, but no other, rights of way: a right of way on foot and a right of way on horseback or leading a horse, with or without a right to drive animals of any description along the way,

'carriage of goods' includes the haulage of goods,

'cycle' means a bicycle, a tricycle, or a cycle having four or more wheels, not being in any case a motor vehicle,

'driver', where a separate person acts as a steersman of a motor vehicle, includes (except for the purposes of section 1 of this Act) that person as well as any other person engaged in the driving of the vehicle, and 'drive' is to be interpreted accordingly,

'footpath', in relation to England and Wales, means a way over which the public have a right of way on foot only,

'goods' includes goods or burden of any description,

'goods vehicle' means a motor vehicle constructed or adapted for use for the carriage of goods, or a trailer so constructed or adapted,

'highway authority', in England and Wales, means—

(a) in relation to a road for which he is the highway authority within the meaning of the Highways Act 1980, the Secretary of State, and

(b) in relation to any other road, the council of the county, metropolitan district or London borough, or the Common Council of the City of London, as the case may be;

. . .

'owner', in relation to a vehicle which is the subject of a hiring agreement or hire-purchase agreement, means the person in possession of the vehicle under that agreement,

'prescribed' means prescribed by regulations made by the Secretary of State,

'road'

(a) in relation to England and Wales, means any highway and any other road to which the public has access, and includes bridges over which a road passes, and

. . .

'the Road Traffic Acts' means the Road Traffic Offenders Act 1988, the Road Traffic (Consequential Provisions) Act 1988 (so far as it reproduces the effect of provisions repealed by that Act) and this Act,

'statutory', in relation to any prohibition, restriction, requirement or provision, means contained in, or having effect under, any enactment (including any enactment contained in this Act),

'the Traffic Acts' means the Road Traffic Acts and the Road Traffic Regulation Act 1984,

'traffic sign' has the meaning given by section 64(1) of the Road Traffic Regulation Act 1984,

'tramcar' includes any carriage used on any road by virtue of an order under the Light Railways Act 1896, and

'trolley vehicle' means a mechanically propelled vehicle adapted for use on roads without rails under power transmitted to it from some external source (whether or not there is in addition a source of power on board the vehicle).

- Whether an area is a 'public place' is a matter that will need consideration on a case-by-case basis.

- Where an area is restricted to a special category or class of person, it is unlikely to be a public place (*R v Spence* [1999] EWCA Crim 808).
- However, where a person is in essence a member of the public and the process is simply to subject them to payment, or other conditions imposed by the landowner, then the area will remain capable of forming a public place (*DPP v Vivier* [1991] 4 All ER 18).

B10.2 Causing death by dangerous or careless driving/causing serious injury by dangerous driving

Road Traffic Act 1988

s 1 'Causing death by dangerous driving'

(1) A person who causes the death of another person by driving a mechanically propelled vehicle dangerously on a road or other public place is guilty of an offence.

B10.2.1 Related offences

- Causing death by careless or inconsiderate driving.

Road Traffic Act 1988

s 2B 'Causing death by careless, or inconsiderate, driving'

(1) A person who causes the death of another person by driving a mechanically propelled vehicle on a road or other public place without due care and attention, or without reasonable consideration for other persons using the road or place is guilty of an offence.

- Causing serious injury by dangerous driving.

Road Traffic Act 1988

s 1A 'Causing serious injury by dangerous driving'

(1) A person who causes serious injury to another person by driving a mechanically propelled vehicle dangerously on a road or other public place is guilty of an offence.

(2) In this section 'serious injury' means—

(a) in England and Wales, physical harm which amounts to grievous bodily harm for the purposes of the Offences against the Person Act 1861…

See also:

- Dangerous driving **B10.3**.
- Causing death by driving whilst under the influence **B10.4**.
- Causing death by driving: disqualified drivers **J1.3.1**.
- Causing death while driving when disqualified/no insurance/no licence **B10.5**.
- Wanton/furious driving **B10.6**.

B10.2.2 Breakdown

Offence	Elements of the Offence	Defence
s 1 Road Traffic Act 1988 'Death by dangerous driving'	• Caused the death of another person • By driving a mechanically propelled vehicle • Dangerously • On a road/public place	• Negative any element of the offence • General Defences **C**
s 2B Road Traffic Act 1988 'Causing death by careless, inconsiderate driving'	• Caused the death of another person • By driving a mechanically propelled vehicle • On a road/public place • Without due care and attention/ reasonable consideration for others	• Negative any element of the offence • General Defences **C**
s 1A Road Traffic Act 1988 'Causing serious injury by dangerous driving'	• Caused the serious injury of another person • By driving a mechanically propelled vehicle • Dangerously • On a road/public place	• Negative any element of the offence • General Defences **C**

B10.2.3 Interpretation

- See road traffic interpretations **B10.1**.

Road Traffic Act 1988

s 2A 'Meaning of dangerous driving'

(1) For the purposes of sections 1, 1A and 2 above a person is to be regarded as driving dangerously if (and, subject to subsection (2) below, only if)—

(a) the way he drives falls far below what would be expected of a competent and careful driver, and

(b) it would be obvious to a competent and careful driver that driving in that way would be dangerous.

(2) A person is also to be regarded as driving dangerously for the purposes of sections 1, 1A and 2 above if it would be obvious to a competent and careful driver that driving the vehicle in its current state would be dangerous.

(3) In subsections (1) and (2) above 'dangerous' refers to danger either of injury to any person or of serious damage to property; and in determining for the purposes of those subsections what would be expected of, or obvious to, a competent and careful driver in a particular case, regard shall be had not only to the circumstances of which he could be expected to be aware but also to any circumstances shown to have been within the knowledge of the accused.

(4) In determining for the purposes of subsection (2) above the state of a vehicle, regard may be had to anything attached to or carried on or in it and to the manner in which it is attached or carried.

B10.2.4 Defences

- See General Defences C.

B10.2.5 Key point

- *R v Hennigan* [1971] RTR 305—there is nothing in the statute to indicate that the driving must be a substantial cause; it must simply be more than the *de minimis* cause.

B10.2.6 Sentencing

s 1 Road Traffic Act 1988

Indictable only: 14 years' imprisonment, obligatory disqualification until extended test passed, obligatory endorsement of 3–11 penalty points.

s 2B Road Traffic Act 1988

Summary: 6 months' imprisonment and/or a fine Indictment: 5 years' imprisonment and/or a fine. Obligatory disqualification and obligatory endorsement with 3 to 11 penalty points

s 1B Road Traffic Act 1988

Summary: 12 months' imprisonment/a fine/both

Indictment: 5 years' imprisonment/a fine/both

Youth Gravity Matrix

OFFENCE	Gravity Score	Offence type	AGGRAVATING FACTORS	MITIGATING FACTORS
Causing death by dangerous driving (s 1 Road Traffic Act 1988)	4	I	Always refer to the CPS	

B10.3 Dangerous/careless driving

Road Traffic Act 1988

s 2 'Dangerous driving'

(1) A person who drives a mechanically propelled vehicle dangerously on a road or other public place is guilty of an offence.

B10.3.1 Related offences

- Driving without due care and attention.

Road Traffic Act 1988

s 3 'Careless and inconsiderate driving'

(1) If a person drives a mechanically propelled vehicle on a road or other public place without due care and attention, or without reasonable consideration for other persons using the road or place, he is guilty of an offence.

B10.3.2 Breakdown

Offence	Elements of the Offence	Defence
s 2 Road Traffic Act 1988 'Dangerous driving'	• Being the driver of a mechanically propelled vehicle • On a road/public place • Drove dangerously	• Negative any element of the offence • General Defences **C**
s 3 Road Traffic Act 1988 'Driving without due care and attention'	• Being the driver of a mechanically propelled vehicle • On a road/public place • Without due care and attention/reasonable consideration for others	• Negative any element of the offence • General Defences **C**

B10.3.3 Interpretation

Road Traffic Act 1988

s 2A 'Meaning of dangerous driving'

(1) For the purposes of sections 1, 1A and 2 above a person is to be regarded as driving dangerously if (and, subject to subsection (2) below, only if)—

(a) the way he drives falls far below what would be expected of a competent and careful driver, and

(b) it would be obvious to a competent and careful driver that driving in that way would be dangerous.

(2) A person is also to be regarded as driving dangerously for the purposes of sections 1, 1A and 2 above if it would be obvious to a competent and careful driver that driving the vehicle in its current state would be dangerous.

(3) In subsections (1) and (2) above 'dangerous' refers to danger either of injury to any person or of serious damage to property; and in determining for the purposes of those subsections what would be expected of, or obvious to, a competent and careful driver in a particular case, regard shall be had not only to the circumstances of which he could be expected to be aware but also to any circumstances shown to have been within the knowledge of the accused.

(4) In determining for the purposes of subsection (2) above the state of a vehicle, regard may be had to anything attached to or carried on or in it and to the manner in which it is attached or carried.

s 3ZA 'Meaning of careless, or inconsiderate, driving'

(1) This section has effect for the purposes of sections 2B and 3 above and section 3A below.

(2) A person is to be regarded as driving without due care and attention if (and only if) the way he drives falls below what would be expected of a competent and careful driver.

(3) In determining for the purposes of subsection (2) above what would be expected of a careful and competent driver in a particular case, regard shall be had not only to the circumstances of which he could be expected to be aware but also to any circumstances shown to have been within the knowledge of the accused.

(4) A person is to be regarded as driving without reasonable consideration for other persons only if those persons are inconvenienced by his driving.

B10.3.4 Defences

- See General Defences C.

B10.3.5 Key point

- Whether driving is dangerous is an objective test and any special skill of the driver will not be a consideration (*R v Bannister* [2009] EWCA Crim 1571).

B10.3.6 Sentencing

s 2 Road Traffic Act 1988

Summary: 6 months' imprisonment and/or a fine.

Indictment: 2 years' imprisonment and/or a fine.

Obligatory disqualification for 12 months

Must endorse and disqualify for a minimum period of 12 months; must order extended re-test; must disqualify for at least 2 years if offender has had two or more disqualifications for periods of 56 days or more in preceding 3 years.

s 3 Road Traffic Act 1988

Summary only: fine.

Must endorse and may disqualify. If no disqualification, impose 3–9 points

Youth Gravity Matrix

OFFENCE	Gravity Score	Offence type	AGGRAVATING FACTORS	MITIGATING FACTORS
Dangerous driving (s 2 Road Traffic Act 1988)	4	S	• Avoiding detection or apprehension • Competitive driving, racing, showing off • Disregard of warnings eg, from passengers or others in vicinity • Evidence alcohol/ drugs • Excessive speed • Prolonged, persistent, deliberate bad driving • Serious risk	• Continuing for only a short period • Contributed to by action of another
Careless driving (s 3 Road Traffic Act 1988) Inconsiderate driving (s 3 Road Traffic Act 1988)	3 3	S S	• Major error of judgement • Excessive speed • Driving with disregard for safety relating to road, weather, traffic conditions • Re-test may be appropriate—s 36 Road Traffic Offenders Act 1988 • Disability—s 22 RTOA 1988 • Deliberate act of selfishness, impatience or aggressiveness causing inconvenience	• Minor error of judgement • Defect in road surface/signing, etc • Momentary lapse • Adverse weather conditions • Both (or more) drivers may have been at fault

B10.4 Causing death by careless driving when under the influence

Road Traffic Act 1988

s 3A 'Causing death by careless driving when under influence of drink or drugs'

(1) If a person causes the death of another person by driving a mechanically propelled vehicle on a road or other public place without due care and attention, or without reasonable consideration for other persons using the road or place, and—
  (a) he is, at the time when he is driving, unfit to drive through drink or drugs, or
  (b) he has consumed so much alcohol that the proportion of it in his breath, blood or urine at that time exceeds the prescribed limit, or
  (c) he is, within 18 hours after that time, required to provide a specimen in pursuance of section 7 of this Act, but without reasonable excuse fails to provide it, or
  (d) he is required by a constable to give his permission for a laboratory test of a specimen of blood taken from him under section 7A of this Act, but without reasonable excuse fails to do so,

he is guilty of an offence.

(2) For the purposes of this section a person shall be taken to be unfit to drive at any time when his ability to drive properly is impaired.

(3) Subsection (1)(b), (c) and (d) above shall not apply in relation to a person driving a mechanically propelled vehicle other than a motor vehicle.

B10.4.1 Related offences

- Driving without due care and attention **B10.3.1**.
- Driving/attempting to drive whilst unfit through drink/drugs **B10.7/B10.8**.

B10.4.2 Breakdown

Offence	Elements of the Offence	Defence
s 3A Road Traffic Act 1988 'Causing death by dangerous driving when under the influence of drink or drugs'	• On a road/public place • Causing the death of another person • By driving a motor vehicle • Without due care/reasonable consideration for other road users; and • At the time of driving was unfit through drink/drugs; or • Was over the prescribed limit; or	• Negative any element of the offence • General Defences **C**

Offence	Elements of the Offence	Defence
	• Within 18 hours of the incident failed to provide a specimen for analysis; or • On being required, failed to give permission to take a specimen of blood	

B10.4.3 Interpretation

- See road traffic interpretations **B10.1**.

B10.4.4 Defences

- See General Defences C.

B10.4.5 Key point

- By the wording of the section it is the careless driving that must be the cause of the death. It is not necessary to prove that the influence of drink or drugs was the cause of the careless driving.

B10.4.6 Sentencing

s 3A Road Traffic Act 1988

Indictable only: 14 years' imprisonment. Must disqualify and must endorse 3–11 penalty points

Youth Gravity Matrix

OFFENCE	Gravity Score	Offence type	AGGRAVATING FACTORS	MITIGATING FACTORS
Causing death by careless driving under the influence of drink or drugs (s 3 Road Traffic Act 1988)	4	I	Always refer to the CPS	

B10.5 Causing death while driving when no insurance/no licence

For offences of causing death when disqualified and causing serious injury when disqualified see **J1.3**.

Road Traffic Act 1988

s 3ZB 'Causing death by driving: unlicensed or uninsured drivers'

A person is guilty of an offence under this section if he causes the death of another person by driving a motor vehicle on a road and, at the time when he is driving, the circumstances are such that he is committing an offence under—

(a) section 87(1) of this Act (driving otherwise than in accordance with a licence),

or

(c) section 143 of this Act (using motor vehicle while uninsured or unsecured against third party risks).

B10.5.1 Related offences

- Driving without insurance **B10.10**.
- Driving not in accordance with a licence **B10.9**.

B10.5.2 Breakdown

Offence	Elements of the Offence	Defence
s 3ZB Road Traffic Act 1988 'Causing death by driving: unlicensed, or uninsured drivers'	• Caused the death of another person • By driving a motor vehicle • Without a licence/without insurance	• Negative any element of the offence • *R v Hughes* **B10.5.4** • General Defences **C**

B10.5.3 Interpretation

- See road traffic interpretations **B10.1**.

B10.5.4 Defences

- See General Defences **C**.
- Section 3ZB requires at least some act or omission in the control of the car, which involves some element of fault, whether amounting to careless/inconsiderate driving or not, and which contributes in some more than minimal way to the death. It is not necessary that such act or omission be the principal cause of the death (*R v Hughes* [2013] UKSC 56).

B10.5.5 Key point

- This offence is committed when a fatality occurs and the driver is committing one of the specified offences.

B10.5.6 Sentencing

s 3ZB Road Traffic Act 1988

Summary: 12 months' imprisonment or a fine or both

Indictment: 2 years' imprisonment and/or fine. Obligatory disqualification and obligatory endorsement

B10.6 Wanton or furious driving

Offences Against the Person Act 1861

s 35 'Drivers of carriages injuring persons by furious driving'

(1) Whosoever, having the charge of any carriage or vehicle, shall by wanton or furious driving or racing, or other wilful misconduct, or by wilful neglect, do or cause to be done any bodily harm to any person whatsoever, shall be guilty of an offence.

B10.6.1 Breakdown

Offence	Elements of the Offence	Defence
s 35 Offences Against the Person Act 1861 'Wanton of furious driving'	• In charge of a carriage/vehicle • By wanton/furious driving/racing or other wilful misconduct/neglect • Did/caused bodily harm to be done to another	• Negative any element of the offence • General Defences **C**

B10.6.2 Defences

- See General Defences C.

B10.6.3 Sentencing

s 35 Offences Against the Person Act 1861

Indictable only: 2 years' imprisonment. If a mechanically propelled vehicle—discretionary disqualification and obligatory endorsement of 3–9 penalty points.

B10.7 Driving/attempting to drive whilst unfit through drink/drugs and drive/in charge of a motor vehicle with alcohol concentration above the prescribed limit

Road Traffic Act 1988

s 4 'Driving, or being in charge, when under influence of drink or drugs'

(1) A person who, when driving or attempting to drive a mechanically propelled vehicle on a road or other public place, is unfit to drive through drink or drugs is guilty of an offence

(2) Without prejudice to subsection (1) above, a person, who, when in charge of a mechanically propelled vehicle which is on a road or other public place, is unfit to drive through drink or drugs is guilty of an offence.

B10.7.1 Related offences

Road Traffic Act 1988

s 5 'Driving or being in charge of a motor vehicle with alcohol concentration above prescribed limit'

(1) If a person—

(a) drives or attempts to drive a motor vehicle on a road or other public place, or

(b) is in charge of a motor vehicle on a road or other public place,

after consuming so much alcohol that the proportion of it in his breath, blood or urine exceeds the prescribed limit he is guilty of an offence.

B10.7.2 Breakdown

Offence	Elements of the Offence	Defence
s 4(1) Road Traffic Act 1988 'Drive while unfit'	• Drove or attempted to drive • A mechanically propelled vehicle • On a road or other public place • When unfit to drive though drink or drugs	• Negative any element of the offence • s 4 Road Traffic Act 1988 **B10.7.4** • General Defences **C**
s 4(2) Road Traffic Act 1988 'In charge while unfit'	• In charge of a mechanically propelled vehicle • On a road or other public place • Being unfit to drive through drink/drugs	• Negative any element of the offence • s 4 Road Traffic Act 1988 **B10.7.4** • General Defences **C**
s 5(1) Road Traffic Act 1988 'Drive with a concentration of alcohol above the prescribed limit'	• Drove or attempted to drive • A motor vehicle • On a road or other public place • After consuming so much alcohol that the proportion of it in breath/blood/urine exceeds the prescribed limit	• Negative any element of the offence • s 5 Road Traffic Act 1988 **B10.7.4** • General Defences **C**

Offence	Elements of the Offence	Defence
s 5(2) Road Traffic Act 1988 'In charge with a concentration of alcohol above the prescribed limit'	• In charge of • A motor vehicle • On a road or other public place • After consuming so much alcohol that the proportion of it in breath/blood/urine exceeds the prescribed limit	• Negative any element of the offence • s 5 Road Traffic Act 1988 **B10.7.4** • General Defences **C**

B10.7.3 Interpretation

- See road traffic interpretations **B10.1**.

B10.7.4 Defences

Road Traffic Act 1988

s 4 'Driving, or being in charge, when under influence of drink or drugs'

(3) For the purposes of section (2) above, a person shall be deemed not to have been in charge of a mechanically propelled vehicle if he proves that at the material time the circumstances were such that there was no likelihood of his driving it so long as he remained unfit to drive through drink or drugs.

s 5 'Driving or being in charge of a motor vehicle with alcohol concentration above prescribed limit'

(2) It is a defence for a person charged with an offence under subsection (1)(b) above to prove that at the time he is alleged to have committed the offence the circumstances were such that there was no likelihood of his driving the vehicle whilst the proportion of alcohol in his breath, blood or urine remained likely to exceed the prescribed limit.

(3) The court may, in determining whether there was such a likelihood as is mentioned in subsection (2) above, disregard any injury to him and any damage to the vehicle.

- See General Defences **C**.

B10.7.5 Sentencing

s 4/s 5 Road Traffic Act 1988

Drive/attempt to drive:

Summary only: 6 months' imprisonment and/or a fine. Must endorse and disqualify for at least 12 months. Must disqualify for at least 2 years if offender has had two or more disqualifications for periods of 56 days or more in preceding years.

In charge:

Summary only: 3 months' imprisonment and/or level 4 fine. Must endorse and may disqualify. If no disqualification, impose 10 points.

Drive above the prescribed limit:

Summary only: 6 months' imprisonment/a fine. Must disqualify, must endorse with 3–10 penalty points.

In charge above the prescribed limit:

Summary only: 3 months' imprisonment/a fine. Discretion to disqualify, must endorse with up to 10 penalty points.

Youth Gravity Matrix

OFFENCE	Gravity Score	Offence type	AGGRAVATING FACTORS	MITIGATING FACTORS
Excess alcohol/driving when unfit through drink/drugs	4	S		
Drunk in charge	4	S		

See *Blackstone's Criminal Practice* C3.35

B10.8 Driving or being in charge of a motor vehicle with concentration of specified controlled drug above specified limit

Road Traffic Act 1988

s 5A 'Driving or being in charge of a motor vehicle with concentration of specified controlled drug above specified limit'

(1) This section applies where a person ('D')—
  (a) drives or attempts to drive a motor vehicle on a road or other public place, or
  (b) is in charge of a motor vehicle on a road or other public place, and there is in D's body a specified controlled drug.

(2) D is guilty of an offence if the proportion of the drug in D's blood or urine exceeds the specified limit for that drug.

B10.8.1 Related offences

- Driving, or being in charge, when under influence of drink or drugs **B10.7**.

B10.8.2 Breakdown

Offence	Elements of the Offence	Defence
s 5A(1)(a) Road Traffic Act 1988 'Driving or attempting to drive with concentration of specified controlled drug above specified limit'	• Drive or attempt to drive • A motor vehicle • On a road or public place • With a proportion of a drug in blood or urine • Which exceeds the prescribed limit	• Negative any element of the offence • General Defences **C** • 'Medical Defence' **B10.8.3**
s 5A(1)(b) Road Traffic Act 1988 'Being in charge of a motor vehicle with concentration of specified controlled drug above specified limit'	• Be in charge of a motor vehicle • On a road or public place • With a proportion of a drug in blood or urine • Which exceeds the prescribed limit	• Negative any element of the offence • General Defences **C** • 'Medical Defence' **B10.8.3**

B10.8.3 Defences

Road Traffic Act 1988

s 5A 'Driving or being in charge of a motor vehicle with concentration of specified controlled drug above specified limit'

(3) It is a defence for a person ('D') charged with an offence under this section to show that—
   (a) the specified controlled drug had been prescribed or supplied to D for medical or dental purposes,
   (b) D took the drug in accordance with any directions given by the person by whom the drug was prescribed or supplied, and with any accompanying instructions (so far as consistent with any such directions) given by the manufacturer or distributor of the drug, and
   (c) D's possession of the drug immediately before taking it was not unlawful under section 5(1) of the Misuse of Drugs Act 1971 (restriction of possession of controlled drugs) because of an exemption in regulations made under section 7 of that Act (authorisation of activities otherwise unlawful under foregoing provisions).

(4) The defence in subsection (3) is not available if D's actions were—
   (a) contrary to any advice, given by the person by whom the drug was prescribed or supplied, about the amount of time that should elapse between taking the drug and driving a motor vehicle, or

(b) contrary to any accompanying instructions about that matter (so far as consistent with any such advice) given by the manufacturer or distributor of the drug.

(5) If evidence is adduced that is sufficient to raise an issue with respect to the defence in subsection (3), the court must assume that the defence is satisfied unless the prosecution proves beyond reasonable doubt that it is not.

(6) It is a defence for a person ('D') charged with an offence by virtue of subsection (1)(b) to prove that at the time D is alleged to have committed the offence the circumstances were such that there was no likelihood of D driving the vehicle whilst the proportion of the specified controlled drug in D's blood or urine remained likely to exceed the specified limit for that drug.

(7) The court may, in determining whether there was such a likelihood, disregard any injury to D and any damage to the vehicle.

- See General Defences C.

B10.8.4 Interpretation

Road Traffic Act 1988

s 5A 'Driving or being in charge of a motor vehicle with concentration of specified controlled drug above specified limit'

(8) In this section, and in sections 3A, 6C(1), 6D and 10, 'specified' means specified in regulations made—

(a) by the Secretary of State, in relation to driving or attempting to drive, or being in charge of a vehicle, in England and Wales;

(b) by the Scottish Ministers, in relation to driving or attempting to drive, or being in charge of a vehicle, in Scotland.

(9) A limit specified under subsection (2) may be zero.

Controlled drug	Limit (microgrammes per litre of blood)
Benzoylecgonine	50
Clonazepam	50
Cocaine	10
Delta-9-Tetrahydrocannabinol (cannabis)	2
Diazepam	550
Flunitrazepam	300
Ketamine	20
Lorazepam	100
Lysergic Acid Diethylamide	1

Methadone	500
Methylamphetamine	10
Methylenedioxymethamphetamine	10
6-Monoacetylmorphine	5
Morphine	80
Oxazepam	300
Temazepam	1000
Amphetamine (for offences on or after 14 April 2015)	250

B10.8.5 Sentencing

s 5A(1)(a) and (2) 'Driving or attempting to drive with concentration of specified controlled drug above specified limit'

Summary only: 6 months and /or a fine

Must disqualify/must endorse/3–11 penalty points

s 5A(1)(b) and (2) 'Being in charge of a motor vehicle with concentration of specified controlled drug above specified limit'

Summary only: 6 months/a fine

May disqualify/must endorse/10 points

B10.9 Driving whilst disqualified

Road Traffic Act 1988

s 103 'Obtaining licence, or driving, while disqualified'

(1) A person is guilty of an offence, if, while disqualified for holding or obtaining a licence, he—
- (a) obtains a licence, or
- (b) drives a motor vehicle on a road.

B10.9.1 Breakdown

Offence	Elements of the Offence	Defence
s 103(1)(a) Road Traffic Act 1988 'Driving whilst disqualified'	• While disqualified for holding/obtaining a licence • Drove a motor vehicle on a road	• Negative any element of the offence • General Defences **C**

Offence	Elements of the Offence	Defence
s 103(1)(b) Road Traffic Act 1988 'Obtain a licence whilst disqualified'	• While disqualified for holding/obtaining a licence • Obtained a licence	• Negative any element of the offence • General Defences **C**

B10.9.2 Interpretation

Road Traffic Act 1988

s 108 'Interpretation'

(1) ...'disqualified' means disqualified for holding or obtaining a licence (or, in cases where the disqualification is limited, a licence to drive motor vehicles of the class to which the disqualification relates), and 'disqualification' is to be interpreted accordingly,

...

'licence' (except where the context otherwise requires) means a licence to drive a motor vehicle granted under this Part of this Act...

B10.9.3 Defences

- See General Defences C.

B10.9.4 Key point

- Strict proof that the person disqualified by the court is the offender will be required. This will normally arise from (a) admission, (b) fingerprints, (c) evidence of identity from someone in court when the disqualification was made (*R v Derwentside Justices, ex p Heavside* [1996] RTR 384).

B10.9.5 Sentencing

s 103 Road Traffic Act 1988

Summary only: 6 months' imprisonment and/or a fine. Must endorse and may disqualify. If no disqualification, impose 6 points.

Youth Gravity Matrix

OFFENCE	Gravity Score	Offence type	AGGRAVATING FACTORS	MITIGATING FACTORS
Driving whilst disqualified	4	S		• Driving whilst disqualified

B10.10 Driving otherwise than in accordance with a licence

Road Traffic Act 1988

s 87 'Drivers of motor vehicles to have driving licences'

(1) It is an offence for a person to drive on a road a motor vehicle of any class otherwise than in accordance with a licence authorising him to drive a motor vehicle of that class.

(2) It is an offence for a person to cause or permit another person to drive on a road a motor vehicle of any class otherwise that in accordance with a licence authorising that other person to drive a motor vehicle of that class.

B10.10.1 Breakdown

Offence	Elements of the Offence	Defence
s 87 Road Traffic Act 1988 'Drive otherwise than in accord-ance with a licence'	• Drove a motor vehicle • On a road • Otherwise than in accordance with a licence • Authorising driving of that class of vehicle; or • Caused/permitted • Another person to commit this offence	• Negative any element of the offence • General Defences **C**

B10.10.2 Defences

- See General Defences C.

B10.10.3 Sentencing

s 87(1) Road Traffic Act 1988

Summary only: fine not exceeding level 3 on the standard scale. Must endorse and may disqualify—3–6 penalty points.

s 87(2) Road Traffic Act 1988

Summary only: fine not exceeding level 3 on the standard scale. Must endorse—3 penalty points.

Youth Gravity Matrix

OFFENCE	Gravity Score	Offence type	AGGRAVATING FACTORS	MITIGATING FACTORS
Driving other than in accordance with driving licence, ie no 'L' plates	3	S		L plate fell off
'L' driver unaccompanied	3			
'L' driver carrying passengers	3			
No driving licence	3			

B10.11 **Driving without insurance**

Road Traffic Act 1988

s 143 'Users of motor vehicles to be insured or secured against third-party risks'

(1) Subject to the provisions of this act—

(a) A person must not use a motor vehicle on a road [or other public place] unless there is in force in relation to the use of the vehicle by that person such a policy of insurance or such a security in respect of third party risks as complies with the requirements of this Part of this act,

(b) A person must not cause or permit any person to use a motor vehicle on a road [or other public place] unless there is in force in relation to the use of that vehicle by that other person such a policy of insurance or such a security in respect of third party risks as complies with the requirements of this Part of this Act.

(2) If a person acts in contravention of subsection (1) above he is guilty of an offence.

B10.11.1 Breakdown

Offence	Elements of the Offence	Defence
s 143 Road Traffic Act 1988 'Users of motor vehicles to be insured or secured against third-party risks'	• Used/caused/permitted another to use • Motor vehicle • On a road/public place • Without insurance/security for third party risks	• Negative any element of the offence • s 143 Road Traffic Act 1988 **B10.11.3** • General Defences **C**

B10.11.2 Interpretation

- *Newbury v Davis* [1974] RTR 367—a person permits use when he allows or authorizes use. If A gives B permission to use his vehicle, on the condition that B insures it and then B fails to insure it, B does not have permission to use the vehicle and A does not commit an offence.

B10.11.3 Defences

Road Traffic Act 1988

s 143 'Users of motor vehicles to be insured or secured against third-party risks'

(3) A person charged with using a motor vehicle in contravention of this section shall not be convicted if he proves—
  (a) That the vehicle did not belong to him and was not in his possession under a contract of hiring or of loan,
  (b) That he was using the vehicle in the course of his employment, and
  (c) That he neither knew nor had reason to believe that there was not in force in relation to the vehicle such a policy of insurance or security as is mentioned in subsection (1) above.

- See General Defences C.

B10.11.4 Key point

- It is for the defendant to show that he was insured, once it is established that a motor vehicle was used on a road or other public place (*DPP v Hay* [2005] EWHC 1395 (Admin), QBD).

B10.11.5 Sentencing

s 143 Road Traffic Act 1988

Summary only: a fine Must endorse and may disqualify—6–8 penalty points.

Youth Gravity Matrix

OFFENCE	Gravity Score	Offence type	AGGRAVATING FACTORS	MITIGATING FACTORS
No insurance	3	S	• Deliberate offence • Offence involving TWOC or other offence giving rise to danger	• Genuine mistake/ technicality • Duty to provide insurance resting with another, eg parent, company, hirer, etc

B10.12 **Vehicle interference**

Criminal Attempts Act 1981

s 9 'Interference with vehicles'

(1) A person is guilty of the offence of vehicle interference if he interferes with a motor vehicle or trailer or with anything carried in or on a motor vehicle or trailer or with anything carried in or on a motor vehicle or trailer with the intention that an offence specified in subsection (2) below shall be committed by himself or some other person.

(2) The offences mentioned in subsection (1) above are—
  (a) Theft of the motor vehicle or part of it;
  (b) Theft of anything carried in or on the motor vehicle or trailer; and
  (c) An offence under section 12(1) of the Theft Act 1968 (taking a conveyance)

and if it is shown that a person accused of an offence under this section intended that one of those offences should be committed, it is immaterial that it cannot be shown which it was.

B10.12.1 Related offences

- Tampering with a motor vehicle.

Road Traffic Act 1988

s 25 'Tampering with motor vehicles'

(1) If while a motor is on a road or on a parking place provided by a local authority, a person—
  (a) Gets on to the vehicle, or
  (b) Tampers with the brake or other part of its mechanism

without lawful authority or reasonable cause he is guilty of an offence.

B10.12.2 Breakdown

Offence	Elements of the Offence	Defence
s 9 Criminal Attempts Act 1981 'Interference with vehicles'	• Interfere with • A motor vehicle/trailer or part of anything carried in or on it • With intent that an offence of theft or taking and driving away without consent • Should be committed	• Negative any element of the offence • General Defences **C**

Offence	Elements of the Offence	Defence
s 25 Road Traffic Act 1988 'Tampering with a motor vehicle'	• Without lawful authority or reasonable excuse • Go on to or tampered with • The brakes or other mechanism of a motor vehicle • On a road or parking place provided by a local authority	• Negative any element of the offence • s 25 Road Traffic Act 1988 **B10.12.3** • General Defences **C**

B10.12.3 Defences

Road Traffic Act 1988

s 25 'Tampering with motor vehicles'

(1) If while a motor is on a road or on a parking place provided by a local authority, a person—
(a) Gets on to the vehicle, or
(b) Tampers with the brake or other part of its mechanism
without lawful authority or reasonable cause he is guilty of an offence.

- See General Defences C.

B10.12.4 Sentencing

s 9 Criminal Attempts Act 1981

Summary only: 3 months' imprisonment or a fine not exceeding level 4 on the standard scale, or both

s 25 Road Traffic Act 1988

Summary only: fine, not exceeding level 3 on the standard scale

B10.13 Taking a conveyance without owner's consent/aggravated vehicle taking/allowing to be carried

Theft Act 1968

s 12 'Taking motor vehicle or other conveyance without authority'

(1) Subject to sections (5) and (6) below, a person shall be guilty of an offence if, without having the consent of the owner or other lawful authority, he

takes any conveyance for his own or another's use or, knowing that any conveyance has been taken without such authority, drives it or allows himself to be carried in or on it.

B10.13.1 Related offences

- Aggravated vehicle taking.

Theft Act 1968

s 12A 'Aggravated vehicle taking'

(1) Subject to subsection 12A (3) a person is guilty of aggravated vehicle taking if—
  (a) he commits an offence under section 12(1) (taking a conveyance without consent (in this section referred to as the 'basic offence')) in relation to a mechanically propelled vehicle, and
  (b) it is proved that, at any time after the vehicle was unlawfully taken (whether by him or another) and before it was recovered, the vehicle was driven or injury or damage was caused, in one or more of the circumstances set out in paragraphs (a) to (d) of subsection (2) below.
(2) the circumstances referred to in subsection 1(b) are—
  (a) that the vehicle was driven dangerously on a road or other public place;
  (b) that, owing to the driving of the vehicle, an accident occurred by which injury was caused to a person;
  (c) that, owing to the driving of the vehicle, an accident occurred by which damage was caused to any property, other than the vehicle;
  (d) that damage was caused to the vehicle.

B10.13.2 Breakdown

Offence	Elements of the Offence	Defence
s 12 Theft Act 1968 'Taking motor vehicle or other conveyance without authority'	• Without consent • Of the owner/other lawful authority • Took a conveyance • For own/another's use; or • Knowing that any conveyance has been taken • Without such authority • Allows himself to be carried in or on it	• Negative any element of the offence • s 12(6) Theft Act 1968 **B10.13.4** • General Defences **C**

Offence	Elements of the Offence	Defence
s 12A Theft Act 1968 'Aggravated vehicle taking'	• Without consent • Of the owner/other lawful authority • Took a mechanically propelled vehicle • For own/another's use; and • After it was taken; and • Before it was recovered • The vehicle was driven dangerously on a road/ public place; or • An accident occurred which caused injury to a person/ damage to property/damage to a vehicle	• Negative any element of the offence • s 12A(3) Theft Act 1968 **B10.13.4** • General Defences **C**

B10.13.3 Interpretation

Theft Act 1968

s 12 'Taking motor vehicle or other conveyance without authority'

(7) For the purposes of this section—
- (a) 'conveyance' means any conveyance constructed or adapted for carriage of a person or persons whether by land, water or air, except that it does not include a conveyance constructed or adapted for use only under control of a person not carried in or on it, and 'drive' shall be construed accordingly; and
- (b) 'owner', in relation to a conveyance which is the subject of a hiring agreement or hire-purchase agreement, means the person in possession of the conveyance under that agreement.

s 12A 'Aggravated vehicle taking'

(7) For the purposes of this section a vehicle is driven dangerously if—
- (a) it is driven in a way which falls far below what would be expected of a competent and careful driver; and
- (b) it would be obvious to a competent and careful driver that driving the vehicle in that way would be dangerous.

(8) For the purposes of this section a vehicle is recovered when it is restored to its owner or to other lawful possession or custody; and in this subsection 'owner' has the same meaning as in section 12 above.

B10.13.4 Defences

- Taking a conveyance without owner's consent.

Theft Act 1968

s 12 'Taking motor vehicle or other conveyance without authority'

(6) A person does not commit this offence under this section by anything done in the belief that he has lawful authority to do it or that he would have the owner's consent if the owner knew of his doing it and the circumstances of it.

- Aggravated vehicle taking.

Theft Act 1968

s 12A 'Aggravated vehicle taking'

(3) A person is not guilty of an offence under this section if he proves that, as regards any such proven driving, injury or damage as is referred to in subsection (1)(b) (aggravating factors) above, either—
   (a) The driving, accident or damage referred to above occurred before he committed the basic offence; or
   (b) He was neither in, nor on, nor in the immediate vicinity of, the vehicle when that driving, accident or damage occurred.

- See General Defences C.

B10.13.5 Key point

- In order to be convicted of an offence under s 12(1), it must be shown that there was some movement of the vehicle (*R v Bogacki* (1973) 57 Cr App R 593).

B10.13.6 Sentencing

s 12 Theft 1968

Summary only: 6 months' imprisonment/ a fine

s 12A Theft Act 1968

Summary: 6 months' imprisonment/ a fine

Indictment:

Where injury results—2 years' imprisonment

Where death results—14 years' imprisonment

Youth Gravity Matrix

OFFENCE	Gravity Score	Offence type	AGGRAVATING FACTORS	MITIGATING FACTORS
Taking vehicle without consent	3	S	• Premeditated • Group action • Organized team • Commercial basis (stole to order) • Causes damage to vehicle or other property • Excessive speed to avoid apprehension • Evidence of drugs/ alcohol	• Taking from family member • The taking is a technical offence • Employee using outside working hours • Keys left in vehicle
Aggravated vehicle taking where owing to the driving of the vehicle, an accident occurred causing injury to any person	4	E		• The taking is a technical offence • Injured is member of drivers family
Aggravated vehicle taking where: (a) Damage to any property other than the vehicle (b) Damage was caused to the vehicle (c) The vehicle was driven dangerously on a road or other public place (s 1 Aggravated Vehicle Taking Act 1992)	4	E or S But all types are included in the Charging Scheme	• Competitive driving or racing • Drives furiously/ recklessly to avoid apprehension/ detection • Excessive speed • Evidence of drugs/ alcohol • Disregards warnings from passengers or others • Premeditated • Group action • Evidence of alcohol or drugs • Serious risk	• Minor damage • The taking is a technical offence • Damage to own family property

TO

B11 **Immigration Offences**

B11.1 **Illegal entry**

Immigration Act 1971

s 24 'Illegal entry and similar offences'

(1) It is an offence—

(a) if contrary to this Act he knowingly enters the United Kingdom in breach of a deportation order or without leave;

(b) if, having only a limited leave to enter or remain in the United Kingdom, he knowingly either—

(i) remains beyond the time limited by the leave; or

(ii) fails to observe a condition of the leave;

(c) if, having lawfully entered the United Kingdom without leave by virtue of section 8(1) above, he remains without leave beyond the time allowed by section 8(1);

(d) if, without reasonable excuse, he fails to comply with any requirement imposed on him under Schedule 2 to this Act to report to a medical officer of health, or to attend, or submit to a test or examination, as required by such an officer;

(e) if, without reasonable excuse, he fails to observe any restriction imposed on him under Schedule 2 or 3 to this Act as to residence, as to his employment or occupation or as to reporting to the police, to an immigration officer or to the Secretary of State;

(f) if he disembarks in the United Kingdom from a ship or aircraft after being placed on board under Schedule 2 or 3 to this Act with a view to his removal from the United Kingdom;

(g) if he embarks in contravention of a restriction imposed by or under an Order in Council under section 3(7) of this Act.

(1A) A person commits an offence under subsection (1)(b)(i) above on the day when he first knows that the time limited by his leave has expired and continues to commit it throughout any period during which he is in the United Kingdom thereafter; but a person shall not be prosecuted under that provision more than once in respect of the same limited leave.

...

(3) The extended time limit for prosecutions which is provided for by section 28 below shall apply to offences under subsection (1)(a) and (c) above.

(4) In proceedings for an offence against subsection (1)(a) above of entering the United Kingdom without leave—

(a) any stamp purporting to have been imprinted on a passport or other travel document by an immigration officer on a particular date for the purpose of giving leave shall be presumed to have been duly so imprinted, unless the contrary is proved;

(b) proof that a person had leave to enter the United Kingdom shall lie on the defence if, but only if, he is shown to have entered within six months before the date when the proceedings were commenced.

B11.1.1 Related offences

- Obtaining unlawful entry by deception.

Immigration Act 1971

s 24A 'Deception'

(1) A person who is not a British citizen is guilty of an offence if, by means which include deception by him—
  (a) he obtains or seeks to obtain leave to enter or remain in the United Kingdom; or
  (b) he secures or seeks to secure the avoidance, postponement or revocation of enforcement action against him.

(2) *'Enforcement action'*, in relation to a person, means—
  (a) the giving of directions for his removal from the United Kingdom ('directions') under Schedule 2 to this Act or section 10 of the Immigration and Asylum Act 1999;
  (b) the making of a deportation order against him under section 5 of this Act; or
  (c) his removal from the United Kingdom in consequence of directions or a deportation order.

- Assisting unlawful entry—sections 25, 25A, and 25B.

Immigration Act 1971

s 25 'Assisting unlawful immigration to member State'

(1) A person commits an offence if he—
  (a) does an act which facilitates the commission of a breach of immigration law by an individual who is not a citizen of the European Union,
  (b) knows or has reasonable cause for believing that the act facilitates the commission of a breach of immigration law by the individual, and
  (c) knows or has reasonable cause for believing that the individual is not a citizen of the European Union.

(2) In subsection (1) *'immigration law'* means a law which has effect in a member State and which controls, in respect of some or all persons who are not nationals of the State, entitlement to—
  (a) enter the State,
  (b) transit across the State, or
  (c) be in the State.

s 25A 'Helping asylum-seeker to enter United Kingdom'

(1) A person commits an offence if—
  (a) he knowingly and for gain facilitates the arrival in, or the entry into, the United Kingdom of an individual, and
  (b) he knows or has reasonable cause to believe that the individual is an asylum-seeker.

s 25B 'Assisting entry into the United Kingdom in breach of deportation or exclusion order'

(1) A person commits an offence if he—

(a) does an act which facilitates a breach of a deportation order in force against an individual who is a citizen of the European Union, and
(b) knows or has reasonable cause for believing that the act facilitates a breach of the deportation order.

B11.1.2 Breakdown

Offence	Elements of the Offence	Defence
s 24(1)(a) Immigration Act 1971 'Illegal entry and similar offences'	• Entered the United Kingdom • In breach of a deportation order; or • Without leave to remain	• Negative any element of the offence • General Defences **C**
s 24(1)(b) Immigration Act 1971 'Illegal entry and similar offences'	• Entered the United Kingdom • Having limited leave to enter/remain • Knowingly • Remain beyond the time limited by the leave; or • Fail to observe a condition of the leave	• Negative any element of the offence • General Defences **C**
s 24(1)(c) Immigration Act 1971 'Illegal entry and similar offences'	• Lawfully entered without leave under the provisions of s 8 • Remain without leave beyond the time allowed	• Negative any element of the offence • General Defences **C**
s 24(1)(d) Immigration Act 1971 'Illegal entry and similar offences'	• Without reasonable excuse • Fail to comply with any requirement imposed under Schedule 2	• Negative any element of the offence • General Defences **C**
s 24(1)(e) Immigration Act 1971 'Illegal entry and similar offences'	• Without reasonable excuse • Fail to observe any restriction imposed under Schedule 2 or 3	• Negative any element of the offence • General Defences **C**
s 24(1)(f) Immigration Act 1971 'Illegal entry and similar offences'	• Disembark in the United Kingdom • From a ship or aircraft • After being placed on board with a view to removal	• Negative any element of the offence • General Defences **C**
s 24A Immigration Act 1971 'Deception'	• By means which include deception • Obtained/sought to obtain leave to remain in the United Kingdom	• Negative any element of the offence • s 31 Immigration and Asylum Act 1999 **B11.1.3** • General Defences **C**

Offence	Elements of the Offence	Defence
s 25 Immigration Act 1971 'Assisting unlawful immigration to member State'	• Do an act which facilitates a breach of immigration law • By an individual who is not a citizen of the EU • Knowing or having reasonable cause for believing that it did so; and • Knowing or having reasonable cause for believing that the individual is not a citizen of the EU	• Negative any element of the offence • General Defences **C**
s 25A Immigration Act 1971 'Helping asylum-seeker to enter United Kingdom'	• Knowingly and for gain • Facilitated the arrival in/entry into the UK • Of an individual	• Negative any element of the offence • General Defences **C**
s 25B Immigration Act 1971 'Assisting entry into the United Kingdom in breach of deportation or exclusion order'	• A deportation order was in force against an individual • The defendant did an act which facilitated a breach of that order • Knowing or having reasonable cause for believing that the act facilitated the breach	• Negative any element of the offence • General Defences **C**

B11.1.3 Defences

Immigration and Asylum Act 1999

s 31 'Defences based on Article 31(1) of the Refugee Convention'

(1) It is a defence for a refugee charged with an offence to which this section applies to show that, having come to the United Kingdom directly from a country where his life or freedom was threatened (within the meaning of the Refugee Convention), he—

(a) presented himself to the authorities in the United Kingdom without delay;

(b) showed good cause for his illegal entry or presence; and

(c) made a claim for asylum as soon as was reasonably practicable after his arrival in the United Kingdom.

(2) If, in coming from the country where his life or freedom was threatened, the refugee stopped in another country outside the United Kingdom, subsection (1) applies only if he shows that he could not reasonably have expected to be given protection under the Refugee Convention in that other country.

(3) In England and Wales and Northern Ireland the offences to which this section applies are any offence, and any attempt to commit an offence, under—
  (a) Part I of the Forgery and Counterfeiting Act 1981 (forgery and connected offences);
  (aa) section 4 or 6 of the Identity Documents Act 2010;
  (b) section 24A of the 1971 Act (deception); or
  (c) section 26(1)(d) of the 1971 Act (falsification of documents).

...

(5) A refugee who has made a claim for asylum is not entitled to the defence provided by subsection (1) in relation to any offence committed by him after making that claim.

(6) '*Refugee*' has the same meaning as it has for the purposes of the Refugee Convention.

(7) If the Secretary of State has refused to grant a claim for asylum made by a person who claims that he has a defence under subsection (1), that person is to be taken not to be a refugee unless he shows that he is.

- See General Defences **C**.

B11.1.4 Sentencing

s 24 Immigration Act 1971

Summary only: a fine/6 months' imprisonment

s 24A Immigration Act 1971

Summary: a fine/6 months' imprisonment

Indictment: 2 years' imprisonment

s 25, s 25A, s 25B Immigration Act 1971

Summary: a fine/6 months' imprisonment

Indictment: 14 years' imprisonment

B11.2 Possession of false identity documents with improper intent

Identity Documents Act 2010

s 4 'Possession of false identity documents etc with improper intention'

(1) It is an offence for a person 'P' with an improper intention to have in P's possession or under P's control—

(a) an identity document that is false and that P knows or believes to be false,
(b) an identity document that was improperly obtained and that P knows or believes to have been improperly obtained, or
(c) an identity document that relates to someone else.

B11.2.1 Related offences

- Possession of false identity documents etc without reasonable excuse.

Identity Documents Act 2010

s 6 'Possession of false identity documents etc without reasonable excuse'

(1) It is an offence for a person 'P', without reasonable excuse, to have in P's possession or under P's control—
(a) an identity document that is false,
(b) an identity document that was improperly obtained,
(c) an identity document that relates to someone else,
(d) any apparatus which, to P's knowledge, is or has been specially designed or adapted for the making of false identity documents, or
(e) any article or material which, to P's knowledge, is or has been specially designed or adapted to be used in the making of such documents.

B11.2.2 Breakdown

Offence	Elements of the Offence	Defence
s 4 Identity Documents Act 2010 'Possession of false identity documents etc with improper intention'	• (A) Possessed/controlled • With improper intention • An identity document • That is false/improperly obtained; and • A knows or believes it to be false/improperly obtained; or • That it relates to someone else	• Negative any element of the offence • Immigration and Asylum Act 1999 **B11.1.3** • General Defences **C**
s 6 Identity Documents Act 2010 'Possession of false identity documents etc without reasonable excuse'	• (A) Without reasonable excuse • Possessed/controlled • An identity document • That is false/improperly obtained/relates to someone else; or • Any apparatus which A knows is designed/adapted for the making of such documents; or • Any article or material which A knows has been specially designed or adapted to be used in the making of such documents	• Negative any element of the offence • Immigration and Asylum Act 1999 **B11.1.3** • General Defences **C**

B11.2.3 Interpretation

- Improper intention.

Identity Documents Act 2010

s 4 'Possession of false identity documents etc with improper intention'

(2) Each of the following is an improper intention—
  (a) the intention of using the document for establishing personal information about P;
  (b) the intention of allowing or inducing another to use it for establishing, ascertaining or verifying personal information about P or anyone else.

- Identity document.

Identity Documents Act 2010

s 7 'Meaning of "identity document"'

(1) For the purposes of sections 4 to 6 'identity document' means any document that is or purports to be—
  (a) an immigration document,
  (b) a United Kingdom passport (within the meaning of the Immigration Act 1971),
  (c) a passport issued by or on behalf of the authorities of a country or territory outside the United Kingdom or by or on behalf of an international organisation,
  (d) a document that can be used (in some or all circumstances) instead of a passport,
  (e) a licence to drive a motor vehicle granted under Part 3 of the Road Traffic 1988 or under Part 2 of the Road Traffic (Northern Ireland) Order 1981, or
  (f) a driving licence issued by or on behalf of the authorities of a country or territory outside the United Kingdom.

B11.2.4 Defences

- See General Defences C.

B11.2.5 Key points

- If the document itself is false and the defendant intends to use it to establish a registrable fact then, it is no defence that the document contains the correct details of the defendant (*R v Jamalov* [2010] EWCA Crim 309).
- Ignorance that a document is false could amount to a reasonable excuse for possessing it but will depend on the particular circumstances of the case (*R v Unah* [2011] EWCA Crim 1837).

B11.2.6 Sentencing

s 4 Identity Document Act 2010

Indictable only: 10 years' imprisonment

s 6 Identity Document Act 2010

Summary: 6 months' imprisonment and/or a fine

Indictment: 2 years' imprisonment

B12 **Damage to Property**

B12.1 **Criminal damage**

Criminal Damage Act 1971

s 1 'Destroying or damaging property'

(1) A person who without lawful excuse destroys or damages any property belonging to another intending to destroy or damage any such property or being reckless as to whether any such property would be destroyed or damaged shall be guilty of an offence.

(2) A person who without lawful excuse destroys or damages any property, whether belonging to himself or another—

(a) intending to destroy or damage any property or being reckless as to whether any property would be destroyed or damaged; and

(b) intending by the destruction or damage to endanger the life of another or being reckless as to whether the life of another would be thereby endangered;

shall be guilty of an offence.

(3) An offence committed under this section by destroying or damaging property by fire shall be charged as arson.

B12.1.1 **Related offences**

- Criminal damage s 1(3):
  - Any offence committed under this section by destroying/damaging property by fire shall be charged as arson **B12.2**.
  - An offence under s 1(3) is triable only on indictment.
- Threats to destroy or damage property.

Criminal Damage Act 1971

s 2 'Threats to destroy or damage property'

A person who without lawful excuse makes to another a threat, intending that that other would fear it would be carried out—

(a) to destroy or damage any property belonging to that other or a third person; or

(b) to destroy or damage his own property in a way which he knows is likely to endanger the life of that other or third person;

shall be guilty of an offence.

s 3 'Possessing anything with intent to destroy or damage property'

A person who has anything in his custody or under his control intending without lawful excuse to use it or cause or permit another to use it—

(a) to destroy or damage any property belonging to some other person; or
(b) to destroy or damage his own or the user's property in a way which he knows is likely to endanger the life of some other person;

shall be guilty of an offence.

B12.1.2 Breakdown

Offence	Elements of the Offence	Defence
s 1(1) Criminal Damage Act 1971 'Destroying or damaging property'	• Without lawful excuse • Destroys/damages • Any property belonging to another • Intending/reckless as to whether such property would be destroyed/damaged	• Negative any element of the offence • s 5 Criminal Damage Act 1971 **B12.1.4** • General Defences **C**
s 1(2) Criminal Damage Act 1971 'Destroying or damaging property'	• Without lawful excuse • Destroys/damages • Any property • Intending/reckless as to whether such property would be destroyed/damaged • Intending/reckless as to whether the destruction/damage would endanger the life of another	• Negative any element of the offence • General Defences **C**
s 2 Criminal Damage Act 1971 'Threats to Destroy or Damage Property'	• Without lawful excuse • Makes a threat to another • Intending that the other would fear it would be carried out • To destroy/damage property belonging to that other or a third person; or • To destroy/damage his own property in a way in which he knows is likely to endanger the life of the other or a third person	• Negative any element of the offence • s 5 Criminal Damage Act 1971 **B12.1.4** • General Defences **C**
s 3 Criminal Damage Act 1971 'Possessing anything with intent to destroy or damage property'	• Has anything in his custody/ control intending • Without lawful excuse to use/ permit another to use • To destroy/damage property belonging to some other person; or • To destroy/damage his own/the user's property in a way in which he knows is likely to endanger the life of another person	• Negative any element of the offence • s 5 Criminal Damage Act 1971 **B12.1.4** • General Defences **C**

B12.1.3 Interpretation

Criminal Damage Act 1971

s 10 'Interpretation'

(1) In this Act 'property' means of a tangible nature, whether real or personal, including money and—
  (a) including wild creatures which have been tamed or are ordinarily kept in captivity, and any other wild creatures or their carcasses if, but only if, they have been reduced into possession which has not been lost or abandoned or are in the course of being reduced into possession; but
  (b) not including mushrooms growing wild on any land or flowers, fruit or foliage of a plant growing wild on any land.

  For the purposes of this subsection 'mushroom' includes any fungus and 'plant' includes any shrub or tree.

(2) Property shall be treated for the purposes of this Act as belonging to any person—
  (a) having the custody or control of it;
  (b) having in it any proprietary right or interest (not being an equitable interest arising only from an agreement to transfer or grant an interest); or
  (c) having a charge on it.

(3) Where property is subject to a trust, the persons to whom it belongs shall be so treated as including any person having a right to enforce the trust.

(4) Property of a corporation sole shall be so treated as belonging to the corporation notwithstanding a vacancy in the corporation.

B12.1.4 Defences

Criminal Damage Act 1971

s 5 '"Without lawful excuse"'

(1) This section applies to any offence under section 1(1) above and any offence under section 2 or 3 above other than one involving a threat by the person charged to destroy or damage property in a way which he knows is likely to endanger the life of another or involving an intent by the person charged to use or cause or permit the use of something in his custody or under his control so to destroy or damage property.

(2) A person charged with an offence to which this section applies, shall, whether or not he would be treated for the purposes of this Act as having a lawful excuse apart from this subsection, be treated for those purposes as having a lawful excuse—
  (a) if at the time of the act or acts alleged to constitute the offence he believed that the person or persons whom he believed to be entitled to consent to the destruction of or damage to the property in question had so consented, or would have so consented to it if he or they had known of the destruction or damage and its circumstances; or

(b) if he destroyed or damaged or threatened to destroy or damage the property in question or, in the case of a charge of an offence under section 3 above, intended to use or cause or permit the use of something to destroy or damage it, in order to protect property belonging to himself or another or a right or interest in property which was or which he believed to be vested in himself or another, and at the time of the act or acts alleged to constitute the offence he believed—

(i) that the property, right or interest was in immediate need of protection; and

(ii) that the means of protection adopted or proposed to be adopted were or would be reasonable having regard to all the circumstances.

(3) For the purposes of this section it is immaterial whether a belief is justified or not if it is honestly held.

(4) For the purposes of subsection (2) above a right or interest in property includes any right or privilege in or over land, whether created by grant, licence or otherwise.

(5) This section shall not be construed as casting doubt on any defence recognised by law as a defence to criminal charges.

- See General Defences **C**.

B12.1.5 Key points

- The term 'without lawful excuse' is defined in section 5 of the Act (above).
- A person can avail himself of the defence of lawful excuse, notwithstanding the fact that he was intoxicated (*Jaggard v Dickinson* (1981) 72 Cr App R 33). The test is subjective, ie whether the belief is held honestly, not whether it is justified or reasonable.
- Whilst the test of recklessness is subjective the question of whether or not a particular act of destruction or damage was done in order to protect property is an objective test (*R v Hunt* [1977] 66 Cr App R 105).
- Damaging something that can be restored constitutes damage (*Cox v Riley* (1986) 83 Cr App R 54). The soaking of a blanket and the flooding of the floor of a police cell was held to amount to damage in (*R v Fiak* [2005] EWCA 2381), and the daubing of water-soluble paint on a pavement was equally found to amount to damage in *Hardman v Chief Constable of Avon and Somerset* [1986] Crim LR 330.
- Spitting on a police officer's uniform is unlikely to cause damage (*A v R* [1978] Crim LR 689); however this is a matter of fact and should be considered alongside *Hardman* (above). It involved an allegation of spittle on an officer's rain jacket which left a faint mark, while no attempt had been made to clean the coat it is likely that wiping with a damp cloth could have removed the mark.

- Whether a threat has been made under section 2(a) is to be assessed objectively with reference to the words and actions of the defendant (*R v Cakmak* [2002] EWCA Crim 500).

B12.1.6 Sentencing

s 1 Criminal Damage Act 1971

Summary only if the value does not exceed £5,000

Summary: (if value is less than £5,000): a fine/3 months' imprisonment (if value > £5,000): 6 months' imprisonmentand/or fine

Indictment: 10 years' imprisonment

s 2 Criminal Damage Act 1971

Summary: a fine/6 months' imprisonment

Indictment: 10 years' imprisonment

s 3 Criminal Damage Act 1971

Summary: a fine/6 months' imprisonment

Indictment: 10 years' imprisonment

Youth Gravity Matrix

OFFENCE	Gravity Score	Offence type	AGGRAVATING FACTORS	MITIGATING FACTORS
Criminal damage valued at £300 (Home Office) £500 (max)	2	E If over £5,000, otherwise S But all types are included in the Charging Scheme	• Damage deliberate rather than reckless • Potential of greater danger • Group offence • Damage £300+ (approx)	• Damage £100 or less
Threat to destroy property of another	2	E	• Intent to cause fear • Ongoing intimidation	• Did not think victim would believe threats
Possession of articles with intent to commit criminal damage	2	E	• Evidence of intent to commit serious damage • Potential value of damage £200+ (approx)	• Potential value of damage £100 or less

See *Blackstone's Criminal Practice* **B8.1**

B12.2 Arson

Criminal Damage Act 1971

s 1 'Destroying or damaging property'

(3) An offence committed under this section by destroying or damaging property by fire shall be charged as arson.

B12.2.1 Related offences

- Arson with intent to endanger life.

Criminal Damage Act 1971

s 1 'Destroying or damaging property'

(2) A person who (without lawful excuse), destroys or damages any property, whether belonging to himself or another—
  (a) Intending to destroy or damage any property or being reckless as to whether any property would be destroyed or damages; and
  (b) Intending by the destruction or damage to endanger the life of another being or being reckless as to whether the life of another would be thereby endangered;

shall be guilty of an offence.

B12.2.2 Breakdown

Offence	Elements of the Offence	Defence
s 1(3) Criminal Damage Act 1971 'Arson'	• Without lawful excuse • Destroy or damage • By fire • Property with intent to destroy/damage it; or • Being reckless as to whether such property was destroyed or damaged	• Negative any element of the offence • s 5 Criminal Damage Act 1971 **B12.1.4** • General Defences **C**
s 1(2) Criminal Damage Act 1971 'Arson with intent to endanger life'	• All points to prove for arson; and • Intending by destruction/damage to endanger life of another; or • Being reckless as to whether such life would be endangered	• Negative any element of the offence • General Defences **C**

B12.2.3 Interpretation

Criminal Damage Act 1971

s 10 'Interpretation'

In this Act 'property' means of a tangible nature, whether real or personal, including money and—

(a) including wild creatures which have been tamed or are ordinarily kept in captivity, and any other wild creatures or their carcasses if, but only if, they have been reduced into possession which has not been lost or abandoned or are in the course of being reduced into possession; but

(b) not including mushrooms growing wild on any land or flowers, fruit or foliage of a plant growing wild on any land.

For the purposes of this subsection 'mushroom' includes any fungus and 'plant' includes any shrub or tree.

B12.2.4 Defences

- See General Defences C.

B12.2.5 Key point

- By virtue of section 5 of the Act, the statutory defence of lawful excuse does not apply to arson or arson with intent to endanger life.

B12.2.6 Sentencing

s 1 Criminal Damage Act 1971

Summary: 6 months' imprisonment/a fine or both

Indictment: life imprisonment

s 1(2) Criminal Damage Act 1971

Indictable only: life imprisonment

Youth Gravity Matrix

OFFENCE	Gravity Score	Offence type	AGGRAVATING FACTORS	MITIGATING FACTORS
Arson—life not endangered	3	E	• Damage deliberate • Potential of greater danger • Group offence • Damage £300+ (approx)	• Damage £100 or less
Criminal damage (including arson) with intent to Endanger life or reckless as to whether life is endangered	4	I	Defer decision to the CPS	

B13 Offences Interfering with the Course of Public Justice

B13.1 Concealing or false information and wasting police time

Criminal Law Act 1967

s 5 'Penalties for concealing offences or giving false information'

(1) Where a person has committed a relevant offence, any other person who, knowing or believing that the offence, or some other relevant offence has been committed, and that he has information which might be of material assistance in securing the prosecution or conviction of an offender for it, accepts or agrees to accept for not disclosing that information any consideration other than the making good of loss or injury caused by the offence, or the making of reasonable compensation for that loss or injury, shall be liable on conviction on indictment to imprisonment for not more that two years.

(2) Where a person causes any wasteful employment of the police by knowingly making to any person a false report tending to show that an offence has been committed, or to give rise to apprehension for the safety of any persons or property, or tending to show that he has information material to any police inquiry, he shall be liable on summary conviction to imprisonment for not more than six months or to a fine of not more than two hundred pounds or to both.

B13.1.1 Related offences

- Perverting the course of justice **B13.2**.

B13.1.2 Breakdown

Offence	Elements of the Offence	Defence
s 5(1) Criminal Law Act 1967 'Concealing offences or giving false information'	• (A) commits an offence • (B) knows or believes that an offence has been committed by A; and • B knowing that he has information that might be of material assistance in securing the prosecution • Accepts or agrees to not disclose that material	• Negative any element of the offence • General Defences **C**

Offence	Elements of the Offence	Defence
s 5(2) Criminal Law Act 1967 'Wasting police time'	• Knowingly making a false report • Tending to show an offence has been committed/giving rise to apprehension for the safety of any person or property/tending to show that he has information material to any police enquiry	• Negative any element of the offence • General Defences **C**

B13.1.3 Defences

- See General Defences **C**.

B13.1.4 Sentencing

s 5(1) Criminal Law Act 1967

Summary: 6 months' imprisonment/fine

Indictment: 2 years' imprisonment/fine

s 5(2) Criminal Law Act 1967 'Wasting police time'

Summary only: 6 months' imprisonment/level 4 fine

B13.2 Perverting the course of justice

An act tending and intended to pervert the course of public justice (*R v Verones* [1891] 1 QB 360).

B13.2.1 Related offences

- Perjury **B13.3**.
- Witness intimidation **B13.4**.
- Wasting police time **B13.1**.

B13.2.2 Breakdown

Offence	Elements of the Offence	Defence
***R v Verones* [1891] 1 QB 360 'Perverting the course of justice'**	• Do an act • Tending or intended to • Pervert the course of public justice	• Negative any element of the offence • General Defences **C**

B13.2.3 Interpretation

- There must be a positive action taken by the defendant, acquiescence is not sufficient (*R v Headley* [1996] RTR 173).
- The course of justice includes the police investigation of a possible crime. An act that makes that investigation more difficult, or which may mislead the police in their investigation, may tend to pervert the course of justice (*R v T* [2011] EWCA Crim 729).

B13.2.4 Defences

- See General Defences C.

B13.2.5 Key point

- Where there is found to be an intention to impede police investigations before an investigation has begun, there is an intention to pervert the course of public justice (*R v Rafique* (1993) 97 Cr App R 395).

B13.2.6 Sentencing

Perverting the course of justice

Indictable only: life/and or a fine

Youth Gravity Matrix

OFFENCE	Gravity Score	Offence type	AGGRAVATING FACTORS	MITIGATING FACTORS
Conspiracy/attempt to pervert the course of justice	4	I	Always refer to the CPS	

B13.3 Perjury

Perjury Act 1911

s 1 'Perjury'

(1) If any person lawfully sworn as a witness or as an interpreter in a judicial proceedings wilfully makes a statement material in that proceeding, which he knows to be false or does not believe to be true, he shall be guilty of perjury.

B13.3.1 Related offences

- Perverting the course of justice **B13.2**.

B13.3.2 Breakdown

Offence	Elements of the Offence	Defence
s 1 Perjury Act 1911 'Perjury'	• When lawfully sworn as a witness or interpreter in judicial proceedings • Make any wilful statement • That he knows to be false or does not believe to be true	• Negative any element of the offence • s 13 Perjury Act 1911 **B13.3.4** • General Defences **C**

B13.3.3 Interpretation

Perjury Act 1911

s 1 'Perjury'

(2) The expression 'judicial proceeding' includes a proceeding before any court, tribunal, or person having by law power to hear, receive, and examine evidence on oath.

(3) Where a statement made for the purposes of a judicial proceeding is not made before the tribunal itself, but is made on oath before a person authorised by law to administer an oath to the person who makes the statement, and to record or authenticate the statement, it shall, for the purposes of this section, be treated as having been made in a judicial proceeding.

s 15 'Interpretation'

(1) For the purposes of this Act, the forms and ceremonies used in administering an oath are immaterial, if the court or person before whom the oath is taken has power to administer an oath for the purpose of verifying the statement in question, and if the oath has been administered in a form and with ceremonies which the person taking the oath has accepted without objection, or has declared to be binding on him.

(2) In this Act—

The expression 'oath' includes 'affirmation' and 'declaration', and the expression 'swear' includes 'affirm' and 'declare'; and

The expression 'statutory declaration' means a declaration made by virtue of the Statutory Declarations Act 1835, or of any Act, Order in Council, rule or regulation applying or extending the provisions thereof.

B13.3.4 Defences

Perjury Act 1911

s 13 'Corroboration'

A person shall not be liable to be convicted of any offence against this Act, or of any offence declared by any other Act to be perjury or subornation of perjury, or to be punishable as perjury or subornation of perjury, solely upon the evidence of one witness as to the falsity of any statement alleged to be false.

- See General Defences C.

B13.3.5 Key points

- To commit perjury the following must be present:
  1. that the witness was lawfully sworn as a witness;
  2. in a judicial proceeding;
  3. that the witness made a statement wilfully, that is to say deliberately and not inadvertently or by mistake;
  4. that that statement was false;
  5. that the witness knew it was false or did not believe it to be true;
  6. that the statement was, viewed objectively, material in the judicial proceeding.

  This last requirement is, by virtue of section 1(6) of the 1911 Act, a matter to be decided by the judge (*R v Millward* (1985) 80 Cr App R 280).

B13.3.6 Sentencing

s 1 Perjury Act 1911

Indictable only: 7 years' imprisonment/a fine

Youth Gravity Matrix

OFFENCE	Gravity Score	Offence type	AGGRAVATING FACTORS	MITIGATING FACTORS
Perjury	4	I	Always refer to the CPS	

B13.4 Witness/juror intimidation

Criminal Justice and Public Order Act 1994

s 51 'Intimidation, etc., of witnesses, jurors and others'

(1) A person commits an offence if—
- (a) he does an act which intimidates, and is intended to intimidate, another person ('the victim'),
- (b) he does the act knowing or believing that the victim is assisting in the investigation of an offence or is a witness or potential witness or a juror or potential juror in proceedings for an offence, and
- (c) he does it intending thereby to cause the investigation or the course of justice to be obstructed, perverted or interfered with.

(2) A person commits an offence if—
- (a) he does an act which harms, and is intended to harm, another person or, intending to cause another person to fear harm, he threatens to do an act which would harm that other person,
- (b) he does or threatens to do the act knowing or believing that the person harmed or threatened to be harmed ('the victim'), or some other person, has assisted in an investigation into an offence or has given evidence or particular evidence in proceedings for an offence, or has acted as a juror or concurred in a particular verdict in proceedings for an offence, and
- (c) he does or threatens to do it because of that knowledge or belief.

B13.4.1 Related offences

- Perverting the course of justice **B13.2**.

B13.4.2 Breakdown

Offence	Elements of the Offence	Defence

s 51(1) Criminal Justice and Public Order Act 1994 'Intimidation, etc., of witnesses, jurors and others'	• (A) does an act intending to intimidate another person (B)
	• The act does in fact intimidate B
	• When doing the act A knows or believes B is:
	  • A witness or potential witness; or
	  • Juror or potential juror; or
	  • Is assisting police with the investigation of an offence
	• A does the act intending the investigation will be obstructed, perverted, or interfered with
		• Negative any element of the offence
		• General Defences **C**

Offence	Elements of the Offence	Defence
s 51(2) Criminal Justice and Public Order Act 1994 'Intimidation, etc., of witnesses, jurors and others'	• (A) does an act intending to harm another person (B) which does in fact harm them; or • Intending to cause B to fear harm threatens to do an act which would harm B • A does or threatens the act knowing or believing B, or some other person, has assisted an investigation into an offence, or has given evidence in proceedings, or has acted as a juror, or has concurred in a verdict in proceedings • A does or threatens the act because of the knowledge or belief described immediately above	• Negative any element of the offence • General Defences **C**

B13.4.3 Interpretation

Criminal Justice and Public Order Act 1994

s 51 'Intimidation, etc., of witnesses, jurors and others'

(3) For the purposes of subsections (1) and (2) it is immaterial that the act is or would be done, or that the threat is made—
  (a) otherwise than in the presence of the victim, or
  (b) to a person other than the victim.

(4) The harm that may be done or threatened may be financial as well as physical (whether to the person or a person's property) and similarly as respects an intimidatory act which consists of threats.

(5) The intention required by subsection (1)(c) and the motive required by subsection (2)(c) above need not be the only or the predominating intention or motive with which the act is done or, in the case of subsection (2), threatened.

...

(7) If, in proceedings against a person for an offence under subsection (1) above, it is proved that he did an act falling within paragraph (a) with the knowledge or belief required by paragraph (b), he shall be presumed, unless the contrary is proved, to have done the act with the intention required by paragraph (c) of that subsection.

(8) If, in proceedings against a person for an offence under subsection (2) above, it is proved that within the relevant period—
  (a) he did an act which harmed, and was intended to harm, another person, or
  (b) intending to cause another person fear of harm, he threatened to do an act which would harm that other person, and that he did the act, or (as the case may be) threatened to do the act, with the knowledge or belief

required by paragraph (b), he shall be presumed, unless the contrary is proved, to have done the act or (as the case may be) threatened to do the act with the motive required by paragraph (c) of that subsection.

B13.4.4 Defences

- See General Defences C.

B13.4.5 Key points

- The suspect cannot commit the offence where he wrongly believes there to be an investigation in progress, as it requires the belief to be correct (*R v Singh (B)* [1999] Crim LR 681 CA.
- Physical harm under ss 51(1) and (4) must involve some physical injury (*R v Normanton* [1998] Crim LR 220 CA).

B13.4.6 Sentencing

s 51 Criminal Justice and Public Order Act

Summary: a fine and/or 6 months' imprisonment

Indictment: 5 years' imprisonment and/or a fine

B14 **Animal Offences**

B14.1 **Possession of a fighting dog**

Dangerous Dogs Act 1991

s 1 'Dogs bred for fighting'

(2) No person shall—
- (a) breed, or breed from, a dog to which this section applies;
- (b) sell or exchange such a dog or offer, advertise or expose such a dog for sale or exchange;
- (c) make or offer to make a gift of such a dog or advertise or expose such a dog as a gift;
- (d) allow such a dog of which he is the owner or of which he is for the time being in charge to be in a public place without being muzzled and kept on a lead; or
- (e) abandon such a dog of which he is the owner or, being the owner or for the time being in charge of such a dog, allow it to stray.

(3) After such day as the Secretary of State may by order appoint for the purposes of this subsection no person shall have any dog to which this section applies in his possession or custody except—
- (a) in pursuance of the power of seizure conferred by the subsequent provisions of this Act; or
- (b) in accordance with an order for its destruction made under those provisions...

B14.1.1 **Breakdown**

Offence	Elements of the Offence	Defence
s 1(2) Dangerous Dogs Act 1991 'Possession of a fighting dog'	• Breed, or breed from; or • Sell, exchange, offer, advertise, or expose for sale or exchange; or • Make, offer to make a gift or advertise, or expose as a gift; or • Allow in a public place without muzzle or lead; or • Abandon; or • Allow to stray • A dog to which s 1 applies	• Negative any element of the offence • s 1 Dangerous Dogs Act 1991 **B14.1.3** • General Defences **C**
s 1(3) Dangerous Dogs Act 1991 'Possession of a fighting dog'	• Have in possession; or • In custody • A dog to which s 1 applies	• Negative any element of the offence • General Defences **C**

B14.1.2 Interpretation

- Fighting dog.

Dangerous Dogs Act 1991

s 1 'Dogs bred for fighting'

(1) This section applies to—
- (a) any dog of the type known as the pit bull terrier;
- (b) any dog of the type known as the Japanese tosa; and
- (c) any dog of any type designated for the purposes of this section by an order of the Secretary of State, being a type appearing to him to be bred for fighting or to have the characteristics of a type bred for that purpose.

The Dangerous Dogs (Designated Types) Order 1991 (SI 1991 No 1743)

Article 2

There are hereby designated for the purposes of section 1 of the Dangerous Dogs Act 1991 dogs of the following types, being types appearing to be bred for fighting or to have the characteristics of types bred for that purpose, namely:
- (a) any dog of the type known as the Dogo Argentino; and
- (b) any dog of the type known as the Fila Braziliero.

Dangerous Dogs Act 1991

s 10 'Short title, interpretation, commencement and extent'

(2) In this Act—

'public place' means any street, road or other place (whether or not enclosed) to which the public have or are permitted to have access whether for payment or otherwise and includes the common parts of a building containing two or more separate dwellings.

s 6 'Dogs owned by young persons'

Where a dog is owned by a person who is less than sixteen years old any reference to its owner in section 1(2)(d) or (e) or 3 above shall include a reference to the head of the household, if any, of which that person is a member...

s 10 'Short title, interpretation, commencement and extent'

(2) In this Act—

'*advertisement*' includes any means of bringing a matter to the attention of the public and '*advertise*' shall be construed accordingly...

B14.1.3 Defences

Dangerous Dogs Act 1991

s 1 'Dogs bred for fighting'

(7) Any person who contravenes this section is guilty of an offence... except that a person who publishes an advertisement in contravention of subsection (2)(b) or (c)—

(a) shall not on being convicted be liable to imprisonment if he shows that he published the advertisement to the order of someone else and did not himself devise it; and

(b) shall not be convicted if, in addition, he shows that he did not know and had no reasonable cause to suspect that it related to a dog to which this section applies.

- See General Defences C.

B14.1.4 Key points

- Intoxication is not a defence to the offences listed within s 1, which is an offence of strict liability (*R v Kellet* [1994] Crim LR 916).
- 'Type' as per s 1(1) has a broader meaning than 'breed' and is to be construed more widely and with regard to the physical and behavioural characteristics of the dog in question (*R v Knightsbridge Crown Court ex parte Dunne, Brock v DPP* [1993] 4 All ER 491).
- A dog within a car is considered to be in a public place if the car itself is in a public place (*Bates v DPP* (1993) 157 JP 1004).

B14.1.5 Sentencing

s 1 Dangerous Dogs Act 1991

Summary: 6 months' imprisonment and/or a fine

Youth Gravity Matrix

OFFENCE	Gravity Score	Offence type	AGGRAVATING FACTORS	MITIGATING FACTORS
Possession without exemption of a pit bull terrier, Japanese tosa or other designated fighting dog which appears to have been bread for fighting (s 1(3) Dangerous Dogs Act 1991)	3	S		• Dog destroyed

B14.2 Dangerous dog out of control

Dangerous Dogs Act 1991

s 3 'Keeping dogs under proper control'

(1) If a dog is dangerously out of control (whether or not in a public place)—
(a) the owner; and
(b) if different, the person for the time being in charge of the dog,
is guilty of an offence, or, if the dog while so out of control injures any person, an aggravated offence, under this subsection.

...

(3) If the owner or, if different, the person for the time being in charge of a dog allows it to enter a place which is not a public place but where it is not permitted to be and while it is there—
(a) it injures any person; or
(b) there are grounds for reasonable apprehension that it will do so,
he is guilty of an offence, or, if the dog injures any person, an aggravated offence, under this subsection.

B14.2.1 Breakdown

Offence	Elements of the Offence	Defence
s 3(1) Dangerous Dogs Act 1991 'Possession of a fighting dog'	• Dog out of control • Whilst in a public place NB Aggravated offence: • And it injures any person	• Negative any element of the offence • s 3 Dangerous Dogs Act 1991 **B14.2.3** • s 10 Dangerous Dogs Act 1991 **B14.2.3** • General Defences **C**
s 3(3) Dangerous Dogs Act 1991 'Possession of a fighting dog'	• Allows dog to enter • A place not being a public place • Where it is not permitted to be • Whilst there, there is reasonable apprehension it may injure NB Aggravated offence: • And it injures any person	• Negative any element of the offence • s 3 Dangerous Dogs Act 1991 **B14.2.3** • s 10 Dangerous Dogs Act 1991 **B14.2.3** • General Defences **C**

B14.2.2 Interpretation

- Public place B14.1.2.
- Owner B14.1.2.

Dangerous Dogs Act 1991

s 10 'Short title, interpretation, commencement and extent'

(3) For the purposes of this Act a dog shall be regarded as dangerously out of control on any occasion on which there are grounds for reasonable apprehension that it will injure any person, whether or not it actually does so . . .

B14.2.3 Defences

Dangerous Dogs Act 1991

s 3 'Keeping dogs under proper control'

(2) In proceedings for an offence under subsection (1) above against a person who is the owner of a dog but was not at the material time in charge of it, it shall be a defence for the accused to prove that the dog was at the material time in the charge of a person whom he reasonably believed to be a fit and proper person to be in charge of it.

s 10 'Short title, interpretation, commencement and extent'

(3) . . . references to a dog injuring a person or there being grounds for reasonable apprehension that it will do so do not include references to any case in which the dog is being used for a lawful purpose by a constable or a person in the service of the Crown.

- See General Defences **C**.

B14.2.4 Key points

- The offences under s 3(1) and s 3(3) are of strict liability. Intoxication is not a defence to an offence of strict liability; *R v Kellet* as before **B14.1.4**.
- More than one person may be 'in charge' of a dog at any given time. A short and temporary transfer of physical control (eg by giving another control of the dog's lead) does not prevent someone from remaining in charge of the dog if they are able to influence it by command, or retake physical control of it (*L v CPS* [2010] EWHC 341 (Admin)).
- A dog may be deemed dangerously out of control even if there is no previous history but on a single occasion it acted in a way which gave a reasonable apprehension that the dog would injure a person. The apprehension necessary to satisfy s 10(3) can be formed at the same moment as an injury occurs (*R v Gedminintaite* [2008] EWCA Crim 814).

B14.2.5 Sentencing

s 3(1) and 3(3) Dangerous Dogs Act 1991 (Without injury)

Summary: 6 months' imprisonment and/or a fine

s 3(1) and 3(3) Dangerous Dogs Act 1991 (Where injury is caused—aggravated offence)

Summary: 6 months' imprisonment and/or a fine

Indictment: 14 years if a person dies as a result of being injured

5 years in any other case where a person is injured

3 years in any case where an assistance dog is injured (whether or not it dies)

Youth Gravity Matrix

OFFENCE	Gravity Score	Offence type	AGGRAVATING FACTORS	MITIGATING FACTORS
Owner or person in charge allowing dog to be dangerously out of control in a public place injurig any person (s 3(1) Dangerous Dogs Act 1991)	3	E	• Serious injury • No effort to control	• Minor injury • Dog destroyed • Beyond physical limitation of owner/person in charge • First time in charge

B15 **Other Offences Against Property**

B15.1 **Enclosed premises or area**

Vagrancy Act 1824

s 4 'Persons committing certain offences to be deemed rogues and vagabonds'

Every person committing any of the offences herein-before mentioned...every person being found in or upon any dwelling house, warehouse, coach-house, stable, or outhouse, or in any inclosed yard, garden, or area, for any unlawful purpose.... shall [be liable to] imprisonment for any time not exceeding three calendar months.

B15.1.1 **Breakdown**

Offence	Elements of the Offence	Defence
s 4 Vagrancy Act 1824 'Persons committing certain offences to be deemed rogues and vagabonds'	• Being found in or on • A dwelling house, warehouse, coach-house, stable or outhouse; or • In an enclosed yard, garden or area • For any unlawful purpose	• Negative any element of the offence • General Defences **C**

B15.1.2 **Defences**

- See General Defences C.

B15.1.3 Key points

- For there to be an 'unlawful purpose', there had to be some criminal activity in mind at the time of being found on or in premises or area. Hiding from the police does not by itself constitute an 'unlawful purpose' (*L v DPP* [2007] EWHC 1843 (Admin)).
- A university campus of a substantial area will not constitute an enclosed area (*Ankhurst and Ankhurst v DPP* [2009] EWHC 806 (Admin)).

B15.1.4 Sentencing

s 4 Vagrancy Act 1824

Summary: 3 months' imprisonment/level 3 fine

B15.2 Violence to secure entry

Criminal Law Act 1977

s 6 'Violence for securing entry'

(1) Subject to the following provisions of this section, any person who, without lawful authority, uses or threatens violence for the purpose of securing entry into any premises for himself or for any other person is guilty of an offence, provided that—

(a) there is someone present on those premises at the time who is opposed to the entry which the violence is intended to secure; and

(b) the person using or threatening the violence knows that that is the case.

...

(5) A person guilty of an offence under this section shall be liable on summary conviction to imprisonment for a term not exceeding six months and/or to a fine.

B15.2.1 Breakdown

Offence	Elements of the Offence	Defence
s 6 Criminal Law Act 1977 'Violence for securing entry'	• (A) without lawful authority • Uses/threatens violence • For the purpose of securing entry into any premises • Knowing that there is someone present on those premises opposed to A's entry	• Negative any element of the offence • s 1A Criminal Law Act 1977 **B15.2.3** • General Defences **C**

B15.2.2 Interpretation

Criminal Law Act 1977

s 6 'Violence for securing entry'

(2) Subject to subsection (1A) [below], The fact that a person has any interest in or right to possession or occupation of any premises shall not for the purposes of subsection (1) above constitute lawful authority for the use or threat of violence by him or anyone else for the purpose of securing his entry into those premises.

...

(4) It is immaterial for the purposes of this section—
  (a) whether the violence in question is directed against the person or against property; and
  (b) whether the entry which the violence is intended to secure is for the purpose of acquiring possession of the premises in question or for any other purpose.

...

(7) Section 12 below contains provisions which apply for determining when any person is to be regarded for the purposes of this Part of this Act as a displaced residential occupier of any premises or of any access to any premises and section 12A below contains provisions which apply for determining when any person is to be regarded for the purposes of this Part of this Act as a protected intending occupier of any premises or of any access to any premises.

s 12 'Supplementary provisions'

(1) In this Part of this Act—
  (a) 'premises' means any building, any part of a building under separate occupation, any land ancillary to a building, the site comprising any building or buildings together with any land ancillary thereto, and (for the purposes only of sections 10 and 11 above) any other place; and
  (b) 'access' means, in relation to any premises, any part of any site or building within which those premises are situated which constitutes an ordinary means of access to those premises (whether or not that is its sole or primary use).

(2) References in this section to a building shall apply also to any structure other than a movable one, and to any movable structure, vehicle or vessel designed or adapted for use for residential purposes; and for the purposes of subsection (1) above—
  (a) part of a building is under separate occupation if anyone is in occupation or entitled to occupation of that part as distinct from the whole; and
  (b) land is ancillary to a building if it is adjacent to it and used (or intended for use) in connection with the occupation of that building or any part of it.

(3) Subject to subsection (4) below, any person who was occupying any premises as a residence immediately before being excluded from occupation by anyone who entered those premises, or any access to those premises, as a trespasser is a displaced residential occupier of the premises for the purposes of this Part of this Act so long as he continues to be excluded from occupation of the premises by the original trespasser or by any subsequent trespasser.

(4) A person who was himself occupying the premises in question as a trespasser immediately before being excluded from occupation shall not by virtue of subsection (3) above be a displaced residential occupier of the premises for the purposes of this Part of this Act.

(5) A person who by virtue of subsection (3) above is a displaced residential occupier of any premises shall be regarded for the purposes of this Part of this Act as a displaced residential occupier also of any access to those premises.

(6) Anyone who enters or is on or in occupation of any premises by virtue of—
   (a) any title derived from a trespasser; or
   (b) any licence or consent given by a trespasser or by a person deriving title from a trespasser, shall himself be treated as a trespasser for the purposes of this Part of this Act (without prejudice to whether or not he would be a trespasser apart from this provision); and references in this Part of this Act to a person's entering or being on or occupying any premises as a trespasser shall be construed accordingly.

(7) Anyone who is on any premises as a trespasser shall not cease to be a trespasser for the purposes of this Part of this Act by virtue of being allowed time to leave the premises, nor shall anyone cease to be a displaced residential occupier of any premises by virtue of any such allowance of time to a trespasser.

(7A) Subsection (6) also applies to the Secretary of State if the tenancy or licence is granted by him under Part III of the Housing Associations Act 1985.

(8) No rule of law ousting the jurisdiction of magistrates' courts to try offences where a dispute of title to property is involved shall preclude magistrates' courts from trying offences under this Part of this Act.

s 12A 'Protected intending occupiers: supplementary provisions'

(1) For the purposes of this Part of this Act an individual is a protected intending occupier of any premises at any time if at that time he falls within subsection (2), (4) or (6) below.

(2) An individual is a protected intending occupier of any premises if—
   (a) he has in those premises a freehold interest or a leasehold interest with not less than two years still to run;
   (b) he requires the premises for his own occupation as a residence;
   (c) he is excluded from occupation of the premises by a person who entered them, or any access to them, as a trespasser; and
   (d) he or a person acting on his behalf holds a written statement—
      (i) which specifies his interest in the premises;
      (ii) which states that he requires the premises for occupation as a residence for himself; and
      (iii) with respect to which the requirements in subsection (3) below are fulfilled.

(3) The requirements referred to in subsection (2)(d)(iii) above are—
   (a) that the statement is signed by the person whose interest is specified in it in the presence of a justice of the peace or commissioner for oaths; and
   (b) that the justice of the peace or commissioner for oaths has subscribed his name as a witness to the signature.

(4) An individual is also a protected intending occupier of any premises if—
   (a) he has a tenancy of those premises (other than a tenancy falling within subsection (2)(a) above or (6)(a) below) or a licence to occupy those premises granted by a person with a freehold interest or a leasehold interest with not less than two years still to run in the premises;
   (b) he requires the premises for his own occupation as a residence;

(c) he is excluded from occupation of the premises by a person who entered them, or any access to them, as a trespasser; and
(d) he or a person acting on his behalf holds a written statement—
(i) which states that he has been granted a tenancy of those premises or a licence to occupy those premises;
(ii) which specifies the interest in the premises of the person who granted that tenancy or licence to occupy ('the landlord');
(iii) which states that he requires the premises for occupation as a residence for himself; and
(iv) with respect to which the requirements in subsection (5) below are fulfilled.

(5) The requirements referred to in subsection (4)(d)(iv) above are—
(a) that the statement is signed by the landlord and by the tenant or licensee in the presence of a justice of the peace or commissioner for oaths;
(b) that the justice of the peace or commissioner for oaths has subscribed his name as a witness to the signatures.

(6) An individual is also a protected intending occupier of any premises if—
(a) he has a tenancy of those premises (other than a tenancy falling within subsection (2)(a) or (4)(a) above) or a licence to occupy those premises granted by an authority to which this subsection applies;
(b) he requires the premises for his own occupation as a residence;
(c) he is excluded from occupation of the premises by a person who entered the premises, or any access to them, as a trespasser; and
(d) there has been issued to him by or on behalf of the authority referred to in paragraph (a) above a certificate stating that—
(i) he has been granted a tenancy of those premises or a licence to occupy those premises as a residence by the authority; and
(ii) the authority which granted that tenancy or licence to occupy is one to which this subsection applies, being of a description specified in the certificate.

(7) Subsection (6) above applies to the following authorities—
(a) any body mentioned in section 14 of the Rent Act 1977 (landlord's interest belonging to local authority etc.);
(b) the Regulator of Social Housing;
(ba) a non-profit registered provider of social housing;
(bb) a profit-making registered provider of social housing, but only in relation to premises which are social housing within the meaning of Part 2 of the Housing and Regeneration Act 2008;

...

(d) a registered social landlord within the meaning of the Housing Act 1985 (see section 5(4) and (5) of that Act).

(8) A person is guilty of an offence if he makes a statement for the purposes of subsection (2)(d) or (4)(d) above which he knows to be false in a material particular or if he recklessly makes such a statement which is false in a material particular.

...

(10) A person guilty of an offence under subsection (8) above shall be liable on summary conviction to imprisonment for a term not exceeding six months and/or to a fine

(11) A person who is a protected intending occupier of any premises shall be regarded for the purposes of this Part of this Act as a protected intending occupier also of any access to those premises.

B15.2.3 Defences

Criminal Law Act 1977

s 6 'Violence for securing entry'

(1A) Subsection (1) above does not apply to a person who is a displaced residential occupier or a protected intending occupier of the premises in question or who is acting on behalf of such an occupier; and if the accused adduces sufficient evidence that he was, or was acting on behalf of, such an occupier he shall be presumed to be, or to be acting on behalf of, such an occupier unless the contrary is proved by the prosecution.

- See General Defences C.

B15.2.4 Key point

- A freeholder of a former matrimonial home, even when they are not excluded from the home under a provision of the *Matrimonial Homes Act*, is not a protected intended occupier under s 12A of this Act (*Wakolo v DPP* [2012] EWHC 611 (Admin)).

B15.2.5 Sentencing

s 6 Criminal Law Act 1977

Summary only: 6 months' imprisonment/a fine

B16 **Terrorist Offences**

B16.1 **Interpretation for terrorism offences**

B16.1.1 **Definition of terrorism**

The definition of terrorism for the purposes of the offences stated in this chapter is found in s 1 of the Terrorism Act 2000 and reads as follows:

Terrorism Act 2000

s 1 'Terrorism: interpretation'

(1) In this Act 'terrorism' means the use or threat of action where—
- (a) the action falls within subsection (2),
- (b) the use or threat is designed to influence the government or an international governmental organisation or to intimidate the public or a section of the public, and
- (c) the use or threat is made for the purpose of advancing a political, religious, racial or ideological cause.

(2) Action falls within this subsection if it—
- (a) involves serious violence against a person,
- (b) involves serious damage to property,
- (c) endangers a person's life, other than that of the person committing the action,
- (d) creates a serious risk to the health or safety of the public or a section of the public, or
- (e) is designed seriously to interfere with or seriously to disrupt an electronic system.

(3) The use or threat of action falling within subsection (2) which involves the use of firearms or explosives is terrorism whether or not subsection (1)(b) is satisfied.

(4) In this section—
- (a) 'action' includes action outside the United Kingdom,
- (b) a reference to any person or to property is a reference to any person, or to property, wherever situated,
- (c) a reference to the public includes a reference to the public of a country other than the United Kingdom, and
- (d) 'the government' means the government of the United Kingdom, of a part of the United Kingdom or of a country other than the United Kingdom.

(5) In this Act a reference to action taken for the purposes of terrorism includes a reference to action taken for the benefit of a proscribed organisation.

s 121 'Interpretation'

In this Act—

'act' and 'action' include omission

'organization' includes any association or combination of persons.

- The reference to government in 1(b) and 4(d) applies to countries which are governed by tyrants and dictators. There is no exemption from criminal liability for terrorist activities which are motivated or said to be morally justified by the alleged nobility of the terrorist cause (*R v F* [2007] EWCA Crim 243).

B16.1.2 Definition of terrorist

Terrorism Act 2000

s 40 'Terrorist: interpretation'

(1) In this Part 'terrorist' means a person who—

(a) has committed an offence under any of sections 11, 12, 15 to 18, 54 and 56 to 63, or

(b) is or has been concerned in the commission, preparation or instigation of acts of terrorism.

- The definition of 'terrorism' includes military attacks by a non-state armed group against any state or inter-governmental organisation armed forces in the context of a non-international armed conflict (*R v Gul UKSC* [2013] UKSC 64).

B16.1.3 Key points

The specific offences mentioned in s 40(a) above refer to the following:

- s 11 membership of a proscribed organization
- s 12 support of a proscribed organization
- s 15 invite, receive, provide funds
- s 16 use, possess money/property
- s 17 being concerned in the raising of funds
- s 18 money laundering
- s 54 weapons training
- s 56 directing a terrorist organization
- s 57 possession for terrorism purposes
- s 58 collection of information
- ss 59–61 inciting terrorism overseas

- s 62 terrorist bombing: jurisdiction
- s 63 terrorist finance offences.

B16.1.4 'Acts of Terrorism'

Terrorism Act 2006

s 20 'Interpretation of Part 1'

(2) In this Part—

'Act of terrorism' includes anything constituting an action taken for the purposes of terrorism, within the meaning of the Terrorism Act 2000.

B16.1.5 'Convention offence'

Terrorism Act 2006

s 20 'Interpretation of Part 1'

(2) In this part . . .

'convention offence' means an offence listed in Schedule 1 or an equivalent offence under the law of a country or territory outside the United Kingdom.

Schedule 1 convention offences include the following:

- Explosives offences contrary to s. 28 to 30 of the Offences Against the Person Act 1861
- Explosives offences contrary to s. 2 to 5 of the Explosive Substances Act 1883
- Biological weapons offences contrary to s. 1 of the Biological Weapons Act 1974
- Offences against internationally protected persons contrary to s. 1 of the Internationally Protected Persons Act 1978
- Hostage taking offences contrary to s. 1 of the Taking Hostages Act 1982
- Hijacking and other offences against aircraft contrary to s. 1 to 3 and 6 of the Aviation Security Act 1982.
- Offences involving nuclear material contrary to s. 1 and 2 of the Nuclear Material (Offences) Act 1983 and s. 50, 68 and 170 of the Customs and Excise Management Act 1979.
- Aviation and Maritime offences under s. 1, 9, 10, 11, 12, 13 and 14 of the Aviation and Maritime Security Act 1990
- Chemical weapons offences contrary to s. 2 of the Chemical Weapons Act 1996
- Terrorist funding offences contrary to s. 15, 16, 17, 18 of the Terrorism Act 2000.
- Directing terrorist organisations contrary to s. 56 of the Terrorism Act 2000

- Offences involving nuclear weapons contrary to s. 47 of the Anti-terrorism, Crime and Security Act 2001
- Conspiracy to commit a convention offence.

B16.1.6 Jurisdiction

Various Terrorism Act offences can be committed abroad and still be prosecuted in the UK. Section 17 of the TA 2006 states which offences fall into this category.

Terrorism Act 2006

s 17 'Commission of offences abroad'

(1) If—
  (a) a person does anything outside the United Kingdom, and
  (b) his action, if done in a part of the United Kingdom, would constitute an offence falling within subsection (2),

he shall be guilty in that part of the United Kingdom of the offence.

(2) The offences falling within this subsection are—
  (a) an offence under section 1 or 6 of this Act so far as it is committed in relation to any statement, instruction or training in relation to which that section has effect by reason of its relevance to the commission, preparation or instigation of one or more Convention offences;
  (b) an offence under any of sections 8 to 11 of this Act;
  (c) an offence under section 11(1) of the Terrorism Act 2000 (c. 11) (membership of proscribed organisations);
  (d) an offence under section 54 of that Act (weapons training);
  (e) conspiracy to commit an offence falling within this subsection;
  (f) inciting a person to commit such an offence;
  (g) attempting to commit such an offence;
  (h) aiding, abetting, counselling or procuring the commission of such an offence.

(3) Subsection (1) applies irrespective of whether the person is a British citizen or, in the case of a company, a company incorporated in a part of the United Kingdom.

B16.1.7 s 41 Arrest without warrant/detention for interview

A person can be detained and questioned under s 41 or under Schedule 7 of the Terrorism Act 2000 if they are suspected of being a terrorist. For further procedural information regarding detention at the police station under the Terrorism Act 2000 see Code H of PACE.; and The Terrorism Act 2000 Code of Practice for examining officers and review officers 2014.

Section 41 deals with those arrested in any part of the UK whilst Schedule 7 deals specifically with those detained at UK ports and borders.

Terrorism Act 2000

s 41 'Arrest without warrant'

(1) A constable may arrest without a warrant a person whom he reasonably suspects to be a terrorist.
(2) Where a person is arrested under this section the provisions of Schedule 8 (detention: treatment, review and extension) shall apply.
(3) Subject to subsections (4) to (7), a person detained under this section shall (unless detained under any other power) be released not later than the end of the period of 48 hours beginning—
  (a) with the time of his arrest under this section, or
  (b) if he was being detained under Schedule 7 when he was arrested under this section, with the time when his examination under that Schedule began.
(4) If on a review of a person's detention under Part II of Schedule 8 the review officer does not authorise continued detention, the person shall (unless detained in accordance with subsection (5) or (6) or under any other power) be released.
(5) Where a police officer intends to make an application for a warrant under paragraph 29 of Schedule 8 extending a person's detention, the person may be detained pending the making of the application.
(6) Where an application has been made under paragraph 29 or 36 of Schedule 8 in respect of a person's detention, he may be detained pending the conclusion of proceedings on the application.
(7) Where an application under paragraph 29 or 36 of Schedule 8 is granted in respect of a person's detention, he may be detained, subject to paragraph 37 of that Schedule, during the period specified in the warrant.
(8) The refusal of an application in respect of a person's detention under paragraph 29 or 36 of Schedule 8 shall not prevent his continued detention in accordance with this section.
(9) A person who has the powers of a constable in one Part of the United Kingdom may exercise the power under subsection (1) in any Part of the United Kingdom.

B16.1.8 Key points

- Arrest under s 41 does not require a necessity test to be fulfilled unlike those arrested under the Police and Criminal Evidence Act 1984.
- There is no requirement under s 41 that the suspect be given detailed information of the reasons for the arrest, merely basic factual details and legal grounds.

B16.1.9 Schedule 7 interviews

Schedule 7 Terrorism Act 2000

Para 2

(1) An examining officer may question a person to whom this paragraph applies for the purpose of determining whether he appears to be a person falling within section 40(1)(b). (I.e. is or has been concerned in the commission, preparation or instigation of acts of terrorism.)

...

(4) An examining officer may exercise his powers under this paragraph whether or not he has grounds for suspecting that a person falls within section 40(1)(b).

Para 6

(1) For the purposes of exercising a power under paragraph 2 or 3 an examining officer may—
  (a) stop a person or vehicle;
  (b) detain a person.

...

(4) A person detained under this paragraph shall (unless detained under any other power) be released not later than the end of the period of nine hours beginning with the time when his examination begins.

B16.1.10 Key point

- *R (CC) v Commr of Police of the Metropolis* [2012] 1 WLR 1913, QBD—in relation to para 2(1) the power to question could not be used if the predominant purpose was other than that specified.

B16.1.11 Schedule 8

Schedule 8 of the Terrorism Act 2000 details how the police should deal with those detained under s 41 or Schedule 7 of the Act.

Schedule 8 Terrorism Act 2000

Place of detention

Para 1

(3) Where a person is detained under Schedule 7, he may be taken in the custody of an examining officer or of a person acting under an examining officer's authority to and from any place where his attendance is required for the purpose of—
  (a) his examination under that Schedule,
  (b) establishing his nationality or citizenship, or
  (c) making arrangements for his admission to a country or territory outside the United Kingdom.

(4) A constable who arrests a person under section 41 shall take him as soon as is reasonably practicable to the police station which the constable considers the most appropriate.

Identification

Para 2

(1) An authorised person may take any steps which are reasonably necessary for—

(a) photographing the detained person,
(b) measuring him, or
(c) identifying him.

Rights

Para 6

(1) Subject to paragraph 8, a person detained under Schedule 7 or section 41 at a police station in England, Wales or Northern Ireland shall be entitled, if he so requests, to have one named person informed as soon as is reasonably practicable that he is being detained there.

Para 7

(1) Subject to paragraphs 8 and 9, a person detained under Schedule 7 or section 41 at a police station in England, Wales or Northern Ireland shall be entitled, if he so requests, to consult a solicitor as soon as is reasonably practicable, privately and at any time.

Para 8

(1) Subject to sub-paragraph (2), an officer of at least the rank of superintendent may authorise a delay—

(a) in informing the person named by a detained person under paragraph 6;
(b) in permitting a detained person to consult a solicitor under paragraph 7.

(2) But where a person is detained under section 41 he must be permitted to exercise his rights under paragraphs 6 and 7 before the end of the period mentioned in subsection (3) of that section.

(3) Subject to sub-paragraph (5), an officer may give an authorisation under sub-paragraph (1) only if he has reasonable grounds for believing—

(a) in the case of an authorisation under sub-paragraph (1)(a), that informing the named person of the detained person's detention will have any of the consequences specified in sub-paragraph (4), or
(b) in the case of an authorisation under sub-paragraph (1)(b), that the exercise of the right under paragraph 7 at the time when the detained person desires to exercise it will have any of the consequences specified in sub-paragraph (4).

(4) Those consequences are—

(a) interference with or harm to evidence of a serious offence,
(b) interference with or physical injury to any person,
(c) the alerting of persons who are suspected of having committed a serious offence but who have not been arrested for it,

(d) the hindering of the recovery of property obtained as a result of a serious offence or in respect of which a forfeiture order could be made under section 23 or 23A,
(e) interference with the gathering of information about the commission, preparation or instigation of acts of terrorism,
(f) the alerting of a person and thereby making it more difficult to prevent an act of terrorism, and
(g) the alerting of a person and thereby making it more difficult to secure a person's apprehension, prosecution or conviction in connection with the commission, preparation or instigation of an act of terrorism.

Para 9

(1) A direction under this paragraph may provide that a detained person who wishes to exercise the right under paragraph 7 may consult a solicitor only in the sight and hearing of a qualified officer.
(3) A direction under this paragraph may be given only if the officer giving it has reasonable grounds for believing—
 (a) that, unless the direction is given, the exercise of the right by the detained person will have any of the consequences specified in paragraph 8(4), or
 (b) that the detained person has benefited from his criminal conduct and that, unless the direction is given, the exercise of the right by the detained person will hinder the recovery of the value of the property constituting the benefit.

B16.1.12 Key points

- People arrested under the Terrorism Act 2000 can be subject to detention of up to 14 days, unlike those under PACE who are subject to a maximum of 96 hours.
- Para 9(1) should be considered according to para 9 of Home Office Circular 42/2003 'there will only be limited circumstances where this power can be exercised compatibly with Article 6 and that there must be a thorough assessment of those circumstances and of proportionality before it is applied'. At para 15 the circular mentions factors that should be taken account of in reaching this evaluation:
  - Whether the suspect has been initially co-operative and answering questions: if the suspect has been co-operating and making admissions that could prejudice his defence it may indicate that the suspect is in need of legal advice and as such requires uninhibited access to his solicitor.
  - Whether the suspect could be considered vulnerable.

B16.2 Port controls—failing to cooperate with a Schedule 7 enquiry

Schedule 7 Terrorism Act 2000

Para 18(1)

A person commits an offence if he—

(a) wilfully fails to comply with a duty imposed under or by virtue of this Schedule...

B16.2.1 Related offences

B16.2.1.1 *Contravenes a prohibition under Schedule 7*

Schedule 7 Terrorism Act 2000

Para 18(2)

A person commits an offence if he—

(b) wilfully contravenes a prohibition imposed under or by virtue of this Schedule...

Obstructs or seeks to frustrate... Schedule 7

Para 18(3)

(c) wilfully obstructs, or seeks to frustrate, a search or examination under or by virtue of this schedule.

B16.2.2 Breakdown

Offence	Elements of the Offence	Defence
Sch 7, para 18(1) Terrorism Act 2000 'Fail to cooperate with a Schedule 7 enquiry'	• Wilfully fails to comply • With a duty imposed • Under Schedule 7 Terrorism Act 2000	• Negative any element of the offence • General Defences **C**
Sch 7, para 18(1) Terrorism Act 2000 'Contravene a prohibition under Schedule 7'	• Wilful contravention • Of a prohibition imposed • Under Schedule 7 Terrorism Act 2000	• Negative any element of the offence • General Defences **C**
Sch 7, para 18(3) Terrorism Act 2000 'Obstruct or seek to frustrate a search'	• Wilful obstruction/seek to frustrate • A search or examination • Under/by virtue of Schedule 7 Terrorism Act 2000	• Negative any element of the offence • General Defences **C**

B16.2.3 Interpretation

Schedule 7 Terrorism Act 2000

Duties

Para 5

A person who is questioned under paragraph 2 or 3 must—

(a) give the examining officer any information in his possession which the officer requests;
(b) give the examining officer on request either a valid passport which includes a photograph or another document which establishes his identity;
(c) declare whether he has with him documents of a kind specified by the examining officer;
(d) give the examining officer on request any document which he has with him and which is of a kind specified by the officer.

Para 13(2)

Where owners or agents of a ship or aircraft receive notice under sub-paragraph (1) in relation to a port they shall take all reasonable steps to ensure, in respect of the ship or aircraft—

(a) that passengers do not embark or disembark at the port outside a control area, and
(b) that any specified conditions are met and any specified restrictions are complied with.

Para 14(2)

Where port managers receive notice under sub-paragraph (1) they shall take all reasonable steps to comply with any requirement set out in the notice.

Para 15(2)

(2) The captain shall ensure—

(a) that passengers and members of the crew do not disembark at a port in Great Britain or Northern Ireland unless either they have been examined by an examining officer or they disembark in accordance with arrangements approved by an examining officer;
(b) that passengers and members of the crew do not embark at a port in Great Britain or Northern Ireland except in accordance with arrangements approved by an examining officer;
(c) where a person is to be examined under this Schedule on board the ship or aircraft, that he is presented for examination in an orderly manner.

Para 16(2)

An order under this paragraph may require the owners or agents of a ship or aircraft employed to carry passengers for reward to supply their passengers with cards in the form required by virtue of sub-paragraph (1).

Para 17(2)

If an examining officer gives the owners or agents of a ship or aircraft to which this paragraph applies a written request to provide specified information, the owners or agents shall comply with the request as soon as is reasonably practicable.

Para 17(5)

A passenger or member of the crew on a ship or aircraft shall give the captain any information required for the purpose of enabling the owners or agents to comply with a request under this paragraph.

Prohibitions

Para 12(2)

(2) Where a ship or aircraft is employed to carry passengers for reward on a journey to which this paragraph applies the owners or agents of the ship or aircraft shall not arrange for it to call at a port in Great Britain or Northern Ireland for the purpose of disembarking or embarking passengers unless—
  (a) the port is a designated port, or
  (b) an examining officer approves the arrangement.

Para 12(3)

Where an aircraft is employed on a journey to which this paragraph applies otherwise than to carry passengers for reward, the captain of the aircraft shall not permit it to call at or leave a port in Great Britain or Northern Ireland unless—
  (a) the port is a designated port, or
  (b) he gives at least 12 hours' notice in writing to a constable for the police area in which the port is situated (or, where the port is in Northern Ireland, to a member of the Royal Ulster Constabulary).

Searches/examinations

Para 2

See Police powers section

Para 7

For the purpose of satisfying himself whether there are any persons whom he may wish to question under paragraph 2 an examining officer may—
  (a) search a ship or aircraft;
  (b) search anything on a ship or aircraft;
  (c) search anything which he reasonably believes has been, or is about to be, on a ship or aircraft.

Para 8

(1) An examining officer who questions a person under paragraph 2 may, for the purpose of determining whether he falls within section 40(1)(b)—
  (a) search the person;
  (b) search anything which he has with him, or which belongs to him, and which is on a ship or aircraft;
  (c) search anything which he has with him, or which belongs to him, and which the examining officer reasonably believes has been, or is about to be, on a ship or aircraft;
  (d) search a ship or aircraft for anything falling within paragraph (b)
  (e) search a vehicle which is on a ship or aircraft;

(f) search a vehicle which the examining officer reasonably believes has been, or is about to be, on a ship or aircraft.

(2) Where an examining officer questions a person in the border area under paragraph 2 he may (in addition to the matters specified in sub-paragraph (1)), for the purpose of determining whether the person falls within section 40(1)(b)—
   (a) search a vehicle;
   (b) search anything in or on a vehicle;
   (c) search anything which he reasonably believes has been, or is about to be, in or on a vehicle.

Para 9

(1) An examining officer may examine goods to which this paragraph applies for the purpose of determining whether they have been used in the commission, preparation or instigation of acts of terrorism.
(2) This paragraph applies to—
   (a) goods which have arrived in or are about to leave Great Britain or Northern Ireland on a ship or vehicle, and
   (b) goods which have arrived at or are about to leave any place in Great Britain or Northern Ireland on an aircraft (whether the place they have come from or are going to is within or outside Great Britain or Northern Ireland).
(3) In this paragraph 'goods' includes—
   (a) property of any description, and
   (b) containers.
(4) An examining officer may board a ship or aircraft or enter a vehicle for the purpose of determining whether to exercise his power under this paragraph.

B16.2.4 Defences

- See General Defences C.

B16.2.5 Key points

- *Elosta v Commissioner of Police of the Metropolis* [2013] EWHC 3397 (Admin)—A detainee under the Terrorism Act 2000 Sch 7 had the right to consult a solicitor before being interviewed, so his questioning after his request for a solicitor and prior to the solicitor's arrival was unlawful.
- Contra *Sylvie Beghal v Director of Public Prosecutions* [2013] EWHC 2573 (Admin)—A detainee under the Terrorism Act 2000 Sch 7 will be committing an offence under para 18 of that Schedule if he refuses to answer questions at interview, regardless of whether he has requested and is awaiting the presence of a solicitor before answering. However, any answer given in the absence of a solicitor is likely to be excluded from use at trial under s 78 PACE.

- *R (CC) v Commr of Police of the Metropolis* [2012] 1 WLR 1913, QBD—in relation to para 2(1) the power to question could not be used if the predominant purpose was other than that specified.
- **Para 2**—applies when an examining officer wishes to determine whether a person is concerned in the commission, preparation, or instigation of acts of terrorism (s 40(1)(b) TA 2000).
- **Para 12**—applies to a journey to Great Britain from the Republic of Ireland, Northern Ireland or any of the Islands, from Great Britain to any of those places, to Northern Ireland from Great Britain, the Republic of Ireland or any of the Islands, or from Northern Ireland to any of those places (para 12(1)).
- **Para 13**—applies when the Secretary of State designates control areas in any port in the UK by notice in writing to the owners or agents of ships or aircraft, and specifies conditions for or restrictions on the embarkation or disembarkation of passengers in a control area (para 13(1)(a)).
  - This para also applies if person is in the border area and examining officer wishes to establish whether his presence in the area is connected with entering or leaving NI (para 3).
- **Para 14**—applies when the Secretary of State gives notice in writing to the port managers to designate control areas in the port and:
  - requires them to provide at their own expense specified facilities in a control area for the purposes of the embarkation or disembarkation of passengers or their examination under this Schedule;
  - requires conditions to be met and restrictions to be complied with in relation to the embarkation or disembarkation of passengers in a control area;
  - requires the port managers to display, in specified locations in control areas, notices containing specified information about the provisions of this Schedule in such form as may be specified (para 14(1)).
- **Para 15**—applies to a ship employed to carry passengers for reward, or an aircraft, which:
  - arrives in Great Britain from the Republic of Ireland, Northern Ireland, or any of the Islands,
  - arrives in Northern Ireland from Great Britain, the Republic of Ireland, or any of the Islands,
  - leaves Great Britain for the Republic of Ireland, Northern Ireland, or any of the Islands, or
  - leaves Northern Ireland for Great Britain, the Republic of Ireland, or any of the Islands (para 15(1)).
- **Para 16**—applies when the Secretary of State makes an order requiring a person to whom this paragraph applies, if required to do so by an examining officer, to complete and produce to the

officer a card containing such information in such form as the order may specify.

- **Para 17**—applies to a ship or aircraft which arrives/leaves or is expected to arrive/leave in any place in the United Kingdom.

B16.2.6 Sentencing

Schedule 7, para 18(2)

Summary only: 3 months' imprisonment and/or a fine not exceeding level 4 on the standard scale

B16.3 Uniforms

Terrorism Act 2000

s 13 'Uniform'

(1) A person in a public place commits an offence if he—
 (a) wears an item of clothing, or
 (b) wears, carries or displays an article,
 in such a way or in such circumstances as to arouse reasonable suspicion that he is a member or supporter of a proscribed organization.

B16.3.1 Breakdown

Offence	Elements of the Offence	Defence
s 13 Terrorism Act 2000 'Uniforms'	• In a public place • Wear an item of clothing; or • Wear/carry/display an article • In such a way or in such circumstances as to arouse • Reasonable suspicion that he is a member/supporter of • A proscribed organisation	• Negative any element of the offence • General Defences **C**

B16.3.2 Defences

- See General Defences C.

B16.3.3 Sentencing

s 13(4) Terrorism Act 2000

Summary only: 6 months' imprisonment and/or a fine

B16.4 Attendance at a place used for terrorist training

Terrorism Act 2006

s 8 'Attendance at a place used for terrorist training'

(1) A person commits an offence if—
- (a) he attends at any place, whether in the United Kingdom or elsewhere;
- (b) while he is at that place, instruction or training of the type mentioned in section 6(1) of this Act or section 54(1) of the Terrorism Act 2000 (c. 11) (weapons training) is provided there;
- (c) that instruction or training is provided there wholly or partly for purposes connected with the commission or preparation of acts of terrorism or Convention offences; and
- (d) the requirements of subsection (2) are satisfied in relation to that person.

(2) The requirements of this subsection are satisfied in relation to a person if—
- (a) he knows or believes that instruction or training is being provided there wholly or partly for purposes connected with the commission or preparation of acts of terrorism or Convention offences; or
- (b) a person attending at that place throughout the period of that person's attendance could not reasonably have failed to understand that instruction or training was being provided there wholly or partly for such purposes.

B16.4.1 Breakdown

Offence	Elements of the Offence	Defence
s 6 Terrorism Act 2006 'Attendance at a place used for terrorist training'	• A person (A) attends a place • Whilst at that place, instruction/training in accordance with s 6(1) TA 2006 or s 54(1) TA 2006 is being provided there • The instruction/training provided is wholly or partly for purposes related to the commission/preparation of acts of terrorism/Convention offences • A knows/believes/could not reasonably have failed to understand that training/instruction was being provided for the above purposes	• Negative any element of the offence • General Defences **C**

B16.4.2 Interpretation

Terrorism Act 2006

s 8 'Attendance at a place used for terrorist training'

(3) It is immaterial for the purposes of this section—
   (a) whether the person concerned receives the instruction or training himself; and
   (b) whether the instruction or training is provided for purposes connected with one or more particular acts of terrorism or Convention offences, acts of terrorism or Convention offences of a particular description or acts of terrorism or Convention offences generally.

...

(6) References in this section to instruction or training being provided include references to its being made available.

B16.4.3 Defences

- See General Defences C.

B16.4.4 Key points

- Convention offence—see interpretation section at **B16.1.5** for definition.
- Act of terrorism—see interpretation section at **B16.1.4** for definition.

B16.4.5 Sentencing

s 8 Terrorism Act 2006

Summary: 6 months' imprisonment and/or a fine

Indictment: 10 years' imprisonment and/or a fine

B16.5 Disclosure of information

Terrorism Act 2000

s 39 'Disclosure of information &c.'

(1) Subsection (2) applies where a person knows or has reasonable cause to suspect that a constable is conducting or proposes to conduct a terrorist investigation.

(2) The person commits an offence if he—
   (a) discloses to another anything which is likely to prejudice the investigation, or (b) interferes with material which is likely to be relevant to the investigation.

B16.5.1 Failure to disclose information about acts of terrorism

Terrorism Act 2000

s 38B 'Information about acts of terrorism'

(1) This section applies where a person has information which he knows or believes might be of material assistance—
  (a) in preventing the commission by another person of an act of terrorism, or
  (b) in securing the apprehension, prosecution or conviction of another person, in the United Kingdom, for an offence involving the commission, preparation or instigation of an act of terrorism.

(2) The person commits an offence if he does not disclose the information as soon as reasonably practicable in accordance with subsection (3).

B16.5.2 Breakdown

Offence	Elements of the Offence	Defence
s 39 Terrorism Act 2000 'Disclosure of information'	• Knows/has reasonable cause to suspect • Constable is conducting/proposes to conduct a terrorist investigation; and • Discloses to another anything likely to prejudice the investigation; or • Interferes with material which is likely to be relevant to the investigation	• Negative any element of the offence • s 39 Terrorism Act 2000 **B16.5.4** • General Defences **C**
s 38B Terrorism Act 2000 'Failure to disclose information'	• Has information • Which he knows/believes might be of material assistance in preventing act of terrorism • Securing apprehension, prosecution, or conviction of someone in the UK for an offence involving commission/preparation/instigation of an act of terrorism • Does not disclose the information to a constable as soon as reasonably practicable	• Negative any element of the offence • s 38B Terrorism Act 2000 **B16.5.4** • General Defences **C**

B16.5.3 Interpretation

Terrorism Act 2000

s 39 'Disclosure of information &c.'

(8) For the purposes of this section—
  (a) a reference to conducting a terrorist investigation includes a reference to taking part in the conduct of, or assisting, a terrorist investigation, and
  (b) a person interferes with material if he falsifies it, conceals it, destroys it or disposes of it, or if he causes or permits another to do any of those things.

s 38B 'Information about acts of terrorism'

(3) Disclosure is in accordance with this subsection if it is made—
  (a) in England and Wales, to a constable...

B16.5.4 Defences

Terrorism Act 2000

s 39 'Disclosure of information &c.'

(5) It is a defence for a person charged with an offence under subsection (2) or (4) to prove—
  (a) that he did not know and had no reasonable cause to suspect that the disclosure or interference was likely to affect a terrorist investigation, or
  (b) that he had a reasonable excuse for the disclosure or interference.
(6) Subsections (2) and (4) do not apply to a disclosure which is made by a professional legal adviser—
  (a) to his client or to his client's representative in connection with the provision of legal advice by the adviser to the client and not with a view to furthering a criminal purpose, or
  (b) to any person for the purpose of actual or contemplated legal proceedings and not with a view to furthering a criminal purpose.
(6A) Subsections (2) and (4) do not apply if—
  (a) the disclosure is of a matter within section 21D(2) or (3)(a) (terrorist property: tipping off), and
  (b) the information on which the disclosure is based came to the person in the course of a business in the regulated sector.

s 38B 'Information about acts of terrorism'

(4) It is a defence for a person charged with an offence under subsection (2) to prove that he had a reasonable excuse for not making the disclosure.

- Representatives should be mindful of the law society guidance issued on 24 October 2011 which notes that s 38B does not automatically override legal professional privilege and detailed consideration of the Law Society guidance should be immediately sought in these circumstances.
- See General Defences C.

B16.5.5 Sentencing

s 39 Terrorism Act 2000

Summary: 6 months' imprisonment and/or a fine

Indictment: 5 years' imprisonment and/or a fine

s 38B Terrorism Act 2000

Summary: 6 months' imprisonment and/or a fine

Indictment: 5 years' imprisonment and/or a fine

B16.6 Encouragement of terrorism

Terrorism Act 2006

s 1 'Encouragement of terrorism'

(1) This section applies to a statement that is likely to be understood by some or all of the members of the public to whom it is published as a direct or indirect encouragement or other inducement to them to the commission, preparation or instigation of acts of terrorism or Convention offences.

(2) A person commits an offence if—
(a) he publishes a statement to which this section applies or causes another to publish such a statement; and
(b) at the time he publishes it or causes it to be published, he—
(i) intends members of the public to be directly or indirectly encouraged or otherwise induced by the statement to commit, prepare or instigate acts of terrorism or Convention offences; or
(ii) is reckless as to whether members of the public will be directly or indirectly encouraged or otherwise induced by the statement to commit, prepare or instigate such acts or offences.

B16.6.1 Breakdown

Offence	Elements of the Offence	Defence
s 1 Terrorism Act 2006 'Encouragement of Terrorism'	• Publishes or causes another to publish a statement • Likely to be understood by some/all members of public to whom it is published as direct or indirect encouragement/ inducement for commission, preparation, or instigation of act of terrorism or convention offence	• Negative any element of the offence • s 1 Terrorism Act 2000 **B16.6.3** • General Defences **C**

Offence	Elements of the Offence	Defence
	• At the time of publishing intends public to be so encouraged/induced; or • Is reckless as to whether they will be so encouraged/ induced	

B16.6.2 Interpretation

Terrorism Act 2006

s 1 'Encouragement of terrorism'

(3) For the purposes of this section, the statements that are likely to be understood by members of the public as indirectly encouraging the commission or preparation of acts of terrorism or Convention offences include every statement which—

(a) glorifies the commission or preparation (whether in the past, in the future or generally) of such acts or offences; and

(b) is a statement from which those members of the public could reasonably be expected to infer that what is being glorified is being glorified as conduct that should be emulated by them in existing circumstances.

(4) For the purposes of this section the questions how a statement is likely to be understood and what members of the public could reasonably be expected to infer from it must be determined having regard both—

(a) to the contents of the statement as a whole; and

(b) to the circumstances and manner of its publication.

(5) It is irrelevant for the purposes of subsections (1) to (3)—

(a) whether anything mentioned in those subsections relates to the commission, preparation or instigation of one or more particular acts of terrorism or Convention offences, of acts of terrorism or Convention offences of a particular description or of acts of terrorism or Convention offences generally; and,

(b) whether any person is in fact encouraged or induced by the statement to commit, prepare or instigate any such act or offence.

s 20 'Interpretation of Part 1'

(2) in this part...

'glorification' includes any form of praise or celebration, and cognate expressions are to be construed accordingly

(3) In this Part references to the public—

(a) are references to the public of any part of the United Kingdom or of a country or territory outside the United Kingdom, or any section of the public; and

(b) except in section 9(4), also include references to a meeting or other group of persons which is open to the public (whether unconditionally or on the making of a payment or the satisfaction of other conditions).

(4) In this Part references to a person's publishing a statement are references to—
   (a) his publishing it in any manner to the public;
   (b) his providing electronically any service by means of which the public have access to the statement; or
   (c) his using a service provided to him electronically by another so as to enable or to facilitate access by the public to the statement;

but this subsection does not apply to the references to a publication in section 2.

...

(6) In this Part references to a statement are references to a communication of any description, including a communication without words consisting of sounds or images or both.

(7) In this Part references to conduct that should be emulated in existing circumstances include references to conduct that is illustrative of a type of conduct that should be so emulated.

B16.6.3 Defences

Terrorism Act 2006

s 1 'Encouragement of terrorism'

(6) In proceedings for an offence under this section against a person in whose case it is not proved that he intended the statement directly or indirectly to encourage or otherwise induce the commission, preparation or instigation of acts of terrorism or Convention offences, it is a defence for him to show—
   (a) that the statement neither expressed his views nor had his endorsement (whether by virtue of section 3 or otherwise); and
   (b) that it was clear, in all the circumstances of the statement's publication, that it did not express his views and (apart from the possibility of his having been given and failed to comply with a notice under subsection (3) of that section) did not have his endorsement.

s 3 'Application of ss 1 and 2 to internet activity etc.'

(1) This section applies for the purposes of sections 1 and 2 in relation to cases where—
   (a) a statement is published or caused to be published in the course of, or in connection with, the provision or use of a service provided electronically; or
   (b) conduct falling within section 2(2) was in the course of, or in connection with, the provision or use of such a service.

(2) The cases in which the statement, or the article or record to which the conduct relates, is to be regarded as having the endorsement of a person ('the relevant person') at any time include a case in which—

(a) a constable has given him a notice under subsection (3);
(b) that time falls more than 2 working days after the day on which the notice was given; and
(c) the relevant person has failed, without reasonable excuse, to comply with the notice.

(3) A notice under this subsection is a notice which—
(a) declares that, in the opinion of the constable giving it, the statement or the article or record is unlawfully terrorism-related;
(b) requires the relevant person to secure that the statement or the article or record, so far as it is so related, is not available to the public or is modified so as no longer to be so related;
(c) warns the relevant person that a failure to comply with the notice within 2 working days will result in the statement, or the article or record, being regarded as having his endorsement; and
(d) explains how, under subsection (4), he may become liable by virtue of the notice if the statement, or the article or record, becomes available to the public after he has complied with the notice.

(4) Where—
(a) a notice under subsection (3) has been given to the relevant person in respect of a statement, or an article or record, and he has complied with it, but
(b) he subsequently publishes or causes to be published a statement which is, or is for all practical purposes, the same or to the same effect as the statement to which the notice related, or to matter contained in the article or record to which it related, (a 'repeat statement');

the requirements of subsection (2)(a) to (c) shall be regarded as satisfied in the case of the repeat statement in relation to the times of its subsequent publication by the relevant person.

(5) In proceedings against a person for an offence under section 1 or 2 the requirements of subsection (2)(a) to (c) are not, in his case, to be regarded as satisfied in relation to any time by virtue of subsection (4) if he shows that he—
(a) has, before that time, taken every step he reasonably could to prevent a repeat statement from becoming available to the public and to ascertain whether it does; and
(b) was, at that time, a person to whom subsection (6) applied.

(6) This subsection applies to a person at any time when he—
(a) is not aware of the publication of the repeat statement; or
(b) having become aware of its publication, has taken every step that he reasonably could to secure that it either ceased to be available to the public or was modified as mentioned in subsection (3)(b).

(7) For the purposes of this section a statement or an article or record is unlawfully terrorism-related if it constitutes, or if matter contained in the article or record constitutes—
(a) something that is likely to be understood, by any one or more of the persons to whom it has or may become available, as a direct or indirect encouragement or other inducement to the commission, preparation or instigation of acts of terrorism or Convention offences; or
(b) information which—

(i) is likely to be useful to any one or more of those persons in the commission or preparation of such acts; and
(ii) is in a form or context in which it is likely to be understood by any one or more of those persons as being wholly or mainly for the purpose of being so useful.

(8) The reference in subsection (7) to something that is likely to be understood as an indirect encouragement to the commission or preparation of acts of terrorism or Convention offences includes anything which is likely to be understood as—
(a) the glorification of the commission or preparation (whether in the past, in the future or generally) of such acts or such offences; and
(b) a suggestion that what is being glorified is being glorified as conduct that should be emulated in existing circumstances.

(9) In this section 'working day' means any day other than—
(a) a Saturday or a Sunday;
(b) Christmas Day or Good Friday; or
(c) a day which is a bank holiday under the Banking and Financial Dealings Act 1971 in any part of the United Kingdom.

- See General Defences C.

B16.6.4 Sentencing

s 1 Terrorism Act 2006

Summary: 6 months' imprisonment and/or a fine

Indictment: 7 years' imprisonment and/or a fine

B16.7 Incite terrorism overseas

Terrorism Act 2000

s 59 'England and Wales'

(1) A person commits an offence if—
(a) he incites another person to commit an act of terrorism wholly or partly outside the United Kingdom, and
(b) the act would, if committed in England and Wales, constitute one of the offences listed in subsection (2).

(2) Those offences are—
(a) murder,
(b) an offence under section 18 of the Offences against the Person Act 1861 (wounding with intent),
(c) an offence under section 23 or 24 of that Act (poison),
(d) an offence under section 28 or 29 of that Act (explosions), and
(e) an offence under section 1(2) of the Criminal Damage Act 1971 (endangering life by damaging property).

B16.7.1 Breakdown

Offence	Elements of the Offence	Defence
s 59 Terrorism Act 2000 'Incite terrorism overseas'	• Incites another person • To commit murder/ wounding s 18, poisoning ss 23–24, explosions ss 28–29 of OAP Act 1861/endangering life by damaging property s 1(2) Criminal Damage Act 1971 • Wholly or partly outside the UK	• Negative any element of the offence • s 59 Terrorism Act 2000 **B16.7.3** • General Defences **C**

B16.7.2 Interpretation

Terrorism Act 2000

s 59 'England and Wales'

(4) For the purposes of subsection (1) it is immaterial whether or not the person incited is in the United Kingdom at the time of the incitement.

B16.7.3 Defences

Terrorism Act 2000

s 59 'England and Wales'

(5) Nothing in this section imposes criminal liability on any person acting on behalf of, or holding office under, the Crown.

B16.7.4 Sentencing

Terrorism Act 2000

s 59 'England and Wales'

A person guilty of an offence under this section shall be liable to any penalty to which he would be liable on conviction of the offence listed in subsection (2) which corresponds to the act which he incites.

B16.8 Weapons training

Terrorism Act 2000

s 54 'Weapons training'

(1) A person commits an offence if he provides instruction or training in the making or use of—
- (a) firearms,
- (aa) radioactive material or weapons designed or adapted for the discharge of any radioactive material,
- (b) explosives, or
- (c) chemical, biological or nuclear weapons.

B16.8.1 Related offences

- Receiving training.

Terrorism Act 2000

s 54 'Weapons training'

(2) A person commits an offence if he receives instruction or training in the making or use of—
- (a) firearms,
- (aa) radioactive material or weapons designed or adapted for the discharge of any radioactive material,
- (b) explosives, or
- (c) chemical, biological or nuclear weapons.

- Inviting to train.

Terrorism Act 2000

s 54 'Weapons training'

(3) A person commits an offence if he invites another to receive instruction or training and the receipt—
- (a) would constitute an offence under subsection (2), or
- (b) would constitute an offence under subsection (2) but for the fact that it is to take place outside the United Kingdom.

B16.8.2 Breakdown

Offence	Elements of the Offence	Defence
s 54(1) Terrorism Act 2000 'Provides training'	• Provide instruction or training • In the making or use of • Firearms, radioactive material, or weapons designed or adapted for the discharge of any radioactive material, explosives or chemical, biological or nuclear weapons.	• Negative any element of the offence • s 54 Terrorism Act 2000 **B16.8.4** • General Defences **C**
s 54(2) Terrorism Act 2000 'Receives training'	• Receives instruction or training • In the making or use of • Firearms, radioactive material, or weapons designed or adapted for the discharge of any radioactive material, explosives, or chemical, biological or nuclear weapons.	• Negative any element of the offence • s 54 Terrorism Act 2000 **B16.8.4** • General Defences **C**
s 54(3) 'Inviting to train'	• Invites another to receive instruction or training; and • The receipt would constitute an offence under subsection (2); or • Would have been an offence under subsection (2) but for it taking place outside the UK	• Negative any element of the offence • General Defences **C**

B16.8.3 Interpretation

Terrorism Act 2000

s 54 'Weapons training'

(4) For the purpose of subsections (1) and (3)—

(a) a reference to the provision of instruction includes a reference to making it available either generally or to one or more specific persons, and

(b) an invitation to receive instruction or training may be either general or addressed to one or more specific persons.

s 55 'Weaons training: interpretation'

'biological weapon'—means a biological agent or toxin (within the meaning of the Biological Weapons Act 1974) in a form capable of use for hostile purposes or anything to which section 1(1)(b) of that Act applies.

'Chemical weapon' has the meaning given by section 1 of the Chemical Weapons Act 1996, and

'Radioactive material' means material capable endangering life or causing harm to human health.

s 121 'Interpretation'

'explosive' means—

(a) an article or substance manufactured for the purpose of producing a practical effect by explosion,
(b) materials for making an article or substance within paragraph (a),
(c) anything used or intended to be used for causing or assisting in causing an explosion, and
(d) a part of anything within paragraph (a) or (c),

'firearm' includes an air gun or air pistol...

Chemical Weapons Act 1996

s 1 'General interpretation'

(1) Chemical weapons are—
  (a) toxic chemicals and their precursors;
  (b) munitions and other devices designed to cause death or harm through the toxic properties of toxic chemicals released by them;
  (c) equipment designed for use in connection with munitions and devices falling within paragraph (b).

B16.8.4 Defences

Terrorism Act 2000

s 54 'Weapons training'

(5) It is a defence for a person charged with an offence under this section in relation to instruction or training to prove that his action or involvement was wholly for a purpose other than assisting, preparing for or participating in terrorism.

- See General Defences C.

B16.8.5 Sentencing

s 54(6) Terrorism Act 2000

Summary: 6 months' imprisonment and/or a fine

Indictment: 10 years' imprisonment and/or a fine

B16.9 Possession of articles/collection of information

Terrorism Act 2000

s 57 'Possession for terrorist purposes'

(1) A person commits an offence if he possesses an article in circumstances which give rise to a reasonable suspicion that his possession is for a purpose connected with the commission, preparation or instigation of an act of terrorism.

B16.9.1 Related offences

Terrorism Act 2000

s 58 'Collection of information'

(1) A person commits an offence if—
 (a) he collects or makes a record of information of a kind likely to be useful to a person committing or preparing an act of terrorism, or
 (b) he possesses a document or record containing information of that kind.

B16.9.2 Breakdown

Offence	Elements of the Offence	Defence
s 57 Terrorism Act 2000 'Possession of articles'	• Possession of an article • In circumstances which give rise to a reasonable suspicion • That possession is for a purpose connected with commission, preparation, or instigation of an act of terrorism	• Negative any element of the offence • s 57 Terrorism Act 2000 **B16.9.4** • General Defences **C**
s 58 Terrorism Act 2000 'Collection of information'	• Collect/make/possess • Record/document of information • Likely to be useful to a person • Committing/preparing an act of terrorism	• Negative any element of the offence • s 58 Terrorism Act 2000 **B16.9.4** • General Defences **C**

B16.9.3 Interpretation

Terrorism Act 2000

s 57 'Possession for terrorist purposes'

(3) In proceedings for an offence under this section, if it is proved that an article—
- (a) was on any premises at the same time as the accused, or
- (b) was on premises of which the accused was the occupier or which he habitually used otherwise than as a member of the public,

the court may assume that the accused possessed the article, unless he proves that he did not know of its presence on the premises or that he had no control over it.

s 118 'Defences'

(3) Subsection (4) applies where in accordance with a provision mentioned in subsection (5) a court—
- (a) may make an assumption in relation to a person charged with an offence unless a particular matter is proved, or
- (b) may accept a fact as sufficient evidence unless a particular matter is proved.

(4) If evidence is adduced which is sufficient to raise an issue with respect to the matter mentioned in subsection (3)(a) or (b) the court shall treat it as proved unless the prosecution disproves it beyond reasonable doubt.

s 58 'Collection of information'

(2) In this section 'record' includes a photographic or electronic record.

s 121 'Interpretation'

...article includes substance and any other thing...

B16.9.4 Defences

Terrorism Act 2000

s 57 'Possession for terrorist purposes'

(2) It is a defence for a person charged with an offence under this section to prove that his possession of the article was not for a purpose connected with the commission, preparation or instigation of an act of terrorism.

s 58 'Collection of information'

(3) It is a defence for a person charged with an offence under this section to prove that he had a reasonable excuse for his action or possession.

- See General Defences C.

B16.9.5 Key points

- A direct link between the article and the act of terrorism is required for the offence to be applicable. The section should be interpreted as if it reads: 'A person commits an offence if he possesses an article in circumstances which give rise to a reasonable suspicion that he intends it to be used for the purpose of the commission, preparation or instigation of an act of terrorism.' (*R v Zafar, Butt, Iqbal, Raja and Malik* [2008] EWCA Crim 184)
- s 57 must be construed having regard to the normal meaning of instigate. (*R v Zafar, Butt, Iqbal, Raja and Malik* [2008] EWCA Crim 184)
- Documents and records can be articles for the purpose of this offence. (*R v Rowe* [2007] EWCA Crim 635)
- A document or record will only fall within s 58 if it is of a kind that is likely to provide practical assistance to a person committing or preparing an act of terrorism. A document that simply encourages the commission of acts of terrorism does not fall with s 58. (*R v K* [2008] EWCA Crim 185)
- In order to obtain a conviction under s 58(1)(b), the Crown must prove beyond reasonable doubt that the defendant (1) had control of a record which contained information that was likely to provide practical assistance to a person committing or preparing an act of terrorism, (2) knew that he had the record, and (3) knew the kind of information which it contained. If the Crown establishes all three elements, then it has proved its case against the defendant and he falls to be convicted—unless he establishes a defence under subsection (3). (*R v G; R v J* [2009] UKHL 13)

B16.9.6 Sentencing

s 57 Terrorism Act 2000

Summary: 6 months' imprisonment and/or a fine

Indictment: 15 years' imprisonment and/or a fine

s 58 Terrorism Act 2000

Summary: 6 months' imprisonment and/or a fine

Indictment: 10 years' imprisonment and/or a fine

B16.10 **Preparation of terrorist acts**

Terrorism Act 2006

s 5 'Preparation of terrorist acts'

(1) A person commits an offence if, with the intention of—
(a) committing acts of terrorism, or
(b) assisting another to commit such acts,
he engages in any conduct in preparation for giving effect to his intention.

B16.10.1 **Breakdown**

Offence	Elements of the Offence	Defence
s 5 Terrorism Act 2006 'Preparation of terrorist acts'	• P engages in conduct in preparation of • Committing acts of terrorism; or • Assisting another to commit such acts • With the intention of so doing	• Negative any element of the offence • General Defences **C**

B16.10.2 **Interpretation**

Terrorism Act 2006

s 5 'Preparation of terrorist acts'

(2) It is irrelevant for the purposes of subsection (1) whether the intention and preparations relate to one or more particular acts of terrorism, acts of terrorism of a particular description or acts of terrorism generally.

B16.10.3 **Defences**

- See General Defences **C**.

B16.10.4 Key point

- s 5 Terrorism Act 2006 captures preparation in the UK for acts abroad. (*R v Iqbal (Abbas Niazi) and Iqbal (Ilyas Niazi)* [2010] EWCA Crim 3215)

B16.10.5 **Sentencing**

s 5(3) Terrorism Act 2006

Indictment: life imprisonment

B16.11 Support of a proscribed organization

Terrorism Act 2000

s 12 'Support'

(1) A person commits an offence if—
  (a) he invites support for a proscribed organisation, and
  (b) the support is not, or is not restricted to, the provision of money or other property (within the meaning of section 15).

B16.11.1 Related offences

Terrorism Act 2000

s 12 'Support'

(2) A person commits an offence if he arranges, manages or assists in arranging or managing a meeting which he knows is—
  (a) to support a proscribed organisation,
  (b) to further the activities of a proscribed organisation, or
  (c) to be addressed by a person who belongs or professes to belong to a proscribed organisation.
(3) A person commits an offence if he addresses a meeting and the purpose of his address is to encourage support for a proscribed organisation or to further its activities.

B16.11.2 Breakdown

Offence	Elements of the Offence	Defence
s 12(1) Terrorism Act 2000 'Support a proscribed organisation'	• Invites support • For a prescribed organisation; and • Support is not/not restricted to • Provision of money or other • Property	• Negative any element of the offence • s 12 Terrorism Act 2000 **B16.11.4** • General Defences **C**
s 12(2) Terrorism Act 2000 'Support a proscribed organisation'	• Arranges, manages, or assists in arranging or managing; of • A meeting which he knows is to support/is to further activities of/will be attended by a person who belongs or professes to belong to • A proscribed organisation	• Negative any element of the offence • s 12 Terrorism Act 2000 **B16.11.4** • General Defences **C**

Offence	Elements of the Offence	Defence
s 12(3) Terrorism Act 2000 'Support a proscribed organisation'	• Addresses a meeting; and • The purpose of the address is to encourage support for proscribed organisation; or • Further its activities	• Negative any element of the offence • s 12 Terrorism Act 2000 **B16.11.4** • General Defences **C**

B16.11.3 Interpretation

Terrorism Act 2000

s 12 'Support'

(5) In subsections (2) to (4)—

(a) 'meeting' means a meeting of three or more persons, whether or not the public are admitted, and

(b) a meeting is private if the public are not admitted.

B16.11.4 Defences

Terrorism Act 2000

s 12 'Support'

(4) Where a person is charged with an offence under subsection (2)(c) in respect of a private meeting it is a defence for him to prove that he had no reasonable cause to believe that the address mentioned in subsection (2)(c) would support a proscribed organisation or further its activities.

- See General Defences C.

B16.11.5 Sentencing

s 12 Terrorism Act 2000

Summary: 6 months' imprisonment and/or a fine

Indictment: 10 years' imprisonment and/or a fine

B16.12 Membership of a proscribed organization

Terrorism Act 2000

s 11 'Membership'

(1) A person commits an offence if he belongs or professes to belong to a proscribed organisation...

B16.12.1 Breakdown

Offence	Elements of the Offence	Defence
s 11 Terrorism Act 2000 'Membership of a proscribed organisation'	• Belongs/professes to belong to • A proscribed organisation	• Negative any element of the offence • s 11 Terrorism Act 2000 **B16.12.3** • General Defences **C**

B16.12.2 Interpretation

Terrorism Act 2000

s 3 'Proscription'

(1) For the purposes of this Act an organisation is proscribed if—
   (a) it is listed in Schedule 2, or
   (b) it operates under the same name as an organisation listed in that Schedule.

...

(6) Where the Secretary of State believes—
   (a) that an organisation listed in Schedule 2 is operating wholly or partly under a name that is not specified in that Schedule (whether as well as or instead of under the specified name), or
   (b) that an organisation that is operating under a name that is not so specified is otherwise for all practical purposes the same as an organisation so listed,

   he may, by order, provide that the name that is not specified in that Schedule is to be treated as another name for the listed organisation.

(7) Where an order under subsection (6) provides for a name to be treated as another name for an organisation, this Act shall have effect in relation to acts occurring while—
   (a) the order is in force, and
   (b) the organisation continues to be listed in Schedule 2,

   as if the organisation were listed in that Schedule under the other name, as well as under the name specified in the Schedule.

B16.12.3 Defences

Terrorism Act 2000

s 11 'Membership'

(2) It is a defence for a person charged with an offence under subsection (1) to prove—
   (a) that the organisation was not proscribed on the last (or only) occasion on which he became a member or began to profess to be a member, and

(b) that he has not taken part in the activities of the organisation at any time while it was proscribed.

- See General Defences C.

B16.12.4 Key points

- ... the core elements of membership within the meaning of section 11, namely voluntary and knowing association with others with a view to furthering the aims of the proscribed organization ... In some cases it will be necessary to make clear that unilateral sympathy with the aims of an organisation, even coupled with acts designed to promote similar objectives, will, whilst being clear evidence of belonging, not always be sufficient; the jury may need to consider whether there is the necessary element of acceptance or reciprocity which will be involved in belonging. (*R v Ahmed (Rangzieb) and Ahmed (Habib)* [2011] EWCA Crim 184)
- In order to establish that the person concerned is a member of the proscribed organization, evidence can be given that the person joined the organization from abroad or when abroad. That would not in itself make that person guilty of an offence. He would only be guilty of an offence when he was in this country. Either he would have to travel to this country in order to commit an offence after he became a member or he would already have had to be in this country and joined the local foreign branch of the proscribed organization while in this country. (*R v Hundal and Dhaliwal* [2004] EWCA Crim 389)

B16.12.5 Sentencing

s 11 Terrorism Act 2000

Summary: 6 months' imprisonment and/or a fine

Indictment: 10 years' imprisonment and/or a fine

B16.13 Directing a terrorist organization

Terrorism Act 2000

s 56 'Directing terrorist organisation'

(1) A person commits an offence if he directs, at any level, the activities of an organisation which is concerned in the commission of acts of terrorism.

B16.13.1 Breakdown

Offence	Elements of the Offence	Defence
s 56 Terrorism Act 2000 'Direct a terrorist organisation'	• Directs • At any level • Activities of an organisation • Concerned in the commission of acts of terrorism	• Negative any element of the offence • General Defences **C**

B16.13.2 Interpretation

- See interpretations for terrorist offences **B16.1**.

B16.13.3 Defences

- See General Defences C.

B16.13.4 Sentencing

s 56 Terrorism Act 2000

Indictable only

Indictment: life imprisonment

B16.14 Training for terrorist acts etc

Terrorism Act 2006

s 6 'Training for terrorism'

(1) A person commits an offence if—

(a) he provides instruction or training in any of the skills mentioned in subsection (3); and

(b) at the time he provides the instruction or training, he knows that a person receiving it intends to use the skills in which he is being instructed or trained—

(i) for or in connection with the commission or preparation of acts of terrorism or Convention offences; or

(ii) for assisting the commission or preparation by others of such acts or offences.

...

(3) The skills are—

(a) the making, handling or use of a noxious substance, or of substances of a description of such substances;

(b) the use of any method or technique for doing anything else that is capable of being done for the purposes of terrorism, in

connection with the commission or preparation of an act of terrorism or Convention offence or in connection with assisting the commission or preparation by another of such an act or offence; and
(c) the design or adaptation for the purposes of terrorism, or in connection with the commission or preparation of an act of terrorism or Convention offence, of any method or technique for doing anything.

B16.14.1 Related offences

Terrorism Act 2006

s 6 'Training for terrorism'

(2) A person commits an offence if—
  (a) he receives instruction or training in any of the skills mentioned in subsection (3); and
  (b) at the time of the instruction or training, he intends to use the skills in which he is being instructed or trained—
    (i) for or in connection with the commission or preparation of acts of terrorism or Convention offences; or
    (ii) for assisting the commission or preparation by others of such acts or offences.
(3) The skills are—
  (a) the making, handling or use of a noxious substance, or of substances of a description of such substances;
  (b) the use of any method or technique for doing anything else that is capable of being done for the purposes of terrorism, in connection with the commission or preparation of an act of terrorism or Convention offence or in connection with assisting the commission or preparation by another of such an act or offence; and
  (c) the design or adaptation for the purposes of terrorism, or in connection with the commission or preparation of an act of terrorism or Convention offence, of any method or technique for doing anything.

B16.14.2 Breakdown

Offence	Elements of the Offence	Defence
s 6 (1) Terrorism Act 2006 'Provides training for terrorist acts'	• Provides instructions or training • In any skills listed in subsection (3); and • Knows at the time of instruction/training that the person intends to use these skills • For/to assist in/in connection with the commission/preparation of acts of terrorism/Convention offences	• Negative any element of the offence • General Defences **C**

Offence	Elements of the Offence	Defence
s 6 (2) Terrorism Act 2006 'Receives training for terrorist acts'	• Receives instructions or training • In any skills listed in subsection (3); and • At the time of instruction/training he intends to use skills • For/to assist in/in connection with the commission/preparation of acts of terrorism/Convention offences	• Negative any element of the offence • General Defences **C**

B16.14.3 Interpretation

Terrorism Act 2006

s 6 'Training for terrorism'

(4) It is irrelevant for the purposes of subsections (1) and (2)—

(a) whether any instruction or training that is provided is provided to one or more particular persons or generally;

(b) whether the acts or offences in relation to which a person intends to use skills in which he is instructed or trained consist of one or more particular acts of terrorism or Convention offences, acts of terrorism or Convention offences of a particular description or acts of terrorism or Convention offences generally; and

(c) whether assistance that a person intends to provide to others is intended to be provided to one or more particular persons or to one or more persons whose identities are not yet known.

...

(7) In this section—

'noxious substance' means—

(a) a dangerous substance within the meaning of Part 7 of the Anti-terrorism, Crime and Security Act 2001 (c. 24); or

(b) any other substance which is hazardous or noxious or which may be or become hazardous or noxious only in certain circumstances;

'substance' includes any natural or artificial substance (whatever its origin or method of production and whether in solid or liquid form or in the form of a gas or vapour) and any mixture of substances.

B16.14.4 Defences

- See General Defences C.

B16.14.5 Key point

- s 6(1) does not make the test whether the provider of training intends that his training should be used for terrorist purposes; it makes the test whether he knows that someone present does in fact intend to use his training for terrorist purposes (*Regina v Kibley Da Costa* [2009] EWCA Crim 482).

B16.14.6 Sentencing

s 6 Terrorism Act 2006

Summary: 6 months' imprisonment and/or fine

Indictment: 10 years' imprisonment and/or fine

Part C
General Defences

C1 Self-Defence/Householder Self-Defence

There are two questions to be answered in relation to self-defence

1. Were the facts as the suspect honestly, however mistakenly, believed them to be such that the use of force was reasonably necessary; and
2. Was the degree of force used reasonable in the circumstances as the defendant believed them to be.

It is for the defence to raise the defence, which may be best done in the police station, and the Crown must then prove that there was not self-defence to the criminal standard.

Section 76 Criminal justice and Immigration Act 2008 sought to embody a summary of the common law, and the householder defence has since been added.

Criminal Justice and Immigration Act 2008

s 76 'Reasonable force for use of self-defence etc'

(1) This section applies where in proceedings for an offence—
 (a) an issue arises as to whether a person charged with the offence ('D') is entitled to rely on a defence within subsection (2), and
 (b) the question arises whether the degree of force used by D against a person ('V') was reasonable in the circumstances.

(2) The defences are—
 (a) the common law defence of self-defence;
 (aa) the common law defence of defence of property; and
 (b) the defences provided by section 3(1) of the Criminal Law Act 1967 (c. 58)...(use of force in prevention of crime or making arrest).

(3) The question whether the degree of force used by D was reasonable in the circumstances is to be decided by reference to the circumstances as D believed them to be, and subsections (4) to (8) also apply in connection with deciding that question.

(4) If D claims to have held a particular belief as regards the existence of any circumstances—
 (a) the reasonableness or otherwise of that belief is relevant to the question whether D genuinely held it; but
 (b) if it is determined that D did genuinely hold it, D is entitled to rely on it for the purposes of subsection (3), whether or not—
  (i) it was mistaken, or
  (ii) (if it was mistaken) the mistake was a reasonable one to have made.

(5) But subsection (4) (b) does not enable D to rely on any mistaken belief attributable to intoxication that was voluntarily induced.

(5A) In a householder case, the degree of force used by D is not to be regarded as having been reasonable in the circumstances as D believed them to be if it was grossly disproportionate in those circumstances.

(6) In a case other than a householder case, the degree of force used by D is not to be regarded as having been reasonable in the circumstances as D believed them to be if it was disproportionate in those circumstances.

(6A) In deciding the question mentioned in subsection (3), a possibility that D could have retreated is to be considered (so far as relevant) as a factor to be taken into account, rather than as giving rise to a duty to retreat.

(7) In deciding the question mentioned in subsection (3) the following considerations are to be taken into account (so far as relevant in the circumstances of the case)—
  - (a) that a person acting for a legitimate purpose may not be able to weigh to a nicety the exact measure of any necessary action; and
  - (b) that evidence of a person's having only done what the person honestly and instinctively thought was necessary for a legitimate purpose constitutes strong evidence that only reasonable action was taken by that person for that purpose.

(8) Subsections (6A) and (7) are not to be read as preventing other matters from being taken into account where they are relevant to deciding the question mentioned in subsection (3).

(8A) For the purposes of this section 'a householder case' is a case where—
  - (a) the defence concerned is the common law defence of self-defence,
  - (b) the force concerned is force used by D while in or partly in a building, or part of a building, that is a dwelling or is forces accommodation (or is both),
  - (c) D is not a trespasser at the time the force is used, and
  - (d) at that time D believed V to be in, or entering, the building or part as a trespasser.

(8B) Where—
  - (a) a part of a building is a dwelling where D dwells,
  - (b) another part of the building is a place of work for D or another person who dwells in the first part, and
  - (c) that other part is internally accessible from the first part, that other part, and any internal means of access between the two parts, are each treated for the purposes of subsection (8A) as a part of a building that is a dwelling.

(8C) Where—
  - (a) a part of a building is forces accommodation that is living or sleeping accommodation for D,
  - (b) another part of the building is a place of work for D or another person for whom the first part is living or sleeping accommodation, and
  - (c) that other part is internally accessible from the first part, that other part, and any internal means of access between the two parts, are each treated for the purposes of subsection (8A) as a part of a building that is forces accommodation.

(8D) Subsections (4) and (5) apply for the purposes of subsection (8A)(d) as they apply for the purposes of subsection (3).

(8E) The fact that a person derives title from a trespasser, or has the permission of a trespasser, does not prevent the person from being a trespasser for the purposes of subsection (8A).

(8F) In subsections (8A) to (8C)—

'building' in cludes a vehicle or vessel, and

'forces accommodation' means service living accommodation for the purposes of Part 3 of the Armed Forces Act 2006 by virtue of section 96(1)(a) or (b) of that Act.

...

(10) In this section—

(a) 'legitimate purpose' means—

(i) the purpose of self-defence under the common law,

(ia) the purpose of defence of property under the common law, or

(ii) the prevention of crime or effecting or assisting in the lawful arrest of persons mentioned in the provisions referred to in subsection (2)(b);

(b) references to self-defence include acting in defence of another person; and

(c) references to the degree of force used are to the type and amount of force used.

See *Blackstone's Criminal Practice* A3.54

C2 Force Used in the Prevention of Crime

Criminal Law Act 1967

s 3 'Use of force in making arrest, etc.'

(1) A person may use such force as is reasonable in the circumstances in the prevention of crime, or in effecting or assisting in the lawful arrest of offenders or suspected offenders or of persons unlawfully at large.

(2) Subsection (1) above shall replace the rules of the common law on the question when force used for a purpose mentioned in the subsection is justified by that purpose.

The test is subjective as to the suspect's belief as to whether a crime is being prevented (*R v Morris* [2013] EWCA Crim 436).

C3 Duress

The principal questions for duress were considered in *R v Graham* [1981] EWCA Crim 5 where it was held that the following questions must be addressed:

> (1) Was the defendant, or may he have been, impelled to act as he did because, as a result of what he reasonably believed ['A'] had said or done, he had good cause to fear that if he did not so act ['A'] would kill him or (if this is to be added) cause him serious physical injury? (2) If so, have the prosecution made the jury sure that a sober person of reasonable firmness, sharing the characteristics of the defendant, would not have responded to whatever he reasonably believed ['A'] said or did by taking part in the [act]? The fact that a defendant's will to resist has been eroded by the voluntary consumption of drink or drugs or both is not relevant to this test.

- Duress is not a defence to murder (*R v Howe* [1986] UKHL 4).
- Where a person has voluntarily, and with knowledge of its nature, joined a criminal organization or gang which he knew might bring pressure on him to commit an offence and was an active member when he was put under such pressure, he cannot avail himself of the defence of duress (*R v Sharp* (1987) 85 Cr App R 207).
- If a person can avoid the effects of duress by escaping from the threats, without damage to himself, he must do so (*R v Sharp* (1987) 85 Cr App R 207). The possibility of seeking official protection (such as reporting the matter to the police) must be considered in that context (see *R v Hasan* [2005] UKHL 22).
- The defence must raise the issue of duress by evidence and the burden of proof then passes to the Crown. This can be done at the police station interview and in *R v Van Dao* [2012] EWCA Crim 1717 the lack of detail given in the defendant's interview in respect of the duress on which they (unsuccessfully) intended to rely was said to be, 'telling'. However the policy grounds on which duress may be disallowed are so complex that caution may be required.

See *Blackstone's Criminal Practice* A3.35

C4 Insanity/Automatism

C4.1 Insanity

- If insanity is to be relied upon as a defence it must be raised by the defendant (*R v Smith* (1911) 6 Cr App R 19). It is not fatal to the defence of insanity if it is not raised at the police station.
- At detainee may request a clinical examination by a medical practitioner of their choice at their expense while in a police station (Code C para 9.8).
- The question of insanity was considered in *R v McNaughten* [1843] UKHL J16. Colloquially known as the M'Naughten rules. The questions that must be addressed are:

> [whether] at the time of the committing of the act, the party accused was labouring under such a defect of reason, from disease of the mind, as not to know the nature and quality of the act he was doing, or, if he did know it, that he did not know he was doing what was wrong.

C4.2 Automatism

- The onus of proving automatism is on the defendant (*Hill v Baxter* (1958) 42 Cr App R 51). A proper foundation for the defence must be laid by introducing evidence. This can be done at the police station or at court.
- The term automatism requires a totally involuntary movement of the body or limbs of a person (*Broome v Perkins* (1987) 85 Cr App R 321). This defence is confined to acts done while unconscious or the result of spasms, reflex actions, and convulsions (*R v Beatty* [1963] AC 386). The defence is physical not moral involuntariness.
- The defence is not available if induced by voluntary intoxication.
- The actus reus of the offence cannot be made out if the defendant is in a state of automatism. If the automatism was caused by a disease of the mind the defence is not guilty by reason of insanity. In other circumstances the finding is one of not guilty. Automatism caused by cerebral tumour or epilepsy or diabetes arises from a disease of the mind. These are internal factors. External factors leading to a finding of not guilty include concussion, the administration of an anaesthetic, or hypnosis. If the administration of insulin induces hypoglycaemia this is an external factor leading to acquittal.

See *Blackstone's Criminal Practice* A3.23

C5 **Mistake**

- Where a defendant is mistaken as to a fact which is an element of an offence this may constitute a defence in negating the required mens rea, see *W (A minor) v Dolbey* (1983) 88 Cr App R 1, where the defendant believed his gun was unloaded and so could not be guilty of an offence under s 20 Offences against the Person Act 1861.
- This will apply to offences requiring intention or subjective recklessness. For mistake to amount to a defence to an offence requiring only objective recklessness the mistake would have to rule out any possibility of risk. The mistake must be honest but need not be reasonable.
- Mistake of fact will not amount to a defence to an offence requiring negligence or where there is an offence of strict liability (*R v Howells* (1977) 65 Cr App R 86).
- A mistake of criminal law can never amount to a defence.
- A mistake of civil law may occasionally amount to a defence is it means the relevant *mens rea* is lacking, for instance where damage was done to property which the defendant believed still to be his own (*R v Smith* [1974] QB 354).

C6 Intoxication

- Intoxication is not itself a defence. In some cases it may remove defences but it may serve, in permitted cases, to negative the *mens rea* of an offence.
- Involuntary intoxication may provide a defence if it negatives an element of the offence.
- However voluntary intoxication, whether with alcohol or drugs, is only available as a defence for crimes of specific intent.
- Crimes of specific intent include murder, s 18 grievous bodily harm, theft, robbery, burglary under s 9(1)(a) Theft Act 1968, and all attempts. They require an intent to do something beyond committing the actus reus of the offence. Sexual touching contrary to s 3 Sexual Offences Act 2003 is a crime of basic intent (*R v Heard* [2007] EWCA Crim 125).

See *Blackstone's Criminal Practice* A3.15

C7 Victims of Trafficking

Crown prosecutors should be mindful of the *CPS Policy for Prosecuting Cases of Human Trafficking* issued in May 2011 in which it was noted:

> If new information or evidence supports the fact that the suspect has been trafficked and has committed the offence whilst in a coerced situation, there is a strong public interest to stop the prosecution.

This has subsequently seen judicial consideration in *R v O* [2008] EWCA Crim 2835 by Laws LJ who noted:

> Prosecutors must be aware of the protocols which, although not in the text books are enshrined in their Code. Defence lawyers must respond by making enquiries, if there is before them credible material showing that they have a client who might have been the victim of trafficking, especially a young client. Where there is doubt about the age of a defendant who is a possible victim of trafficking, proper inquiries must be made, indeed statute so required.

Part D
Pre-Attendance

D1 Initial Rights and Entitlements of those Detained

- The custody officer must ensure that the detained person is treated in accordance with PACE 1984 *and* the PACE Codes of Practice (s 39(1) PACE 1984). 'The detainee must be dealt with expeditiously and released as soon as the need for detention no longer applies' (PACE Code C para 1.1).
- For a period of 12 months after the release from police custody, a detainee, or their legal representative, shall be given, on request, a copy of their custody record as soon as practicable (PACE Code C para 2.4A).
- At the conclusion of a sound recorded interview the interviewee shall be handed a notice which will advise that a copy of the tape of the interview shall be supplied as soon as practicable if the person is charged or informed that he will be prosecuted (PACE Code E para 4.19 (replicated by PACE Code F para 4.19 for visually recorded (with sound) interviews)).

D1.1 Communication with those outside the police station

- Under s 56 PACE 1984 the detainee is entitled to have someone informed of their arrest and whereabouts, unless the police have grounds to delay this right according to the grounds set out in s 56(5) PACE. In addition, the detainee should be allowed writing materials and allowed to speak to someone on the telephone for a reasonable period, though this right can be delayed or denied in certain cases. Any delay or denial of rights to communicate with those outside the police station should be proportionate and should last no longer than necessary (PACE Code C paras 5.1, 5.6, and 5.7A).

D1.2 Rights of juveniles and vulnerable adults

- The police must take steps to ascertain the identity of a person responsible for the welfare of children or young persons in custody, and where those persons are identified they must be informed of the detainee's whereabouts where it is practicable to do so (s 57 PACE 1984).
- Additionally, for both juveniles and vulnerable adults the custody officer must as soon as is practicable inform the appropriate adult of the detainee's whereabouts and the grounds for their detention,

and must request that the appropriate adult attends the police station to see the detainee (PACE Code C para 3.15).

- 'If the detainee is blind, seriously visually impaired, or unable to read the custody officer must ensure that their solicitor, appropriate adult, or someone else likely to take an interest in them who is not connected to the investigation is available to help check any documentation' (PACE Code C para 3.20).
- Further details for these clients and for those requiring medical treatment and attention are set out in **Chapter E**.

D1.3 Access to legal advice

- All detainees have the right to consult a solicitor, protected by Art 6(3)(c) ECHR. Further, under s 58 PACE 1984 and PACE Code C para 6 an arrested person has the right to consult a solicitor in private at any time, and the request must be permitted as soon as practicable.
- The police do have the power to delay the suspect's right of access to legal advice where the suspect has been arrested but not charged for an indictable offence and an officer of at least the rank of superintendent authorizes it (s 58(2) PACE 1984). The superintendent must have reasonable grounds for believing that the access to a solicitor at that time will either:
  - (a) lead to interference with or harm to evidence connected with an indictable offence, or interference with or physical injury to another person; or
  - (b) lead to the alerting of other persons suspected of having committed such an offence but not yet arrested for it; or
  - (c) Hinder the recovery of property obtained as a result of the offence ((s 58(8) PACE 1984)).
- 'An officer may also authorize delay where he has reasonable grounds for believing that:
  - (a) the person detained for the indictable offence has benefitted from his criminal conduct; and
  - (b) the recovery of the value of property constituting the benefit will be hindered by telling the named person of the arrest' (s 58(8A) PACE 1984).

NB s 58(8A) is related to the proceeds of crime under POCA 2002 Part 2.

- The right may be delayed for as long as the grounds continue to exist, but in any event this must not be more than 36 hours from the relevant time and the suspect must be allowed to consult with a solicitor for a reasonable time before a court hearing (PACE Code C Annex B paras 6–7).

- The detainee must be informed of the arrival at the police station of their legal representative and they must be given the opportunity to consult with the representative in private (PACE Code C para 6.15).
- Where an appropriate adult is required 'a detainee should always be given an opportunity…to consult privately with a solicitor in the appropriate adult's absence if they want. An appropriate adult is not subject to legal privilege' (PACE Code C NfG 1E).
- Detainees must be allowed access to a copy of the PACE Codes of Practice.
- Detainees must be provided promptly with a written Letter of Rights. They shall be given an opportunity to read the Letter of Rights and shall be allowed to keep it in their possession throughout the time that they are deprived of liberty (Art 4 Directive 2012/13/EU).

D1.4 Access to legal materials and disclosure

- Detainees have the right of access to the materials of the case (Art 4 para 2(a) Directive 2012/13/EU).
- 'Documents and materials which are essential to effectively challenging the lawfulness of the detainee's arrest and detention must be made available to the detainee or their solicitor. Documents and materials will be "essential" for this purpose if they are capable of undermining the reasons and grounds which make the detainee's arrest and detention necessary. The decision about whether particular documents or materials must be made available for the purpose of this requirement therefore rests with the custody officer who determines whether detention is necessary, in consultation with the investigating officer who has the knowledge of the documents and materials in a particular case necessary to inform that decision. A note should be made in the detainee's custody record of the fact that documents or materials have been made available under this sub-paragraph and when. The investigating officer should make a separate note of what is made available and how it is made available in a particular case. This sub-paragraph also applies (with modifications) for the purposes of sections 15 (Reviews and extensions of detention) and 16 (Charging detained persons). See Note 3ZA and paragraphs 15.0 and 16.7A' (Pace Code C para 3.4(b)).
- 'An interview is the questioning of a person regarding their involvement or suspected involvement in a criminal offence or offences which, under paragraph 10.1, must be carried out under caution. Before a person is interviewed, they and, if they are

represented, their solicitor must be given sufficient information to enable them to understand the nature of any such offence, and why they are suspected of committing it (see *paragraphs 3.4(a)* and *10.3*), in order to allow for the effective exercise of the rights of the defence' (PACE Code C para 11.1A).

- 'However, whilst the information must always be sufficient for the person to understand the nature of any offence (see PACE Code C NfG 11ZA), this does not require the disclosure of details at a time which might prejudice the criminal investigation' (PACE Code C para 11.1A).
- 'The decision about what needs to be disclosed for the purpose of this requirement therefore rests with the investigating officer who has sufficient knowledge of the case to make that decision. The officer who discloses the information shall make a record of the information disclosed and when it was disclosed. This record may be made in the interview record, in the officer's pocket book or other form provided for this purpose' (PACE Code C para 11.1A).
- 'The requirement in paragraph 11.1A for a suspect to be given sufficient information about the offence applies prior to the interview and whether or not they are legally represented. What is sufficient will depend on the circumstances of the case, but it should normally include, as a minimum, a description of the facts relating to the suspected offence that are known to the officer, including the time and place in question. This aims to avoid suspects being confused or unclear about what they are supposed to have done and to help an innocent suspect to clear the matter up more quickly' (PACE Code C NfG 11ZA).
- 'Facts and information relevant to a person's suspected involvement in an offence should not be confined to those which tend to indicate the person has committed or attempted to commit the offence. Before making a decision to arrest, a constable should take account of any facts and information that are available, including claims of innocence made by the person that might dispel the suspicion' (PACE Code G NfG 2).
- 'Particular examples of facts and information which might point to a person's innocence and may tend to dispel suspicion include those which relate to the statutory defence provided by the Criminal Law Act 1967, section 3(1) which allows the use of reasonable force in the prevention of crime or making an arrest and the common law of self-defence. This may be relevant when a person appears, or claims, to have been acting reasonably in defence of themselves or others or to prevent their property or the property of others from being stolen, destroyed or damaged, particularly if the offence alleged is based on the use of unlawful force, e.g. a

criminal assault. When investigating allegations involving the use of force by school staff, the power given to all school staff under the Education and Inspections Act 2006, section 93, to use reasonable force to prevent their pupils from committing any offence, injuring persons, damaging property or prejudicing the maintenance of good order and discipline may be similarly relevant. The Association of Chief Police Officers and the Crown Prosecution Service have published joint guidance to help the public understand the meaning of reasonable force and what to expect from the police and CPS in cases which involve claims of self defence. Separate advice for school staff on their powers to use reasonable force is available from the Department for Education' (PACE Code G NfG 2A).

- 'If a constable who is dealing with an allegation of crime and considering the need to arrest becomes an investigator for the purposes of the Code of Practice under the Criminal Procedure and Investigations Act 1996, the officer should, in accordance with paragraph 3.5 of that Code, "pursue all reasonable lines of inquiry, whether these point towards or away from the suspect. What is reasonable in each case will depend on the particular circumstances"' (PACE Code G NfG 2B).

D1.5 Questioning outside the police station

- The police must not question a person in police detention at a hospital without the agreement of the responsible doctor. Also, a detainee must not be questioned, other than to clarify any voluntary statements made, where he is being transported to another police area to be questioned there in respect of an offence (PACE Code C para 14).

D1.6 Property

- On release from detention the suspect is entitled to the return of any property taken from him except where: (i) the property constitutes evidence of an offence, (ii) forensic examination or investigation is required of it in connection with an offence, (iii) in order to establish the item's lawful owner where there are reasonable grounds for believing it has been obtained in consequence of the commission of an offence (s 54C PACE 1984).

D1.7 Interpreters

- Where the detainee cannot communicate with the representative because of language, hearing, or speech difficulties an interpreter must be called. Further, detainees who require an interpreter or other assistance to enable effective communication because they do not appear to speak or understand English, or because of a hearing or speech impediment must not be interviewed in the absence of a person capable of interpreting (PACE Code C paras 13.2, 13.5, and 13.9).

D2 Rights of Representatives before Attendance

D2.1 Gaining access

- The detainee must be informed of the representative's arrival at the police station and the detainee must be given the opportunity to consult with the representative in private (PACE Code C para 6.15).
- When trying to obtain access to a client at the police station PACE does discriminate between solicitors and accredited or probationary representatives, in that under PACE Code C para 6.12A the latter can be refused admission to the police station if an officer of inspector rank or above considers their presence will hinder the investigation. The factors allowed to be taken into consideration are whether: (i) the identity and status of the representative has been established, (ii) whether they are of suitable character to provide legal advice, and (iii) any other matters in a written letter of authorization provided by the solicitor on whose behalf they are attending (PACE Code C para 6.13). In the situation where an accredited or probationary representative is refused access the solicitor must be informed and given the opportunity to make alternative arrangements (PACE Code C para 6.14).

D2.2 Being told the suspect no longer wants a solicitor

- The suspect, having initially requested legal representation at the police station, is perfectly able to change their mind and proceed to interview unrepresented. However, according to PACE Code C para 6.6(d), in such cases an officer of the rank of at least inspector must:
  - (i) Speak to the suspect to enquire about their reasons for changing their mind;
  - (ii) Make reasonable efforts to inform the representative that the suspect has changed their mind and to ascertain the representative's estimated time of arrival. If the representative is on their way or is to set off immediately it will not normally be appropriate to begin an interview before their arrival;
  - (iii) Ensure the suspect confirms in writing that they wish to proceed with the interview without speaking to a legal representative or having a legal representative present;

(iv) Record on the custody record the suspect's reasons for changing their mind and that proceeding without a solicitor present has been authorized;
(v) Make reasonable efforts to inform the solicitor of the time the interview is expected to start and that authority to proceed without them being present has been given.

- If this procedure is not followed it *may* be arguable that an inference from silence in the resulting interview should not be drawn.

D3 Rights of Representatives at the Police Station

D3.1 Role of the representative

- The representative's only role at the police station is, 'to protect and advance the legal rights of their client'. This may involve intervening to seek clarification, to challenge improper conduct by the police, and to advise their client (PACE Code C NfG 6D).

D3.2 Custody record

- The representative has the right to inspect the whole of the suspect's custody record (including any entries made in respect of medical attention—though this may require the suspect's consent) as soon as practicable after arrival at the police station, and thereafter at any other time during the suspect's detention (PACE Code C para 2.4). However, the property record does not form part of the custody record and it is up to the custody officer whether or not to allow the representative to see it (PACE Code C para 4.4).
- The representative is entitled to a copy of the detainee's custody record for up to 12 months after the detainee has left police detention, and is entitled to inspect a copy of the original without time limit (PACE Code C paras 2.4A–2.5).

D3.3 Removal from interview

- 'The [representative] may only be removed from the interview by the police where their conduct is such that the interviewer is unable properly to put questions to the suspect.' Bearing in mind the representative's role, the ability to exclude a representative only applies where their conduct prevents or unreasonably obstructs proper questions being put to the suspect or the suspect's response from being recorded (PACE Code C para 6.9 and PACE Code C NfG 6D). Only a superintendent, or inspector where a superintendent is unavailable, can make the decision to remove a representative from an interview (PACE Code C para 6.10).

D3.4 Advising the client

- In accordance with the representative's role, they have the right to consult with the client in private at any time (s 58 PACE 1984 and PACE Code C Annex B).

D4 Custody Time Limits

D4.1 General rule

- Section 41(1) PACE 1984 states that generally someone shall not be kept in police detention for more than 24 hours without being charged. There are, however, provisions for the extension of detention beyond 24 hours.

D4.2 'Relevant time'

- In most cases the time at which the 24-hour detention period starts to count down is called the 'relevant time' and it is governed by s 41(2) PACE 1984. It is the earlier of either (i) the suspect's arrival at a police station, or (ii) 24 hours after their arrest. The following exceptions apply:
  1. If a suspect is arrested outside England & Wales the relevant time is the earlier of: (i) when they first arrive at a police station in England & Wales in which the offence for which they have been arrested is being investigated, or (ii) 24 hours after their entry into England & Wales;
  2. Where a suspect attends a police station voluntarily and is subsequently arrested, the relevant time is the time of arrest;
  3. Where a suspect attends a police station to answer street bail, the relevant time is the time of arrival;
  4. Where a suspect is detained in police area 1, and his arrest is sought in police area 2 for questioning in relation to another offence, the relevant time is the earlier of: (i) his arrival at a police station in area 2, or (ii) 24 hours after leaving the police station in area 1. This is provided questioning has taken place about the subsequent offence in area 1;
  5. Where a suspect is detained and re-arrested for a further offence the relevant time remains that for the first offence.

D4.3 Extension of detention for 12 hours

- In case of an indictable offence an officer of the rank of superintendent or above can extend the initial 24-hour period of detention, by one or more further periods adding up to a further 12 hours, if they have reasonable grounds for believing that:
  - Further detention is necessary to secure or preserve evidence relating to an offence for which the suspect is under arrest, or to obtain further evidence by questioning him.
  - The investigation is being conducted diligently and expeditiously.

- Before making the decision to extend the detention the officer must allow the suspect or their legal representative to make representations (s 42(6) PACE).

D4.4 Interruption to the period of detention

- Where a suspect is taken from police detention to a hospital for medical treatment the time spent travelling to, from, and the time at the hospital do not count toward the detention period (s 41(6) PACE).
- Where a suspect is released on bail and returns to the police station the relevant time is that for the initial detention and the period resumes on any subsequent detention. However, should the suspect be re-arrested when returning on bail the relevant time will be the time of re-arrest (s 41 PACE).

D4.5 Warrants of further detention

- On application by a constable a magistrate may issue a warrant of further detention for a period, or periods totalling a maximum of 36 hours (s 43 PACE).

D4.6 Expiry of custody time limit

- On expiry of the custody time limit the suspect must be charged, released on bail, or released without charge (s 41 PACE).

NB For terrorism offences, detention periods differ and powers to extend them are greater. Reference should be made to Code H.

D5 Volunteers at the Police Station

(In relation to interviews see also G5.1).

- A volunteer is entitled to leave at will unless they are arrested (s 29 PACE; Code C para 3.21). PACE Code C applies to those attending the police station as volunteers and as such they must be treated in the same manner as detained persons, with access to many of the same rights, such as the right to legal advice at any time (PACE Code C para 1.10 and PACE Code C NfG 1A).
- If a volunteer is cautioned (such as at the start of a tape recorded interview) they must be informed they are not under arrest and that they may leave at any time, and that they are entitled to free and independent legal advice (PACE Code C para 3.21).
- The routine arrest of a volunteer on arrival at the police station without further justification is unlawful (*Richardson v Chief Constable of West Midlands Police* [2011] EWHC 733 (QB)) and officers must consider other alternatives short of arrest.
- The police have the power to take photographs of volunteers who are not detained, but force may not be used. Indeed, force may not be used to take photographs of identifying marks, or to perform a search in order to establish identity or discover identifying marks (PACE Code D paras 5.19–5.21). Photographs taken of a volunteer must be destroyed unless they are warned or reprimanded, cautioned, charged, or prosecuted, or indeed they give permission for the retention (PACE Code D para 5.22).
- The police do not have the power to take intimate samples from volunteers under s 62 PACE 1984 as they are not in police detention, though this position is changed following the volunteer's arrest (s 118(2) PACE 1984).

See *Blackstone's Criminal Practice* D1.40–D2

Part E
Vulnerable Clients

E1 Youths

E1.1 Assumptions

- 'If any suspect appears to be under 17 they shall, in the absence of clear evidence that they are older, be treated as under 17' (PACE Code C para 1.5).

E1.2 Entitlements

- These provisions apply to those under 18 years of age unless otherwise stated.
- To have identified and informed someone responsible for their welfare, which is in addition to their right in section 5 of this Code not to be held incommunicado (PACE Code C para 3.13).
- To have notified a person who has statutory responsibility under a court order to supervise or monitor them (PACE Code C para 3.14).
- Not normally to be placed in cell accommodation; and to be kept separate from adults (PACE Code C para 8.8).
- To call a person in relation to testing for the presence of Class A drugs, to fulfil the role of the appropriate adult (PACE Code C para 17.7(a)and PACE Code C NfG 17G).
- To have an appropriate adult present when:
    - They are informed of their rights and entitlements and the grounds for their detention (PACE Code C paras 3.17 and 3.18);
    - They are cautioned or given a special warning (PACE Code C paras10.12 and 10.11A);
    - They are being interviewed in accordance with this Code C 11 and 12 or Codes E or F unless PACE Code C para 11.18 applies which exceptionally allows the interview to go ahead without the adult being present;
    - Their detention is being reviewed or an extension is being considered (PACE Code C paras 15.3(c) and 15.3C(a));
    - They are charged, cautioned or conditionally cautioned and related action is taken (PACE Code C paras 16.1, 16.3, 16.4A, and 16.6);
    - Samples to test for Class A drugs are requested (PACE Code C para 17.7);
    - An intimate search is carried out (PACE Code C Annex A paras 2A, 2B, and 5);
    - A strip search is carried out (PACE Code C Annex A para 11(c));
    - An x-ray or ultrasound scan is carried out (PACE Code C Annex K paras 2 and 3);
    - Procedures in Code D involving witness identification, taking fingerprints, samples, footwear impressions, and photographs

and when evidential searches and examinations are carried out (PACE Code D paras 2.14 and 2.15).

To be allowed:

- the adult to inspect their custody record and to have a copy of their record (PACE Code C paras 2.4, 2.4A, and 2.5);
- to consult the adult in private (PACE Code C para 3.18);
- the adult to request legal advice on their behalf to advise and assist them.

NB Until the necessary legislative amendments have been passed, of those rights the following will only apply to 17-year-olds:

(a) The statutory provisions in section 38 of PACE (Detention after charge) which apply only to an arrested juvenile as defined in s 37(15) of PACE, shall not apply to a person who appears to have attained the age of 17 for the purposes of:
  (i) the grounds to keep them in police detention after charge; and
  (ii) the requirement to transfer a person who has been kept in police detention after charge to local authority accommodation.

(b) the statutory provisions in s 65(1) of PACE (appropriate consent) which require appropriate consent for a person who has not attained the age of 17 to be given by them and their parent or guardian shall not apply to a person who appears to have attained the age of 17 and whose consent alone shall be sufficient.

Section 65(1) applies to PACE Code C Annex A paras 2(b) and 2B (Intimate searches) and PACE Code C Annex K paras 1(b) and 3 (X-ray and ultrasound scan) and in PACE Code D (Identification) to para 2.12 and NfG 2A with regards to taking fingerprints, samples, footwear impressions, photographs, and evidential searches and examinations (PACW Code C para1.5A).

E2 The Rights of the Blind, Seriously Visually Impaired, Deaf, etc.

- 'If a person appears to be blind, seriously visually impaired, deaf, unable to read or speak or has difficulty orally because of a speech impediment, they shall be treated as such for the purposes of this Code in the absence of clear evidence to the contrary' (PACE Code C para 1.6).

E3 Identifying Vulnerability before Interview

Extracts from PACE Code C Annex G

- 'A detainee may be at risk in an interview if it is considered that:
  (a) conducting the interview could significantly harm the detainee's physical or mental state;
  (b) anything the detainee says in the interview about their involvement or suspected involvement in the offence about which they are being interviewed might be considered unreliable in subsequent court proceedings because of their physical or mental state' (PACE Code C Annex G 2).
- '... The following must be considered:
  (a) how the detainee's physical or mental state might affect their ability to understand the nature and purpose of the interview, to comprehend what is being asked and to appreciate the significance of any answers given and make rational decisions about whether they want to say anything;
  (b) the extent to which the detainee's replies may be affected by their physical or mental condition rather than representing a rational and accurate explanation of their involvement in the offence;
  (c) how the nature of the interview, which could include particularly probing questions, might affect the detainee' (PACE Code C Annex G 3).
- 'It is essential healthcare professionals who are consulted consider the functional ability of the detainee rather than simply relying on a medical diagnosis, e.g. it is possible for a person with severe mental illness to be fit for interview' (PACE Code C Annex G 4).
- 'Healthcare professionals should advise on the need for an appropriate adult to be present, whether reassessment of the person's fitness for interview may be necessary if the interview lasts beyond a specified time, and whether a further specialist opinion may be required' (PACE Code C Annex G 5).
- '... The healthcare professional's determination and any advice or recommendations should be made in writing and form part of the custody record' (PACE Code C Annex G 7).

E4 Provisions Relating to Mentally Disordered and Otherwise Mentally Vulnerable People

Extracts from PACE Code C Annex E:

- 'If an officer has any suspicion, or is told in good faith, that a person of any age may be mentally disordered or otherwise mentally vulnerable, or mentally incapable of understanding the significance of questions or their replies that person shall be treated as mentally disordered or otherwise mentally vulnerable for the purposes of this Code (see PACE Code C para 1.4 and note E4)' (PACE Code C Annex E 1)).
- 'If the custody officer authorises the detention of a person who is mentally vulnerable or appears to be suffering from a mental disorder, the custody officer must as soon as practicable inform the appropriate adult of the grounds for detention and the person's whereabouts, and ask the adult to come to the police station to see them. If the appropriate adult:
  - is already at the station when information is given as in PACE Code C paras 3.1 to 3.5 the information must be given in their presence;
  - is not at the station when the provisions of PACE Code C paras 3.1 to 3.5 are complied with these provisions must be complied with again in their presence once they arrive (see PACE Code C paras 3.15 to 3.17)' (PACE Code C Annex E 3).
- 'If the appropriate adult, having been informed of the right to legal advice, considers legal advice should be taken, the provisions of section 6 apply as if the mentally disordered or otherwise mentally vulnerable person had requested access to legal advice (see PACE Code C para 3.19 and Note E1)' (PACE Code C Annex E 4).
- 'The custody officer must make sure a person receives appropriate clinical attention as soon as reasonably practicable if the person appears to be suffering from a mental disorder or in urgent cases immediately call the nearest appropriate healthcare professional or an ambulance. It is not intended these provisions delay the transfer of a detainee to a place of safety under the Mental Health Act 1983, section 136 if that is applicable. If an assessment under that Act is to take place at a police station, the custody officer must consider whether an appropriate healthcare professional should be called to conduct an initial clinical check on the detainee (see PACE Code C paras 9.5 and 9.6)' (PACE Code C Annex E 5).

- 'It is imperative a mentally disordered or otherwise mentally vulnerable person detained under the Mental Health Act 1983, section 136 be assessed as soon as possible. A police station should only be used as a place of safety as a last resort but if that assessment is to take place at the police station, an approved social worker and registered medical practitioner shall be called to the station as soon as possible to carry it out. Once the detainee has been assessed and suitable arrangements been made for their treatment or care, they can no longer be detained under section 136. A detainee should be immediately discharged from detention if a registered medical practitioner, having examined them, concludes they are not mentally disordered within the meaning of the Act (see PACE Code C pars 3.16)' (PACE Code C Annex E 6).
- 'If a mentally disordered or otherwise mentally vulnerable person is cautioned in the absence of the appropriate adult, the caution must be repeated in the appropriate adult's presence (see PACE Code C para10.12)' (PACE Code C Annex E 7).
- 'A mentally disordered or otherwise mentally vulnerable person must not be interviewed or asked to provide or sign a written statement in the absence of the appropriate adult unless the provisions of C11.1 or 11.18 to 11.20 apply. Questioning in these circumstances may not continue in the absence of the appropriate adult once sufficient information to avert the risk has been obtained. A record shall be made of the grounds for any decision to begin an interview in these circumstances (see PACE Code C paras 11.1, 11.15 and 11.18 to 11.20)' (PACE Code C Annex E 8).
- 'If the detention of a mentally disordered or otherwise mentally vulnerable person is reviewed by a review officer or a superintendent, the appropriate adult must, if available at the time, be given an opportunity to make representations to the officer about the need for continuing detention (see PACE code C para 15.3)' (PACE Code C Annex E 10).
- 'If the custody officer charges a mentally disordered or otherwise mentally vulnerable person with an offence or takes such other action as is appropriate when there is sufficient evidence for a prosecution this must be carried out in the presence of the appropriate adult if they are at the police station. A copy of the written notice embodying any charge must also be given to the appropriate adult (see PACE Code C paras 16.1 to 16.4A)' (PACE Code C Annex E 11).
- 'An intimate or strip search of a mentally disordered or otherwise mentally vulnerable person may take place only in the presence of the appropriate adult of the same sex, unless the detainee specifically requests the presence of a particular adult of the opposite sex. A strip search may take place in the absence of an appropriate adult

only in cases of urgency when there is a risk of serious harm to the detainee or others (PACE Code C Annex A, paras 5 and 11(c))' (see PACE Code C Annex E 12).

- 'Particular care must be taken when deciding whether to use any form of approved restraints on a mentally disordered or otherwise mentally vulnerable person in a locked cell (see PACE Code C para 8.2)'

PACE Code C Annex E 13. Notes for guidance

- 'The purpose of the provision at paragraph 3.19 is to protect the rights of a mentally disordered or otherwise mentally vulnerable detained person who does not understand the significance of what is said to them. If the detained person wants to exercise the right to legal advice, the appropriate action should be taken and not delayed until the appropriate adult arrives. A mentally disordered or otherwise mentally vulnerable detained person should always be given an opportunity, when an appropriate adult is called to the police station, to consult privately with a solicitor in the absence of the appropriate adult if they want' (PACE Code C Annex E NfG E1).
- 'Although people who are mentally disordered or otherwise mentally vulnerable are often capable of providing reliable evidence, they may, without knowing or wanting to do so, be particularly prone in certain circumstances to provide information that may be unreliable, misleading or self-incriminating. Special care should always be taken when questioning such a person, and the appropriate adult should be involved if there is any doubt about a person's mental state or capacity. Because of the risk of unreliable evidence, it is important to obtain corroboration of any facts admitted whenever possible' (PACE Code C Annex E NfG E2).
- 'Because of the risks referred to in Note E2, which the presence of the appropriate adult is intended to minimise, officers of superintendent rank or above should exercise their discretion to authorise the commencement of an interview in the appropriate adult's absence only in exceptional cases, if it is necessary to avert an immediate risk of serious harm (see PACE Code C paras 11.1, 11.18 to 11.20)' (PACE Code C Annex E NfG E3).
- 'There is no requirement for an appropriate adult to be present if a person is detained under section 136 of the Mental Health Act 1983 for assessment' (PACE Code C Annex E NfG E4).

E5 Appropriate Adult

E5.1 Meaning of appropriate adult

- In the case of a:
  - (a) juvenile (which extends to all those under 18):
    - (i) 'The parent, guardian or, if the juvenile is in the care of a local authority or voluntary organisation, a person representing that authority or organisation (see PACE Code C Note 1B);
    - (ii) A social worker of a local authority (see PACE Code C Note 1C);
    - (iii) Failing these, some other responsible adult aged 18 or over who is not a police officer or employed by the police' (PACE Code C Para 1.7(a).
  - (b) person who is mentally disordered or mentally vulnerable:
    - (i) 'A relative, guardian or other person responsible for their care or custody;
    - (ii) Someone experienced in dealing with mentally disordered or mentally vulnerable people but who is not a police officer or employed by the police;
    - (iii) Failing these, some other responsible adult aged 18 or over who is not a police officer or employed by the police (PACE Code C para 1.7(b) and NfG 1D (PACE Code C Annex E2))' (PACE Code C para 1.7(b)).
- '"Mentally vulnerable" applies to any detainee who, because of their mental state or capacity, may not understand the significance of what is said, of questions or of their replies. "Mental disorder" is defined in the Mental Health Act 1983, section 1(2) as "any disorder or disability of mind". When the custody officer has any doubt about the mental state or capacity of a detainee, that detainee should be treated as mentally vulnerable and an appropriate adult called' (PACE Code C NfG 1G).
- 'In the case of people who are mentally disordered or otherwise mentally vulnerable, it may be more satisfactory if the appropriate adult is someone experienced or trained in their care rather than a relative lacking such qualifications. But if the detainee prefers a relative to a better qualified stranger or objects to a particular person their wishes should, if practicable, be respected' (PACE Code C NfG 1D).

E5.2 When a person is not appropriate

- 'A person, including a parent or guardian, should not be an appropriate adult if they are:
  - suspected of involvement in the offence;
  - the victim;
  - a witness;
  - involved in the investigation;
  - received admissions prior to attending to act as the appropriate adult.

  Note: If a juvenile's parent is estranged from the juvenile, they should not be asked to act as the appropriate adult if the juvenile expressly and specifically objects to their presence' (PACE Code C NfG 1B).
- 'If a juvenile admits an offence to, or in the presence of, a social worker or member of a youth offending team other than during the time that person is acting as the juvenile's appropriate adult, another appropriate adult should be appointed in the interest of fairness' (PACE Code C NfG 1C).

E5.3 Role of the appropriate adult

- 'If the appropriate adult is present at an interview, they shall be informed they are not expected to act simply as an observer and the purposes of their presence are to:
  - advise the interviewee;
  - observe whether or not the interview is being conducted properly and fairly;
  - facilitate communication with the interviewee' (PACE Code C para 11.17).
- 'A detainee should always be given an opportunity, when an appropriate adult is called to the police station, to consult privately with a solicitor in the appropriate adult's absence if they want. An appropriate adult is not subject to legal privilege' (PACE Code C NfG 1E).
- 'A solicitor or independent custody visitor present at the police station in that capacity may not be the appropriate adult' (PACE Code C NfG 1F).

E6 Those who may Require Clinical Treatment and Attention

- 'The custody officer must make sure a detainee receives appropriate clinical attention as soon as reasonably practicable if the person:
  (a) appears to be suffering from physical illness; or
  (b) is injured; or
  (c) appears to be suffering from a mental disorder; or
  (d) appears to need clinical attention' (PACE Code C para 9.5).
- 'This applies even if the detainee makes no request for clinical attention and whether or not they have already received clinical attention elsewhere. If the need for attention appears urgent, e.g. when indicated as in Annex H, the nearest available healthcare professional or an ambulance must be called immediately' (PACE Code C para 9.5A).
- 'The custody officer must also consider the need for clinical attention as set out in Note 9C in relation to those suffering the effects of alcohol or drugs' (PACE Code C para 9.5B).
- 'Paragraph 9.5 is not meant to prevent or delay the transfer to a hospital if necessary of a person detained under the Mental Health Act 1983, section 136. See Note 9D. When an assessment under that Act is to take place at a police station, see paragraph 3.16, the custody officer must consider whether an appropriate healthcare professional should be called to conduct an initial clinical check on the detainee. This applies particularly when there is likely to be any significant delay in the arrival of a suitably qualified medical practitioner' (PACE Code C para 9.6).
- 'If a detainee requests a clinical examination, an appropriate healthcare professional must be called as soon as practicable to assess the detainee's clinical needs. If a safe and appropriate care plan cannot be provided, the appropriate healthcare professional's advice must be sought. The detainee may also be examined by a medical practitioner of their choice at their expense' (PACE Code C para 9.8).
- 'If the detainee has in their possession, or claims to need, medication relating to a heart condition, diabetes, epilepsy, or condition of comparable potential seriousness then medical advice must be obtained' (PACE Code C para 9.12).
- 'A record must be made in the custody record of:
  (a) The arrangements made for an examination by an appropriate healthcare professional under paragraph 9.2 and of any

complaint reported under that paragraph together with any relevant remarks by the custody officer;

(b) Any arrangements made in accordance with paragraph 9.5;

(c) Any request for a clinical examination under paragraph 9.8 and any arrangements made in response;

(d) The injury, ailment, condition or other reason which made it necessary to make the arrangements in (a) to (c); (See Note 9G).

(e) Any clinical directions and advice, including any further clarifications, given to police by a healthcare professional concerning the care and treatment of the detainee in connection with any of the arrangements made in (a) to (c); (See Notes 9E and 9F).

(f) If applicable, the responses received when attempting to rouse a person using the procedure in Annex H. See Note 9H' (PACE Code C para 9.15).

- 'If a healthcare professional does not record their clinical findings in the custody record, the record must show where they are recorded. See Note 9G. However, information which is necessary to custody staff to ensure the effective ongoing care and well being of the detainee must be recorded openly in the custody record, see paragraph 3.8 and Annex G, paragraph 7' (PACE Code C para 9.16).
- 'It is important to respect a person's right to privacy and information about their health must be kept confidential and only disclosed with their consent or in accordance with clinical advice when it is necessary to protect the detainee's health or that of others who come into contact with them' (PACE Code C NfG 9E).
- 'Paragraphs 9.15 and 9.16 do not require any information about the cause of any injury, ailment or condition to be recorded on the custody record if it appears capable of providing evidence of an offence' (PACE Code C NfG 9G).

Part F
Ancillary Procedures

F1 Identity Procedures

F1.1 Records

- 'A record shall be made of the suspect's description as first given by a potential witness... [this shall] unless otherwise specified—be made before the witness takes part in any identification procedures' (PACE Code D para 3.1(b)).

F1.2 No known suspect

- 'In cases where the suspect's identity is not known, a witness may be taken to a particular... place to see whether they can identify the person they saw on a previous occasion' (PACE Code D para 3.2).

F1.3 Nature of the procedure

- An identification procedure *shall* (emphasis added) be held 'whenever there is a witness available who [has identified, purported to identify or expressed an ability to identify the suspect]... and the suspect disputes being the person who the witness claims to have seen... unless it is not practicable or it would serve no useful purpose in proving or disproving whether the suspect was involved in committing the offence' (PACE Code D para 3.12).
- 'If... an identification procedure is to take place then the suspect shall initially be offered a video identification unless: a video identification is not practicable; an identification parade is both practicable and more suitable than a video identification; or [the officer in charge of the investigation offers a group identification as it is considered more suitable than a video identification or an identification parade]...' (PACE Code D para 3.14).
- 'Where a known suspect is not available or ceased to be available [NB this will include refusal by a defendant to take part in identification proceedings] the identification officer may still follow the video identification procedures but using still images' (PACE Code D para 3.21).
- '[If no alternative identification procedures are available] the identification officer may arrange for the suspect to be confronted by the witness... this does not require the consent of the suspect' (PACE Code D para 3.23).

F1.4 Obtaining images

- '[When a] detainee is unwilling to co-operate sufficiently to enable a suitable [custody] photograph to be taken and it is not reasonably practicable to take the photograph covertly, an officer may use reasonable force' (PACE Code D para 5.14).
- 'For the purposes of this Code, a photograph may be obtained without the person's consent by making a copy of an image of them taken at any time on a camera system installed anywhere in the police station' (PACE Code D para 5.15).

F1.5 Distinctive features

- 'The identification officer has the discretion whether to conceal or replicate a distinctive feature and the method to be used. If an unusual physical feature has been described by a witness [this should be replicated if practicable]. If an [unusual physical feature] has not been described then concealment may be more appropriate' (PACE Code D Annex A para 2A).
- 'If a witness requests to view an image, where an unusual physical feature has been concealed or replicated, without the concealment or replication, they may be allowed to do so' (PACE Code D Annex A para 2C).

F1.6 Viewing

- 'The suspect, or their solicitor, friend, or appropriate adult must be given a reasonable opportunity to see the complete set of images before it is shown to any witness. If the suspect has a reasonable objection to the set of images or any participants they shall be asked to state the reason for the objection. Steps shall, if practicable, be taken to remove the grounds for objection' (PACE Code D Annex A para 7).

F2 Provisions Relating to Youths and the Mentally Disordered

- Consent to identification procedures involving the mentally disordered is only valid if given in the presence of an appropriate adult (PACE Code D para 2.12).
- Consent to identification procedures involving youths is only valid if the parent's or guardian's consent is also given. However when a youth is under the age of 14 the necessary consent can be provided by a parent or guardian alone (PACE Code D para 2.12).
- Where a young person is under the care of a local authority or voluntary organization the respective organization may provide the relevant consent in the place of a parent or guardian (PACE Code D NfG 2A).
- [Any identification procedure involving a youth or the mentally disordered] must take place in the presence of an appropriate adult (PACE Code D para 2.15).

F3 Intimate Samples

- 'An intimate sample means a dental impression or sample of blood, semen, or any other tissue fluid, urine or pubic hair, or a swab taken from any part of a person's genitals or from a person's body orifice other than the mouth (PACE Code D para 6.1) (s 65 PACE).
- Intimate samples may only be taken with the suspect's written consent and an inspector's authority because of reasonable grounds for believing that a recordable offence has been committed and that the sample will tend to prove or disprove the suspect's involvement (s 62 PACE).
- A suspect at a police station may refuse to give an intimate sample but if they refuse without good reason a court may draw such inference from the refusal as appear proper (s 62(10) PACE).
- If there is no other evidence against the suspect, an inference alone will not be sufficient to prove the offence. However, a judge, when faced with an application to dismiss, may draw an inference from the refusal to provide an intimate sample.
- 'Intimate samples will be subject to a speculative search. However, a speculative search may only be conducted in relation to a person who is not arrested, charged, or reported with their written consent' (PACE Code D para 6E).

F4 Non-Intimate Samples

- These include samples taken from the suspect's mouth. They may be taken without the suspect's consent in certain circumstances, including, if the suspect is detained at the police station in relation to a recordable offence; or the person has been charged with, reported for, or convicted of a recordable offence (s 63 PACE) (PACE Code D para 6.6).

Part G
Other Interviews

G1 Volunteers under Caution

- Any individual legal person or authority may invite a suspect to take part in an interview under caution so that the result may be introduced into evidence in any proceedings. In particular this includes local authorities; the Deportment of Work and Pensions; Serious Fraud Office; Financial Conduct Authority, and organizations such as British Gas and the Vehicle Inspectorate.
- However, only a constable may arrest. A volunteer may leave at any time. The fact that a suspect may leave cannot justify a constable making an arrest until the time that the volunteer chooses to leave (PACE Code C para 3.21). The possibility of an arrest must be considered when offering advice.
- If there is no power to arrest and there is no interview there can be no inference from silence in relation to individual questions (*R v Argent* [1996] EWCA Crim 1728). A volunteer must be treated with no less consideration than a person under arrest (PACE Code C NfG 1A), told that they are not obliged to remain, but may obtain free and independent legal advice (PACE Code C para 3.21).
- When a volunteer is interviewed at a location at which the interviewer requires the volunteer's informed consent to remain, the volunteer may withdraw their consent and require the interviewer to leave (PACE Code C para 3.22).
- Force may not be used to search/examine or take any photograph of a volunteer where they attend a police station as a volunteer (PACE Code D para 5.21).

G1.1 Compulsory interviews

- Statute provides for situations where persons are required to take part in compulsory interviews and to provide relevant documents to an enquiry. These are not interviews under caution. The content of such an interview cannot self-incriminate the provider although the interview may lead to other evidence that will be admissible. To fail to comply is a criminal offence. For this reason a solicitor cannot advise against compliance. However a solicitor must still advise on the consequences of compliance in the identification of other relevant evidence and of non-compliance. The powers described in the following sections exist.

G2 Serious Fraud Office Investigating Fraud, Bribery, and Corruption

Criminal Justice Act 1987

s 2 'Director's investigation powers'

(2) The Director may by notice in writing require the person whose affairs are to be investigated ('the person under investigation') or any other person whom he has reason to believe has relevant information to answer questions or otherwise furnish information with respect to any matter relevant to the investigation at a specified place and either at a specified time or forthwith.

(3) The Director may by notice in writing require the person under investigation or any other person to produce at such place as may be specified in the notice and either forthwith or at such time as may be so specified, any specified documents which appear to the Director to relate to any matter relevant to the investigation or any documents of a specified description which appear to him so to relate; and—
- (a) if any such documents are produced, the Director may—
  - (i) take copies or extracts from them;
  - (ii) require the person producing them to provide an explanation of any of them;
- (b) if any such documents are not produced, the Director may require the person who was required to produce them to state, to the best of his knowledge and belief, where they are.

...

(8) A statement by a person in response to a requirement imposed by virtue of this section may only be used in evidence against him—
- (a) on a prosecution for an offence under subsection (14) below; or
- (b) on a prosecution for some other offence where in giving evidence he makes a statement inconsistent with it.

(8AA) However, the statement may not be used against that person by virtue of paragraph (b) of subsection (8) unless evidence relating to it is adduced, or a question relating to it is asked, by or on behalf of that person in the proceedings arising out of the prosecution.

...

(13) Any person who without reasonable excuse fails to comply with a requirement imposed on him under this section shall be guilty of an offence and liable on summary conviction to imprisonment for a term not exceeding six months or to an unlimited fine on the standard scale or to both.

(14) A person who, in purported compliance with a requirement under this section—
- (a) makes a statement which he knows to be false or misleading in a material particular; or

(b) recklessly makes a statement which is false or misleading in a material particular,

shall be guilty of an offence.

(15) A person guilty of an offence under subsection (14) above shall—

(a) on conviction on indictment, be liable to imprisonment for a term not exceeding two years or to a fine or to both; and

(b) on summary conviction, be liable to imprisonment for a term not exceeding six months or to an unlimited fine or to both.

(16) Where any person—

(a) knows or suspects that an investigation by the police or the Serious Fraud Office into serious or complex fraud is being or is likely to be carried out; and

(b) falsifies, conceals, destroys or otherwise disposes of, or causes or permits the falsification, concealment, destruction or disposal of documents which he knows or suspects are or would be relevant to such an investigation, he shall be guilty of an offence unless he proves that he had no intention of concealing the facts disclosed by the documents from persons carrying out such an investigation.

(17) A person guilty of an offence under subsection (16) above shall—

(a) on conviction on indictment, be liable to imprisonment for a term not exceeding 7 years or to a fine or to both; and

(b) on summary conviction, be liable to imprisonment for a term not exceeding 6 months or to an unlimited fine or to both.

G3 Financial Conduct Authority in relation to Investigations within the Financial Services and Markets Act 2000

Financial Services and Markets Act 2000

s 171 'Powers of persons appointed under section 167'

(1) An investigator may require the person who is the subject of the investigation ('the person under investigation') or any person connected with the person under investigation—
   (a) to attend before the investigator at a specified time and place and answer questions; or
   (b) otherwise to provide such information as the investigator may require.

(2) An investigator may also require any person to produce at a specified time and place any specified documents or documents of a specified description.

(3) A requirement under subsection (1) or (2) may be imposed only so far as the investigator concerned reasonably considers the question, provision of information or production of the document to be relevant to the purposes of the investigation.

s 172 'Additional power of persons appointed as a result of section 168(1) or (4)'

(1) An investigator has the powers conferred by section 171.

(2) An investigator may also require a person who is neither the subject of the investigation ('the person under investigation') nor a person connected with the person under investigation—
   (a) to attend before the investigator at a specified time and place and answer questions; or
   (b) otherwise to provide such information as the investigator may require for the purposes of the investigation.

s 173 'Powers of persons appointed as a result of section 168(2)'

(1) Subsections (2) to (4) apply if an investigator considers that any person ('A') is or may be able to give information which is or may be relevant to the investigation.

(2) The investigator may require A—
   (a) to attend before him at a specified time and place and answer questions; or
   (b) otherwise to provide such information as he may require for the purposes of the investigation.

(3) The investigator may also require A to produce at a specified time and place any specified documents or documents of a specified description which appear to the investigator to relate to any matter relevant to the investigation.

(4) The investigator may also otherwise require A to give him all assistance in connection with the investigation which A is reasonably able to give.

s 174 'Admissibility of statements made to investigators'

(1) A statement made to an investigator by a person in compliance with an information requirement is admissible in evidence in any proceedings, so long as it also complies with any requirements governing the admissibility of evidence in the circumstances in question.

(2) But in criminal proceedings in which that person is charged with an offence to which this subsection applies or in proceedings in relation to action to be taken against that person under section 123—

(a) no evidence relating to the statement may be adduced, and

(b) no question relating to it may be asked, by or on behalf of the prosecution or (as the case may be) a regulator, unless evidence relating to it is adduced, or a question relating to it is asked, in the proceedings by or on behalf of that person.

(3) Subsection (2) applies to any offence other than one—

(a) under section 177(4) or 398;

(b) under section 5 of the Perjury Act 1911 (false statements made otherwise than on oath); . . .

s 177 'Offences'

(1) If a person other than the investigator ('the defaulter') fails to comply with a requirement imposed on him under this Part the person imposing the requirement may certify that fact in writing to the court.

(2) If the court is satisfied that the defaulter failed without reasonable excuse to comply with the requirement, it may deal with the defaulter (and in the case of a body corporate, any director or other officer) as if he were in contempt; and 'officer', in relation to a limited liability partnership, means a member of the limited liability partnership.

(3) A person who knows or suspects that an investigation is being or is likely to be conducted under this Part is guilty of an offence if—

(a) he falsifies, conceals, destroys or otherwise disposes of a document which he knows or suspects is or would be relevant to such an investigation, or

(b) he causes or permits the falsification, concealment, destruction or disposal of such a document, unless he shows that he had no intention of concealing facts disclosed by the documents from the investigator.

(4) A person who, in purported compliance with a requirement imposed on him under this Part—

(a) provides information which he knows to be false or misleading in a material particular, or

(b) recklessly provides information which is false or misleading in a material particular, is guilty of an offence.

(5) A person guilty of an offence under subsection (3) or (4) is liable—

(a) on summary conviction, to imprisonment for a term not exceeding six months or an unlimited fine, or both;

(b) on conviction on indictment, to imprisonment for a term not exceeding two years or a fine, or both.

NB A person found to be in contempt of court is liable to imprisonment for maximum of 1 month on summary conviction and 2 years on indictment or to a fine (s 14 Contempt of Court Act 1981).

- Those advising must be aware that the protection offered in section 2 interviews (under s 8AA Criminal Justice Act 1987 is not replicated under the Financial Services and Markets Act 2000 ('FSMA'). Therefore, while a prosecutor cannot use a compulsory interview under FSMA in related proceedings it can be used by other parties in the proceedings (ie co-defendants).

G4 An Examiner at the Border or Port under Schedule 7 Terrorism Act 2000

Terrorism Act 2000

Schedule 7 'Port and border controls'

Para 2 'Power to stop, question and detain'

(1) An examining officer may question a person to whom this paragraph applies for the purpose of determining whether he appears to be a person falling within section 40(1)(b) [a person connected with terrorism].

(2) This paragraph applies to a person if—
   (a) he is at a port or in the border area, and
   (b) the examining officer believes that the person's presence at the port or in the area is connected with his entering or leaving Great Britain or Northern Ireland or his travelling by air within Great Britain or within Northern Ireland.

(3) This paragraph also applies to a person on a ship or aircraft which has arrived at any place in Great Britain or Northern Ireland (whether from within or outside Great Britain or Northern Ireland).

(4) An examining officer may exercise his powers under this paragraph whether or not he has grounds for suspecting that a person falls within section 40(1)(b).

Para 5

A person who is questioned under paragraph 2 or 3 must—
   (a) give the examining officer any information in his possession which the officer requests;
   (b) give the examining officer on request either a valid passport which includes a photograph or another document which establishes his identity;
   (c) declare whether he has with him documents of a kind specified by the examining officer;
   (d) give the examining officer on request any document which he has with him and which is of a kind specified by the officer.

Para 6

(1) For the purposes of exercising a power under paragraph 2 or 3 an examining officer may—
   (a) stop a person or vehicle;
   (b) detain a person.

(2) For the purpose of detaining a person under this paragraph, an examining officer may authorise the person's removal from a ship, aircraft or vehicle.

(3) Where a person is detained under this paragraph the provisions of Part I of Schedule 8 (treatment) shall apply.

(4) A person detained under this paragraph shall (unless detained under any other power) be released not later than the end of the period of nine hours beginning with the time when his examination begins.

Para 18 'Offences'

(1) A person commits an offence if he—
   (a) wilfully fails to comply with a duty imposed under or by virtue of this Schedule,
   (b) wilfully contravenes a prohibition imposed under or by virtue of this Schedule, or
   (c) wilfully obstructs, or seeks to frustrate, a search or examination under or by virtue of this Schedule.

(2) A person guilty of an offence under this paragraph shall be liable on summary conviction to—
   (a) imprisonment for a term not exceeding three months,
   (b) a fine not exceeding level 4 on the standard scale, or
   (c) both.

- Although there is no statutory protection against self-incrimination yet in place, responses to a compulsory interview under these provisions should not be admitted in evidence for that purpose (though the court may consider evidence identified as a result of any reply) as it would be unfair in the proceedings under s 78 Police and Criminal Evidence Act 1984 (*Beghal v DPP* [2013] EWHC 2573 (Admin)).
- By analogy with Schedule 8 Terrorism Act 2000, a detainee has a right to legal advice at any time, wherever they may be detained. Repeated consultation may not be used so as to frustrate the proper purpose of the examination. If a solicitor attends in person they may be present during the interview and a reasonable delay must be allowed to await the arrival of the solicitor but not so as to frustrate the purpose (*R (Elosta) v CMP* [2013] EWHC 3397 (Admin) ('developing' the decision in *R Beghal v DPP* above)). This is now confirmed by the Code of Practice for examining officers and review officers (2014) made under the Terrorism Act 2000 which took effect on 31 July 2014.

G5 'Intelligence' Interviews

- Interviews for the police to gain intelligence may be informal or formal in accordance with Chapter 2 Serious Organised Crime Act 2005.
- Careful consideration should be given to the advantages and disadvantages of taking part in such interviews. There is no obligation to do so.

G5.1 Informal intelligence interviews

Detention for voluntary intelligence interview is unlawful as the questioning does not relate to a matter for which the suspect is under arrest (s 37(2) Police and Criminal Evidence Act 1984). The mitigation benefits should be weighed against the risk of self-incrimination and risks to the suspect's own safety.

G5.2 Formal intelligence interviews

More formal arrangements can be made under Part 2 Chapter 2 Serious Organised Crime and Police Act 2005 either before charge or after conviction.

The DPP may offer immunity from prosecution (s 71) and give appropriate undertakings not to use self-incriminating material (s 72) This can lead to a reduction in sentence (s 73) even after conviction (s 74). However for immunity to be considered a full declaration of criminality will be required and this could make the suspect's position more serious.

After conviction a modified caution is used to the effect that nothing said will be relied upon as part of a prosecution case against the suspect, save for attempting to pervert the course of justice if the police are given misleading information. At all stages the safety of the suspect must be carefully considered if information is given to the police.

G6 TICs

The guideline issued by the Sentencing Council states:

> When sentencing an offender who requests offences to be taken into consideration (TICs), courts should pass a total sentence which reflects all the offending behaviour.
>
> ...
>
> The court has discretion as to whether or not to take TICs into account. In exercising its discretion the court should take into account that TICs are capable of reflecting the offender's overall criminality. The court is likely to consider that the fact that the offender has assisted the police (particularly if the offences would not otherwise have been detected) and avoided the need for further proceedings demonstrates a genuine determination by the offender to 'wipe the slate clean'.

There is therefore a difficult balancing exercise to be carried out. Admissions to more offences may increase the eventual sentence but the court may take a different view if it considers that the defendant genuinely wishes to move away from crime. The decision whether to sign TICs is seldom best made at the police station. Officers should be invited to raise relevant issues with the CPS for consideration later.

G7 Interviews in relation to Seized Cash under the Proceeds of Crime Act 2002 Part 5

G7.1 During an investigation

Financial investigators seek to interview suspects about their financial affairs but such interviews are not under caution and not subject to PACE protections. However any disclosure made by the financial investigator may provide useful information when advising in the criminal investigation. The suspect is under no obligation to answer and any answers given may provide a link to admissible evidence or be used in confiscation proceedings and affect whether a restraint order is sought.

G7.2 In relation to cash seized under Part 5

A magistrates' court has jurisdiction under s 298 Proceeds of Crime Act 2000 to forfeit cash seized by the authorities if it is satisfied that the cash or any part of it is recoverable property or intended by any person for use in unlawful conduct. Recoverable property is defined by s 304 as property obtained through criminal conduct. The burden of proof to the civil standard lies on the police.

Interviews in relation to such issues are not technically part of a criminal investigation but are often closely examined and used substantially by the police in later forfeiture proceedings. The suspect is free to leave at any time.

Part H
Representations

H1 Lawful Arrest

The police powers of arrest are very extensive; they apply to every offence so there is a need for balance between the rights of individuals and the need for investigative powers by the police.

- Arrest can be carried out either after warrant issued or without warrant being issued; the powers derive from two sources:
  1. Police and Criminal Evidence Act 1984 ('PACE');
  2. Common law power to arrest for breach of peace.

H1.1 PACE

Police and Criminal Evidence Act 1984

s 24 'Arrest without warrant: constables'

(1) A constable may arrest without a warrant—
  (a) anyone who is about to commit an offence;
  (b) anyone who is in the act of committing an offence;
  (c) anyone whom he has reasonable grounds for suspecting to be about to commit an offence;
  (d) anyone whom he has reasonable grounds for suspecting to be committing an offence.

(2) If a constable has reasonable grounds for suspecting that an offence has been committed, he may arrest without a warrant anyone whom he has reasonable grounds to suspect of being guilty of it.

(3) If an offence has been committed, a constable may arrest without a warrant—
  (a) anyone who is guilty of the offence;
  (b) anyone whom he has reasonable grounds for suspecting to be guilty of it.

(4) But the power of summary arrest conferred by subsection (1), (2) or (3) is exercisable only if the constable has reasonable grounds for believing that for any of the reasons mentioned in subsection (5) it is necessary to arrest the person in question.

(5) The reasons are—
  (a) to enable the name of the person in question to be ascertained (in the case where the constable does not know, and cannot readily ascertain, the person's name, or has reasonable grounds for doubting whether a name given by the person as his name is his real name);
  (b) correspondingly as regards the person's address;
  (c) to prevent the person in question—
    (i) causing physical injury to himself or any other person;
    (ii) suffering physical injury;
    (iii) causing loss of or damage to property;

(iv) committing an offence against public decency (subject to subsection (6)); or
(v) causing an unlawful obstruction of the highway;
(d) to protect a child or other vulnerable person from the person in question;
(e) to allow the prompt and effective investigation of the offence or of the conduct of the person in question;
(f) to prevent any prosecution for the offence from being hindered by the disappearance of the person in question.

(6) Subsection (5)(c)(iv) applies only where members of the public going about their normal business cannot reasonably be expected to avoid the person in question.

H1.2 Common law

H1.2.1 *Breach of the peace*

- 'Whenever harm is actually done or is likely to be done to a person or in his presence to his property or a person is in fear of being so harmed through an assault, an affray, a riot or other disturbance' (R v Howell (1981) 73 Cr App R 31).
- Where a breach of the peace occurs in the presence (or the reasonable apprehension of it taking place) of a constable, or anyone else, a constable may arrest an offender without warrant (*R v Howell* (1981) 73 Cr App R 31).

H1.3 The necessity requirement

Extracts from PACE Code G:

- 'Facts and information relevant to a person's suspected involvement in an offence should not be confined to those which tend to indicate the person has committed or attempted to commit the offence. Before making a decision to arrest, a constable should take account of any facts and information that are available, including claims of innocence made by the person, that might dispel the suspicion' (PACE Code G NfG 2).
- 'The power of arrest is only exercisable if the constable has reasonable grounds for believing that it is necessary to arrest the person...' (PACE Code G para 2.4).
- '...Applying the necessity criteria requires the constable to examine and justify the reason or reasons why a person needs to be arrested...' (PACE Code G para 2.6).
- 'In considering the individual circumstances, the constable must take into account the situation of the victim, the nature of the offence, the circumstances of the suspect and the needs of the investigative process' (PACE Code G para 2.8).

- The statutory criteria in sub-paragraphs (a) to (f), namely:
  (a) To enable the name of the person in question to be ascertained (in the case where the constable does not know, and cannot readily ascertain, the person's name, or has reasonable grounds for doubting whether a name given by the person as his name is his real name);
  (b) Correspondingly as regards the person's address;
  (c) To prevent the person in question;
    (i) Causing physical injury to himself or any other person;
    (ii) Suffering physical injury;
    (iii) Causing loss or damage to property;
    (iv) Committing an offence against public decency (only applies where members of the public going about their normal business cannot reasonably be expected to avoid the person in question);
    (v) Causing an unlawful obstruction of the highway;
  (d) To protect a child or other vulnerable person from the person in question;
  (e) To allow the prompt and effective investigation of the offence or of the conduct of the person in question (see NfG 2E) (PACE Code G para 2.9).
- 'The meaning of "prompt" should be considered on a case by case basis taking account of all the circumstances. It indicates that the progress of the investigation should not be delayed to the extent that it would adversely affect the effectiveness of the investigation…' (PACE Code G NfG 2E).
- 'This may arise when it is thought likely that unless the person is arrested and then taken in custody to the police station further action considered necessary to properly investigate their involvement in the offence would be frustrated, unreasonably delayed or otherwise hindered and therefore be impracticable. Examples of such actions include:
  (i) interviewing the suspect on occasions when the person's voluntary attendance is not considered to be a practicable alternative to arrest, because for example:
    - it is thought unlikely that the person would attend the police station voluntarily to be interviewed;
    - it is necessary to interview the suspect about the outcome of other investigative action for which their arrest is necessary, see (ii) to (v) below;
    - arrest would enable the special warning to be given in accordance with Code C paragraphs 10.10 and 10.11;
    - the person has made false statements and/or presented false evidence;
    - it is thought likely that the person:

- may steal or destroy evidence;
- may collude or make contact with co-suspects or conspirators;
- may intimidate or threaten or make contact with, witnesses (PACE Code G para 2.9).

See PACE Code G NfG 2F and 2G.

- 'An officer who believes that it is necessary to interview the person suspected of committing the offence must then consider whether their arrest is necessary in order to carry out the interview. The officer is not required to interrogate the suspect to determine whether they will attend a police station voluntarily to be interviewed but they must consider whether the suspect's voluntary attendance is a practicable alternative for carrying out the interview. If it is, then arrest would not be necessary. Conversely, an officer who considers this option but is not satisfied that it is a practicable alternative, may have reasonable grounds for deciding that the arrest is necessary at the outset "on the street". Without such considerations, the officer would not be able to establish that arrest was necessary in order to interview' (PACE Code G NfG 2F).
- 'When the person attends the police station voluntarily for interview by arrangement (as in Note 2F above), their arrest on arrival at the station prior to interview would only be justified if:
  - New information coming to light after the arrangements were made indicates that from that time, voluntary attendance ceased to be a practicable alternative and the person's arrest became necessary; and
  - It was not reasonably practicable for the person to be arrested before they attended the station.

  If a person who attends the police station voluntarily to be interviewed decides to leave before the interview is complete, the police would at that point be entitled to consider whether their arrest was necessary to carry out the interview. The possibility that the person might decide to leave during the interview is therefore not a valid reason for arresting them before the interview has commenced (see Code C paragraph 3.21)' (PACE Code G NfG 2G).

(ii) When considering arrest in connection with the investigation of an indictable offence (see Note 6), there is a need:
- To enter and search without a search warrant any premises Occupied or controlled by the arrested person or where the person was when arrested or immediately before arrest;
- To prevent the arrested person from having contact with others;
- To detain the arrested person for more than 24 hours before charge.

(iii) When considering arrest in connection with any recordable offence and it is necessary to secure or preserve evidence of that offence by taking fingerprints, footwear impressions, or samples from the suspect for evidential comparison or matching with other material relating to that offence, for example, from the crime scene (see Note 2H).

(iv) When considering arrest in connection with any offence and it is necessary to search, examine or photograph the person to obtain evidence (see Note 2H) (PACE Code G para 2.9).

- 'The necessity criteria do not permit arrest solely to enable the routine taking, checking (speculative searching) and retention of fingerprints, samples, footwear impressions and photographs when there are no prior grounds to believe that checking and comparing the fingerprints etc. or taking a photograph would provide relevant evidence of the person's involvement in the offence concerned or would help to ascertain or verify their real identity' (PACE Code G NfG 2H).
- When considering arrest in connection with an offence to which the statutory Class A drug testing requirements in Code C section 17 apply, to enable testing when it is thought that drug misuse might have caused or contributed to the offence (see Note 2I) (PACE Code G para 2.9).
- 'The necessity criteria do not permit arrest for an offence solely because it happens to be one of the statutory drug testing "trigger offences" (see Code C Note 17E) when there is no suspicion that Class A drug misuse might have caused or contributed to the offence' (PACE Code G NfG 2I).
- To prevent any prosecution for the offence from being hindered by the disappearance of the person in question (PACE Code G para 2.9).

H1.4 Lawful arrest

- Police can use 'reasonable force' to conduct arrest (s 117 (a) and (b) PACE).
- An arresting officer must tell the suspect:
  - He is under arrest (as soon as practicable) (s 28(1) PACE);
  - Grounds for arrest (as soon as practicable) (s 28(3) PACE).
- A suspect must be cautioned in accordance with PACE Code C para 10.5.
- The caution may be delayed due to suspect's behaviour (PACE Code G para 3.4(a)).
- Where a person has been arrested for an offence and is at a police station for that offence, and it appears to police that he might be

involved in another offence, the person must be arrested for that other offence (s 31 PACE). The detention time runs from the original offence.

- If an arrest is unlawful, subsequent detention at the police station is arguably unlawful.
- If a volunteer decides to leave the station prior to interview and the police decide not to allow it, the volunteer must be arrested (PACE Code C para 3.21).

H2 **Bail at Police Station**

- Bail at police station is ultimately a decision for the Custody Sargent.
- There are three scenarios at the pre-charge stage where the police may decide to grant bail with or without conditions or withhold bail altogether:

Police and Criminal Evidence Act 1984

s 37 'Duties of custody officer before charge'

(1) Where—
  (a) a person is arrested for an offence—
    (i) without a warrant; or
    (ii) under a warrant not endorsed for bail, the custody officer at each police station where he is detained after his arrest shall determine whether he has before him sufficient evidence to charge that person with the offence for which he was arrested and may detain him at the police station for such period as is necessary to enable him to do so.

(2) If the custody officer determines that he does not have such evidence before him, the person arrested shall be released either on bail or without bail, unless the custody officer has reasonable grounds for believing that his detention without being charged is necessary to secure or preserve evidence relating to an offence for which he is under arrest or to obtain such evidence by questioning him.

(3) If the custody officer has reasonable grounds for so believing, he may authorise the person arrested to be kept in police detention.

(4) Where a custody officer authorises a person who has not been charged to be kept in police detention, he shall, as soon as is practicable, make a written record of the grounds for the detention.

...

(7) Subject to section 41(7) below, if the custody officer determines that he has before him sufficient evidence to charge the person arrested with the offence for which he was arrested, the person arrested—
  (a) shall be—
    (i) released without charge and on bail, or
    (ii) kept in police detention,

  for the purpose of enabling the Director of Public Prosecutions to make a decision under section 37B below,
  (b) shall be released without charge and on bail but not for that purpose,
  (c) shall be released without charge and without bail, or
  (d) shall be charged.

(7A) The decision as to how a person is to be dealt with under subsection (7) above shall be that of the custody officer.

(7B) Where a person is dealt with under subsection (7)(a) above, it shall be the duty of the custody officer to inform him that he is being released, or (as the case may be) detained, to enable the Director of Public Prosecutions to make a decision under section 37B below.

(8) Where—

(a) a person is released under subsection (7)(b) or (c) above; and

(b) at the time of his release a decision whether he should be prosecuted for the offence for which he was arrested has not been taken, it shall be the duty of the custody officer so to inform him.

(8A) Subsection (8B) applies if the offence for which the person is arrested is one in relation to which a sample could be taken under section 63B below and the custody officer—

(a) is required in pursuance of subsection (2) above to release the person arrested and decides to release him on bail, or

(b) decides in pursuance of subsection (7)(a) or (b) above to release the person without charge and on bail.

(8B) The detention of the person may be continued to enable a sample to be taken under section 63B, but this subsection does not permit a person to be detained for a period of more than 24 hours after the relevant time.

(9) If the person arrested is not in a fit state to be dealt with under subsection (7) above, he may be kept in police detention until he is.

(10) The duty imposed on the custody officer under subsection (1) above shall be carried out by him as soon as practicable after the person arrested arrives at the police station or, in the case of a person arrested at the police station, as soon as practicable after the arrest.

H2.1 Key points

- Bail at police station shall be granted in accordance with the Bail Act 1976, s 1(1)(a)(b) Bail Act 1976.
- The custody officer is required to include a note of the reasons for varying or imposing bail conditions at the police station and shall give a copy of the note to the person in relation to which the decision was taken (s 5A Bail Act 1976).
- Conditions imposed by an officer may be varied by the magistrates' court on application by the suspect (s 47(1E) PACE). This is not subject to a means test. For legally aided cases, form CRM3 should be held on file.
- Under s 3A Bail Act 1976, where a constable grants bail to a person no conditions shall be imposed under subsections (4), (5), (6), or (7) of section 3 of the Bail Act 1976 unless it appears to the constable that it is necessary to do so for the purpose of preventing that person from—
  (a) failing to surrender to custody, or
  (b) committing an offence while on bail, or
  (c) interfering with witnesses or otherwise obstructing the course of justice, whether in relation to himself or any other person

H2.2 Bail for youths

- The United Nations Convention on the Rights of the Child provides under Article 37(b) that:

  No child shall be deprived of his or her liberty unlawfully or arbitrarily. The arrest, detention or imprisonment of a child shall be in conformity with the law and shall be used only as a measure of last resort and for the shortest appropriate period of time.

- 'When a juvenile is charged with an offence and the custody officer authorises their continued detention after charge, the custody officer must make arrangements for the juvenile to be taken into the care of a local authority to be detained pending appearance in court unless the custody officer certifies in accordance with PACE, section 38(6), that:
  (a) For any juvenile; it is impracticable to do so; or,
  (b) In the case of a juvenile of at least 12 years old, no secure accommodation is available and other accommodation would not be adequate to protect the public from serious harm from that juvenile (see Note 16D).

  Note: The 16 year old maximum age limit for transfer to local authority accommodation, the power of the local authority to detain the person transferred and take over responsibility for that person from the police are determined by section 38 of PACE. For this reason, this paragraph and Note 16D do not apply to detainees who appear to have attained the age of 17 (see paragraph 1.5A(a))' (PACE Code C para 16.7) until s 42 Criminal Justice and Courts Act 2015 is brought into force.
- 'Except as in paragraph 16.7, neither a juvenile's behaviour nor the nature of the offence provides grounds for the custody officer to decide it is impracticable to arrange the juvenile's transfer to local authority care. Impracticability concerns the transport and travel requirements and the lack of secure accommodation which is provided for the purposes of restricting liberty does not make it impracticable to transfer the juvenile. The availability of secure accommodation is only a factor in relation to a juvenile aged 12 or over when other local authority accommodation would not be adequate to protect the public from serious harm from them. The obligation to transfer a juvenile to local authority accommodation applies as much to a juvenile charged during the daytime as to a juvenile to be held overnight, subject to a requirement to bring the juvenile before a court under PACE, section 46' (PACE Code C NfG 16D).

See *Blackstone's Criminal Practice* **B7.136**

H3 Drug Testing

H3.1 Key points

- Testing for a specified Class A drug may take place in notified areas if a person aged 14 or over is detained for a trigger offence. Note that such a test must be conducted in the presence of an appropriate adult for those who have been charged and are aged under 17 but above 14.
- Trigger offences are listed in Code C, Note 17E and are denoted by the presence of TO next to the substantive offence in this handbook.
- A person who fails without good cause to give any sample which may be taken from him under section s 63B(8) PACE shall be guilty of an offence.
- If analysis of the sample reveals that a specified Class A drug may be present in the person's body, a police officer may—so long as the defendant is aged 18 or over—at any time before the person is released from detention at the police station, require him to attend an initial assessment and remain for its duration: s 9(2) Drugs Act 2005. The failure to do so may lead to the defendant committing an offence under s 12 Drugs Act 2005.
- Section 38(1)(a) PACE enables police custody officers to detain a person after charge where necessary for the purposes of taking a sample to test for the presence of a specified Class A drug subject to the provisions of s 63B PACE (above).
- Force may not be used to take any sample for the purpose of drug testing (PACE Code C para 17.14).

H4 Intervening in Interview

- '[A] solicitor may only be required to leave the interview if their conduct is such that the interviewer is unable properly to put questions to the suspect' (PACE Code C para 6.9).
- 'The solicitor's only role in the police station is to protect and advance the legal rights of their client... The solicitor may intervene in order to seek clarification, challenge an improper question to their client or the manner in which it is put, advise their client not to reply to particular questions, or if they wish to give their client further legal advice. Paragraph 6.9 only applies if the solicitor's approach or conduct prevents or unreasonably obstructs proper questions being put to the suspect or the suspect's response being recorded. Examples of unacceptable conduct include answering questions on a suspect's behalf or providing written replies for the suspect to quote' (PACE Code C, NfG 6D).
- 'An officer who takes the decision to exclude a solicitor must be in a position to satisfy the court the decision was properly made. In order to do this they may need to witness what is happening' (PACE Code C para 6E).
- 'An interview is the questioning of a person regarding their involvement or suspected involvement in a criminal offence or offences which... must be carried out under caution. Whenever a person is interviewed they must be informed of the nature of the offence, or further offence...' (PACE Code C para 11.1A).
- 'No interviewer may try to obtain answers or elicit a statement by the use of oppression...' (PACE Code C para 11.5).
- The term 'oppression' should be given its ordinary dictionary meaning and is likely to involve some impropriety on the part of the interrogator (*R v Fulling* (1987) 85 Cr App R 136).
- 'Breaks from interviewing should be made at recognised meal times or at other times that take account of when an interviewee last had a meal. Short refreshment breaks shall be provided at approximately two hour intervals, subject to the interviewer's discretion to delay a break if there are reasonable grounds for believing it would:
  - (i) involve a: risk of harm to people;
  - (ii) serious loss of, or damage to, property
  - (iii) unnecessarily delay the detainee's release;
  - (iv) otherwise prejudice the outcome of the investigation' (PACE Code C para 12.8).

Part I
Out of Court Disposal Options

I1 Introduction

The Ministry of Justice issues guidance on the disposal options available. The use of these disposals is intended to assist the police in dealing proportionately with low-level, often first-time, offending.

Where out-of-court disposals may result in required disclosure as part of an enhanced Disclosure and Barring Service ('DBS') request this is indicated in the relevant sub-section.

12 Suspended Prosecutions

On 1 November 2014 the Justice Secretary announced plans to introduce a new system of out of court disposals ('OOCDs') for England and Wales. The scheme will be piloted for 1 year in the Staffordshire, West Yorkshire, and Leicestershire regions.

On 3 November 2014 the Ministry of Justice and College of Policing produced the consultation response for out of court disposals. This response outlined the proposed new framework for OOCDs and the content of this chapter comes from this response.

This new scheme is devised of two levels:

1. A new statutory community resolution, which is envisaged to resolve minor offences and first time offenders; and
2. Suspended prosecutions, which are designed to deal with more serious offending.

12.1 Community resolution

- The new community resolution is aimed at lower-level and/or first-time offending. The community resolution could include a requirement for the offender to apologize to the victim and may include elements of financial compensation.

12.2 Suspended prosecution

- A suspended prosecution is aimed at more serious offending. It is intended for offending where there is sufficient evidence to prosecute but the public interest is better served through the offender complying with one or more of the conditions of a suspended prosecution.
- The conditions of a suspended prosecution dealing with punishment are expected to include financial penalties.
- The reparation element of a suspended prosecution is expected to repair the damage done by the offender either directly or indirectly. It is expected that this element will contain financial compensations, verbal or written apologies, or other restorative justice methods.
- The element of a suspended prosecution dealing with rehabilitation is expected to include sobriety testing (for alcohol related offending) or restricting an offender from visiting a specific place or area.

- Police officers will need to take account of the views of the victim and be prepared to justify why this course of action was the most appropriate way of dealing with the offender.
- If the offender failed to comply with any condition imposed upon him as part of a suspended prosecution they would face prosecution for the original offence.
- It is expected that failure to comply with a suspended prosecution (without good reason) would preclude an offender from being eligible to receive another OOCD for a subsequent offence.
- A suspended prosecution is expected only to be available for use with indictable-only offences in exceptional circumstances and with approval of the CPS.

13 Community Resolutions

- The current community resolutions can be used for adults or youths and are a non-statutory disposal. A suspect *must* admit an offence for a community resolution to be appropriate.
- For a community resolution to be appropriate it must be clear that an offence has been committed and the suspect *must* admit committing the offence.
- A suspect must consent to accepting a community resolution but there is no requirement for the victim to consent to this disposal option being used (although a victim must be consulted).
- A community resolution may be disclosed as part of an enhanced DBS request.

14 Restorative Justice

Restorative justice ('RJ') in an initiative to reduce recidivism by making defendants directly accountable to complainants. Each police force may chose to implement RJ with their own procedures; however the following is considered the minimum standard.

The following four elements must be present for a matter to be considered for disposal by RJ:

1. The offender must take responsibility;
2. There must be the involvement of the victim, community, or other affected party;
3. There must be a structured process that establishes what has occurred and what the impact has been; and
4. There must be an outcome that seeks to put right the harm that has been caused or an outcome that makes other reparation that may not be directly related to the original case.

The use of RJ should be proportionate to the offence and the evidence does not have to be beyond reasonable doubt.

There are three levels of RJ and the approach and delivery differs in each case:

Level 1	• An instant or on street disposal; this can be used by Police Community Support Officers
Level 2 (alternative to a formal criminal justice disposal)	• A conference is arranged to seek risk assessment and longer-term solutions • For offending where a 'level 1' disposal could not take place immediately or where the offence is more serious • A neighbourhood justice panel can be used and will help identify reparation to assist the offender to understand their behaviour and 'give something back' to the community
Level 2 (in addition to formal criminal justice disposal)	• This is to be considered as part of a formal criminal justice disposal and is aimed at the rehabilitation of the offender. An example of this is face-to-face contact between the offender and the complainant.
Level 3	• Deals with offenders mainly post sentence and while serving the custodial element of their sentence.

The following decision matrix provides guidance to considerations of whether RJ is appropriate:

Decision	Issues and Considerations
Green—Usually safe to RJ	• No public interest factors • No reason to make referral to, or need support from, other agencies • No vulnerability with any parties involved
Amber—Not always straightforward, just think	• Crime that is a local priority • Serious crimes by definition by minor in the individual circumstances • Serious acquisitive crime • Consider risk of reoccurrence • Consider offending history
Red—The most risky, consider cautiously and take advice from supervisor or other agency experts	• Domestic abuse—risk of re-victimization • Hate crimes • Sex offences—risk of re-victimization • A crime where formal sanction offers more appropriate support or intervention to either party • A crime where formal sanction is essential to ensure that proper record is made of behaviour that is of 'significant risk'

(Source: Associataion of Chief Police Officers Restorative Justice Guidelines and Minimum Standards August 2014)

15 Adult Cannabis and Khat Warning

Cannabis warnings are a non-statutory disposal and are used by police officers to deliver an informal verbal warning to adults found in possession of cannabis. Each constabulary will have individual guidance covering the issuance of cannabis or khat warnings.

A cannabis warning may be disclosed as part of an enhanced DBS check.

16 Penalty Notices for Disorder ('PNDs')

- PNDs were introduced as a statutory disposal and are provided for by ss 1–11 Criminal Justice and Police Act 2001. Section 132 and Schedule 23 of Legal Aid, Sentencing and Punishment of Offenders Act 2012 amended the scope of PNDs and repealed the power for the issuing of PNDs to those aged under 18 years.
- A PND can only be given where a constable has reason to believe that a person aged 18 or over has committed a penalty offence and they have sufficient evidence to support a prosecution.
- A suspect does *not* have to admit guilt for a PND to be issued and the payment of a PND is not an admission of guilt. A PND will not be appropriate where a satisfactory address for enforcement is not provided.

Where a PND may be Appropriate	
PND may be appropriate	Where a simple caution or conditional caution might be used. In some cases that would normally result in a charge.
PND may not be appropriate	Where custody or sentence more serious than a fine would be expected if the case were to be tried at court.
PND will not be appropriate	Where there has been any injury to any person or any realistic threat or risk of injury. Where there has been substantial financial or material loss to private property of an individual. Where a penalty offence is committed in association with another offence, including a penalty offence. Where the offence involves domestic violence (follow ACPO guidance). For any football-related offences. Where an offence has been committed jointly with a person below the age of 18 years. Where the provisions of the Protection from Harassment Act 1997 might apply.

Source: MoJ Penalty Notices for Disorder www.justice.gov.uk/downloads/oocd/pnd-guidance-oocd.pdf

- A PND can only be issued for offences of shoplifting where the value of goods is less that £100. A PND can only be issued for criminal damage where the value of the damage is less that £300.
- A PND may only be issued for offences specified in s 1 Criminal Justice and Police Act 2001.
- A PND may be disclosed on an enhanced DBS check if the offence is reasonably believed to be relevant.
- A PND is available for the following offences:

Penalty offences Upper Tier—£90 penalty				
PND Code	**CJS Code**	**Act**	**Description**	**Notifiable/ Recordable**
DA01	CL67008	s 5(2) Criminal Law Act 1967	Wasting police time, giving false report	Recordable
DA02	CA03007	s 127(2) Communications Act 2003	Send false message/ persistently use a public electronic communications network in order to cause annoyance, inconvenience, or needless anxiety	Recordable
DA03	FS04009	s 49 Fire and Rescue Services Act 2004	Knowingly gives a false alarm to a person acting on behalf of a fire and rescue authority.	Recordable
DA04	PU86107	s 5 Public Order Act 1986	Words/behaviour likely to cause harassment, alarm, or distress	Notifiable & recordable
DA05	EP75006	s 80 Explosives Act 1875	Fire or throw firework(s)	Non-recordable
DA06	CJ67002	s 91 Criminal Justice Act 1967	Drunk & disorderly in a public place	Recordable
DA11	CD71039	s 1 Criminal Damage Act 1971	Destroying or damaging property **(under £300 and may only be given on one occasion)**	Notifiable & recordable
DA12	TH68010	s 1(1) Theft Act 1968	Retail theft **(under £100 and may only be given on one occasion)**	Notifiable & recordable
DA13	FW04003	reg 7 Fireworks Regulations 2004 under s 11 of the Fireworks Act 2003	Breach of fireworks curfew (11pm–7am)	Recordable
DA14	FW04002	reg 5 Fireworks Regulations 2004 under s 11 of the Fireworks Act 2003	Possession of a category 4 firework	Recordable
DA16	LG03036	s 141 Licensing Act 2003 (c 17)	Sells or attempts to sell alcohol to a person who is drunk.	Recordable

Penalty offences Upper Tier—£90 penalty				
PND Code	**CJS Code**	**Act**	**Description**	**Notifiable/ Recordable**
DA17	LG03067	s 146(3) Licensing Act 2003	Supply of alcohol by or on behalf of a club to a person aged under 18	Recordable
DA18	LG03064	s 146(1) Licensing Act 2003	Sale of alcohol anywhere to a person under 18	Recordable
DA19	LG03081	s 149(3) Licensing Act 2003	Buys or attempts to buy alcohol on behalf of person under 18	Recordable
DA20	LG03083	s 149(4) Licensing Act 2003	Buys or attempts to buy alcohol for consumption on relevant premises by person under 18.	Recordable
DA21	LG03088	s 151 Licensing Act 2003	Delivery of alcohol to person under 18 or allowing such delivery	Recordable
DA 22	MD71530	s 5(2) and Sch 2 Misuse of Drugs Act 1971	Possess a controlled drug of Class B—cannabis/cannabis resin	Notifiable & recordable

Lower Tier—£60 penalty				
PND Code	**CJS Code**	**Act**	**Description**	
DB03	BT49005	s 55 British Transport Commission Act 1949	Trespassing on a railway	Non-recordable
DB04	BT49006	s 56 British Transport Commission Act 1949	Throwing stones/ matter/thing at a train or railway	Non-recordable
DB05	LG72008	s 12 Licensing Act 1872	Drunk in a highway, other public place or licensed premises	Recordable
DB07	CJ01002	s 12 Criminal Justice & Police Act 2001	Consume alcohol in designated public place, contrary to requirement by constable not to do so	Non-recordable
DB08	EP90046	s 87 Environmental Protection Act 1990	Depositing and leaving litter	Non-recordable
DB13	LG03086	s 150(2) Licensing Act 2003	Allowing consumption of alcohol by a person under 18 on relevant premises	Recordable
DB29	RP97006	reg 3(3) of the Royal Parks and Other Open Spaces Regulations 1997	Drop/leave litter/refuse except in a receptacle provided for the purpose in a Royal Park or other open space	Non-recordable
DB30	RP97007	reg 3(4) of the Royal Parks and Other Open Spaces Regulations 1997	Use pedal cycle/ skates/blade/board/ foot-propelled device in a Royal Park or other open spaces	Non-recordable
DB31	RP97057	reg 3(6) of the Royal Parks and Other Open Spaces Regulations 1997	Unless the person is registered blind, failing to immediately remove animal faeces from a Royal Park or other open space	Non-recordable

Source: MoJ Penalty Notices for Disorder www.justice.gov.uk/downloads/oocd/pnd-guidance-oocd.pdf

17 Simple Adult Caution

Criminal Justice and Courts Act 2015

s 17 'Restrictions on use of cautions'

(1) This section applies where, in England and Wales, a person aged 18 or over admits that he or she has committed an offence.

(2) If the offence is an indictable-only offence, a constable may not give the person a caution except—
   (a) in exceptional circumstances relating to the person or the offence, and
   (b) with the consent of the Director of Public Prosecutions.

(3) If the offence is an either-way offence specified by order made by the Secretary of State, a constable may not give the person a caution except in exceptional circumstances relating to the person or the offence.

(4) If—
   (a) the offence is a summary offence or an either-way offence not specified under subsection (3), and
   (b) in the two years before the commission of the offence the person has been convicted of, or cautioned for, a similar offence, a constable may not give the person a caution except in exceptional circumstances relating to the person, the offence admitted or the previous offence.

(5) It is for a police officer not below a rank specified by order made by the Secretary of State to determine—
   (a) whether there are exceptional circumstances for the purposes of subsection (2), (3) or (4), and
   (b) whether a previous offence is similar to the offence admitted for the purposes of subsection (4)(b).

(6) A determination under subsection (5) must be made in accordance with guidance issued by the Secretary of State.

(7) The Secretary of State may by order amend this section so as to provide for a different period for the purposes of subsection (4)(b).

(8) For the purposes of this section—
   (a) 'caution' does not include a conditional caution under Part 3 of the Criminal Justice Act 2003, but
   (b) a person has been 'cautioned for' an offence if he or she has been given a caution, a conditional caution or a youth caution or youth conditional caution under Chapter 1 of Part 4 of the Crime and Disorder Act 1998.

(9) In this section—
   'either-way offence' means an offence triable either way;
   'indictable-only offence' means an offence which, if committed by an adult, is triable only on indictment.

(10) This section applies whether the offence admitted was committed before or after the time when this section comes into force.

The Criminal Justice and Courts Act 2015 (Simple Cautions) (Specification of Police Ranks) Order 2015 provides the specified ranks for determinations made under s 17(2)–(4)(b) Criminal Justice and Courts Act 2015; which are:

Section	Rank
s 17(2)	Superintendent
s 17(3)	Inspector
s 17(4)	Inspector
s 17(5)	Inspector

The Criminal Justice and Courts Act 2015 (Simple Cautions) (Specification of Either-Way Offences) Order 2015 provides a list of offences specified by the Secretary of State under s 17(3); the offences relevant to this text are:

s 1(1) Children and Young Persons Act 1933 **B4.1**	s 1(1) Prevention of Crime Act 1953 **B9.6**	s 1A(1) Prevention of Crime Act 1953 **B9.6**	s 4(2) Misuse of Drugs Act 1971, where the offence was committed in relation to a Class A drug and is triable either way **B2.1**	s 4(3) Misuse of Drugs Act 1971, where the offence was committed in relation to a Class A drug and is triable either way **B2.2**
s 5(3) Misuse of Drugs Act 1971, where the offence was committed in relation to a Class A drug and is triable either way **B2.4**	s 1(1) Protection of Children Act 1978 **B3.25**	s 170(2) Customs and Excise Management Act 1979 **B2.3**	s 160(1) Criminal Justice Act 1988 **B3.25.1**	s 139(1) Criminal Justice Act 1988 **B9.7**
s 139AA(1) Criminal Justice Act 1988 **B9.7.1**	s 139A(2) Criminal Justice Act 1988 **B9.6.1**	s 139AA(1) Criminal Justice Act 1988 **B9.6.1**	s 3(1) Sexual Offences Act 2003, where the victim of the offence was under the age of 16 at the time of the offence **B3.6**	s 4(1) and (5) Sexual Offences Act 2003, where the victim of the offence was under the age of 16 at the time of the offence **B3.18**

s 7(1) Sexual Offences Act 2003 **B3.17**	s 8(1) and (3) Sexual Offences Act 2003 **B3.7**	s 9(1) and (3) Sexual Offences Act 2003 **B3.19**	s 10(1) and (3) Sexual Offences Act 2003 **B3.22**	s 14(1) Sexual Offences Act 2003 **B3.23**
s 15(1) Sexual Offences Act 2003 **B3.24**	s 16(1) Sexual Offences Act 2003 **B3.20**	s 17(1) Sexual Offences Act 2003 **B3.21**		

- A simple caution is spent immediately (**see J4**) but an offender may be placed on the sex offenders register if the caution is administered for a relevant sexual offence and cautions may affect the ability to travel to certain countries including the United States of America.
- A simple caution may be disclosed as part of a DBS check.

18 Youth Caution

- The Ministry of Justice and Youth Justice Board provide guidance for youth cautions and excerpts of this guidance are reproduced later in the chapter.

Crime and Disorder Act 1998

s 66ZA 'Youth cautions'

(1) A constable may give a child or young person ('Y') a caution under this section ('a youth caution') if—
   (a) the constable decides that there is sufficient evidence to charge Y with an offence,
   (b) Y admits to the constable that Y committed the offence, and
   (c) the constable does not consider that Y should be prosecuted or given a youth conditional caution in respect of the offence.
(2) A youth caution must be given in the presence of an appropriate adult.
(3) If a constable gives a youth caution to a person, the constable must explain the matters referred to in subsection (4) in ordinary language to—
   (a) that person, and
   (b) the appropriate adult.

- In dealing with any offence committed by a young person the police have a range of options:
  1. No further action
  2. Community resolution
  3. Youth caution
  4. Youth conditional caution
  5. Charge.
- Youth cautions were introduced by the Legal Aid, Sentencing and Punishment of Offenders Act 2012.
- A youth caution is available to those aged 10 to 17 (on the date upon which the youth caution is given). Where a person is aged 18 or above an adult caution should be used.
- There are three requirements before a youth caution can be given:
  1. There is sufficient evidence to charge the young person with an offence;
  2. The young person admits that they committed the offence, and
  3. The constable does not consider that the young person should be prosecuted or given a youth conditional caution in respect of the offence.
- Previous convictions or out of court disposals (including previous youth cautions or youth conditional cautions) do not preclude the use of a youth caution. However, consideration is needed to

establish whether the offence in question forms part of a pattern of offending that would require a prosecution.

- Where a young person is accused of a serious offence (such as those that would normally attract a high-level community order or immediate custody), a youth caution will not generally be a suitable disposal.
- Youth cautions are considered spent as soon as they are delivered but may appear on DBS certificates.

19 Conditional Caution

- A conditional caution is a statutory disposal introduced by the Criminal Justice Act 2003. The conditions attached to a caution must be rehabilitative, reparative, or a punitive financial penalty.
- Conditional cautions are not generally suitable for offences where the likely sentence would be a substantial community order or imprisonment.
- There must be sufficient evidence for a realistic prospect of conviction and the matter must be in the public interest to conditionally caution rather than prosecute. A suspect must admit an offence to be conditionally cautioned. The suspect must also explicitly agree to the conditions attached to the proposed caution.
- For a conditional caution to be issued, the offender must sign a document containing: details of the offence, an admission that the offender committed the offence, consent to be given a conditional caution, and details of the conditions attached to the conditional caution.
- If the conditions attached to a caution are not complied with an offender may be prosecuted for the original offence s 24(2) of the Criminal Justice Act 2003 provides that the document recording the conditional caution and signed by the offender is admissible in such proceedings.
- If the conditions of the caution are complied with then the caution will be spent after three months. An offender may be placed on the sexual offenders register where a caution is administered for a relevant sexual offence and travel restrictions may apply.
- A conditional caution may be disclosed as part of a DBS check.

(Source: Ministry of Justice Code of Practice for Adult Conditional Cautions)

I10 Youth Conditional Caution

Crime and Disorder Act 1998

s 66A 'Youth conditional cautions'

(1) An authorised person may give a youth conditional caution to a child or young person ('the offender') if—
 (a) *repealed*
 (b) each of the five requirements in section 66B is satisfied.

(2) In this Chapter, 'youth conditional caution' means a caution which is given in respect of an offence committed by the offender and which has conditions attached to it with which the offender must comply.

(3) The conditions which may be attached to such a caution are those which have one or more of the following objectives—
 (a) facilitating the rehabilitation of the offender;
 (b) ensuring that the offender makes reparation for the offence;
 (c) punishing the offender.

(4) The conditions that may be attached to a youth conditional caution include—
 (a) (subject to section 66C) a condition that the offender pay a financial penalty;
 (b) a condition that the offender attend at a specified place at specified times.
 'Specified' means specified in the condition

(5) Conditions attached by virtue of subsection (4)(b) may not require the offender to attend for more than 20 hours in total, not including any attendance required by conditions attached for the purpose of facilitating the offender rehabilitation.

s 66B 'The five requirements'

(1) The first requirement is that the authorised person has evidence that the offender has committed an offence.

(2) The second requirement is that a relevant prosecutor or the authorised person decides—
 (a) that there is sufficient evidence to charge the offender with the offence, and
 (b) that a youth conditional caution should be given to the offender in respect of that offence.

(3) The third requirement is that the offender admits to the authorised person that he committed the offence.

(4) The fourth requirement is that the authorised person explains the effect of the youth conditional caution to the offender and warns him that failure to comply with any of the conditions attached to the caution may result in his being prosecuted for the offence.

(5) The explanation and warning mentioned in subsection (4) must be given in the presence of an appropriate adult.

(6) The fifth requirement is that the offender signs a document which contains—
 (a) details of the offence,
 (b) an admission by him that he committed the offence,
 (c) his consent to be given the youth conditional caution, and
 (d) the conditions attached to the caution.

A code of practice is in force for youth conditional cautions (<https://www.gov.uk/government/uploads/system/uploads/attachment_data/file/243443/9780108512179.pdf>)

and excerpts of this code are reproduced below:

- 'A youth conditional caution allows an authorised person (usually a police officer) or a relevant prosecutor (usually a member of the CPS) to decide to give a caution with one or more conditions attached. When a young person is given a conditional caution for an offence, criminal proceedings for that offence are halted while the young person is given an opportunity to comply with the conditions. Where the conditions are complied with, the prosecution is not normally commenced. However, where there is no reasonable excuse for non-compliance, criminal proceedings may be commenced for the original offence and the conditional caution will cease to have effect' (2.1).
- 'Youth conditional cautions can only be given to an offender aged 10 to 17 years inclusive. Offenders aged 18 and over, irrespective of their age when the offence was committed, should be given a conditional caution rather than a youth conditional caution' (2.2).
- 'Section 66B of the [Crime and Disorder Act] 1998 Act sets out five requirements that must all be met before a youth conditional caution may be given. These requirements should be addressed in order.
  1. The authorised person must have evidence that the young person has committed an offence;
  2. The authorised person or relevant prosecutor must determine that there is sufficient evidence to charge the young person with the offence...;
  3. The young person must admit to the authorised person that he has committed the offence;
  4. The authorised person must explain the effect of the youth conditional caution and warn the young person that failure to comply with any of the conditions may result in prosecution for the original offence. Where the young person is aged 16 years or under, the explanation and warning must be given in the presence of an appropriate adult;
  5. The young person must sign a document containing details of the offence, the admission to the authorised person, consent to be given a youth conditional caution and details of the conditions attached' (4.1).
- 'A second youth conditional caution should not generally be given for the same or similar offence unless there are exceptional circumstances indicating that it may be appropriate; for example, where the previous youth conditional caution was more than two years earlier. Generally, it will not be appropriate to give a second youth conditional caution where the offender failed to comply with the conditions of the previous youth conditional caution' (6.6).

- 'The conditions that can be attached to a youth conditional caution must have one or more of the following objectives:
  - **Rehabilitation**—conditions which help to modify the behaviour of the young person, serve to reduce the likelihood of re-offending or help to reintegrate the young person into society [such as substance misuse programmes];
  - **Reparation**—conditions which serve to repair the damage done either directly or indirectly by the young person [e.g. an apology/making good any damage that has been caused];
  - **Punishment**—unpaid work or financial penalty conditions which punish or penalise the young person for their unlawful conduct [unpaid work must not exceed 20 hours (7.4)]' (7.1).
- 'All rehabilitative, reparative and punitive conditions must be capable of being completed within 16 weeks of the date of the original offence where it is a summary only offence. Exceptionally a period of longer than 16 weeks from the date the conditional caution is administered may be suitable for an offence triable either way or an indictable only offence depending on the facts of the particular case but must not exceed 20 weeks' (9.2).
- 'In any case where an authorised person or prosecutor is considering offering a youth conditional caution the case should be referred to the local YOT' (15.1).
- 'A specific power allowing a police officer to arrest and detain offenders is provided by s.24A(1) of the Criminal Justice Act 2003 (as amended). The power arises when a constable has *reasonable* grounds for believing that a young person has failed without reasonable excuse to comply with any conditions attached to a youth conditional caution but should only be exercised where considered necessary. In determining when arrest might be necessary regard should be had to the criteria in s.24(4) and (5) of the Police and Criminal Evidence Act 1984. Once arrested, detention may be authorised where it is necessary to investigate reasons for any non-compliance or to seek a charging decision from a prosecutor and formally charge a young person' (18.1).
- 'The young person should only be detained for as long as is necessary to explore the reasons for any breach and/or to undertake any charging procedures. This should be done as soon as practicable after arrest or arrival at the police station. Where it is clear that this cannot be achieved in a short period of time, the young person should be released on bail under s.24A(2)(b) of the Criminal Justice Act 2003' (18.2).
- A youth conditional caution is spent three months after its imposition but may appear on a DBS certificate **J5**.

I11 Triage

- Triage is a post-charge disposal option available in some parts of the country for youth offenders when dealing with low gravity offences. **See J3**.
- The purpose of a triage is to divert young people away from a charge and to a restorative intervention managed by a Youth Offending Team ('YOT').
- There are three triage routes:
  - Triage One: Early Diversion
  - Triage Two: Joint Risk Assessment
  - Triage Three: Criminal Justice Disposal.
- A youth will *not* be eligible for triage if:
  - They do not admit the offence;
  - The offence has a gravity score of 4 or more;
  - The youth is a serious or persistent offender.
- Triage One applies when a young person:
  - Is arrested for the first time; and
  - Admits the offence; and
  - The offence has a gravity score of 1 or 2.
- If the requirements for Triage One are fulfilled, the custody staff should divert the young person to the YOT for a restorative intervention. This will be recorded as 'NFA—Triage Diversion'.
- Triage Two applies when a young person admits the offence but:
  - The offence has a gravity score of 3; or
  - The young person has a reprimand, final warning, or has previously had a triage referral; or
  - The police custody or YOT staff have concerns about the offence and the risk or behaviour of the young person.
- If the requirements for Triage Two are fulfilled then a YOT triage worker would be expected to carry out a rapid assessment at the police station and then consult the Police Evidential Review Officer ('ERO'). If the case is a gravity 3 offence (**see J2.1.1**) then the CPS should be consulted. A decision will then be made regarding the disposal. The young person may be bailed (for a short period of around 10 days) whilst this takes place.
- If the young person engages then the bail to return date should be cancelled. If the young person fails to engage then the police may still reprimand/warn/charge as appropriate.
- The minimum YOT intervention is:
  - a restorative conversation; and
  - a statement of apology written by the young person.
- Triage is not recorded as a criminal justice disposal.

Part J
Appendices

J1 New Offences Created by the Criminal Justice and Courts Act and Serious Crime Act 2015

J1.1 Ill-treatment or wilful neglect: care worker offence

Criminal Justice and Courts Act 2015

s 20 'Ill-treatment or wilful neglect: care worker offence'

(1) It is an offence for an individual who has the care of another individual by virtue of being a care worker to ill-treat or wilfully neglect that individual.
(2) An individual guilty of an offence under this section is liable—
  (a) on conviction on indictment, to imprisonment for a term not exceeding 5 years or a fine (or both);
  (b) on summary conviction, to imprisonment for a term not exceeding [6] months or a fine (or both).

J1.1.1 *Breakdown*

Offence	Elements of the Offence	Defence
s 20 Criminal Justice and Courts Act 2015 'Ill-treatment or wilful neglect: care worker offence'	• An individual (a) who has care of another individual (b) • By virtue of (a) being a care worker • Ill-treats or neglects (b)	• Negative any element of the offence • General Defences **C**

J1.1.2 *Interpretation*

Criminal Justice and Courts Act 2015

s 20 'Ill-treatment or wilful neglect: care worker offence'

(3) 'Care worker' means an individual who, as paid work, provides—
  (a) health care for an adult or child, other than excluded health care, or
  (b) social care for an adult, including an individual who, as paid work, supervises or manages individuals providing such care or is a director or similar officer of an organisation which provides such care.
(4) An individual does something as 'paid work' if he or she receives or is entitled to payment for doing it other than—
  (a) payment in respect of the individual's reasonable expenses,
  (b) payment to which the individual is entitled as a foster parent,

(c) a benefit under social security legislation, or
(d) a payment made under arrangements under section 2 of the Employment and Training Act 1973 (arrangements to assist people to select, train for, obtain and retain employment).

(5) 'Health care' includes—
(a) all forms of health care provided for individuals, including health care relating to physical health or mental health and health care provided for or in connection with the protection or improvement of public health, and
(b) procedures that are similar to forms of medical or surgical care but are not provided in connection with a medical condition, and 'excluded health care' has the meaning given in Schedule 4.

(6) 'Social care' includes all forms of personal care and other practical assistance provided for individuals who are in need of such care or assistance by reason of age, illness, disability, pregnancy, childbirth, dependence on alcohol or drugs or any other similar circumstances.

(7) References in this section to a person providing health care or social care do not include a person whose provision of such care is merely incidental to the carrying out of other activities by the person.

(8) In this section—
'adult' means an individual aged 18 or over;
'child' means an individual aged under 18;
'foster parent' means—
(a) a local authority foster parent within the meaning of the Children Act 1989,
(b) a person with whom a child has been placed by a voluntary organisation under section 59(1)(a) of that Act, or
(c) a private foster parent within the meaning of section 53 of the Safeguarding Vulnerable Groups Act 2006.

J1.1.3 *Sentencing*

s 20

Summary: level 5 fine/6 months' imprisonment

Indictment: 5 years' imprisonment/a fine

J1.2 Corrupt or other improper exercise of police powers and privileges

J1.2.1 *Corrupt or other improper exercise of police powers and privileges*

Criminal Justice and Courts Act 2015

s 26 'Corrupt or other improper exercise of police powers and privileges'

(1) A police constable listed in subsection (3) commits an offence if he or she—

(a) exercises the powers and privileges of a constable improperly, and
(b) knows or ought to know that the exercise is improper.

(2) A police constable guilty of an offence under this section is liable, on conviction on indictment, to imprisonment for a term not exceeding 14 years or a fine (or both).

J1.2.2 *Related offences*

- Misconduct in public office.

J1.2.3 *Breakdown*

Offence	Elements of the Offence	Defence
s 26 Criminal Justice and Courts Act 2015 'Corrupt or other improper exercise of police powers and privileges'	• A police constable • Exercised the powers and privileges of a constable improperly; and • Knows or ought to know that the exercise is improper	• Negative any element of the offence • General Defences **C**

J1.2.4 *Interpretation*

Criminal Justice and Courts Act 2015

s 26 'Corrupt or other improper exercise of police powers and privileges'

(3) The police constables referred to in subsection (1) are—
(a) a constable of a police force in England and Wales;
(b) a special constable for a police area in England and Wales;
(c) a constable or special constable of the British Transport Police Force;
(d) a constable of the Civil Nuclear Constabulary;
(e) a constable of the Ministry of Defence Police;
(f) a National Crime Agency officer designated under section 9 or 10 of the Crime and Courts Act 2013 as having the powers and privileges of a constable.

(4) For the purposes of this section, a police constable exercises the powers and privileges of a constable improperly if—
(a) he or she exercises a power or privilege of a constable for the purpose of achieving—
(i) a benefit for himself or herself, or
(ii) a benefit or a detriment for another person, and
(b) a reasonable person would not expect the power or privilege to be exercised for the purpose of achieving that benefit or detriment.

(5) For the purposes of this section, a police constable is to be treated as exercising the powers and privileges of a constable improperly in the cases described in subsections (6) and (7).

(6) The first case is where—
  (a) the police constable fails to exercise a power or privilege of a constable,
  (b) the purpose of the failure is to achieve a benefit or detriment described in subsection (4)(a), and
  (c) a reasonable person would not expect a constable to fail to exercise the power or privilege for the purpose of achieving that benefit or detriment.

(7) The second case is where—
  (a) the police constable threatens to exercise, or not to exercise, a power or privilege of a constable,
  (b) the threat is made for the purpose of achieving a benefit or detriment described in subsection (4)(a), and
  (c) a reasonable person would not expect a constable to threaten to exercise, or not to exercise, the power or privilege for the purpose of achieving that benefit or detriment.

(8) An offence is committed under this section if the act or omission in question takes place in England and Wales or in the adjacent United Kingdom waters.

(9) In this section—
'benefit' and 'detriment' mean any benefit or detriment, whether or not in money or other property and whether temporary or permanent;
'United Kingdom waters' means the sea and other waters within the seaward limits of the United Kingdom's territorial sea.

(10) References in this section to exercising, or not exercising, the powers and privileges of a constable include performing, or not performing, the duties of a constable.

(11) Nothing in this section affects what constitutes the offence of misconduct in public office at common law in England and Wales or Northern Ireland.

J1.2.5 *Defences*

- See General Defences C.

J1.2.6 Key point

- This offence can be committed by an omission (s 25(6)(a)).

J1.2.7 *Sentencing*

s 26

Indictable only: 14 years' imprisonment/a fine

J1.3 Offences committed by disqualified drivers

J1.3.1 *Offences committed by disqualified drivers*

Criminal Justice and Courts Act 2015

s 29 'Offences committed by disqualified drivers'

(1) After section 3ZB of the Road Traffic Act 1988 insert [section 3ZC and section 3ZD below]

J1.3.2 *Related offences*

- Causing death by driving: disqualified drivers.

Road Traffic Act 1988

s 3ZC 'Causing death by driving: disqualified drivers'

(1) A person is guilty of an offence under this section if he or she—
  (a) causes the death of another person by driving a motor vehicle on a road, and
  (b) at that time, is committing an offence under section 103(1)(b) of this Act (driving while disqualified).

- Causing serious injury by driving: disqualified drivers.

Road Traffic Act 1988

s 3ZD 'Causing serious injury by driving: disqualified drivers'

(1) A person is guilty of an offence under this section if he or she—
  (a) causes serious injury to another person by driving a motor vehicle on a road, and
  (b) at that time, is committing an offence under section 103(1)(b) of this Act (driving while disqualified).

J1.3.3 *Breakdown*

Offence	Elements of the Offence	Defence
s 3ZC Road Traffic Act 1988 'Causing death by driving: disqualified drivers'	• A person (a) • Causes the death of another person (b) • By driving a motor vehicle on a road; and • At that time (a) is disqualified from driving	• Negative any element of the offence • General Defences **C**

Offence	Elements of the Offence	Defence
s 3ZD Road Traffic Act 1988 'Causing serious injury by driving: disqualified drivers'	• A person (a) • Causes serious injury to another person (b) • By driving a motor vehicle on a road; and • At that time (a) is disqualified from driving	• Negative any element of the offence • General Defences **C**

J1.3.4 *Interpretation*

Road Traffic Act 1988

s 3ZD 'Causing serious injury by driving: disqualified drivers'

(2) In this section 'serious injury' means—

(a) in England and Wales, physical harm which amounts to grievous bodily harm for the purposes of the Offences against the Person Act 1861, and

...

J1.3.5 *Defences*

- See General Defences **C**.

J1.3.6 *Sentencing*

s 3ZC

Indictable only: 10 years' imprisonment/a fine or both

s 3ZD

Indictment: 4 years' imprisonment/a fine or both

Summary: 6 months' imprisonment/a fine or both

J1.4 Disclosing private sexual photographs and films with intent to cause distress

Criminal Justice and Courts Act 2015

s 33 'Disclosing private sexual photographs and films with intent to cause distress'

(1) It is an offence for a person to disclose a private sexual photograph or film if the disclosure is made—

(a) without the consent of an individual who appears in the photograph or film, and

(b) with the intention of causing that individual distress.

...

(9) A person guilty of an offence under this section is liable—
(a) on conviction on indictment, to imprisonment for a term not exceeding 2 years or a fine (or both), and
(b) on summary conviction, to imprisonment for a term not exceeding 6 months or a fine (or both).

J1.4.1 *Breakdown*

Offence	Elements of the Offence	Defence
s 33 Criminal Justice and Courts Act 2015 'Disclosing private sexual photographs and films with intent to cause distress'	• A person (a) discloses • A private sexual photograph or film of (b) • Without the consent of (b) • With the intention of causing (b) distress	• Negative any element of the offence • s 33(2)–(5) Criminal Justice and Courts Act 2015 (below) • General Defences **C**

J1.4.2 *Interpretation*

Criminal Justice and Courts Act 2015

s 33 'Disclosing private sexual photographs and films with intent to cause distress'

(6) A person is taken to have shown the matters mentioned in subsection (4) or (5) if—
(a) sufficient evidence of the matters is adduced to raise an issue with respect to it, and
(b) the contrary is not proved beyond reasonable doubt.
(7) For the purposes of subsections (1) to (5)—
(a) 'consent' to a disclosure includes general consent covering the disclosure, as well as consent to the particular disclosure, and
(b) 'publication' of journalistic material means disclosure to the public at large or to a section of the public.
(8) A person charged with an offence under this section is not to be taken to have disclosed a photograph or film with the intention of causing distress merely because that was a natural and probable consequence of the disclosure.

s 34 'Meaning of "disclose" and "photograph or film"'

(1) The following apply for the purposes of section 33, this section and section 35.
(2) A person 'discloses' something to a person if, by any means, he or she gives or shows it to the person or makes it available to the person.

(3) Something that is given, shown or made available to a person is disclosed—
   (a) whether or not it is given, shown or made available for reward, and
   (b) whether or not it has previously been given, shown or made available to the person.
(4) 'Photograph or film' means a still or moving image in any form that—
   (a) appears to consist of or include one or more photographed or filmed images, and
   (b) in fact consists of or includes one or more photographed or filmed images.
(5) The reference in subsection (4)(b) to photographed or filmed images includes photographed or filmed images that have been altered in any way.
(6) 'Photographed or filmed image' means a still or moving image that—
   (a) was originally captured by photography or filming, or
   (b) is part of an image originally captured by photography or filming.
(7) 'Filming' means making a recording, on any medium, from which a moving image may be produced by any means.
(8) References to a photograph or film include—
   (a) a negative version of an image described in subsection (4), and
   (b) data stored by any means which is capable of conversion into an image described in subsection (4).

s 35 'Meaning of "private" and "sexual"'

(1) The following apply for the purposes of section 33.
(2) A photograph or film is 'private' if it shows something that is not of a kind ordinarily seen in public.
(3) A photograph or film is 'sexual' if—
   (a) it shows all or part of an individual's exposed genitals or pubic area,
   (b) it shows something that a reasonable person would consider to be sexual because of its nature, or
   (c) its content, taken as a whole, is such that a reasonable person would consider it to be sexual.
(4) Subsection (5) applies in the case of—
   (a) a photograph or film that consists of or includes a photographed or filmed image that has been altered in any way,
   (b) a photograph or film that combines two or more photographed or filmed images, and
   (c) a photograph or film that combines a photographed or filmed image with something else.
(5) The photograph or film is not private and sexual if—
   (a) it does not consist of or include a photographed or filmed image that is itself private and sexual,
   (b) it is only private or sexual by virtue of the alteration or combination mentioned in subsection (4), or
   (c) it is only by virtue of the alteration or combination mentioned in subsection (4) that the person mentioned in section 33(1)(a) and (b) is shown as part of, or with, whatever makes the photograph or film private and sexual.

J1.4.3 *Defences*

Criminal Justice and Courts Act 2015

s 33 'Disclosing private sexual photographs and films with intent to cause distress'

(2) But it is not an offence under this section for the person to disclose the photograph or film to the individual mentioned in subsection (1)(a) and (b).

(3) It is a defence for a person charged with an offence under this section to prove that he or she reasonably believed that the disclosure was necessary for the purposes of preventing, detecting or investigating crime.

(4) It is a defence for a person charged with an offence under this section to show that—

- (a) the disclosure was made in the course of, or with a view to, the publication of journalistic material, and
- (b) he or she reasonably believed that, in the particular circumstances, the publication of the journalistic material was, or would be, in the public interest.

(5) It is a defence for a person charged with an offence under this section to show that—

- (a) he or she reasonably believed that the photograph or film had previously been disclosed for reward, whether by the individual mentioned in subsection (1)(a) and (b) or another person, and
- (b) he or she had no reason to believe that the previous disclosure for reward was made without the consent of the individual mentioned in subsection (1)(a) and (b).

J1.4.4 *Sentencing*

s 33 Criminal Justice and Courts Act 2015

Summary: 6 months' imprisonment/a fine or both

Indictment: 2 years' imprisonment/a fine or both

J2 New Offences created by the Serious Crime Act 2015

J2.1 Unauthorised acts causing, or creating risk of, serious damage

J2.1.1 *Computer Misuse Act 1990*

Serious Crime Act 2015

s 41 'Unauthorised acts causing, or creating risk of, serious damage'

(1) The Computer Misuse Act 1990 is amended as follows.
(2) After section 3 insert—

s 3ZA 'Unauthorised acts causing, or creating risk of, serious damage'

(1) A person is guilty of an offence if—
  (a) the person does any unauthorised act in relation to a computer;
  (b) at the time of doing the act the person knows that it is unauthorised;
  (c) the act causes, or creates a significant risk of, serious damage of a material kind; and
  (d) the person intends by doing the act to cause serious damage of a material kind or is reckless as to whether such damage is caused.

(6) A person guilty of an offence under this section is (unless subsection (7) applies) liable, on conviction on indictment, to imprisonment for a term not exceeding 14 years, or to a fine, or to both.

(7) Where an offence under this section is committed as a result of an act causing or creating a significant risk of—
  (a) serious damage to human welfare of the kind mentioned in subsection (3)(a) or (3)(b), or
  (b) serious damage to national security, a person guilty of the offence is liable, on conviction on indictment, to imprisonment for life, or to a fine, or to both."

J2.1.2 *Breakdown*

Offence	Elements of the Offence	Defence
s 3ZA Computer Misuse Act 1990 'Unauthorised acts causing, or creating risk of, serious damage'	• Knowingly undertake an unauthorised act • In relation to any computer; and • Intending/reckless that the act causes or creates • A significant risk of causing serious damage of a material kind	• Negative any element of the offence • General Defences **C**

J2.1.3 *Defences*

- See General Defences C.

J2.1.4 *Interpretation*

Computer Misuse Act 1990

s 3ZA 'Unauthorised acts causing, or creating risk of, serious damage'

(2) Damage is of a 'material kind' for the purposes of this section if it is—
- (a) damage to human welfare in any place;
- (b) damage to the environment of any place;
- (c) damage to the economy of any country; or
- (d) damage to the national security of any country.

(3) For the purposes of subsection (2)(a) an act causes damage to human welfare only if it causes—
- (a) loss to human life;
- (b) human illness or injury;
- (c) disruption of a supply of money, food, water, energy or fuel;
- (d) disruption of a system of communication;
- (e) disruption of facilities for transport; or
- (f) disruption of services relating to health.

(4) It is immaterial for the purposes of subsection (2) whether or not an act causing damage—
- (a) does so directly;
- (b) is the only or main cause of the damage.

(5) In this section—
- (a) a reference to doing an act includes a reference to causing an act to be done;
- (b) 'act' includes a series of acts;
- (c) a reference to a country includes a reference to a territory, and to any place in, or part or region of, a country or territory.

J2.1.5 Key point

- The term 'material kind' is defined in s 3ZA(2), and is to be read with s 3ZA(3) to (5), as damage to human welfare, the environment, the economy, or national security. The other terms used in the definition of a material kind take their normal everyday meaning. It would, in the normal way, be for the jury to determine whether, for example, there had been damage to national security and whether that damage was serious (Serious Crime Act 2015 explanatory note 131).

J2.1.6 *Sentencing*

s 3ZA(6) Computer Misuse Act 1990

Indictable only: 14 years' imprisonment

s 3ZA(7) Computer Misuse Act 1990

(Where an offence under this section is committed as a result of an act causing or creating a significant risk of—

(a) serious damage to human welfare of the kind mentioned in subsection (3)(a) or (3)(b), or

(b) serious damage to national security)

Indictable only: life

J2.2 Participating in activities of organised crime group

J2.2.1 *Participating in activities of organised crime group*

Serious Crime Act 2015

s 45 'Participating in activities of organised crime group'

(1) A person who participates in the criminal activities of an organised crime group commits an offence.

...

(9) A person guilty of an offence under this section is liable on conviction on indictment to imprisonment for a term not exceeding 5 years.

J2.2.2 *Breakdown*

Offence	Elements of the Offence	Defence
s 45 'Participating in activities of organised crime group'	• Participation in any activity • Knowing or reasonably suspecting that the activity is • A criminal activity of an organized crime group; or • Will help organised crime groups carry on criminal activities	• Negative any element of the offence • General Defences **C** • s 45(8) Serious Crime Act 2015 **J2.2.3**

J2.2.3 *Defences*

Serious Crime Act 2015

s 45 'Participating in activities of organised crime group'

(8) It is a defence for a person charged with an offence under this section to prove that the person's participation was necessary for a purpose related to the prevention or detection of crime.

- See General Defences C.

J2.2.4 *Interpretation*

Serious Crime Act 2015

s 45 'Participating in activities of organised crime group'

(2) For this purpose, a person participates in the criminal activities of an organised crime group if the person takes part in any activities that the person knows or reasonably suspects—
  (a) are criminal activities of an organised crime group, or
  (b) will help an organised crime group to carry on criminal activities.

(3) 'Criminal activities' are activities within subsection (4) or (5) that are carried on with a view to obtaining (directly or indirectly) any gain or benefit.

(4) Activities are within this subsection if—
  (a) they are carried on in England or Wales, and
  (b) they constitute an offence in England and Wales punishable on conviction on indictment with imprisonment for a term of 7 years or more.

(5) Activities are within this subsection if—
  (a) they are carried on outside England and Wales,
  (b) they constitute an offence under the law in force of the country where they are carried on, and
  (c) they would constitute an offence in England and Wales of the kind mentioned in subsection (4)(b) if the activities were carried on in England and Wales.

(6) 'Organised crime group' means a group that—
  (a) has as its purpose, or as one of its purposes, the carrying on of criminal activities, and
  (b) consists of three or more persons who act, or agree to act, together to further that purpose.

(7) For a person to be guilty of an offence under this section it is not necessary—
  (a) for the person to know any of the persons who are members of the organised crime group,
  (b) for all of the acts or omissions comprising participation in the group's criminal activities to take place in England and Wales (so long as at least one of them does), or
  (c) for the gain or benefit referred to in subsection (3) to be financial in nature.

J2.2.5 Key point

- The definition of 'criminal activities' is such as to capture participation in only serious criminal conduct which is determined as an offence attracting a sentence of imprisonment of at least seven years. The reference therein to obtaining 'any gain or benefit' should be interpreted broadly so as to include crimes with tangible but non-monetary objectives, for example, when the predominant motivation is sexual gratification, such as the receipt of or trade in images of child sex abuse (Serious Crime Act 2015 explanatory note 158).

J2.2.6 *Sentencing*

s 45 (9) Serious Crime Act 2015

Indictable only: 5 years' imprisonment

J2.3 Possession of paedophile manual

J2.3.1 *Possession of paedophile manual*

Serious Crime Act 2015

s 69 'Possession of paedophile manual'

(1) It is an offence to be in possession of any item that contains advice or guidance about abusing children sexually.

(3) A person guilty of an offence under this section is liable—

(a) on summary conviction in England and Wales, to imprisonment for a term not exceeding 6 months or to a fine, or to both;

...

(c) on conviction on indictment, to imprisonment for a term not exceeding 3 years or to a fine, or to both.

J2.3.2 *Breakdown*

Offence	Elements of the Offence	Defence
s 69 'Possession of paedophile manual'	• Possess any item • Which contains advice or guidance about abusing children sexually	• Negative any element of the offence. • General Defences **C** • s 69(2) Serious Crime Act 2015 **J2.2.3**

J2.3.3 *Defences*

Serious Crime Act 2015

s 69 'Possession of paedophile manual'

(2) It is a defence for a person (D) charged with an offence under this section—
- (a) to prove that D had a legitimate reason for being in possession of the item;
- (b) to prove that—
  - (i) D had not read, viewed or (as appropriate) listened to the item, and
  - (ii) D did not know, and had no reason to suspect, that it contained advice or guidance about abusing children sexually; or
- (c) to prove that—
  - (i) the item was sent to D without any request made by D or on D's behalf, and
  - (ii) D did not keep it for an unreasonable time.

- See General Defences **C**.

J2.3.4 *Interpretation*

Serious Crime Act 2015

s 69 'Possession of paedophile manual'

(4) Proceedings for an offence under this section may be brought—
- (a) in England and Wales, only by or with the consent of the Director of Public Prosecutions;

...

(5) In England and Wales, the following provisions of the Protection of Children Act 1978 apply in relation to prohibited items as they apply in relation to indecent photographs of children (within the meaning of that Act)—
- (a) section 4 (entry, search and seizure);
- (b) the Schedule (forfeiture of photographs).

...

(8) In this section—

'abusing children sexually' means doing anything that constitutes—
- (a) an offence under Part 1 of the Sexual Offences Act 2003, or under Part 2, 3 or 4 of the Sexual Offences (Northern Ireland) Order 2008 (S.I. 2008/1769 (N.I. 2)), against a person under 16, or
- (b) an offence under section 1 of the Protection of Children Act 1978, or under Article 3 of the Protection of Children (Northern Ireland) Order 1978, involving indecent photographs (but not pseudo-photographs),

> or doing anything outside England and Wales or Northern Ireland that would constitute such an offence if done in England and Wales or Northern Ireland;
> 'item' includes anything in which information of any description is recorded;
> 'prohibited item' means an item within subsection (1).

J2.3.5 Key points

- See s 69(7) and Schedule 3 Serious Crime Act 2015 for considerations of the European Union E-Commerce Directive.
- *Subsection (8)* defines the terms 'item', 'prohibited item', and 'abusing children sexually'. The term 'item' has a wide meaning and includes both physical and electronic documents (for example, emails or information downloaded to a computer) (Serious Crime Act 2015 explanatory note 271).
- The standard of proof in making out the defence is the balance of probabilities (Serious Crime Act 2015 explanatory note 272).

J2.3.6 *Sentencing*

s 69(3) Serious Crime Act 2015

Summary: 6 months' imprisonment/a fine/both

Indictment: 3 years' imprisonment/a fine/both

J3 Key Guidance, from the College of Policing, on Youth Cautions

J3.1 Introduction

The College of Policing issues guidance on the grading of youth offences when consideration is given to appropriateness of a caution as a disposal option.

J3.1.1 *Aggravating and mitigating factors*

A gravity score can only be up-graded or down-graded by one point irrespective of the number of aggravating or mitigating features that apply.

FINAL SCORE	ACTION
4	Normally result in charge.
2/3	Normally a youth caution. If the offending behaviour cannot be satisfactorily addressed by a caution consider youth conditional caution. If neither of these addresses the offending behaviour or provides the necessary support then charge.
1	Always the minimum response applicable to the individual offender, ie community resolution or caution, youth conditional caution, or charge.

J4 Retention of Samples

All references below refer to the Police and Criminal Evidence Act 1984 as amended by the Protection of Freedoms Act 2012.

Person not charged with qualifying offence (s 63F)	With conviction that is not an excluded offence.	Retain indefinitely
	Without conviction save for excluded offence where commissioner of biometric material consents (s 63F)	3 years (extendable to 5 years by DJ)
Person not charged with a non-qualifying offence (s 63H)	With conviction that is not an excluded offence	Retain indefinitely
	Without convictions save for an excluded offence	Not retained
Person acquitted of qualifying offence (s 63F)	With conviction that is not an excluded offence	Retain indefinitely
	Without conviction save for an excluded offence	3 years (extendable to 5 years by DJ)
Person acquitted of non-qualifying offence	With conviction other than an excluded offence	Retain indefinitely
	Without conviction save for an excluded offence	Not Retained
Persons convicted of any offence (s 63I)	Receives sentence of 5 years or more	Retain indefinitely
but: Person under 18 convicted of non-qualifying offence (s 63K without convictions)	Receives custodial sentence of under 5 years	Retain for 5 years beyond term of sentence
	If non-custodial	5 years from date sample taken
PND (s 63L)		Retained for 2 years
Sample given voluntarily (s 63N)	No conviction save excluded conviction	Not retained
	With a conviction other than excluded conviction	Retained indefinitely
Person consents (s 63O) to retention beyond statutory rules		Until consent withdrawn

Footwear impressions (s 63S)		Not retained
Arrest under s 41 of the Terrorism Act) 2000 Schedule 8	With conviction other than one exempt conviction	Retained indefinitely
	Only one exempt conviction	Retained for 3 years extendable to 5 years by a DJ
Detained under Schedule 7 Terrorism Act 2000 (para 20C)	Conviction other than an exempt conviction	Retain indefinitely
	Only on exempt conviction	Retained for 6 months

J5 Rehabilitation Periods

J5.1 Basic criminal record certificates

J5.1.1 *Youths*

Rehabilitation of Offenders Act 1974 as amended

For custodial sentences: in each case the rehabilitation period runs from the date on which the sentence (including any licence period) is completed.

Sentence length	Rehabilitation Period (after sentence) for Convictions after 10/04/2014
0–6 months	1½ years
6–30 months	2 years
30 months–4 years	3½ Years

For non-custodial sentences:

Sentence	Rehabilitation Period (after sentence) for Convictions after 10/04/2014
Youth Rehabilitation Order	6 months beginning with the day provided for by or under the order as the last day on which the order is to have effect.
Fine	6 months (from date of conviction)
Conditional discharge, referral order, reparation order, action plan order, supervision order, bind over order, hospital order	Period of order
Absolute discharge; youth caution	None
Compensation order	The date on which the payment is made in full.

J5.1.2 *Adults*

For custodial sentences: in each case the rehabilitation period runs from the date on which the sentence (including any licence period) is completed.

Sentence length	Rehabilitation Period (after sentence) for Convictions after 10/04/2014
0–6 months	2 years
6–30 months	4 years
30 months–4 years	7 years
Over 4 years	Never spent

For non-custodial sentences:

Sentence	Rehabilitation Period (after sentence) for Convictions after 10/04/2014
Community order (and youth rehabilitation order)	1 year beginning with the day provided for by or under the order as the last day on which the order is to have effect.
Fine	1 year (from date of conviction)
Conditional discharge, bind over order, hospital order	Period of order
Absolute discharge, caution, other diversions from prosecution	None
A compensation order	The date on which the payment is made in full.

J5.2 Basic and standard criminal record certificates

'Protected convictions' and 'Protected cautions' are provided for by the (Criminal Record Certificates: Relevant Matters) (Amendment) (England and Wales) Order 2013 (SI 2013/1200); Police Act 1997 (Criminal Records) (Amendment) Regulations 2013 (SI 2013/1194); and Rehabilitation of Offenders Act 1974 (Exceptions) Order 1975 (Amendment) (England and Wales) Order 2013 (SI 2013/1198) make further amendments.

The effect of these amendments in relation to convictions is that:

1. Convictions that resulted in a custodial sentence, convictions for serious sexual or violent offences, and convictions for certain other specified offences will always be disclosed;
2. In relation to all other convictions for persons aged 18 or over, convictions that fall within an 11-year period ending with the day on which the certificate is issued will be disclosed;
3. In relation to all other convictions for persons aged under 18, convictions that fall within a five-and-a-half-year period ending with the day on which the certificate is issued will be disclosed; but
4. Persons with more than one conviction will have all their convictions disclosed.

The effect of the amendments in relation to cautions is that—

5. Cautions for serious sexual and violent offences and certain other offences will always be disclosed;
6. In relation to all other cautions for persons aged 18 or over, cautions that fall within a six-year period ending with the day on which the certificate is issued will be disclosed; and

7. In relation to all other cautions for person aged under 18, cautions that fall within a two-year period ending with the day on which the certificate is issued will be disclosed.

The 1974 Act is no longer disapplied (and so no disclosure need be made), save in defined circumstances, in respect of a 'protected caution' or a 'protected conviction' (as defined in Rehabilitation of Offenders Act 1974 (Exceptions) Order 1975 (SI 1975/1023), art 2A) when a question is asked to assess a person's suitability for certain purposes, or when a decision is made for certain purposes.

J6 **Professional Duties**

J6.1 **Confidentiality**

- A representative must be aware of his duty of confidentiality as imposed by the Solicitors Code of Conduct (O 4.1)—You keep the affairs of clients confidential unless disclosure is required or permitted by law or the client consents.

J6.2 **Disclosure**

- The solicitor must make the client aware of all information material to his case of which the solicitor has personal knowledge (O4.2).

J6.3 **Conflict**

- Where your duty of confidentiality to one client comes into conflict with your duty of disclosure to another client, your duty of confidentiality takes precedence (O4.3).

J6.4 **Privilege**

- The suspect has privilege in confidential information he gives to you so that you may advise appropriately and fully at the police station. The client only may waive that privilege. It may not be overridden by a court, police officer, or general statutory provision.
- In sensitive cases and with the appropriate authority investigators may be able to listen in on privileged conversation at the police station. Make enquiries of the police and if information is refused have this in mind when advising the client. It may be better to delay the taking of detailed instructions.
- Privilege cannot be relied upon when the information is given to the solicitor in furtherance of crime. Privilege amounts to a reasonable excuse for failing to make disclosure which would otherwise be required by statute (eg s 38B of the Terrorism Act 2000).

8 Professional Duties

8.1 Confidentiality

Index